Xiaoting Li, Tsuyoshi Ono (Eds.)
Multimodality in Chinese Interaction

Applications of Cognitive Linguistics

Editors
Gitte Kristiansen
Francisco J. Ruiz de Mendoza Ibáñez

Honorary editor
René Dirven

Volume 34

Multimodality in Chinese Interaction

Edited by
Xiaoting Li
Tsuyoshi Ono

DE GRUYTER
MOUTON

ISBN 978-3-11-073528-4
e-ISBN (PDF) 978-3-11-046239-5
e-ISBN (EPUB) 978-3-11-046051-3
ISSN 1861-4078

Names: Li, Xiaoting, editor. | Ono, Tsuyoshi (Linguist), editor.
Title: Multimodality in Chinese interaction / edited by Xiaoting Li,
   Tsuyoshi Ono.
Description: Berlin ; Boston : De Gruyter, [2019] | Series: Applications of
   cognitive linguistics (ACL) ; band/volume 34 | Includes bibliographical
   references and index.
Identifiers: LCCN 2018025229 (print) | LCCN 2018049299 (ebook) | ISBN
   9783110462395 (pdf) | ISBN 9783110460339 (alk. paper) | ISBN 9783110460513
   (epub)
Subjects: LCSH: Chinese language–Discourse analysis. | Chinese
   language–Grammar. | Modality (Linguistics) | Nonverbal communication. |
   Social interaction–China. | Semiotics.
Classification: LCC P302.15.C4 (ebook) | LCC P302.15.C4 M85 2019 (print) |
   DDC 495.101/41–dc23
LC record available at https://lccn.loc.gov/2018025229

Bibliographic information published by the Deutsche Nationalbibliothek
The Deutsche Nationalbibliothek lists this publication in the Deutsche Nationalbibliografie;
detailed bibliographic data are available on the Internet at http://dnb.dnb.de.

© 2020 Walter de Gruyter GmbH, Berlin/Boston
This volume is text- and page-identical with the hardback published in 2019.
Typesetting: Integra Software Services Pvt. Ltd.
Printing and binding: CPI books GmbH, Leck

www.degruyter.com

Contents

Xiaoting Li, Tsuyoshi Ono
Introduction: A multimodal approach to Chinese interaction —— 1

Part I: Theory and methodology

Sandra A. Thompson
Multimodality and the study of Chinese talk-in-interaction —— 13

Xiaoting Li
Researching multimodality in Chinese interaction: a methodological account —— 24

Part II: Multimodal practices

Hongyin Tao
List gestures in Mandarin conversation and their implications for understanding multimodal interaction —— 65

K.K. Luke and Xiaoling He
Hand gestures and emergent speakership: A study of turn competition and gesticulation in Cantonese conversation —— 99

Kawai Chui
Grounding and gestural repetition in Chinese conversational interaction —— 119

Tomoko Endo
Embodying stance: *wo juede* 'I feel/think' and gaze —— 148

Part III: Multimodal organization of talk and interaction

Xiaoting Li
Multimodal turn construction in Mandarin conversation – Verbal, vocal, and visual practices in the construction of sytactically incomplete turns —— 181

Ni-Eng Lim
On co-operative modalities in the formulation of Mandarin Chinese turn-continuations —— 213

Liang Tao
Self-repair in Mandarin Chinese: The multimodality of conversation —— 255

I-Ni Tsai
A multimodal analysis of tag questions in Mandarin Chinese multi-party conversation —— 300

Index —— 333

Xiaoting Li, Tsuyoshi Ono
Introduction: A multimodal approach to Chinese interaction

The past few years have seen a dramatic increase of interest in the study of multimodality and Chinese interaction. This is partly due to the advancement of technology that allows us to examine social interaction as temporally unfolding multimodal events. In addition, the increasing awareness of the multimodal nature of social interaction has prepared the theoretical ground for studying Chinese interaction from a multimodal perspective. However, in contrast to the heightened interest, empirical multimodal research on Chinese interaction is still scarce. This volume stems from the theme session "Language and the Body in Chinese Spoken Discourse" at the 12th International Cognitive Linguistics Conference and the Workshop "Multimodality and Chinese Interaction" in 2013. It brings together scholars working on the methodology of multimodal analysis and the utilization of multimodal approach in studying Chinese interaction. Some papers in this volume draw on a conversation analytic approach to multimodal interaction, whereas others come from a cognitive linguistic perspective. But they all use data of unscripted Chinese conversational interaction and share the goal to explore the inherently multimodal property of Chinese interaction. In this introduction, we first offer an account of the multimodal approach this volume adopts and some issues related to multimodality. Then we discuss some unique features of Chinese grammar that contribute to the multimodal study of social interaction from a cross-linguistic perspective. Finally, we provide a summary of the chapters in this volume.

1 Multimodality

Multimodality refers to a collection of approaches that perceives and examines human communication as multimodal events involving multiple means of communication including (but not limited to) language, image, gesture, gaze, posture, objects in the environment etc. Multimodality does not prioritize any particular means of communication or modality such as language, but considers communication as a multimodal achievement. These approaches to multimodality are rather heterogeneous ranging from computer science and robotics to linguistics, sociology, and communication studies. Papers in this volume are from

Xiaoting Li and Tsuyoshi Ono, University of Alberta

a linguistic approach (broadly construed) to multimodality. Within the field of linguistics, multimodality is approached from several research traditions such as social semiotics (Halliday 1978; Zlatev 2016) and systemic functional grammar (Halliday 1985), mediated discourse (Scollon 1998, 2001) and multimodal (inter) actional studies (Norris 2004), gesture studies (Kendon 1980; Cienki and Müller 2008; Müller and Cienki 2009; McNeill 2013) and semiotics (Fricke 2012, 2013), corpus linguistics (Cameron and Deignan 2003; Allwood 2008; Bateman 2008; Kipp et al. 2009), and interactional linguistics (Couper-Kuhlen and Selting 2001; Selting 2013) and conversation analysis (Mondada 2007). Li (this volume a) provides a fuller account of these traditions and multimodal approaches.

Although these approaches differ in their research subjects (written or spoken interaction) and views of how to analyze the multimodal resources, they share two interrelated theoretical assumptions. One assumption is multimodal resources work together in expressing meaning and accomplishing action, and language is only one of the multimodal resources. These resources may mutually elaborate each other (convergence) or play off one another (divergence) in interaction (Li 2014, this volume b). The other assumption is each multimodal resource or semiotic system has its own organization. For example, language structure is governed by syntactic rules (Chomsky 1957) and built on various structural units (Bloomfield 1933), whereas gesture is described based on its kinesic properties (McNeill 1992) and can be delimited into gesture phrases and gesture units (Kendon 2004; Schröder 2017). Unveiling the complex working together of these multimodal resources in meaning-making and action-formation in interaction is a central task for students of multimodality and interaction.

2 Chinese interaction

The study of multimodality in Chinese interaction contributes to our understanding of the multimodal nature of human interaction from a cross-linguistic perspective. That is, the Chinese language provides specific resources and sets unique constraints for the organization of interaction in Chinese.

Three typological features of the language are of particular relevance to the organization of Chinese interaction: topic-comment structure, prevalent phrasal structure, and lexical tone. Topic-comment structure is one of the most striking features of Mandarin Chinese sentence structure in contrast to English which is a subject-prominent language (Li and Thompson 1976, 1981). A topic is usually followed by a pause and/or particles in natural speech (Li and Thompson 1981:15). This structure is relevant to turn organization in Mandarin conversation. That is, participants orient to the complete topic-comment structure as relevant to possible turn completion, and refrain from taking the turn at the juncture between the topic and comment (Li 2014). Second, the common unit type for turn construction in Chinese is not necessarily clause, but rather phrasal structure (Tao 1996). It is argued that Mandarin syntax mainly exists at the phrase level (Zhu 1985; Lü 1979). A series of phrasal constructions or elliptical clauses that share a topic (commonly referred to as *liushuiju* 'flowing water sentences' [Lü 1979] in Chinese) are pervasive in Chinese spoken discourse (Tsao 1990; Wang and Li 2014). For example, in Excerpt 1 the phrasal constructions and elliptical clauses in lines 4 to 7 have the same topic: those college applicants with four hundred marks (lines 1–3).

(1) Tao (1996:82) (orthography slightly modified, line numbers added)
01 sì   bǎi   fēn yǐshàng de,
    four hundred mark above NOM
    'those with four hundred marks,'
02 jiùshì kǎoshēng ā,
    indeed examinee PRT
    'those college applicants,'
03 dádào sì   bǎi   fēn yǐshàng de.
    reach four hundred score above NOM
    'those who have achieved four hundred marks and above,'
04 bào   zhíyè gāozhōng de,
    apply vocation high school NOM
    'those who have applied to a vocational school,
05 hái yǒu hǎo duō,
    still have very many
    'there are still a lot of them,'
06 jiù méi yǒu.
    still NEG have
    '(they) haven't,'
07 gēnběn   jiù   tóudàng bù chūqù,
    basically somehow accept NEG out
    '(they) are basically accepted by nobody.'

How these phrases or "fragments" of sentences build speech is not governed by grammar, but pragmatic or discourse factors in Chinese (Qian 1997; Liao 1992). Thus, Chinese grammar is called "discourse grammar" which is not concerned with sentence, but discourse structure (Qian 1997; Liao 1992; Chu 1999; Jiang 2005). Despite the differing opinions regarding the structural level that

Chinese grammar is mainly concerned with, it is generally acknowledged that the position and temporal production of the "fragmented" speech units is fluid and flexible. One implication of the fluid production of syntactic structure is that prosody becomes particularly significant in indicating the possible completion of a unit and a turn. For example, in the midst of a flow of "fragmented" phrasal constructions, prosody at the end of each "fragmented" construction may help indicate if it may (or may not) be the possible completion of a speaker's turn. The importance of prosody in demarcating the basic discourse unit in spoken Chinese has long been acknowledged (Chao 1968; Wang and Li 2014). The third typological feature relevant to multimodal analysis of Chinese interaction is lexical tone. In tone languages such as Chinese, pitch movement or pitch contour is primarily used to distinguish lexical meanings rather than conveying pragmatic information (Liao 1994). The unit-final pitch movement or pitch contour may be affected by lexical tones of the unit-final syllables, and thus may not be very much relevant to turn organization. The projection of possible turn completion may be accomplished through other prosodic/phonetic parameters such as pitch register, pitch range, duration, pause etc. (Li 2014).

From a cross-linguistic perspective, these distinctive features of Chinese grammar and prosody expand our understanding of the practices used in interaction that may not exist in interaction conducted in other languages. However, we are not unaware of the methodological and theoretical issues raised by a cross-linguistic perspective in conversation analysis. Schegloff and Sacks (1974:234–235) refrains from linking findings about interaction to characterizations of data such as participant attributes and ethnicities, unless "warrant can be offered for the relevance of such characterizations of the data from the data themselves." Sidnell (2010:10) also inquires "how can we, for instance, warrant a description of the data as 'requests in Polish', 'French compliments' or whatever where, typically, the participants do not display any overt orientation to the relevance of the language being used or their ethnicity?" As is also pointed out by Sidnell (2010:10), one solution to this challenge is to establish the connection between practices used in interaction to particular linguistic features of the language. In Mandarin Chinese (and other Chinese dialects), the topic-comment structure, pervasive "fragmented" syntactic construction, and lexical tone provide specific resources and set unique constraints for the organization of turns and interaction. An examination of these resources and practices unique to Chinese interaction offers insights into the diversity of conduct used in the organization of human interaction. We use "Chinese interaction" in the title of this volume, as the papers speak about the resources and practices distinctive to the language.

Generally speaking, multimodal analysis of Chinese face-to-face interaction is 1) to explore the interactional function of particular multimodal practices (such as a type of body movement, a lexico-syntactic construction, and a prosodic feature) in Chinese interaction, and 2) to examine how multimodal resources (such as lexico-syntax, prosody, the body, objects in the surround, sequential position) are deployed together to organize talk and accomplish social actions in Chinese interaction. Chapters 3–5 (H. Tao, Luke, and Endo) belong to the first type of research, and Chapters 6–10 (Li, Lim, Chui, L. Tao, and Tsai) represent the second one.

3 The chapters

The subsequent ten chapters are divided into three parts. Part One contains two articles providing overviews of the historical and theoretical backgrounds and a methodological framework in the study of Chinese multimodal interaction:

Sandra Thompson contributes a general overview article examining the intersection between functional linguistics and the study of grammar-in-interaction. She surveys key developments in the areas of conversation analysis and multimodality, and then provides comments on multimodality in the study of Chinese interaction. It highlights theoretical and historical contexts in which scholars recently started to focus on bodily-visual behavior in Chinese interaction.

Xiaoting Li's article is divided into two main parts where she first reviews various approaches to multimodality in general and then lays out the specific steps to make multimodal analysis of Chinese interaction particularly focusing on transcription and analysis. These methodological foci are illustrated using actual Mandarin conversational segments.

Part Two contains three chapters, each focuses on particular linguistic and bodily-visual practices:

Hongyin Tao investigates the role of gesture in constructing list sequences in that a distinction between composite gestures (more or less fixed gestures with distinct listing qualities) and reiterative gestures (a series of gestures of various types produced intermittently with different items of a list) is proposed. These gesture types are shown to correspond to two broader types of discourse functions: to enhance the rhetorical effect for persuasion, exemplification, and clarification, and to do with discourse structuring, tracking, and interlocutor meta-interaction.

Tomoko Endo focuses on how gaze shift and the epistemic marker *wo juede* 'I think/feel' in the initial and final positions of a turn function to facilitate stance expression and turn organization. She shows that, using these resources, speakers take two kinds of stance, one of (dis)affiliation and one of participation. In particular, speakers are found to look away from participants with conflicting opinions, and toward participants who they wish to select as the next speaker.

The previous articles all focus on Mandarin Chinese. **K.K. Luke and Xiaoling He** add another Chinese dialect to our discussion by focusing on two gesture-types in Cantonese multi-party interaction. In particular, Luke and He show that the raised hand/finger and the arm-tap can be used by participants to make a bid for speakership, and to make one in such a way as to display their orientation to their own status as non-current speaker and non-selected next speaker.

Part Three contains five chapters each of which explores how multimodal resources are deployed to organize turns, sequences, repairs, and accomplish social actions in Chinese interaction:

Xiaoting Li's article examines the multimodal construction of syntactically incomplete turns. Specifically, Li examines cases where a bodily-visual behavior such as iconic gesture and head shake completes a syntactically incomplete turn. She also discusses cases where bodily-visual behavior may not play any constitutive role in the incomplete syntactic structure, but are deployed along with prosody and sequential position to indicate and anticipate possible completion of the syntactically incomplete turns.

Ni-Eng Lim highlights the multimodal mechanics of constructing further talk past a possibly complete turn. He finds that syntactically discontinuous constituents after possible completion are still marked as "continuing" by the combination of prosodic cues (i.e. rush-throughs, lack of pitch reset, and declining intonation contour). He also finds that where further talk is prompted by recipient's lack of uptake or intervening talk by others, thereby resulting in prosodic separation between the host-TCU and its turn-continuation, the addition is still syntactically continuous due to the use of grammatical structures available in the language (e.g., serial verb construction, topic-comment structure, verb-resultative complement, etc.).

Kawai Chui examines two grounding sequence types where participants collaborate moment-by-moment to establish mutual understanding in progress. In sequences without gestural repetition, addressees typically manifest their understanding of the speaker's utterance by offering positive responses explicitly while the latter largely express implicit acknowledgements. In sequences with gestural repetition, which provides evidence for the bilateral and interactive nature of speaking, addressees mimic the speaker's previous gesture while expressing understanding mainly in an explicit way and often provide additional information, which is typically followed by the speaker's explicit acknowledgement.

Liang Tao examines same-turn self-repairs where speakers "stop an utterance in progress and then abort, recast or redo that utterance" (Fox et al. 2009: 60) by highlighting language specific tendencies in that a) repair initiation falls on single-syllable words, and dual-syllable 'units' which might not be a grammatical unit, b) on or after the last segment of the syllable (thus rarely on the onset consonant), and c) a single syllable or a dual-syllable phonological unit is recycled to adjust to the tone sandhi rules. She also examines the connection between repair and bodily-visual practices such as head turns, gaze shift from the recipients, and hand gestures.

I-Ni Tsai focuses on tag questions formulated by the two most frequent question tags in spoken Mandarin: *shi bu shi* 'COP not COP' and *dui bu dui* 'right not right'. Based on the study of turn design partly through the inspection of body movement, body position, eye gaze, etc., Tsai finds that the tag questions are commonly deployed in multi-party conversations to embody speaker's differential states of knowledge in relation to different co-participants, and to seek affiliation in a disaffiliating move.

4 Closing remarks

This volume contributes to the growing field of multimodality and embodied interaction by offering new insights into Chinese interaction from a multimodal perspective and proposing methodological framework for multimodal analysis of Chinese interaction. It presents the most recent findings on multimodal practices in aspects of Chinese interaction.

The interdisciplinary nature of multimodal research determines the studies in this volume are necessarily interdisciplinary. The papers are from a range of disciplinary backgrounds including CA/ethnomethodology, interactional linguistics/discourse-functional linguistics, cognitive linguistics, and psycholinguistics to name just three. Regardless of our disciplinary backgrounds, we have the common goal to explore the linguistic and embodied underpinnings of social action and interaction in Chinese. However, the field of multimodality in Chinese interaction is a new, less-studied territory. Few researchers have been trained from the outset to conduct microanalysis of linguistic structure, bodily movement, and action sequence in Chinese interaction. This volume is a small step towards an understanding of Chinese interaction that is closer to the reality of how people interact in their everyday life. We hope that this volume will stimulate interchange between Chinese linguists and researchers on multimodal interaction, and that more researchers will participate in this rapidly-developing conversation on multimodality and Chinese interaction.

References

Allwood, Jens. 2008. Multimodal corpora. In Anke Lüdeling & Merja Kytö (eds.), *Corpus linguistics: An international handbook*, 207–25. Berlin: Mouton de Gruyter.
Bateman, John. 2008. *Multimodality and Genre*. Basingstoke: Palgrave Macmillan.
Bloomfield, Leonard. 1933. *Language*. New York: Henry Holt.
Cameron, Lynne & Alice Deignan. 2003. Combining large and small corpora to investigate tuning devices around metaphor in spoken discourse. *Metaphor and Symbol* 18(3). 149–160.
Chao, Yuen-Ren. 1968. *A grammar of spoken Chinese*. Berkeley: University of California Press.
Chomsky, Noam. 1957. *Syntactic structures*. The Hague: Mouton.
Cienki, Alan & Cornelia Müller. 2008. Metaphor, gesture, and thought. In Raymond W. Gibbs Jr (ed.), *The Cambridge handbook of metaphor and thought*, 483–501. Cambridge: Cambridge University Press.
Couper-Kuhlen, Elizabeth & Margret Selting. 2001. Introducing interactional linguistics. In Margret Selting & Elizabeth Couper-Kuhlen (eds.), *Studies in interactional linguistics*, 1–24. Amsterdam/Philadelphia: John Benjamins.
Chu, Chauncey C. 1999. *A Discourse Grammar of Mandarin Chinese*. New York: Peter Lang.
Fox, Barbara A., Wouk, Fay, Hayashi, Makoto, Fincke, Steven, Tao, Liang, Sorjonen, Marja-Leena, Laakso, Minna and Hernandez, Wilfrido Flores. 2009. A Cross-linguistic investigation of the site of initiation in same-turn self-repair. In Jack Sidnell (ed.), *Conversation analysis: Comparative perspectives*, 60–103. Cambridge: Cambridge University Press.
Fricke, Ellen. 2012. *Grammatik multimodal: Wie Wörter und Gesten zusammenwirken*. Berlin/Boston: Mouton de Gruyter.
Fricke, Ellen. 2013. Towards a unified grammar of gesture and speech: A multimodal approach. In Cornelia Müller, Alan Cienki, Ellen Fricke, Silva H. Ladewig, David McNeill & Sedinha Teßendorf (eds.), *Body – Language – Communication. An International Handbook on Multimodality in Human Interaction (Handbooks of Linguistics and Communication Science 38.1)*, 733–754. Berlin/Boston: Mouton de Gruyter.
Kendon, Adam. 1980. Gesture and speech: two aspects of the process of utterance. In Mary R. Key, (ed.), *Nonverbal communication and language*, 207–227. The Hague: Mouton.
Kendon, Adam. 2004. *Gesture: Visible action as utterance*. Cambridge: Cambridge University Press.
Kipp, Michael, Jean-Claude Martin, Patrizia Paggio & Dirk Heylen. (eds.). 2009. *Multimodal corpora*. Berlin, Germany: Springer.
Halliday, Michael A K. 1978. *Language as social semiotic: The social interpretation of language and meaning*. Baltimore: University Park Press.
Halliday, Michael A K. 1985. *An introduction to functional grammar*. London: Edward Arnold.
Jiang, Wangqi. 2005. Hanyu de 'Juzi' yu yingyu de sentence [Chinese "sentence" and English sentence]. *Journal of PLA University of Foreign Languages* 28(1). 10–15.
Li, Charles N. & Sandra A. Thompson. 1976. Subject and topic: A new typology of language. In Charles N. Li (ed.), *Subject and topic: A new typology of language*, 457–489. New York: Academic Press.
Li, Charles N. & Sandra A. Thompson. 1981. *Mandarin Chinese: A functional reference grammar*. Berkeley, CA: University of California Press.
Li, Xiaoting. 2014. *Multimodality, interaction and turn-taking in Mandarin conversation*. John Benjamins: Amsterdam/Philadelphia.

Liao, Qiuzhong. 1992. *Liao Qiuzhong wenji [Essays of Liao Qiuzhong]*. Beijing: Beijing Yuyan Xueyuan Chubanshe.
Liao, Rongrong. 1994. Pitch contour formation in Mandarin Chinese: A Study of tone and intonation. Ph.D. dissertation, Ohio State University.
Lü, Shuxiang. 1979. *Hanyu Yufa Fenxi Wenti [Analysis of Chinese grammar problems]*. Beijing: Shangwu Yinshuguan.
McNeill, David. 1992. *Hand and mind*. Chicago: University of Chicago Press.
McNeill, David. 2013. Gesture as a window onto mind and brain, and the relationship to linguistic relativity and ontogenesis. In Cornelia Müller, Alan Cienki, Ellen Fricke, Silvia Ladewig, David McNeill & Sedinha Teßendorf (eds.), *Body – language – communication. An international handbook on multimodality in human interaction*. Volume 1, 28–54. Berlin & Boston: De Gruyter Mouton.
Mondada, Lorenza. 2007 Multimodal resources for turn-taking: Pointing and the emergence of possible next speakers. *Discourse Studies* 9(2). 195–226.
Müller, Cornelia & Alan Cienki. 2009. Words, gestures, and beyond: Forms of multimodal metaphor in the use of spoken language. In Charles Forceville & Edurado Urios-Aparisi (eds.), *Multimodal Metaphor*, 297–328. Berlin & New York: Mouton de Gruyter.
Norris, Sigrid. 2004. *Analyzing multimodal interaction: A methodological framework*. London: Routledge.
Qian, Guanlian. 1997. *Hanyu wenhua yuyongxue. [Pragmatics in Chinese culture]*. Beijing: Tsinghua University Press.
Sacks, Harvey, Emanuel A. Schegloff & Gail Jefferson. 1974. A simplest systematics for the organization of turn-taking for conversation. *Language* 50. 696–735.
Schröder, Ulrike. 2017. Multimodal metaphors as cognitive pivots for the construction of cultural otherness in talk. *Intercultural Pragmatics* 14(4). 493–524.
Scollon, Ron. 1998. *Mediated discourse as social interaction: A study of news discourse*. London: Longman.
Scollon, Ron. 2001. *Mediated discourse: The nexus of practice*. London: Routledge.
Selting, Margret. 2013. Verbal, vocal, and visual practices in conversational interaction. In Cornelia Müller, Alan Cienki, Ellen Fricke, Silva H. Ladewig, David McNeill & Sedinha Teßendorf (eds.), *Body – Language – Communication. An International Handbook on Multimodality in Human Interaction (Handbooks of Linguistics and Communication Science 38.1)*, 589–609. Berlin, Boston: Mouton de Gruyter.
Sidnell, Jack. 2010. Comparative perspectives in conversation analysis. In Jack Sidnell (ed.), *Conversation analysis: Comparative perspectives*, 3–27. Cambridge: Cambridge University Press.
Tao, Hongyin. 1996. *Units in Mandarin conversation: Prosody, discourse, and grammar*. Amsterdam: John Benjamins.
Tsao, Fengfu. 1990. *Sentence and clause structure in Chinese: a functional perspective*. Taipei: Student Book.
Wang, Hongjun & Rong Li. 2015. Lun hanyu yupian de jiben danwei he liushuiju de chengyin. [On the basic unit of Chinese discourse and the formation of rundown sentences]. *Yuyanxue Luncong* 49. 11–40.
Zhu, Dexi. 1982. *Yufa Jiangyi [Lectures on Chinese grammar]*. Beijing: Shangwu Yinshuguan.
Zlatev, J. 2016. Mimesis : The role of bodily mimesis for the evolution of human culture and language. In David Dunér & Göran Sonesson (eds.), *Human Lifeworlds: The Cognitive Semiotics of Cultural Evolution*, 63–82. Peter Lang Publishing Group.

Part I: **Theory and methodology**

Sandra A. Thompson
Multimodality and the study of Chinese talk-in-interaction

1 Introduction

Research in conversation analysis and interactional linguistics has long recognized that language and bodily-visual behavior must be considered together in understanding how conversation is organized.

In this brief survey, I offer an overview of the intersection between functional linguistics and the study of interactional linguistics. I survey key developments in the areas of conversation analysis (CA) and multimodality, and then provide a few comments on multimodality in the study of Chinese interaction.

2 Functional linguistics, conversation analysis, and grammar-in-interaction

'Functionalism' as a vibrant subfield of linguistics can be said to have arisen in the 1970's, partially as a reaction to the burgeoning interest at the time in approaching grammar as a formal system. The primary assumption shared by functional linguists has consistently been that the forms and structures of language are adapted to, and shaped by, their communicative functions. Functionalists take the internal organization of language to be a complex adaptive response to the ecological settings in which language is found, the interactional functions which it serves, and the full cognitive, social, and physiological properties of the human user. Functional linguistic research aims to clarify the relationship between linguistic form and function, and to determine the nature of the functions which appear to shape linguistic structure.[1]

At the same time, the field of conversation analysis (CA) was beginning to emerge with the work of Harvey Sacks (cf. Sacks 1974, 1995, Schegloff 1968) and his colleagues and students. Although Sacks originally had no special interest in language in his early explorations of social order (Heritage 1984), his growing

---

[1] For representative references, see Comrie (1978a, 1978b), Dixon (1977, 1979), Givón (1979), Greenberg (1978), Langacker & Munro (1975), Li (1976), Lord (1973), and Schachter (1976).

Sandra A. Thompson, UC Santa Barbara

https://doi.org/10.1515/9783110462395-002

interest in the organization of everyday talk in his work with Emanuel Schegloff eventually drew him to the details of language. When Sacks, Schegloff & Jefferson (1974) appeared, although the field of linguistics at that time was fairly thoroughly dominated by the generative paradigm with its emphasis on language as a 'mental' construct, this article came to have a substantial impact on linguistics.[2]

As early as the late 1970's, some functional linguists were already beginning to realize the need to study linguistic function by examining language in everyday use, working with monologic narratives (e.g., Chafe 1980; Hopper 1979; Hopper & Thompson 1980), but also with dialogic conversation and other everyday interactions (e.g., Duranti & Ochs 1979; Keenan & Schieffelin 1976).

The 1980's saw the beginning of a merger between these two research traditions, with 'discourse-functional' research being more influenced by research in CA, as linguists began to shift their attention away from strictly cognitive considerations, realizing that language may be best understood as a resource for the accomplishment of actions in social interaction, and that by studying people actually talking, we gain a deeper appreciation of the role of grammar in carrying out social actions.[3,4] Three major contributions to our understanding of grammar have arisen from this focus on grammar 'at work'.

The first of these is the understanding that grammar cannot be a fixed property of human brains, but must be seen as emergent, constantly undergoing revision as it is deployed and redesigned in everyday talk, where 'emergent structure' is understood as a set of recurrent patterns in a given language that emerge from humans pursuing their ordinary interactional business of communicating information, needs, identities, attitudes, and desires (Auer & Pfänder 2011; Bybee 2010; Fauconnier and Turner 2008, Hopper 1987).

A second contribution of examining grammar at work is the discovery that if linguistics is to account for language in everyday use, then its perspective on the nature of grammar must be both cognitively realistic as well as interactionally sensible. In other words, as recurrent solutions to speakers' social needs become habitual, these habitually used linguistic forms become cognitively ent-

---

[2] As a primary indication of its influence, it is the most widely cited article ever to have appeared in *Language*; as of October 2016, Google Scholar counts 13,469 citations to this article. For a discussion of the influence of CA on linguistics, and of linguistics on CA, see Fox et al. (2013).

[3] See Langacker (1990) and Taylor (2002) for similar claims from a cognitve perspective.

[4] For discussions of grammar and social action, see, e.g., Clark & Wilkes-Gibbs (1986), Couper-Kuhlen (2014), Evans (2007), Ford (1993), Fox (2007), Goodwin & Goodwin (1987, 1992a), Hopper (2004), Kärkkäinen (2012), Fox & Thompson (2010), Laury, Ono & Suzuki (forthcoming), Curl (2006), Curl & Drew (2008), Thompson & Couper-Kuhlen (2005), Thompson (forthcoming), and Thompson et al. (2015).

renched as the patterns we call the grammar of a language. We could say, then, that 'grammar' is what has been ritualized from social interactions, resulting in a very loosely organized set of richly and complexly categorized memories people have of how they and fellow speakers have resolved recurrent interactional problems (Bybee 2006, 2010; Tomasello 1998, 1999, 2002, 2003).

A third contribution to our understanding of grammar at work is the discovery that grammar is tightly intertwined with the social activities that people are engaged in (Auer 1992, 1996; Clark 1996; Goodwin & Goodwin 1987, 1992a, 1992b; Schegloff 1996). One way in which these activities implicate the nature of grammar is that certain kinds of activities give rise to certain recurrent kinds of grammar. For example, the activities motivating posing questions and giving answers have a number of grammatical consequences (Fox & Thompson 2010; Heritage & Roth 1995; Raymond 2003; Schegloff 1996; Weber 1993; Thompson, Fox & Couper-Kuhlen 2015). Thompson, Fox & Couper-Kuhlen (2015) show, for instance, that English speakers respond to question-word questions such as *What did you have for lunch?* with either a lexical/phrasal response (e.g., *soup*) or a clausal response (e.g., *I had soup (for lunch)*, and that the choice seems to be determined by whether the responder takes the question, or responding to it, as problematic in some way.

3 Multimodality and the study of language and the body

An emphasis on the significance of multiple modalities in joint meaning-making can be traced to the groundbreaking and foundational work of Charles Goodwin, particularly Goodwin (1979, 1981). Among the first to analyze social interaction in terms of video data, Goodwin (1979) forged an entirely new area of research within the study of grammar in talk in interaction by showing how the construction of an ordinary 'sentence' depended on the gaze behavior of the speaker and his recipients. Goodwin (1981) further revealed the extent to which bodies are involved in the way humans use language to interact, and, strikingly, the way the very grammatical shape of their utterances can depend on the use of their bodies. Since that time, a research tradition focusing on the skilled use of multiple modalities by interactants has emerged within studies of language in interaction. For exemplary analyses, see Fox (2001), Goodwin (2000), Hayashi (2003), Mondada (2006, 2011), and Streeck (1993, 1994, 2009); for state-of-the-art treatises see Depperman (2013), Sidnell & Stivers (2005), and Streeck et al. (2011).

4 Multimodality in Chinese

4.1 Chinese discourse-functional linguistics

Just as elsewhere in linguistics, in the late 1970's and early 1980's, the field of Chinese linguistics began to see a growing interest in functional approaches to linguistic structure. Cheng, Li & Tang (1979), Chu (1983), Huang (1982, 1983), Li & Thompson (1981), Lü (1979), Paris (1981), and Teng (1975) capture the essence of this development.

And as research on conversation began to flourish and attract scholarly attention in the late 70's, so the study of Chinese grammar and interaction came into its own at about this time. Tsao (1979) is arguably the first major linguistic work based on Mandarin conversational data, followed by a rich range of studies on such topics as word order, the *ba*-construction, and final particles in everyday conversation. Many important contributions have appeared since then (e.g., Tao & Thompson 1994; for a state-of-the-art discussion, see Biq, Tai & Thompson (1996). More recent contributions include Biq (2001, 2004a, 2004b), Huang (1999), Luke & Zhang (2007), H. Tao (1999, 2001, 2003), L. Tao (2001, 2006), Wu (2002, 2004, 2005, 2006, 2011), Zhang (2012), and papers in *Chinese Language and Discourse* (see just below). An important stimulus to the growth of Chinese interactional linguistics was the founding by K.K. Luke, Hongyin Tao, and Li Wei, in 2010, of a new journal, *Chinese Language and Discourse* (https://benjamins.com/#catalog/journals/cld/main). A number of significant contributions in both interactional linguistics and CA have appeared in the pages of this journal since its inception. Innovative and equally important is the appearance of Huang's *Chinese Grammar at Work* (2013), a masterful discussion of a wide variety of frequently found constructions in Mandarin conversation.

4.2 Chinese CA

Early work in CA arose out of the field of sociology; its earliest practitioners were American and British sociologists. Their ground-breaking work in founding and establishing an entirely new field of endeavor in the study of language notwithstanding, it is also the case that these scholars were neither trained in linguistics nor were they fluent in, or particularly interested in, languages other than English. In the 1980's, however, scholars speaking languages other than English began to study CA and extend its findings to their own languages, and this is when CA scholarship on Chinese was initiated.

The beginning of Chinese CA can be traced directly, then, to the University of York, where K.K. Luke was studying; his 1990 book, *Utterance particles in Cantonese conversation*, is not only the first major contribution to Chinese CA, but Luke courageously takes on the issue of final particles, notoriously one of the most difficult areas of study for any language. Importantly, he also makes explicit the crucial link between CA, that is, the study of the organization of interaction, and grammar, that is, the study of the organization of linguistic patterns: he argues that applying CA techniques to Cantonese final particles reveals both a) what kinds of interactional problems speakers use these particles to address, and b) how solutions to these problems have impinged upon the structure of the Cantonese language.

Since then, more speakers of Chinese languages have joined the community of scholars working on CA and working with Chinese conversation. Following Luke, notable examples include Zhang (1998), the first in-depth study of repair in Chinese, and Wu (2004), the first book-length treatise on the Mandarin final particles *ou* and *a* in conversation, with special consideration of prosody and stance. These scholars have typically had training in both linguistics and CA, and their research, in focusing on grammar as social action happening in real time, has contributed greatly to our appreciation of aspects of Chinese grammar that have resisted analysis with methods utilizing context-free constructed example sentences. At the same time, along with much current research on conversational data in languages other than English (e.g., Cha'palaa, German, Finnish, Japanese, Korean, Lao, Tzeltal, Yélî Dnye),[5] this work on Chinese conversation has in turn helped to change the field of CA, bringing strong awareness of language diversity to the study of the organization of everyday interactions.

4.3 Multimodality in the study of Chinese interactions

As was happening elsewhere in the field of CA, scholars working on Chinese conversation soon began analyzing the use of the body in everyday interactions. Arguably the first such works were Wu (1997) and H. Tao (1999); several articles on gesture followed soon thereafter, e.g., Chui (2003, 2005a, 2005b). Yang (2011) relates nonverbal bodily behavior with taking, yielding, and maintaining turns in everyday conversation.

---

[5] For influential examples of a comparative approach to CA, see Sidnell (2009) and Haakana, Laakso & Lindström (2009).

A major step forward in the study of bodily-visual behavior in Chinese interactions was the appearance of Li (2011), which attracted 'underground' attention even before it appeared as a book (Li 2014). This was the first book-length study of multimodality in Chinese conversation, and its findings on body movements and the construction of turns opened the way for the launching of a lively new research area among students and scholars of Chinese talk-in-interaction, with several conference panels, and now the appearance of the volume of papers you have before you.

References

Auer, Peter. 1992. The neverending sentence: Rightward expansion in spoken language. In Miklós Kontra & Tamás Váradi (eds.), *Studies in spoken languages: English, German, Finno-Ugric*, 41–59. Budapest: Linguistics Institute, Hungarian Academy of Sciences.

Auer, Peter. 1996. On the prosody and syntax of turn-continuations. In Elizabeth Couper-Kuhlen & Margret Selting (eds.), *Prosody in conversation*, 57–100. Cambridge: Cambridge University Press.

Auer, Peter & Stefan Pfänder (eds.). 2011. *Constructions: Emerging and emergent*. Berlin: de Gruyter.

Biq, Yung-O. 2001. The grammaticalization of *jiushi* and *jiushishuo* in Mandarin Chinese. *Concentric: Studies in English Literature and Linguistics* 27(2). 103–124.

Biq, Yung-O. 2004a. Construction, reanalysis, and stance: 'V yi ge N' and variations in Mandarin Chinese. *Journal of Pragmatics* 36(9). 1655–1672.

Biq, Yung-O. 2004b. People, things and stuff: General nouns in spoken Mandarin. *Concentric: Studies in Linguistics* 30(1). 41–64.

Biq, Yung-O, James H-Y Tai, & Sandra A. Thompson. 1996. Recent developments in functional and discourse approaches to Chinese. In James C.T. Huang & Audrey Li (eds.), *New Horizons in Chinese Linguistics*, 97–140. Boston: Kluwer.

Bybee, Joan. 2006. From usage to grammar: The mind's response to repetition. *Language* 82(4). 529–551.

Bybee, Joan. 2010. *Language, usage and cognition*. Cambridge: Cambridge University Press.

Chafe, Wallace (ed.). 1980. The pear stories: Cognitive, cultural, and linguistic aspects of narrative production. Norwood, NJ: Ablex.

Cheng, Robert L., Ying-che Li, & Ting-chi Tang (eds.). 1979. *Proceedings of symposium of Chinese linguistics*. Taipei: Student Book Co.

Chu, Chauncey C. 1983. A reference grammar of Mandarin Chinese for English speakers. New York: Peter Lang.

Chui, Kawai. 2003. Categorization of gestures in communication. In Lily I-Wen Su, Chinfa Lien, & Kawai Chui (eds.), *Form and function: Linguistic studies in honor of Shuanfan Huang*, 105–129. Taipei: Crane.

Chui, Kawai. 2005a. Topicality and gesture in Chinese conversational discourse. *Language and Linguistics* 6(4). 635–654.

Chui, Kawai. 2005b. Temporal patterning of speech and iconic gestures in conversational discourse. *Journal of pragmatics* 37(6). 871–887.

Clark, Herbert H. 1996. *Using language*. Cambridge: Cambridge University Press.

Clark, Herbert H. & Deanna Wilkes-Gibbs. 1986. Referring as a collaborative process. *Cognition* 22. 1–39.
Comrie, Bernard. 1978a. *Aspect*. Cambridge: Cambridge University Press.
Comrie, Bernard. 1978b. Ergativity. In Winfred P. Lehmann (ed.), *Syntactic typology: Studies in the phenomenology of language*, 329–394. Austin: University of Texas Press.
Couper-Kuhlen, Elizabeth. 2014. What does grammar tell us about action? In Ritva Laury, Marja Etelämäki & Elizabeth Couper-Kuhlen (eds.), *Approaches to grammar for Interactional Linguistics*. [Special issue]. *Pragmatics* 24(3). 623–647.
Curl, Traci S. 2006. Offers of assistance: Constraints on syntactic design. *Journal of Pragmatics* 38. 1257–1280.
Curl, Traci S. & Paul Drew. 2008. Contingency and action: A comparison of two forms of requesting. *Research on Language and Social Interaction* 41(2). 1–25.
Deppermann, Arnulf (ed.). 2013. Conversation analytic studies of multimodal interaction. [Special issue]. *Journal of Pragmatics* 46(1).
Dixon, R. M. W. 1977. Where have all the adjectives gone? *Studies in Language* 1. 1–80.
Dixon, R. M. W. 1979. Ergativity. *Language* 55(1). 59–74.
Duranti, Alessandro & Elinor Ochs. 1979. Left-dislocation in Italian conversation. In Talmy Givón (ed.), *Discourse and syntax*, 377–416. New York: Academic Press.
Evans, Nicholas. 2007. Insubordination and its uses. In Irina Nikolaeva (ed.), *Finiteness*, 366–431. Oxford: Oxford University Press.
Fauconnier, Gilles and Mark Turner. 2003. *The Way We Think: Conceptual Blending and the Mind's Hidden Complexities*. New York: Basic Books.
Ford, Cecilia E. 1993. *Grammar in interaction: Adverbial clauses in American English conversations*. Cambridge: Cambridge University Press.
Fox, Barbara A. 2001. On the embodied nature of grammar: Embodied being-in-the-world. In Joan Bybee & Michael Noonan (eds.), *Complex sentences in grammar and discourse*, 79–100. Amsterdam: John Benjamins.
Fox, Barbara A. 2007. Principles shaping grammatical practices: An exploration. *Discourse Studies* 9. 299–318.
Fox, Barbara A. & Sandra A. Thompson. 2010. Responses to WH-questions in English conversation. *Research on Language and Social Interaction* 43(2). 133–156.
Fox, Barbara A., Sandra A. Thompson, Cecilia E. Ford, and Elizabeth Couper-Kuhlen. 2013. Conversation analysis and linguistics. In Jack Sidnell and Tanya Stivers (eds.), *Handbook of Conversation Analysis*, 726–740. London: Blackwell-Wiley.
Givón, Talmy. 1979. *On understanding grammar*. New York: Academic Press.
Goodwin, Charles. 1979. The interactive construction of a sentence in natural conversation. In George Psathas (ed.), *Everyday language: Studies in ethnomethodology*, 97–121. New York: Irvington.
Goodwin, Charles. 1981. *Conversational organization: Interaction between speakers and hearers*. New York: Academic Press.
Goodwin, Charles. 2000. Action and embodiment within situated human interaction. *Journal of Pragmatics* 32. 1489–1522.
Goodwin, Charles & Marjorie H. Goodwin. 1987. Concurrent operations on talk: Notes on the interactive organization of assessments. *IPRA Papers in Pragmatics* 1(1). 1–54.
Goodwin, Charles & Marjorie H. Goodwin. 1992a. Assessments and the construction of context. In Charles Goodwin & Alessandro Duranti (eds.), *Rethinking context*, 147–189. Cambridge: Cambridge University Press.

Goodwin, Charles & Marjorie H. Goodwin. 1992b. Context, activity and participation. In Peter Auer & Aldo di Luzo (eds.), *The contextualization of language*, 77–99. Amsterdam: John Benjamins.

Greenberg, Joseph H. 1978. Universals of human language. Volumes 1–4. Stanford: Stanford University Press.

Haakana, Markku, Minna Laakso & Jan Lindström (eds.). 2009. *Talk in interaction – comparative dimensions*. Helsinki: Finnish Literature Society.

Hayashi, Makoto. 2003. Language and the body as resources for collaborative action: A study of word searches in Japanese conversation. *Research on Language and Social Interaction* 36(2). 109–141.

Heritage, John. 1984. *Garfinkel and ethnomethodology*. Cambridge: Polity Press.

Heritage, John & Andrew L. Roth. 1995. Grammar and institution: Questions and questioning in the broadcast news interview. *Research on language and social interaction* 28(1). 1–60.

Hopper, Paul J. 1979. Aspect and foregrounding in discourse. *Syntax and Semantics* 12. 213–241.

Hopper, Paul J. 1987. Emergent grammar. *Berkeley Linguistics Society* 13. 139–157.

Hopper, Paul J. 2004. The openness of grammatical constructions. *Chicago Linguistic Society* 40. 239–256.

Hopper, Paul J. & Sandra A. Thompson. 1980. Transitivity in Grammar and Discourse. *Language* 56(2). 251–299.

Huang, Shuan-fan. 1982. *Papers in syntax*. Taipei: Crane.

Huang, Shuan-fan. 1983. *Yuyan zhexue* [Philosophy of Language]. Taipei: Crane.

Huang, Shuanfan. 1999. The emergence of a grammatical category definite article in spoken Chinese. *Journal of Pragmatics* 31(1). 77–94.

Huang, Shuan-fan. 2013. *Chinese grammar at work*. Amsterdam: John Benjamins.

Kärkkäinen, Elise. 2012. I thought it was very interesting: Conversational formats for taking a stance. *Journal of Pragmatics* 44(15). 2194–2210.

Keenan, Elinor Ochs & Bambi Schieffelin. 1976. Topic as a discourse notion: A study of topic in the conversation of children and adults. In Charles N. Li (ed.), *Subject and topic*, 335–384. New York: Academic Press.

Langacker, Ronald W. 1990. *Concept, Image, and Symbol: The Cognitive Basis of Grammar*. (Cognitive Linguistics Research 1.) Berlin/New York: Mouton de Gruyter.

Langacker, Ronald W. & Pamela Munro. 1975. Passives and their meaning. *Language* 51(4). 789–830.

Laury, Ritva, Tsuyoshi Ono & Ryoko Suzuki. Forthcoming. Questioning the clause as a crosslinguistic unit in grammar and interaction. [Special issue]. *Studies in Language*.

Li, Charles. 1976. *Subject and Topic*. New York: Academic Press.

Li, Charles & Sandra Thompson. 1981. *A functional reference grammar of Mandarin Chinese*. Berkeley: University of California Press.

Li, Xiaoting. 2011. Syntax, prosody, and body movements in turn organization in everyday Mandarin face-to-face conversation. Beijing: Peking University dissertation.

Li, Xiaoting. 2014. *Multimodality, interaction, and turn-taking in Mandarin conversation*. Amsterdam: John Benjamins.

Lord, Carol. 1973. Serial verbs in transition. *Studies in African Linguistics* 4. 269–297.

Lü, Shuxiang. 1979. *Hanyu yufa fenxi wenti* [Issues in the analysis of Chinese grammar]. Beijing: Shanwu Yinshuguan.

Luke, Kang Kwong. 1990. *Utterance particles in Cantonese conversation*. Amsterdam: John Benjamins.

Luke, Kang Kwong & Wei Zhang. 2007. Retrospective turn continuations in Mandarin Chinese conversation. *Pragmatics* 13(4). 605–635.

Mondada, Lorenza. 2006. Participants' online analysis and multimodal practices: Projecting the end of the turn and the closing of the sequence. *Discourse Studies* 8(1). 117–129.

Mondada, Lorenza. 2011. Understanding as an embodied, situated and sequential achievement in interaction. *Journal of Pragmatics* 43. 542–552.

Paris, Marie-Claude. 1981. *Problèmes de syntaxe et de sémantique en linguistique chinois*. Paris: Presses Universitaires de France.

Raymond, Geoffrey. 2003. Grammar and social organization: Yes/no interrogatives and the structure of responding. *American Sociological Review* 68. 939–967.

Sacks, Harvey. 1974. An analysis of the course of a joke's telling in conversation. In Richard Bauman & Joel Sherzer (eds.), *Explorations in the ethnography of speaking*, 337–353. Cambridge: Cambridge University Press.

Sacks, Harvey. 1995. *Lectures on Conversation*. Oxford: Blackwell.

Sacks, Harvey, Emanuel A. Schegloff & Gail Jefferson. 1974. A simplest systematics for the organization of turn-taking for conversation. *Language* 50(4). 696–735.

Schachter, Paul. 1976. The subject in Philippine languages: Topic, actor, actor-topic or none of the above? In Charles N. Li (ed.), *Subject and topic*, 493–518. New York: Academic Press.

Schegloff, Emanuel A. 1968. Sequencing in conversational openings. *American Anthropologist* 70(6). 1075–1095.

Schegloff, Emanuel. A. 1996. Turn organization: One intersection of grammar and interaction. In Elinor Ochs, Emanuel A. Schegloff & Sandra A. Thompson (eds.), *Interaction and grammar*, 52–133. Cambridge: Cambridge University Press.

Sidnell, Jack (ed.). 2009. *Conversation Analysis: Comparative perspectives*. Cambridge: Cambridge University Press.

Sidnell, Jack & Tanya Stivers (eds.). 2005. Multimodal interaction. [Special issue]. *Semiotica* 156(1/4).

Streeck, Jürgen. 1993. Gesture as communication I: Its coordination with gaze and speech. *Communication monographs* 60. 275–299.

Streeck, Jürgen. 1994. Gesture as communication II: The audience as co-author. *Research on language and social interaction* 27(3). 239–267.

Streeck, Jürgen. 2009. *Gesturecraft: The manufacture of meaning*. Amsterdam: John Benjamins.

Streeck, Jürgen, Charles Goodwin & Curtis LeBaron (eds.). 2011. *Embodied Interaction: Language and body in the material world*. Cambridge: Cambridge University Press.

Tao, Hongyin. 1999. Body movement and participant alignment in Mandarin conversational organization. In *Papers from the 35th Regional Meeting of the Chicago Linguistic Society, Vol. II: The Panels*, 125–139. Chicago: The Chicago Linguistic Society.

Tao, Hongyin. 2001. Some Interactive Functions of Topic Constructions in Mandarin Conversation. In Proceedings of the Joint Meetings of the 10th International Association for Chinese Linguistics and the 13th North American Conference on Chinese Linguistics (Graduate Students in Linguistics Publications), 317–331. Los Angeles: University of Southern California. [Chinese translation by Yue Yao in Yuyanxue Luncong [Studies in Linguistics] 36. 363–376. Beijing: Commercial Press, 2007.

Tao, Hongyin. 2003. Toward an emergent view of lexical semantics. *Language and Linguistics* 4(4). 837–856.

Tao, Hongyin & Sandra A. Thompson. 1994. The discourse and grammar interface: Preferred clause structure in Mandarin conversation. *Journal of the Chinese Language Teachers Association* 29(3). 1–34.

Tao, Liang. 2001. Switch reference and zero anaphora: Emergent reference in discourse processing. In Alan Cienki, Barbara J. Luka & Michael B. Smith (eds.), *Conceptual and discourse factors in linguistic structure*, 253–269. Stanford: CSLI Publications.

Tao, Liang. 2006. Classifier loss and frozen tone in spoken Beijing Mandarin: The YI+GE phono-syntactic conspiracy. *Linguistics* 44(1). 91–133.

Taylor, John R. 2002. *Cognitive Grammar*. Oxford Textbooks in Linguistics. Oxford: Oxford University Press.

Teng, Shou-hsin. 1975. *A semantic study of transitivity relations in Chinese*. Berkeley and Los Angeles: University of California Press.

Thompson, Sandra A. Forthcoming. Understanding 'clause' as an emergent 'unit'. [Special issue]. *Studies in Language*.

Thompson, Sandra A. & Elizabeth Couper-Kuhlen. 2005. The clause as a locus of grammar and interaction. *Discourse Studies* 7(4–5). 481–505.

Thompson, Sandra A., Barbara A. Fox & Elizabeth Couper-Kuhlen. 2015. *Grammar in everyday talk: Building responsive actions*. Cambridge: Cambridge University Press.

Tomasello, Michael. 1999. *The cultural origins of human cognition*. Cambridge, MA: Harvard University Press.

Tomasello, Michael. 2003. Constructing a language: A usage-based theory of language acquisition. Cambridge, MA: Harvard University Press.

Tomasello, Michael (ed.). 1998. The new psychology of language: Cognitive and functional approaches to language structure, volume I. Mahwah, NJ: Laurence Erlbaum Associates.

Tomasello, Michael (ed.). 2002. The new psychology of language: Cognitive and functional approaches to language structure, volume II. Mahwah, NJ: Lawrence Erlbaum Associates.

Tsao, Feng-fu. 1979. A functional study of topic in Chinese: The first step toward discourse analysis. Taipei: Student Book Co.

Weber, Elizabeth. 1993. *Varieties of questions in English conversation*. Amsterdam: John Benjamins.

Wu, Ruey-Jiuan Regina. 1997. "Transforming Participation Frameworks in Multi-Party Mandarin Conversation: The Use of Discourse Particles and Body Behavior." Issues in Applied Linguistics 8(2): 97–118.

Wu, Ruey-Jiuan Regina. 2002. Discourse-pragmatic principles for temporal reference in Mandarin Chinese conversation. *Studies in Language* 26(3). 513–541.

Wu, Ruey-Jiuan Regina. 2004. Stance in talk: A conversation analysis of Mandarin final particles. Amsterdam: John Benjamins.

Wu, Ruey-Jiuan Regina. 2005. "There is more here than meets the eye!": The use of final *ou* in two sequential positions in Mandarin Chinese conversation. *Journal of Pragmatics* 37(7). 967–995.

Wu, Ruey-Jiuan Regina. 2006. Initiating repair and beyond: The use of two repeat-formatted repair initiations in Mandarin conversation. *Discourse Processes* 41(1). 67–109.

Wu, Ruey-Jiuan Regina. 2011. A conversation analysis of self-praising in everyday Mandarin interaction. *Journal of Pragmatics* 43(13). 3152–3176.

Yang, Ping. 2011. "Nonverbal aspects of turn taking in Mandarin Chinese interaction." Chinese Language & Discourse 2(1). 99–130.

Zhang, Wei. 1998. *Repair in Chinese conversation*. Hong Kong: University of Hong Kong dissertation.

Zhang, Wei. 2012. Latching/Rush-Through as a Turn-Holding Device and Its Functions in Retrospectively Oriented Pre-Emptive Turn Continuation: Findings from Mandarin Conversation. Discourse Processes 49(3–4). 163–191.

Xiaoting Li
Researching multimodality in Chinese interaction: a methodological account

> Verbal and nonverbal activity is a unified whole, and theory and methodology should be organized or created to treat it as such.
>
> (Pike, 1976:26)

1 Introduction

People utilize a variety of semiotic systems or modalities to produce talk and perform action in interaction. Sometimes, verbal and vocal behavior is the primary mode of communication such as in telephone conversation, while at other times bodily-visual conduct such as gesture, gaze, and posture may take on primacy; and perhaps even more often, verbal, vocal, and visual practices are orchestrated in nuanced ways to accomplish action in interaction. In order to gain a deeper understanding of how Chinese interaction is conducted and organized, a theoretically grounded methodological framework that deals with multimodal interaction is essential. Chinese linguistic research has advanced our knowledge of the organization, production, and comprehension of the language (though mostly in contrived settings) in numerous ways. But language is just one of the resources necessary for recognizing others' communicative and informative intentions. When looking at real-life interaction, it is apparent that we are still very much at the beginning of multimodal research on interaction.

This chapter is an attempt to propose a way to conduct multimodal analysis of Chinese interaction. Multimodal analysis is immensely multidisciplinary. The methodological framework proposed here is rooted in the research tradition of microanalysis of social interaction represented by conversation analysis and interactional linguistics. Before explicating the methods in conducting multimodal analysis of Chinese interaction in Section 3, I discuss the main approaches to multimodal analysis in linguistics and semiotics in Section 2.

Xiaoting Li, University of Alberta

https://doi.org/10.1515/9783110462395-003

2 Multimodal approaches

In this section, four main approaches to multimodality are briefly discussed. These approaches to multimodality are developed from different fields and disciplines, ranging from social semiotics, systemic functional linguistics, mediated discourse to conversation analysis. Due to the difference in their theoretical orientation, these approaches may have different analytical foci and methods in analyzing multimodal phenomena.

2.1 Multimodal discourse analysis

The first approach to multimodality is multimodal discourse analysis developed from Halliday's theories of social semiotics (Halliday 1978) and systemic functional grammar (Halliday 1985) with an initial focus on the semiotic resources of texts and images (Kress and Van Leeuwen 1996; Forceville 1996; Forceville and Urios-Aparisi 2009). Kress and Van Leeuwen (1996) describes that meaning is realized not only through language, but visually through dynamic selection of texts, images, and other locally available semiotic resources in communicating ideology and discourse. One of the important contributions of the social semiotic approach to multimodality is its proposal of the concept "semiotic resources". According to Van Leeuwen (2005: 285),

> Semiotic resources are the actions, materials and artifacts we use for communicative purposes, whether produced physiologically – for example, with our vocal apparatus, the muscles we use to make facial expressions and gestures – or technologically – for example, with pen and ink, or computer hardware and software – together with the ways in which these resources can be organized.

Although this approach acknowledges the diversity of semiotic resources including both the signs of visual representations (such as text, image, music, space, objects, and mathematical symbols) and embodied actions (such as gesture, gaze, and posture), majority of the research in this approach concentrates on the former, while embodied actions are the focus of microanalysis of social interaction (Li, 2016) and meaning construction (Kappelhoff and Müller 2011; Forceville 2011).

Drawing on Halliday's systemic functional linguistics (SFL), O'Halloran (2000, 2004a, 2004b) explore the metafunctional systems of semiotic resources and how semiotic choices integrate in multimodal discourse such as mathematics texts and film (Müller and Cienki 2009; Forceville and Renckens 2013). Semiotic resources are systems of meaning integrated in multimodal phenomena in specific situational and cultural context. The SFL-oriented multimodal discourse analysis is closely related to the social semiotic theory in that it strives to develop a multimodal social semiotic theory in meaning-making in multimodal objects and events in a culture (Jewitt 2009:33). Thus, the social semiotic and SFL approaches to multimodality are subsumed under the approach of multimodal discourse analysis.

2.2 Multimodal communication

The second approach to multimodality is multimodal communication which is also referred to as "multimodal interactional analysis" by Norris (2004). As this framework addresses communicative awareness and attention and centers on analyzing communicative mode, I will use the term "multimodal communication" to refer to this approach, and "multimodal interaction" to refer to the sequence-oriented microanalysis of social interaction in Section 2.4.

Multimodal communication studies draw on theories of mediated discourse (nexus of practice), interactional sociolinguistics (the ethnographic study of language use and identity construction), and social semiotic approach to multimodality (its attention to other semiotic resources such as gesture, music, and color) (Norris 2004; Norris and Jones 2005). The first step towards "multimodal interactional analysis" is communicative mode (Zima and Brône 2015). Norris (2004:12) adopts the social semiotic theory in viewing communicative modes as semiotic systems with rules and regularities (Kress and Van Leeuwen 2001) that have communicative function in interaction. The basic unit of analysis in this multimodal methodology is mediated action (Scollon 1998, 2001) which is further categorized into higher-level and lower-level actions. Through the analysis of medicated action, Norris (2004) explores how communicative modes are constitutive of action, identities, relations, as well as social interaction. By combining elements from multiple disciplines such as social semiotics, mediated discourse, and interactional sociolinguistics, "multimodal interactional studies" provides a methodological perspective to the complexity of the semiotic systems involved in human interaction.

2.3 Multimodal grammar

The third approach to multimodality is to incorporate gesture as a grammar system called multimodal grammar. It derives from the field of gesture studies. The importance of gesture in meaning-making has long been recognized and underlined by the pioneers in gesture studies (Kendon 1980, 1988; McNeill 1985). Gesture and speech have been considered as "two sides of one process of utterance" (Kendon 1980, 2004). But the use of the term multimodality in the field of gesture studies and the proposal of a multimodal grammar is a relatively recent endeavor (Fricke 2012, 2013).

A body of research in gesture studies has documented the structure of gesture based on four formal parameters of sign language: hand shape, orientation, movement, and position (Stokoe 1960; Cienki 2013; Ladewig and Bressem 2013), and described different types of gestures such as palm up open hand gesture (Müller 1998, 2004), recurrent gesture (Ladewig 2014), and away gesture (Bressem and Müller 2014). Through the systematic documentation of the gesture forms, their meaning, and their syntagmatic and paradigmatic structure from a form-based perspective (what is called "a grammar of gestures", Müller, Bressem, and Ladewig 2013; Zima 2017), gesture is argued to have "potential for language" (Müller 2009) and "emerging linguistic structures" (Müller, Bressem, and Ladewig 2013). That it is being used in conjunction with speech shows that spoken language is inherently multimodal, which points towards a multimodal grammar or multimodal construction grammar (Cienki 2017; Zima & Bergs 2017). Closely related to the linguistic documentation of gestures is the observation that gestures occupy syntactic positions and adopt syntactic functions such as NP, VP, adjectives and adverbs in a syntactic structure (Fricke 2012; Ladewig 2012). Such observations of the integration of gesture into syntactic structure of spoken language prepare the ground for the proposal of "multimodal grammar" (Fricke 2012; Müller, Bressem, and Ladewig 2013:709). Fricke (2012, 2013) argues that gesture goes through the same processes of typification and semantization as spoken language, as is evidenced by two typified forms of pointing gesture in German. Gestural structures also exhibit the same features of constituency and recursion as language. The same principles underlying gesture and language allow the integration of these two (among other sign systems) into a multimodal grammar.

The approach of multimodal grammar broadens the scope of multimodality in linguistics from the study of gesture-speech relations or language-image relations to the theorizing of integrated grammar systems of language and "human faculty of language" (Fricke 2013:751).

2.4 Multimodal interaction

The fourth approach to multimodality is multimodal interaction.[1] It is also the approach adopted in this chapter. Thus, it will be discussed in more detail.

---

[1] Streeck, Goodwin, and LeBaron (2011) uses the term "embodied interaction in the material world" to emphasize the importance of viewing human interaction as situated in and co-constructed by the

Multimodal interaction is characterized by the rigorous microanalysis of the formation of action sequences by taking into account a full array of verbal, vocal, and visual resources in human face-to-face interaction. In contrast to the multimodal discourse analysts' interest in extending social semiotic analysis to text-image-artefact combinations, research in multimodal interaction is concerned with naturally-occurring face-to-face interaction. In this approach, face-to-face interaction is "by definition, multimodal interaction in which participants encounter a steady stream of meaningful facial expressions, gestures, body postures, head movements, words, grammatical constructions, and prosodic contours" (Stivers and Sidnell 2005:1), and located in the material world (Streeck, Goodwin, and LeBaron 2011).

To better understand multimodal interaction, reviewing its intellectual roots is useful. Multimodal interaction is formed through four streams of work: conversation analysis, interactional linguistics, linguistic anthropology, and workplace studies.

Conversation analysis (CA) was developed by American sociologists Harvey Sacks and Emanuel Schegloff in studying recordings of telephone calls for their broader inquiry of establishing an observational science of social action. CA aims to identify and explicate sequential structures and practices in the formation and organization of action and turn in human interaction. It achieves this aim through the microanalysis of the design and the sequential position of each turn and action in sequences of turns and actions in temporally unfolding interaction. The systematic attention to the minutiae of interaction distinguishes it from other multimodal approaches discussed in this section. CA contributes to the development of multimodal interaction by providing a reproducible method of analyzing actions (based on "position" and "composition") applicable to all forms of face-to-face interaction. However, although some early CA work addresses the visual aspects of social interaction (Sacks and Schegloff 2002[1975]), it tends to view bodily-visual conduct as subordinate to verbal conduct and insignificant to the structures and practices identified (Drew 2004:78). Adopting the CA method, research on multimodal interaction does not prioritize verbal conduct, but rather studies the ways in which multimodal practices such as talk, gaze, gesture, and posture are brought together to build coherent courses of actions in interaction (Stivers and Sidnell 2005). An increasing number of studies on multimodal interaction have shown that bodily-visual practices are not only relevant to the formation of action in situated interaction (Goodwin 2000a, 2000b, 2003;

---

material surround. Since material objects and structures in the environments are also modalities, we call this approach "multimodal interaction", which includes both embodied actions involving voice, mouth, hands, face and body, and the material world.

Hayashi 2003, 2005), but also transformative to the (re-) conceptualization of the unit of interaction (Keevallik 2013), and collaborative turn construction and organization (Goodwin 1979; Iwasaki 2009, 2011; Mondada 2007; Li 2014). In particular, Charles Goodwin's work connects the CA method to multimodal analysis of interaction, and illuminatingly demonstrates how action and interaction is constructed and (re-)configured through the mutual elaboration of talk, body, and the material surround (Goodwin 2000a, 2000b, 2003).

The point of departure for CA inquiry is action, rather than specific semiotic system or modality. Language as a semiotic system and its relevance to interaction is the central inquiry of interactional linguistics.

International linguistics is the second stream of work contributing to the formation of multimodal interaction. It is concerned with "how linguistic structures and patterns of use are shaped by, and themselves shape, interaction" (Couper-Kuhlen and Selting 2001:1). It begins with the study of prosody in interaction (Couper-Kuhlen and Selting 1996) by explicating the relevance of different prosodic features such as pitch (Couper-Kuhlen 2001, 2004), rhythm (Auer Couper-Kuhlen, and Müller 1999), and voice quality (Ogden 2001) to action formation and turn/sequence organization in interaction. Another focus of interactional linguistics is the role of lexico-syntactic structures in interaction (Ochs, Schegloff, and Thompson, 1996; Hakulinen and Selting 2005; Auer 2009; Couper-Kuhlen and Thompson 2005). Recently, multimodality begins to gain currency in interactional linguistics with a growing interest in bodily-visual practices and their interplay with linguistic structures in interaction (Selting 2013; Ford, Thompson, and Drake 2012; Walker 2012). A striking methodological feature of CA and interactional linguistics is participants' orientation. This methodology is implemented by demonstrating how a practice is deployed, and how it is treated by participants through their observable behavior displaying such an orientation (Walker 2004). This interactional perspective to prosodic (and linguistic) practices also applies to the analysis of other multimodal practices such as gesture, gaze, and posture. I will return to a fuller account of the concept of participants' orientation and its application to analyzing Chinese interaction in Section 3.3.

The third field of study that contributes to the formation of multimodal interaction is linguistic anthropology. Linguistic anthropology investigates the ways in which linguistic forms (e.g., prosody in Gumperz 1982) and embodied practices (Duranti 1992, 2016; M. H. Goodwin 2006) construct and organize culturally defined events and social life in and through interaction. In linguistic anthropology, taking into account of the human body and the built environment is crucial for the analysis of any situated and embodied interaction (Duranti 1997:322), and for understanding the meaning of composite utterances that are inherently composed of complex semiotics (Enfield 2009). For example, language, gesture, gaze, and the position that a participant occupies (in relation to others) in a house are all constitutive of the negotiation of status and authority in Samoan ceremonial greetings (Duranti 1992). Also, body re-orientation, eyeing each other, and smiling are used by jazz musicians to achieve smooth turn transition in jazz improvisation (Duranti 2016). Lip-pointing is used as a form of deictic gesture and usually coordinated with gaze and hand pointing in Laos (Enfield 2001, 2009). M. H. Goodwin's work on language and embodied practices of children as they play on the street or playground and in family communication demonstrates how they construct their social order and social world in and through moment-by-moment interaction (M. H. Goodwin, C. Goodwin and Yaeger-Dror 2002; M. H. Goodwin 2006). The attention to not only the linguistic and embodied practices and their symbolic meaning, but also the cultural and spatio-temporal environment of interaction is an important contribution of linguistic anthropology to the study of multimodal interaction.

The fourth influence on multimodal interaction comes from workplace studies or studies of institutional interaction. According to Arminen (2005:32), institutional interaction is "a particular type of social interaction in which the participants orient to an institutional context, such as medical, juridical or educational, in and for accomplishing their distinctive institutional actions". The methodological import of workplace studies is the examination of the context's material and procedural relevance, and its documentation of the locally relevant semiotic resources in the context. Workplace interaction is never semiotically simple, which involves talk, body, artefacts and space in the material world, and pre-established procedure etc. In order to make sense of action and activity in workplace interaction, one must have the knowledge of the institutional context in question to recognize "what is going on", just as how we can understand everyday interaction based on our knowledge from being a participant in it. A substantial understanding and explication of the locally relevant semiotic systems in the institutional context to which participants are orienting is key to the analysis of action and activity in workplace interaction. For example, Heath's pioneering work (1984, 1986) on doctor-patient interaction in medical settings elucidates the ways in which patients display recipiency through gaze and posture towards the doctor, and how this display may be coordinated with the doctor's reading of medical records and initiation of a consultation. He also shows that patients adopt the "middle-distance look" away from the doctor during a physical examination, subjecting their body to another's scrutiny (Heath, 1986:111). His work shows that the construction and sequential organization of doctor and patients' talk and bodily-visual practices are largely shaped by the artefacts (e.g., medical record, stethoscope) and procedures (e.g., consultation, examination) made relevant by the particular institutional setting. Medical interaction has been and remains a fruitful site for research on multimodality in interaction, such as studies of psychotherapy sessions (Scheflen

1964; McMartin and LeBaron 2006), prenatal examinations (Nishizaka 2007), medical consultations (Heath 1984, 1986, 2002; Robinson and Stivers, 2001), and surgeries (Koschman et al. 2007; Weldon et al. 2013). Another notable line of work in workplace interaction is Goodwin's research on "professional vision" (Goodwin 1994, 1995, 1996) in the entire "contexture of action" (Goodwin 2000a, 2000b). Through the study of the work of archeologists (Goodwin 1994, 2000a), oceanographers (Goodwin 1995), and airport technicians at operating rooms (Goodwin 1996), Goodwin demonstrates how seeing of work-related phenomena in professional settings is socially situated and how it constructs and shapes the body of knowledge relevant to a profession and/or a work. Further, this activity of seeing links embodied behavior (e.g., gaze) to the larger "activity field" (e.g., in scientific work), and extends the multimodal analysis of interaction from the coordination of talk and embodied practice to the construction of the larger context of action (Goodwin 2000b). The workplace studies bring new analytic dimensions to the methodology of multimodal interaction such as the material and procedural relevance of the context and the perspective to the entire "contextual configuration". They have deepened our understanding of the semiotic richness of various types of human face-to-face interaction.

The preceding discussion of the different approaches to multimodal research in the broad field of linguistics and semiotics shows that multimodal analysis (and multimodality) is a term used by vastly diverse research communities and has differing theoretical and methodological implications. This chapter and other chapters in this book adopt this last interactional approach to Chinese interaction. A turn to multimodal aspect of interaction offers us a richer and deeper understanding of Chinese interaction. The subsequent methodological accounts of the transcription and analysis of Chinese multimodal interaction are grounded in this approach.

3 Doing multimodal analysis of Chinese interaction

Conducting research on Chinese face-to-face interaction from a multimodal analysis approach involves several steps. The first step is collecting data which are audio and video recordings of unscripted natural[2] Chinese face-to-face interaction.

---

[2] Due to the research ethics, it is impossible to claim that any recorded interaction is absolutely "natural" as if participants were not being recorded. In CA, the term "natural" refers to the idea that the recorded interaction is not experimental, not provoked and/or elicited by the researcher (Have 2007:69).

It is recommended that a separate audio recorder is used, in addition to the video recorder, to capture all the phonetic details which may be relevant to the interactional phenomena under investigation. The second step is transcribing data following transcription conventions and methods of a chosen transcription system. The third step is analyzing Chinese interactional data. Analyzing data from a multimodal interactional approach usually involves the analysis of the sequential features and multimodal practices involved in a target phenomenon. The fourth and final step is verifying the analysis, claims and analytical categories through participants' displayed orientation. Data collection is beyond the scope of the current discussion. In this section, I will discuss issues related to multimodal data transcription and annotation, and exemplify the multimodal analysis of Chinese conversation, as well as the method of using participants' displayed orientation as a way to establish and verify claims and analytical categories in Chinese conversational data. But before proceeding, some preliminary methodological issues related to multimodal analysis of Chinese interaction need to be discussed.

3.1 Methodological preliminaries

The first issue in multimodal interaction is the relevance of bodily-visual conduct. Human interaction is formed through the intertwined cooperation of a variety of multimodal resources including but not limited to grammar, prosody, the body, and objects in the environment. People constantly perform a variety of body movement in interaction such as moving of articulators in speaking, blinking, gesticulating, leaning, shrugging, etc. It is neither necessary nor practically possible to document all bodily movements people perform in interaction. Departing from the tenet of CA, the analysis of bodily-visual behavior is based on its relevance to interaction as is displayed in and through participants' observable conduct (Sacks, Schegloff, and Jefferson 1974:729). For example, people can blink 10.5 to 32.5 times per minute while conversing with each other (Doughty 2001). Blinking is a physiological need to wet the cornea. Arguably not all of these blinking behaviors are relevant to interaction. But a type of "long blink" (blinks that are 410ms or longer) produced by the addressee close to the end of a speaker's turn is relevant to interaction and serves as a social feedback signal of understanding (Hömke, Holler, and Levinson 2016). The relevance of this particular type of blinking behavior is shown through a patterned use of this behavior and evidenced through participants' orientation to its relevance. Thus, the multimodal analysis of interaction is not to account for all bodily-visual behaviors that interactants perform in interaction, but to identify its relevance to interaction as is evidenced through participants' displayed orientation.

Second, in studying an interactional phenomenon from a multimodal approach, both holistic and atomistic perspectives are needed. That is, multimodal analysts are to consider a social action being performed in interaction as a holistic experience on the part of interactants, while attending to the structure and organization of each semiotic resource or modality (such as lexico-syntax, prosody, and body movement) that collectively forms the action. A social action is always accomplished through specific practices in talk-in-interaction; and practices of speaking are always used to perform social actions. Thus, one cannot go about studying action and interaction without looking into its constitutive practices, nor can one examine a specific practice without considering the action it is used to accomplish. Thus, attention to both the holistic action as well as to its atomistic local construction through multimodal practices is necessary and would allow us to have a more systematic and deeper understanding of human interaction. On the one hand, action formation and human experience is holistic (Deppermann 2013:2; Streeck 2013). The illuminating work of Goodwin (2002, 2003, 2007) on the situated accomplishment of different types of activities (such as archaeological excavation) through locally relevant semiotic resources (such as maps, charts, pointing gestures) reminds us to attend to the larger activity and participation in interaction. It is only within the "activity framework" that each practice (and object) is endowed with particular kinds of relevance. On the other hand, actions and activities are locally accomplished through practices that are of different properties and organizations. For example, a substantial body of work on prosody/phonetics in interaction demonstrates how particular prosodic/phonetic features in talk such as creaky voice (Ogden 2001), glottal stop (Local and Kelly 1986) and other phonation types, pitch pattern (Couper-Kuhlen 2004), and a constellation of phonetic features (Local and Walker 2004; Local, Kelly, and Wells 1986 etc.) are relevant to the construction of particular actions and activities, and the organization of turns. The knowledge of the physical property and organization of different types of bodily movements such as gaze (Rossano 2012), facial expression (Ekman and Friesen 1976), head movement (McClave 2000), hand gestures (McNeill 1992; Kendon 2004), postural shifts (Scheflen 1964; Li 2013), and spatial-orientational arrangement of the interactants' bodies (Kendon 1990) is also instrumental to the understanding and analysis of *how* they interact with other practices in performing social interaction from a multimodal perspective. Thus, the two perspectives are not mutually exclusive. Multimodal analysis of social interaction ought to carefully analyze both the holistic actions/activities as well as the practices (and their organizations) that jointly constitute and accomplish those actions/activities.

Third, students of multimodal interaction shall look at (Chinese) interaction from a cross-linguistic perspective. Every turn and action is constructed and accomplished through a set of locally available linguistic and non-linguistic resources of some particular language. Although people from different speech communities possess a set of interactional abilities that are arguably universal such as making inference of each other's intention, managing misunderstanding, and conducting transaction (Levinson, 2006), the specific ways in which they are realized and used in differing speech communities are fundamentally different. Thus, the structure of linguistic and non-linguistic resources of a particular language is consequential for interaction with regard to the specific ways in which the interaction is organized. It has been documented that different word-order patterns have a significant impact on practices of turn organization. For example, while the Satzklammer (sentence brackets) in German allows for a turn projection relatively early in a TCU and turn-in-progress (Auer 1996), the early turn projection is not possible in Japanese because of its verb-final word order (Tanaka 1999). Different morphological and syntactic structures in English and Japanese also equip their speakers with different resources to perform self-repair (Fox, Hayashi and Jasperson 1996), and co-construction of a compound TCU (Lerner and Takagi 1999).

Mandarin Chinese (and other Chinese dialects) is typologically different from European languages such as English, German, French, and Finnish, and other East Asian languages such as Japanese and Korean. The typological features of Chinese such as topic-comment structure, the prevalence of "fragmented" phrasal structure in natural speech, and Chinese phonology and prosody are highly relevant to the organization of Chinese interaction. Explorations of the specific resources that the language and the body afford for the organization of Chinese interaction have clear theoretical and methodological implications.

Having discussed the preliminary issues related to multimodal analysis of Chinese interaction, the next section provides a detailed account of how to transcribe and analyze Chinese interaction from a multimodal perspective.

3.2 Transcribing Chinese interaction

Transcribing multimodal Chinese interaction involves a series of content-related and layout-related decisions. These decisions are largely dependent on transcribers' theoretical assumptions, methodological considerations, and the research question and focus (Ochs 1979; Bohle 2013; Bezemer 2014). Transcripts are inherently selective. It is neither necessary nor practically possible to present everything that transpires in interaction through transcripts. Thus, they play an important role in shaping the conceptualization and analysis of an interactional phenomenon.

3.2.1 An overview of transcription systems for multimodal interaction

Transcripts are usually formed through following the transcription methods and conventions of particular transcription systems. Research on multimodal interaction is characterized by a variety of transcription systems from widely different disciplines such as psychology, linguistics, gesture studies, conversation analysis, communication studies, and ethnography. These transcription systems differ (among other aspects) in the types of modalities that they focus on.

One type of transcription system mainly deals with the visual modality of multimodal interaction. For example, Birdwhistell's (1970) kinesic notational system of body movement documents at both the micro- and macro-kinesic level movements of different body parts including head, face, torso, limb, hand, foot etc. Ekman and Friesen's (1978) Facial Acting Coding System (FACS) offers a formal description of the patterns of muscle action in the human face derived from anatomy. It allows for a systematic description of complex behavioral tokens of facial movement. Drawn on parameters describing sign language, Bressem (2013b) proposes a system to notate and transcribe gestures based on their forms such as hand shape, position, movement, and orientation. Note that this system only provides detailed annotation for the *hands* in gestures, because "the hands are of core importance for a notation of gestural forms" (Bressem 2013b:1082).

The other type of transcription system represents both the verbal and visual modalities in interaction, although they may have different foci on the verbal and/or visual modalities. For example, McNeill's (1992) gesture transcription system transcribes not only gesture but also speech. But speech is mainly used as the basis where gestures are annotated, and its primary focus is on the form and function of co-speech gestures. In contrast to McNeill (1992), the transcription systems widely used in CA (Jefferson 1984), interactional linguistics (Selting et al. 2009), and spoken discourse studies (Du Bois et al. 1993) are characterized by an elaborate transcription of verbal and vocal modalities and a notation of gestures and other body movements often with screengrabs or drawings of the movements when they become functionally relevant to interaction.

For example, the CA transcription system established by Jefferson (1984) attempts to capture and represent the sequential aspects of talk-in-interaction based on the organization of turns (Sacks, Schegloff and Jefferson 1974). In this transcription system, the transcripts are sequentially organized where turns are represented based on their linear progression, and overlapping turns are notated by brackets at the onset of the overlap. The system transcribes the prosodic features of utterances through symbols (for pitch change, lengthening, stress, tempo change, and pauses) as well as the "eye dialect" (a nonstandard orthography reflecting the phonetic realization of an utterance). The "eye dialect" is designed to capture how the original speech sounds like through how it looks to the eye (Schenkein 1978:xi). In addition to the problem with the use of "eye dialect" for English conversation itself (see Bucholtz 2000:1456), the nonstandard orthography based on the Roman alphabet cannot be applied to transcribing Chinese conversation due to the different orthographic system and phonological structure of Chinese. The system also notates vocal and visual behaviors such as gestures, laughing, and coughing.

GAT-2 (Gesprächsanalytische Transkriptionssystem 2, Selting et al. 2009) is one of the most widely used transcription systems in interactional linguistics and particularly in German speaking areas. This system abandons the "eye dialect" in CA transcription system and adopts standard orthography to represent spoken language. It also pays closer attention to and offers a fine-grained transcription of the prosodic/phonetic features of interaction such as pitch movement, voice quality, tempo, and accent. The treatment of visual behavior in GAT-2 is similar to Jefferson's CA transcription system where nonverbal events such as gesture and coughing are represented in separate lines in double parenthesis. CA and interactional linguistics are mainly concerned with uncovering the underlying structure of talk. Thus, in contrast to their elaborate transcription of the verbal and vocal modalities and their central position in a transcript, the notation of visual behavior in Jefferson's and GAT-2 transcription systems seems rudimentary.

An alternative approach to transcribing multimodal interaction is to focus on representing action and activity. This approach is best represented by Norris (2004, 2006) and Goodwin's (2001, 2007) transcription of multimodal interaction. From a mediated discourse analytical perspective, Norris (2004, 2006) puts action at the center of her analysis and transcription. She uses sequences of stills with overlaid transcripts of speech and arrows to represent interaction. By placing video stills rather than speech at the center of her transcript, Norris (2006) conveys that relevant actions that "social actors" are engaged in and attend to may not necessarily be solely composed of language but rather a cluster of multimodal practices such as gesture, gaze, posture, head movement etc. With a similar focus on action and activity, Goodwin (2007) examines a mundane activity in everyday interaction where a father helps his daughter do homework. In accomplishing this joint activity, the spatial-orientational arrangement of the bodies of the two interactants towards each other and position of the homework sheet are highly relevant to the formation and organization of this activity. The relevance of the visual practices and the object in the physical surround (i.e., the homework sheet) is explicitly shown in and through his transcript in Figure 1 (Goodwin 2007: 56). In Goodwin's transcription of interaction, drawings or stills of visual practices and relevant objects in the material world are integrated with and related to speech. One commonality of Norris's (2004, 2006) and Goodwin's

Researching multimodality in Chinese interaction: a methodological account — 37

→1 Sandra: ***How*** is it ***fi:ve.***
 2   (2.2)
 3 Father: You mean why the ***five***?
 4 Sandra: °Mm.
 5   (0.4)
 6   Because ***see*** there's a ***five*** on the bottom there.
→7 Sandra: Oh.

Figure 1: A transcript of speech, body movement, and relevant object in interaction.
Source: Goodwin 2007:56, copyright © 2007 by Sage, reused with the permission of Sage and under the STM Guidelines.

(2007) transcription systems is that they do not assume primacy of language, but rather treat and *systematically represent* it as merely one modality among others in forming action and activity.

In addition to the aforementioned transcription systems, there are several other transcription systems used in transcribing verbal and/or visual conduct in face-to-face interaction such as HalbInterpretative ArbeitsTranskriptionen "semi-interpretative working transcription" (HIAT, Ehlich and Rehbein 1976) and the Child Language Data Exchange System (CHILDES, MacWhinney 2000). Since they are not particularly relevant to the theoretical approach to multimodal interaction this chapter adopts, they would not be introduced here and interested readers may refer to Bressem (2013a) for a thorough review of these transcription systems.

From the preceding overview we can see that the choice of transcription system for a multimodal interaction is largely dependent on the researchers' theoretical approach and research interests. In addition, predominantly, the current transcription systems for multimodal interaction are based on and created for European and American languages that use Roman alphabet in their orthography. Some (aspects of the) transcription systems may not be relevant to Chinese interaction due to its distinctive orthography and phonology. In the next section, I discuss some issues unique to transcribing Chinese multimodal interaction and my own practice in dealing with those issues through a specific example.

3.2.2 Transcribing multimodal Chinese interaction

Although the currently existing systems may not be directly applicable to the transcription of multimodal Chinese interaction, they provide valuable insights on the issues that one should attend to in the transcription of multimodal interaction in general. Building on those insights and my own experience working on Chinese conversational data from a multimodal approach, I propose that following aspects be considered in transcribing multimodal Chinese interaction.

1. General verbal features
    - Layout
        - Vertical (sequential)
        - Horizontal (temporal)
    - Speaker identification
    - Sequential structure
        - Representation of spoken Chinese
            - One-line transcription
            - Three-line transcription
            - Four-line transcription
    - Line breaks
    - Overlaps
    etc.
2. Vocal (prosodic) features
    - Segmental features
        - Voice quality (whispery, breathy, creaky, aspirated, etc.)
        - Glottal closure
        - Lengthening
        etc.
    - Suprasegmental features
        - Pitch (register, range, movement)
        - Tempo
        - Stress
        - Loudness
        - Rhythm
        - Pause
        etc.

- Other vocal features
    - In- and outbreaths
    - Laughter
    - Crying
    - Coughing
    - Sighing
    - Lip smacking
    etc.
3. Visual (kinesic) features
    - Gaze
    - Blink
    - Facial expression
    - Head movement
    - Hand gesture
    - Torso movement
    - Postural shift
    - Proxemics (Spatial-orientation change of the body)
    - Touch
    etc.

Four aspects are of particular relevance to the transcription of multimodal Chinese interaction: layout, representation of spoken Chinese, unit-final pitch movement, and the representation of visual behaviors.

When doing transcription of Chinese multimodal interaction, the first decision is usually the layout of a transcript. Two types of layouts are commonly seen in the research on multimodal interaction: vertical and horizontal, defined by the orientation of the page layout. In the vertical layout, a longer stretch of talk is broken into multiple lines, and the verbal, vocal and visual behaviors are organized sequentially in a line-by-line manner (see Excerpt 4). Alternatively, an excerpt of interaction can be presented horizontally based on the temporal emergence of different speakers' turns and their vocal and visual behaviors. Figure 2 illustrates the horizontal layout of a transcript.

The choice of vertical and horizontal layout is often determined by the research focus and theoretical approach. For example, if one conducts a frame-by-frame microanalysis of an action or activity using stills, it would be practically impossible to use the vertical layout due to the large number of stills generated by the frames of a video; and the horizontal layout of transcript can better serve that research purpose (see Bezemer 2014). But for the research focusing on the sequential organization of a course of action through turn-by-turn talk and bodily-visual behavior and patterns of linguistic and embodied actions, the vertical

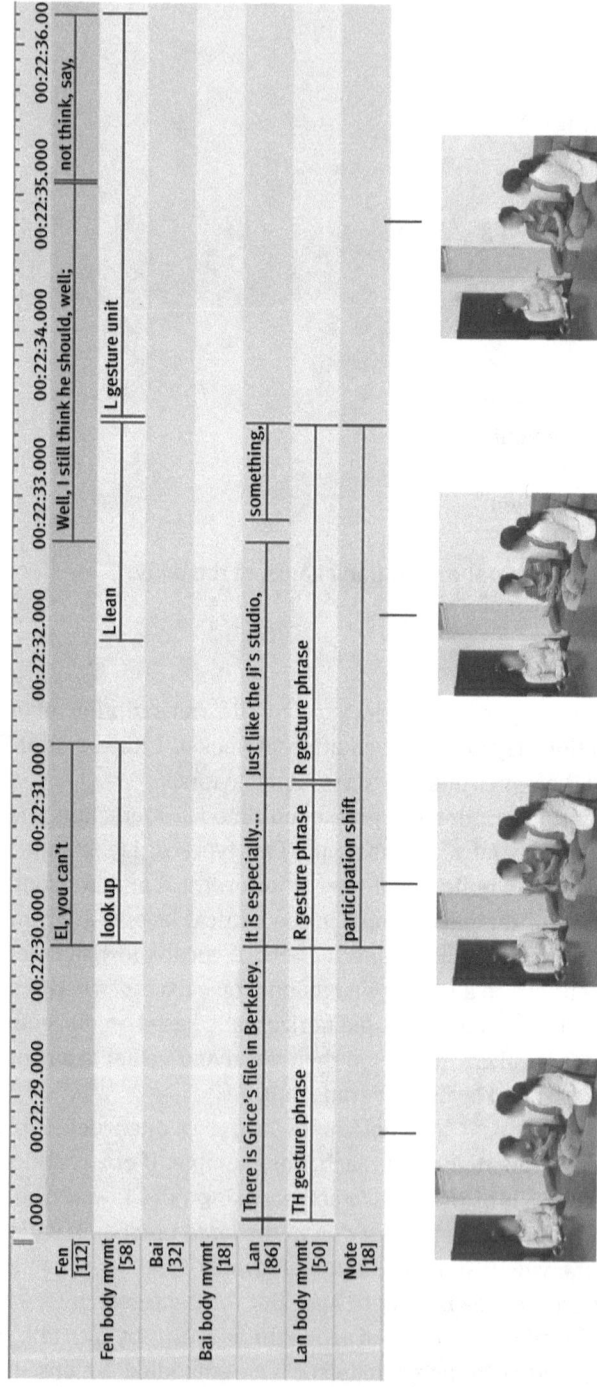

Figure 2: Horizontal layout of a transcript.

layout of transcript is more commonly used. The study that I use to exemplify my transcription of Chinese interaction here is on the interplay of multimodal practices in organizing turns and actions in Mandarin Chinese conversation. As the sequential structure of verbal, vocal and visual practices is central to answering this research question, I use the vertical transcript layout in transcribing the particular excerpt of interaction in Section 3.3.

The second issue that is of relevance to transcribing Chinese interaction is how to represent spoken Chinese orthographically for international audience, since it is written with Chinese characters rather than Roman alphabet. There are three options: one-line transcription, three-line transcription, and four-line transcription.

First, in one-line transcription, Chinese conversation is represented in its original orthography, Chinese characters. This type of transcript is used for readers of Chinese and publication in Chinese-language venues. Second, for English-speaking readers, Chinese conversation is usually represented in three lines: the first line is the original talk represented in *Hanyu pinyin* or *Pinyin* 'Chinese Phonetic Writing', a Romanized system to annotate Modern Standard Chinese pronunciation (Zhou 2003)[3]; the second line is a word-by-word English gloss of the original talk[4]; and the third line is a free translation of the original talk. In the first line of the *Pinyin* Romanization system, there are two further variations: Romanization without tone marks (Excerpt 1), and Romanization with tone marks (Excerpt 2). The Romanization system with tone marks indicates the lexical tone (i.e., pitch contour) of each syllable, and undoubtedly provides more phonological/prosodic information. But it can be a laborious task to represent spoken Chinese as Roman letters with tone marks through regular computer keyboard, and the phonological information conveyed by the tone marks may still be opaque to readers who do not know Chinese language. Thus, three-line transcription without tone marks is commonly seen in publications on Chinese conversation in English-language venues. One issue with three-line transcription is Chinese speakers may find it more difficult to read, because Chinese has a large number of homophonous syllables (Zhou 2003), and the meaning of a word may not be immediately discernible without the help of Chinese characters. The third option for transcribing Chinese conversation is four-line transcription (see Excerpt 3), where the first line represents talk in original Chinese orthography

---

[3] The Romanization system of Pinyin is designed to annotate the phonemes of Modern Standard Chinese or Mandarin Chinese, rather than other Chinese dialects (Zhou 2003). Some Chinese dialects such as Cantonese have developed their own Romanized annotation systems (Zhou 2003).
[4] Strictly speaking, the second line is a combination of word translation and annotation of the grammatical information of certain functional words such as particles and aspect markers in Chinese.

(Chinese characters), the second line is the Romanized *Pinyin* spelling of the original talk (with or without tone mark), the third line is a word-by-word English gloss, and the fourth line is an idiomatic English translation of the original talk. The four-line transcription is friendly to both Chinese-speaking and English-speaking readers. Due to its accessibility to a wide body of audience, I use four-line transcription in this chapter.

(1)
01 Lei: *Wo keyi tongguo zhongjie de fangshi zhaodao zhege fangzi.*
       I can through real estate agent ASSC way find this-CL house
       'I can find this house through real estate agent.'

(2)
01 Lei: *Wǒ kěyǐ tōngguò zhōngjiè de fāngshì zhǎodào zhègè fángzǐ.*
       I can through real estate agent ASSC way find this-CL house
       'I can find this house through real estate agent.'

(3)
01 Lei: 我可以通过 中介的方式找到 这个房子.
       Wo keyi tongguo zhongjie de fangshi zhaodao zhege fangzi.
       I can through real estate agent ASSC way find this-CL house
       'I can find this house through real estate agent.'

The third issue in transcribing Chinese interaction is whether (and if so, how) to transcribe unit-final pitch movement. Unit-final pitch movement is notated in several transcription systems designed for intonation languages such as English (Du Bois et al. 1993) and German (GAT-2, Selting et al. 2009), because unit-final pitch movement has pragmatic function in forming actions performed by a turn of talk. But in tone languages such as Chinese, pitch movement is primarily used to differentiate lexical meanings. Unit-final pitch movement in spoken Chinese is usually affected by both the lexical tone of the unit-final syllables and boundary tone (Cao 2002). Prior research shows that global pitch movement or intonation does exist in spoken Chinese (Chao 1968; Cao 2002; Li 2014), which may have pragmatic function as well. Thus, it is necessary to notate unit-final pitch movement, in spite of the interplay of tones of the unit-final syllables. In my study of turn-final prosody in Mandarin conversation (Li 2014), a significant number of unit-final syllables are unstressed and their tones are neutralized; and thus, many turns end with low fall or high fall pitch movement. Among the transcription systems for interaction, GAT-2 has the most elaborate final pitch movement transcription, including two types of falling pitch movement. I adopt the symbol

";" for low fall, and "." for high fall unit-final pitch movement, among other types (see Appendix).

The final issue is the transcription of visual behavior. In Jefferson's (1984) and GAT-2 (Selting et al. 2009) transcription systems of conversational interaction, nonverbal behavior and event are usually noted as researchers' comments in a separate line in double parenthesis. In Goodwin's (2007) transcription system, they are represented visually through stills or drawings concurrent with verbal exchanges (Figure 1), and gaze is coded in terms of its on- and offsets as well as the performer of gaze above (speaker's gaze) and below (recipient's gaze) the speaker's verbal line (see Goodwin 1979:106–107). In the transcription systems focusing on one particular type of body movement such as hand gesture (Bressem 2013a; McNeill 1992) and facial expression (Ekman and Friesen 1978), other concurrent bodily-visual behaviors such as gaze and torso movement are not considered. Multimodal analysis of interaction ought to take into account not only a particular type of body movement or a particular modality, but also other verbal, vocal, and visual conduct as well as their interplay in the construction of social actions. Stemmed from this theoretical assumption, I represent the verbal, vocal, and visual conduct in my transcription of Chinese interaction. In general, three methods are used to represent visual behavior in my transcription: separate commentary noting non-verbal event (e.g., a speaker's knee hits a bed frame), special notational symbols for different types of visual behaviors (such as gaze, gesture and torso movement), and drawings or photographic stills. The symbols for gesture are from Kendon's (2004) annotation of gesture unit, and those for gaze and torso movement are inspired by Heath's (1986) research on body movement and speech in medical interaction (see Appendix).

Excerpt 4 exemplifies the transcription of different types of concurrent visual behaviors, as well as the verbal and vocal practices. The four relevant issues in the transcription of Chinese interaction (i.e., layout, representation of spoken Chinese, unit-final pitch movement, and representation of visual behaviors) are also exemplified in this excerpt.

(4) The popular instrumentalist (Li 2014:196–197)
031 Bin: 他们 网 上　 就是要 要 要那个 拉二胡那个小 姑　 娘:
　　　　tamen wangshang jiushi yaoyaoyao neige la erhu nage xiaoguniang:
　　　　they internet just ask ask ask that play Erhu thatCL little girl

032　　　那 个 电 话　 号 　码;
　　　　nei ge dianhua haoma;
　　　　that CL telephone number
　　　　'On the Internet, they asked for the telephone number of the girl who played Erhu,'

Figure 3: Bin's body movements at *gao* in line 033.

Figure 4: Bin's body at rest position at the end of line 033.

```
Hand      | ~~~~~~************-.-.-.-. |
Torso     H....... F------------.......H
Head      H....... F------------.......H
033    → 而且   高   价  (.)  求   购.
         erqie  GAO  jia (.) qiu  gou.
         and   high price   ask  buy
         'and even (offered) a high price to buy it.'

034 Pei:  <<aspirated> 真:>    的   呀.
          <<aspirated>ZHEN:>  de   ya.
                              really PRT
          'Really!'
```

(This excerpt is from Li, Xiaoting. 2014. *Multimodality, Interaction and Turn-taking in Mandarin Conversation.* pp 196–197. Reprinted with kind permission from John Benjamins Publishing Company, Amsterdam/Philadelphia. [https://www.benjamins.com/#catalog/books/scld.3/main].)

In the transcript of this excerpt, hand gesture, torso movement, and head movement are annotated directly above the verbal line using specialized symbols, and further represented through drawings (Figures 3 and 4). Prosodic features such as stress (line 033), lengthening (lines 031 and 034), (aspirated) voice quality (line 034), and unit-final pitch movement are represented through notational symbols modified from GAT-2 (Selting et al. 2009). This sequence of interaction is represented in a vertical layout in the four-line transcription format.

Before proceeding, it should be noted that the transcription system presented and exemplified here only shows one way of transcribing Chinese interaction, and it is designed for particular sets of research questions and theoretical approaches. It by no means attempts to *prescribe* how Chinese interaction shall be transcribed. It is hoped that students of conversation analysis, interactional linguistics, and multimodal analysis could contribute to the discussion of the transcription of Chinese interaction from a multimodal perspective.

3.3 Analyzing multimodal interaction

After transcribing a spate of Chinese interaction, the next step is to analyze it. As is clarified in Section 2, this book approaches Chinese interaction from a CA and interactional linguistic perspective. Therefore, the methodology used in the multimodal analysis of Chinese interaction to a large extent aligns with those fields. However, there are some issues related to the methodology of multimodal interaction in general, and multimodal analysis of Chinese interaction in particular. In this section, I outline the typical procedures in analyzing Chinese interaction from a multimodal perspective. Then, I focus on how to establish and evidence one's claims and analytical categories. Finally, I exemplify the analytical procedures through the analysis of the interplay of multimodal practices in turn organization in a short excerpt of Mandarin conversational data.

3.3.1 Procedures in analyzing multimodal interaction

Conducting multimodal analysis of Chinese interaction typically involves the following steps:
- observing video recordings of naturalistic Chinese interactional (such as everyday face-to-face conversation);
- identifying an interactional phenomenon or practice through repeated viewing of data;
- collecting more instances of the phenomenon or practice, and creating a dataset of the targeted phenomenon or practice;
- describing the phenomenon or practice; and
- establishing the validity of analytic claims and/or categories through participants' orientation.

These steps, particularly the first three steps, are similar to doing CA research (see Sidnell 2012). There is a substantial body of literature on the introduction to CA and its methodology (Drew 2004; Have 2007; Hutchby and Wooffitt 1998; Levinson 1983; Sidnell 2012; etc.). An elaborate discussion of the first three steps seems unnecessary. The last two steps are essential to and define the current multimodal approach to Chinese interaction, and thus deserve further discussion.

When describing an interactional phenomenon or practice, all relevant semiotic resources in the immediate semiotic landscape are to be taken into consideration. That is, we as analysts ought to carefully analyze the internal organization of all those semiotic systems without prioritizing (or ignoring) any of them *a priori*. This could pose some challenge due to the constraints of our normally field-specific training background. For example, students of gesture studies may not have the expertise to conduct systematic prosodic/phonetic analysis of conversation, and vice versa. Multimodal analysis of interaction is not (only) an analysis of bodily-visual conduct, but a careful examination of all semiotic resources including (but not limited to) lexico-syntax, prosody, bodily-visual conduct, object in the environment, epistemics, and sequential position. It requires knowledge of the organization of all these semiotic systems or modalities.

After describing a phenomenon or practice, the final step is to establish the validity of the analytic claims and/or categories through demonstrating participants' orientation to them. Analytic claims and/or categories in CA and interactional linguistics arise from and evidenced through how a phenomenon or practice is treated by conversational participants themselves. That is, those claims and/or analytic categories are not the subjective interpretation of the analysts who are outsiders of interaction, or the intuition of the participants when producing/hearing some utterance or action. Rather, they are established and evidenced through *displays* of participants' orientation in terms of the *observable* behavior of participants themselves. This fundamental thrust of CA and interactional linguistics is explained by Sidnell (2012):

> ...instead of examining what persons say they do or did in interaction, we must examine what persons actually *do*, and, from this, discern the analyses they have produced of the circumstances in which they find themselves. .... So, for example, the only evidence we have of a turn-taking system in conversation as described by Sacks, Schegloff and Jefferson (1974) is to be found in conversationalists' displayed orientations to that system.
>
> (Sidnell 2012:79; emphasis in original)

and Selting and Couper-Kuhlen (1996:3):

> The demonstration that participants do indeed orient to the prosodic features in question is used as a warrant for the analytic decisions made. This procedure, which seeks evidence for

its claims in the observable treatment of prosody by participants themselves, frees analysts from the need to rely on intuitions or pre-constructed theories.

The display of participants' treatment through their own observable conduct is called *participants' orientation* in CA. It is the participants' observable behavior that warrants any analytic claims and/or categories, and the relevance of analyses to participants themselves rather than us analysts. The previous steps in analyzing multimodal interaction are exemplified in the next section.

3.3.2 Analyzing multimodal interaction – an exercise

In this section I provide a detailed account of how I analyze a stretch of Mandarin conversation for one particular study from a multimodal perspective. This study is on turn organization in everyday Mandarin face-to-face conversation (Li 2014). In this study, I recorded and examined c.a. 20 hours of everyday face-to-face conversation among native speakers of Mandarin. There are five dyads, three triads, a quartet and a sextet in the data. The current data excerpt is taken from the quartet. The question explored in this excerpt of interaction is: how do participants deploy multimodal resources to construct a turn and indicate possible turn completion in the multi-party conversation?

In this excerpt, Lei (male), Qin (male), Hai (male), and Yin (female) are talking about Lei's problem in his house-hunting in Berlin, Germany. Prior to this sequence, Lei reported that he submitted a rental application to a property management office (referred to as *Hausverwaltung* 'house management' in the excerpt) to rent a house. The prior tenant (referred to as *ta* 'she') of the house asks him to move in to the house after she moves out. But the property management office is rejecting his rental application. In this sequence, Lei expresses his frustration about the confusion regarding who has the say in his rental application (lines 1 to 3). In the current participation framework, Yin and Hai are Lei's addressed recipients, which is made publically visible through Lei's body orientation and gaze towards Hai and Yin across the table (Figure 6).

(5) TO_HLQY_apartment rental
01   Lei: 但 问 题 是．
           dan wenti shi.
           but problem be
           'But the problem is,'

```
02  Lei:   她 不 能   决 定   谁 来  住 进 来;
            ta bu neng jueding shei lai zhu jinlai;
            3SG NEG can decide who come live in
            'she (the prior tenant) can't decide who could move in.'

03  Lei:   Hausver[waltung 决   定.
            Hausver[waltung jueding.
            property management decide
            'The property management office decides (that).'

04  Qin:          [对 对 她 不    能,
                  [dui dui ta bu neng,
                  right right 3SG NEG can
                  'Right, right, she (the prior tenant) can't.'

05  Qin:   Haus[verwaltung   也 不   能  决 定.]
            Haus[verwaltung   ye bu neng jueding.]
            building management also NEG can decide
            'Property management office also can't decide.'
```

Figure 5: Lei's gaze at Qin at *suoyi* in line 06.

Figure 6: Lei's hands and gaze at Hai and Yin at the end of line 06.

```
Gaze          at Qin                ...at Hai and Yin
Hand          |~~~~~~~~~~~~~~~~~~~~~****************~~~~~~~~~~~~~~~~
06  Lei: →   [所以<<f, cresc> 所以 她 (.) 她她自己>]没 有 弄 清 楚 关 系=
              [suoyi<<f, cresc>suoyita (.) tataziji>]meiyou nongqingchuguanxi=
              so              so 3SG 3SG 3SG –self NEG have clear relation
              'So so she herself was confused about the relationship.'
```

```
Gaze        at Hai and Yin
Hand        ****************
07  Lei: →  她 她 她 [把 我;]
            ta ta ta [ba wo;]
            3SG 3SG 3SG BA me
            'she …'

08  Qin:               [不 是-]
                       [bu shi-]
                       NEG be
                       'No.'

09  Qin:    Haus[verwaltung 也 为 难    啊;
            Haus[verwaltung ye weinan a;
            Building management also difficult PRT
            'It's difficult for the property management office too.'
```

Figure 7: Lei's gesture at *jiazai* in line 10.   **Figure 8**: Lei's body position at *banfa* at the end of line 10.

```
Gaze        at Hai and Yin
Hand        ~~~~~~~~~********************.-.-.-.-.|
10  Lei: →  [就 是:(.)夹 在 中    间儿 没 [有  办 法;
            [jiushi: (.) jiazai zhongjianr mei [you banfa;
            just be stick in  middle  NEG have solution
            '(she) put me in the middle (between her and the property
            management company). I'm stuck.'

11  Yin:                                  [没 有-
                                          [mei you-
                                          NEG have
                                          'No.'
```

12 Yin: 有 时 候 是 可 以 的;
            youshihou shi keyi de;
            sometimes be OK PRT
            'Sometimes it's OK.'

Here, the targeted lines are Lei's multi-unit turn in lines 6, 7 and 10. The question is how does Lei design and how other participants treat the (syntactic and/or prosodic) junctures at the end of lines 6, 7 and 10 with regard to possible turn completion?

Lei contrasts the consideration of the previous tenant in asking him to move in to her inability to make such a decision (lines 1–2). Lei then asserts that it is the management office that makes the decision on rental applications (line 3). Immediately after Lei's assertion, Qin produces a strong disagreement that the management office cannot make such a decision (line 5). Lei begins his turn in line 6 "a beat" later than Qin (line 5) with *suoyi* connecting his incipient TCU to his prior talk (Fang 2000). Lei's recycling of his turn-initial element *suoyi* 'so' and his turning to and looking at Qin (Figure 5) at *suoyi* (line 6) verbally and visibly address the possible impairment of his overlapped talk (Schegloff, 1987). The noticeable increase of loudness starting from the recycled turn-beginning element until the end of the overlapping talk in Lei's turn in line 6 displays that Lei designs his incoming speech as turn competitive (French and Local 1983). Lei continues his TCU- and turn-in-progress after the overlap until the possible completion of the TCU and turn at the end of *guanxi* 'relation' (line 6). Lei continues with his turn by accounting of the consequence of the prior tenant's ("her") confusion about the relationship between her and the property management office that puts him in a difficult spot (lines 7 and 10). The turn continuation is produced with no hearable beat of silence between "*guanxi*" (line 6) and "*ta*" (line 7). This pre-emptive "through-produced" turn continuation elaborating the consequence of the prior tenant's confusion inflicted on him shows that Lei treats his report in line 6 as inadequate (Zhang 2012).

In addition to "through-produced" prosody, Lei's bodily-visual behavior also indicates turn continuation at the end of the TCU in line 6. Lei has been gesticulating since the beginning of his projected extended turn in line 1. Towards the end of line 6 at *meiyou*, Lei moves both arms upwards and starts brushing his hair backwards with his hands (Figure 6). His self-grooming action continues across the end of lines 6 and 7 until line 10. At the end of line 6 and during his self-groom, Lei maintains mutual gaze with the addressed recipients Hai and Yin (Figure 6). Here, the raised open-arm self-groom is used as a "turn-holding" gesture.

Thus, at the end of the TCU in line 6, despite the possibly complete syntactic structure and social action (the delivery of "the problem" projected in line 1 being possibly complete), the prosodic and bodily-visual conduct indicate that Lei's turn-so-far is still in progress. That the addressed recipients Hai and Yin refrain from taking the turn at the end of line 6 displays that they also orient to Lei's turn-so-far as incomplete.

As Lei's turn proceeds to the end of line 7, he produces a c.a. 0.5-second pause. At this pause, line 7 forms part of the *BA* construction ([Subject+*BA*+Indirect Object+Verb]) with the final verb or VP missing (see Li and Thompson 1981:463). Visually, Lei is still brushing his hair. At this prosodic juncture, the lexico-syntactic structure and bodily-visual conduct foreshadow turn continuation. Although the un-addressed participant Qin is clearly expressing his disagreement with Lei (lines 8 and 9) *before* and at the pause, the addressed recipients Hai and Yin have not taken the turn. This demonstrates that in the current participation framework they also treat Lei's turn as still in progress.

Lei continues his turn in line 10. After a hedging expression *jiushi* 'just be', Lei completes the *BA* construction by producing the VP *jiazai zhongjian* 'stuck in the middle'. Lei again immediately produces the subsequent TCU *meiyou banfa* 'not solution' without any "beat of silence" and latched it onto the immediately prior TCU. After an iconic gesture concurrent with the VP *jiazai zhongjianr* 'stuck in the middle' (Figure 7), Lei's hands return to a rest position (Figure 8) at the end of line 10. Lei's turn at the end of line 10 is possibly complete as is indicated convergently by the multimodal cues including lexico-syntax, prosody, bodily-visual conduct, and action. Yin initiates her turn disagreeing with Lei's assertive statement about the lack of involvement of the prior tenant in the decision on the next tenant (lines 11 and 12). That Yin starts up in "terminal overlap" shows that she recognizes and attends to Lei's turn at the end of line 10 as transition relevant (Jefferson 1984).

This excerpt demonstrates that multimodal resources such as lexico-syntax, prosody, gesture and gaze work together in a convergent (the end of line 10) *or* divergent (the end of lines 6 and 7) manner in indicating the possible completion of a turn. An accurate account of how turn transition is accomplished requires a close examination of locally relevant verbal, vocal, and visual practices in temporally unfolding interaction. Further, the analytical claims regarding the relevance of multimodal practices to turn transition or continuation is evidenced through how the speaker Lei designs and how the addressed recipients Yin and Hai orient to his ongoing talk, i.e., participants' perspective.

4 Discussions and conclusions

Interaction is fundamental in social life; it is the primordial site of human sociality. Interaction is multimodal by nature. In real-life situation, interactants deploy and attend to a variety of verbal, vocal, visual resources that are made available in and through language, the body, and the physical surround to build talk, accomplish action, and achieve intersubjectivity. It is sensible that our research methodology shall reflect this reality. Traditional linguistic theory and methodology are developed to mainly investigate the verbal aspect of interaction. This chapter demonstrates the importance and necessity to examine interaction from a multimodal perspective, and to expand the theory and methodology to investigate the intricate interplay of multimodal practices in Chinese interaction. In this chapter, I have reviewed different multimodal approaches to the study of interaction, and discussed how to conduct multimodal analysis of Chinese interaction. I focus on and exemplify the transcription and analysis of Chinese face-to-face interaction from a multimodal and interactional perspective.

The current discussion of multimodal analysis of Chinese interaction has several methodological implications. First, it expands the transcription practices for languages that do not use Roman alphabet in their writing system. Transcription conventions for multimodal interaction conducted in English and other European languages that use Roman alphabet are well established. Transcribing languages of other orthographic systems such as Chinese faces unique challenges. The four-line transcription method and conventions in transcribing Mandarin Chinese conversation used in this chapter offers one way to make transcripts accessible to international readers of various linguistic backgrounds. Second, the multimodal research on Chinese interaction contributes to our understanding of the role of prosody in the organization of talk and interaction. In English and other intonation languages pitch movement represents intonation, and unit-final pitch movement conveys pragmatic information. But in tone languages such as Chinese, pitch movement is primarily phonemic rather than pragmatic. Thus, unit-final pitch movement is affected by the lexical tone of the final syllables and does not solely reflect intonation. The link between unit-final intonation pattern and possible turn completion and the type of sentence and action accomplished by the TCU that is observed in English (Bolinger 1957; Quirk et al. 1985) may not exist in Chinese. A close examination of the unique features of Chinese prosody and its role in interaction develops our understanding of the organization and role of prosody in tone languages. Considering that approximately 42% of the world's languages are tone languages (Maddieson 2008), the research on Chinese prosody in multimodal interaction has important methodological implications to the study of interaction in other tone languages.

However, this chapter also shows that we are still very much at the beginning of doing multimodal research on interaction, and Chinese interaction in particular. Our understanding and methodology of multimodal research on Chinese interaction is still very much in the process of development. By sharing a way to conduct multimodal analysis of Chinese interaction in this chapter, I would like to welcome and encourage more researchers to enter into this rapidly-evolving conversation on how to explore the multimodal nature of Chinese interaction.

Appendix

Transcription conventions
The transcription system used for vocal elements in this chapter is GAT 2 (Selting et al., 2009). The following is an abbreviated version adapted from Selting et al. (2009) with a few small modifications.

[ ]	overlap
=	latching
(.)	micro-pause
(-), (--), (---)	short, middle or long pauses of ca. 0.2–0.8 seconds, up to ca. 1 second
(1.0)	pauses of 1.0 second
hehehe	short and syllable-like laughter
((laughing))	description of laughter
:, : :, :::	lengthening of ca. 0.2–0.8 seconds, up to ca. 1 second
ʔ	glottal stop
((cough))	paralinguistic and non-linguistic actions
<<coughing> >	paralinguistic and non-linguistic actions which accompany a stretch of speech
<<creaky>XX>	creaky voice
(XX)	presumed wording
(( ))	omission of text
→	specific line in the transcript which is referred to in the text
?	final pitch movements: high rise to high
,	final pitch movements: mid-rise to high
-	final pitch movements: mid or high level
;	final pitch movements: low fall to low
.	final pitch movements: high fall to low

For a TCU separated in two lines, the final pitch movement is not notated at the end of the first line.

重音	accent (marked by underlining) in Chinese characters
ACcent	primary, or main accent
!AC!cent	extra strong accent
↓	pitch step down
↑	pitch step up
<<f> >	forte, loud
<<ff> >	fortissimo, very loud
<<p> >	piano, soft
<<pp> >	pianissimo, very soft
<<all> >	allegro, fast
<<len> >	lento, slow
<<cresc> >	crescendo, becoming louder
<<dim> >	diminuendo, becoming softer
<<acc> >	accelerando, becoming faster
<<rall> >	rallentando, becoming slower
.h, .hh, .hhh	breathing in, according to its duration
h, hh, hhh	breathing out, according to its duration

The transcription system used for body movements in this chapter can be found below. The transcription system used for gaze and gesture can also be found in C. Goodwin (1981), Heath (1986) and Kendon (2004).

~	preparation of gesticulation
*	stroke of gesticulation
*	holding of stroke
*	superimposed beat
-.	recovery of gesticulation
¦	boundary of gesture phrase
|	boundary of gesture unit
x	head nodding
F	forward movement
H	home position
U	upward movement
......	a series of dots represent movement
------	close dashes indicate the holding of the body movements
away	gaze away
at	gaze at

References

Arminen, Ilkka. 2005. *Institutional interaction: studies of talk at work*. Aldershot: Ashgate.
Auer, Peter. 1996. On the prosody and syntax of turn-taking. In Elizabeth Couper-Kuhlen & Margret Selting (eds.), *Prosody and conversation*, 57–100. Amsterdam/Philadelphia: John Benjamins.
Auer, Peter. On-line syntax: thoughts on the temporality of spoken language. *Language Sciences* 31. 1–13.
Auer, Peter, Elizabeth Couper-Kuhlen & Frank Muller. 1999. *Language in Time: The rhythm and tempo of spoken interaction*. Oxford: Oxford University Press.
Bezemer, Jeff. 2014. How to transcribe multimodal interaction? A case study. In Carmen D. Maier & Sigrid Norris (eds.), *Texts, images and interaction: A reader in multimodality*. Berlin/New York: Mouton de Gruyter.
Birdwhistell, Ray. 1970. *Kinesics and context: eassays on body, motion, communication*. Philadelphia: University of Pennsylvania Press.
Bohle, Ulrike. 2013. Approaching notation, coding, and analysis from a conversational analysis point of view. In Cornelia Müller, Alan Cienki, Ellen Fricke, Silva H. Ladewig, David McNeill & Sedinha Teßendorf (eds.), *Body – Language – Communication. An International Handbook on Multimodality in Human Interaction (Handbooks of Linguistics and Communication Science 38.1)*, 992–1007. Berlin/New York: Mouton de Gruyter.
Bolinger, Dwight L. 1957. *Interrogative structures of American English*. Tuscaloosa AL: University of Alabama Press.
Bressem, Jana. 2013a. Transcription systems for gestures, speech, prosody, postures, gaze. In Cornelia Müller, Alan Cienki, Ellen Fricke, Silva H. Ladewig, David McNeill & Sedinha Teßendorf (eds.), *Body-Language-Communication: An international handbook on multimodality in human interaction. (Handbooks of Linguistics and Communication Science 38.1.)*, 1037–1058. Berlin/New York: De Gruyter: Mouton de Gruyter.
Bressem, Jana. 2013b. A linguistic perspective on the notation of form features in gestures. In Cornelia Müller, Alan Cienki, Ellen Fricke, Silva H. Ladewig, David McNeill & Sedinha Teßendorf (eds.), *Body-Language-Communication: An international handbook on multimodality in human interaction. (Handbooks of Linguistics and Communication Science 38.1.)*, 1079–1098. Berlin/ New York: Mouton de Gruyter.
Bressem, Jana & Cornelia Müller. 2014. The family of AWAY-gestures. In Cornelia Müller, Alan Cienki, Ellen Fricke, Silva H. Ladewig, David McNeill & Jana Bressem (eds.), *Body-Language-Communication: An International Handbook on Multimodality in Human Interaction. (Handbooks of Linguistics and Communication Science 38.2.)*, 1592–1604. Berlin/New York: Mouton de Gruyter.
Bucholtz, Mary. 2000. The Politics of Transcription. *Journal of Pragmatics* 32. 1439–1465.
Cao, Jianfen. 2002. Hanyu Shengdiao yu Yudiao de Guanxi [The Relationship between Tone and Intonation in Chinese]. *Zhongguo Yuwen* 2002(3). 195–202.
Chao, Yuen-Ren. 1968. *A grammar of spoken Chinese*. Berkeley: University of California Press.
Cienki, Alan. 2013. Gesture, space, grammar, and cognition. In Peter Auer, Martin Hilpert, Anja Stukenbrock & Benedikt Szmrecsanyi (eds.), *Space in Language and Linguistics: Geographical, Interactional, and Cognitive Perspectives*, 667–686. Berlin: Walter de Gruyter.
Cienki, Alan. 2017. Utterance Construction Grammar (UCxG) and the variable multimodality of constructions. *Linguistics Vanguard* 3. 1–10.

Couper-Kuhlen, Elizabeth. 2001. Interactional prosody: High onsets in reason-for-the-call turns. *Language in Society* 30. 29–53.

Couper-Kuhlen, Elizabeth. 2004. Prosody and sequence organization: The case of new beginnings. In Elizabeth Couper-Kuhlen & Cecilia E. Ford (eds.), *Sound patterns in interaction*, 335–376. Amsterdam/Philadelphia: John Benjamins.

Couper-Kuhlen, Elizabeth & Margret Selting (eds.) 1996. *Prosody in conversation: Interactional studies*. Cambridge: Cambridge University Press.

Couper-Kuhlen, Elizabeth & Margret Selting. 2001. Introducing interactional linguistics. In Margret Selting & Elizabeth Couper-Kuhlen (eds.), *Studies in interactional linguistics*, 1–24. Amsterdam/Philadelphia: John Benjamins.

Couper-Kuhlen, Elizabeth & Sandra A. Thompson. 2005. The clause as a locus of grammar and interaction. *Discourse Studies* 7. 481–505.

Deppermann, Arnulf. 2013. Multimodal interaction from a conversation analytic perspective. *Journal of Pragmatics* 46(1). 1–7.

Doughty, Michael. 2001. Consideration of three types of spontaneous eyeblink activity in normal humans: During reading and video display terminal use, in primary gaze, and while in conversation. *Optometry & Vision Science* 78(10). 712–725.

Drew, Paul. 2004. Conversation analysis. In Kristine Fitch & Robert Sanders (eds.), *Handbook of language and social interaction*, 71–102. Mahwah, NJ: Lawrence Erlbaum.

Du Bois, John W., Stephan Schuetze-Coburn, Susanna Cumming, & Danae Paolino. 1993. An outline of discourse transcription. In Jane A. Edwards & Martin D. Lampert (eds.), *Talking Data: Transcription and coding in discourse research*, 45–89. Hillsdale, NJ: Lawrence Erlbaum.

Duranti, Alessandro. 1992. Language and bodies in social space: Samoan ceremonial greetings. *American Anthropologist* 94. 657–91.

Duranti, Alessandro. 1997. *Linguistic Anthropology*. Cambridge: Cambridge University Press.

Duranti, Alessandro. 2016. Eyeing each other: Visual access during jazz concerts. Paper presented at the 7th Conference of International Society for Gesture Studies (ISGS) in Paris.

Ehlich, Konrad & Jochen Rehbein. 1976. Halbinterpretative Arbeitstranskriptionen (HIAT). *Linguistische Berichte* 45. 21–41.

Ekman, Paul & Wallace V. Friesen. 1976. Measuring facial movement. *Environmental Psychology and Nonverbal Behavior* 1(1). 56–75.

Ekman, Paul & Wallace V. Friesen. 1978. *Manual for the facial action coding system*. Palo Alto, CA: Consulting Psychologists Press.

Enfield, Nick J. 2001. Lip-pointing: A discussion of form and function with reference to data from Laos. *Gesture* 1(2). 185–211.

Enfield, Nick J. 2009. *The anatomy of meaning: Speech, gesture, and composite utterances*. Cambridge: Cambridge University Press.

Fang, Mei. 2000. Ziran kouyu zhong ruohua lianci de huayu biaoji gongneng [Reduced Conjunctions as Discourse Markers]. *Zhongguo Yuwen* 5. 459–470.

French, Peter & John Local. 1983. Turn Competitive Incomings. *Journal of Pragmatics* 7. 701–715.

Forceville, Charles. 1996. *Pictorial Metaphor in Advertising*. London: Routledge.

Forceville, Charle. 2011. The journey metaphor and the Source-Path-Goal schema in Agnès Varda's autobiographical gleaning documentaries. In Monika Fludernik (ed.), *Beyond Cognitive Metaphor Theory: Perspectives on Literary Metaphor*, 281–297. New York: Routledge.

Forceville, Charles & Eduardo Urios-Aparisi. 2009. *Multimodal Metaphor*. Berlin/New York: Mouton de Gruyter.
Forceville, Charles and Thijs Renckens. 2013. The "good is light" and "bad is dark" Metaphors in Feature Films. *Metaphor and the Social Word* 3, 160–179.
Ford, Cecilia E., Sandra A. Thompson & Veronika Drake. 2012. Bodily-visual practices and turn continuation. *Discourse Processes* 42 (3–4). 192–212.
Fox, Barbara, Makoto Hayashi & Robert Jasperson. 1996. Resources and repair: a cross-linguistic study of the syntactic organization of repair. In Elinor Ochs, Emanuel A. Schegloff & Sandra A. Thompson (eds.), *Interaction and grammar*, 185–227. Cambridge: Cambridge University Press.
Fricke, Ellen. 2012. *Grammatik multimodal: Wie Wörter und Gesten zusammenwirken*. Berlin/New York: Mouton de Gruyter.
Fricke, Ellen. 2013. Towards a unified grammar of gesture and speech: A multimodal approach. In Cornelia Müller, Alan Cienki, Ellen Fricke, Silva H. Ladewig, David McNeill & Sedinha Teßendorf (eds.), *Body – Language – Communication. An International Handbook on Multimodality in Human Interaction (Handbooks of Linguistics and Communication Science 38.1)*, 733–754. Berlin/New York: Mouton de Gruyter.
Goodwin, Charles. 1979. The interactive construction of a sentence in natural conversation. In George Psathas (ed.), *Everyday language: Studies in ethnomethodology*, 97–121. New York: Irvington.
Goodwin, Charles. 1994. Professional vision. *American Anthropologist* 96(3). 606–33.
Goodwin, Charles. 1995. Seeing in depth. *Social Studies of Science* 25. 237–74.
Goodwin, Charles. 1996. Transparent vision. In Elinor Ochs, Emanuel A. Schegloff & Sandra A. Thompson (eds.), *Interaction and grammar*, 370–404. Cambridge: Cambridge University Press.
Goodwin, Charles, 2000a. Practices of seeing, visual analysis: An ethnomethodological approach. In Theo van Leeuwen & Carey Jewitt (eds.) *Handbook of visual analysis*, 157–82. London: Sage.
Goodwin, Charles, 2000b. Action and embodiment within situated human interaction. *Journal of Pragmatics* 32. 1489–1522.
Goodwin, Charles, 2002. Time in action. *Current Anthropology* 43. 19–35.
Goodwin, Charles, 2003. Pointing as situated practice. In Sotaro Kita (ed.), *Pointing: Where language, culture and cognition meet*, 217–241. Mahwah, NJ: Lawrence Erlbaum.
Goodwin, Charles, 2007. Participation, stance, and affect in the organization of activities. *Discourse and Society* 18 (1). 53–73.
Goodwin, Marjorie H. 2006. Participation, affect, and trajectory in family directive/response sequences. *Text and Talk* 26(4/5). 513–542.
Goodwin, Marjorie H. Charles Goodwin and Malcah Yaeger-Dror. 2002. Multi-modality in Girls' game disputes. *Journal of Pragmatics* 34. 1621–49.
Gumperz, John J. 1982. *Discourse strategies*. Cambridge: Cambridge University Press.
Hakulinen, Auli & Margret Selting, (eds.). 2005. *Syntax and lexis in conversation: Studies on the use of linguistic resources in talk-in-interaction*. Amsterdam/Philadelphia: John Benjamins.
Halliday, Michael A K. 1978. *Language as social semiotic: The social interpretation of language and meaning*. Baltimore: University Park Press.
Halliday, Michael A K. 1985. *An introduction to functional grammar*. London: Edward Arnold.
Have, Paul ten. 2007. *Doing conversation analysis: a practical guide*. Second Edition. London: Sage.

Hayashi, Makoto. 2003. *Joint Utterance Construction in Japanese conversation*. Amsterdam/Philadelphia: John Benjamins.

Hayashi, Makoto. 2005. Joint turn construction through language and the body: Notes on embodiment in conjoined participation in situated activities. *Semiotica* 156(1/4). 21–53.

Heath, Christian. 1984. Talk and recipiency: sequential organization in speech and body movement. In Maxwell J. Atkinson & John Heritage (eds.), *Structures of social action: Studies in conversation analysis*, 247–65. Cambridge: Cambridge University Press.

Heath, Christian. 1986. *Body movement and speech in medical interaction*. Cambridge: Cambridge University Press.

Heath, Christian. 2002. Demonstrative suffering: The gestural (re)embodiment of symptoms. *Journal of Communication* 52. 597–617.

Hömke, Paul, Judith Holler & Stephen C. Levinson. 2016. Blinking as addressee feedback in face-to-face conversation. Paper presented at the 7th Conference of the International Society for Gesture Studies (ISGS7). Paris, France.

Hutchby, Ian & Robin Wooffitt. 1998. *Conversation analysis: Principles, practices and applications*. Cambridge: Polity Press.

Iwasaki, Shimako. 2009. Initiating interactive turn spaces in Japanese conversation: local projection and collaborative action. *Discourse Processes* 46(2). 226–246.

Iwasaki, Shimako. 2011. The multimodal mechanics of collaborative unit construction in Japanese conversation. In Jürgen Streeck, Charles Goodwin & Curtis LeBaron (eds.), *Embodied interaction: Language and body in the material world*, 106–120. Cambridge: Cambridge University Press.

Jefferson, Gail. 1984. Transcript notation. In Maxwell J. Atkinson & John Heritage (eds.), *Structures of social action: Studies in conversation analysis*, ix-xvi. Cambridge: Cambridge University Press.

Jewitt, Carey. 2009. Different approaches to multimodality. In Carey Jewitt (ed.), *Routledge handbook of multimodal analysis*, 28–39. London: Routledge.

Kappelhoff, Hermann and Cornelia Müller. 2011. Embodied meaning construction: Multimodal metaphor and expressive movement in speech, gesture, and feature film. *Metaphor and the Social World* 1(2). 121–153.

Keevallik, Leelo. 2013. The interdependence of bodily demonstrations and clausal syntax. *Research on Language and Social Interaction* 46(1). 1–21.

Kendon, Adam. 1980. Gesture and speech: two aspects of the process of utterance. In Mary R. Key, (ed.), *Nonverbal communication and language*, 207–227. The Hague: Mouton.

Kendon, Adam. 1988. How gestures can become like words. In Fernando Poyatos (ed.), *Cross cultural perspectives in nonverbal communication*, 131–141. New York: C. J. Hogrefe, Inc.

Kendon, Adam. 2004. *Gesture: Visible action as utterance*. Cambridge: Cambridge University Press.

Koschmann, Timothy, Curtis LeBaron, Charles Goodwin, Alan Zemel & Gary Dunnington. 2007. Formulating the triangle of doom. *Gesture* 7(1). 97–118.

Kress, Gunther & Theo van Leeuwen. 2001. *Multimodal discourse: The modes and media of contemporary communication*. London: Arnold.

Kress, Gunther & Theo van Leeuwen. 2006. *Reading images: The grammar of visual design*. London: Routledge.

Ladewig, Silva (2012). Syntactic and semantic integration of gestures into speech – Structural, cognitive, and conceptual aspects. PhD thesis, European University Viadrina, Frankfurt (Oder).

Ladewig, Silva H. & Jana Bressem. 2013. New insights into the medium hand – Discovering structures in gestures on the basis of the four parameters of sign language. *Semiotica* 197. 203–231.

Ladewig, Silva H. 2014. Recurrent gestures. In Cornelia Müller, Alan Cienki, Ellen Fricke, Silva H. Ladewig, David McNeill & Jana Bressem (eds.) Body-Language-Communication: *An International Handbook on Multimodality in Human Interaction. (Handbooks of Linguistics and Communication Science 38.2.)*, 1558–1574. Berlin/New York: Mouton de Gruyter.

Lerner, Gene H. & Takagi, Tomoyo. 1999. On the place of linguistic resources in the organization of talk-in-interaction: A co-investigation of English and Japanese grammatical practices. *Journal of Pragmatics* 31(1). 49–76.

Levinson, Stephen C. 1983. *Pragmatics*. Cambridge: Cambridge University Press.

Li, Charles N. & Sandra A. Thompson. 1981. *Mandarin Chinese: A functional reference grammar*. Berkeley, CA: University of California Press.

Li, Xiaoting. 2013. Language and the body in the construction of units in Mandarin face-to-face interaction. In Beatrice Szczepek Reed & Geoffrey Raymond (eds.) *Units of talk—units of action*, 343–375. John Benjamins: Amsterdam/Philadelphia.

Li, Xiaoting. 2014. *Multimodality, interaction and turn-taking in Mandarin conversation*. Amsterdam/Philadelphia: John Benjamins.

Li, Xiaoting. 2016. Researching Body Movement and Interaction in Education. In Kendall King, Yi-Ju Lai & Stephen May (eds.) *Encyclopedia of Language and Education 3rd edition*, Vol. 10, *Research Methods in Language and Education*, 1–12. Berlin/New York: Springer.

Local, John, John Kelly & William H.G. Wells. 1986. Towards a phonology of conversation: turn taking in Tyneside English. *Journal of Linguistics* 22(2). 411–437.

Local, John, & Gareth Walker 2004. Abrupt-joins as a resource for the production of multi-unit, multi-action turns. *Journal of Pragmatics* 36(8). 1375–1403.

MacWhinney, Brain. 2000. *The CHILDES project: Tools for analyzing talk*. 3rd Edition. Mahwah, NJ: Lawrence Erlbaum Associates

Maddieson, Ian. 2008. Tone. In Martin Haspelmath, Matthew S. Dryer, David Gil & Bernard Comrie (eds.), *The World atlas of language structures online*. Munich: Max Planck Digital Library.

McClave, Evelyn. 2000. Linguistic functions of head movements in the context of speech. *Journal of Pragmatics* 32. 855–878.

McMartin, Clare & Curtis D. LeBaron. 2006. Multiple involvements within group interaction: A video-based study of sex offender therapy. *Research on Language and Social Interaction*, 39, 41–80.

McNeill, David. 1985. So you think gestures are nonverbal? *Psychological Review* 92. 350–371.

McNeill, David. 1992. *Hand and mind*. Chicago: University of Chicago Press.

Mondada, Lorenza. 2007 Multimodal resources for turn-taking: Pointing and the emergence of possible next speakers. *Discourse Studies* 9(2). 195–226.

Müller, Cornelia. 1998. *Redebegleitende Gesten. Kulturgeschichte-Theorie-Sprachvergleich*. Berlin: Berlin Verlag.

Müller, Cornelia. 2004. The Palm-Up-Open-Hand. A case of a gesture family? In Cornelia Müller & Roland Posner (eds.), *The semantics and pragmatics of everyday gestures*, 233–256. Berlin: Weidler.

Müller, Cornelia. 2009. Gesture and language. In Kirsten Malmkjaer (ed.), *Routledge's Linguistics Encyclopedia*, 214–217. Abington/ New York: Routledge.

Müller, Cornelia, Jana Bressem & Silva H. Ladewig. 2013. Towards a grammar of gesture – a form based view. In Cornelia Müller, Alan Cienki, Ellen Fricke, Silva H. Ladewig, David McNeill & Sedinha Teßendorf (eds.), *Body – Language – Communication. An International Handbook on Multimodality in Human Interaction (Handbooks of Linguistics and Communication Science 38.1)*, 707–733. Berlin/New York: Mouton de Gruyter.

Müller, Cornelia & Alan Cienki. 2009. Words, gestures, and beyond: forms of multimodal metaphor in the use of spoken language. In Charles Forceville & Eduardo Urios-Aparisi (eds.), *Multimdodal Metaphor* 297–328. Berlin/New York: Mouton de Gruyter.

Nishizaka, Aug. 2007. Hand touching hand: Referential practice at a Japanese midwife house. *Human Studies* 30 (3). 199–217.

Norris, Sigrid. 2004. *Analyzing multimodal interaction: A methodological framework*. London: Routledge.

Norris, Sigrid. 2006. Multiparty interaction: A multimodal perspective on relevance. *Discourse Studies* 8(3). 401–421.

Norris, Sigrid & Rodney Jones (eds.). 2005. *Discourse in action: Introducing mediated discourse analysis*. London/New York: Routledge.

Ochs, E., Schegloff, E., & Thompson, S. 1996 (eds.). *Interaction and grammar*. Cambridge: Cambridge University Press.

Ogden, Richard. 2001. Turn transition, creak and glottal stop in Finnish talk-in-interaction. *Journal of the International Phonetics Association* 31. 139–152.

O'Halloran, Kay L. 2000. Classroom discourse in mathematics: A multisemiotic analysis. *Linguistics and Education* 10(3). 359–388.

O'Halloran, Kay L. 2004a. On the effectiveness of mathematics. In Eija Ventola, Cassily Charles, & Martin Kaltenbacher (eds.), Perspectives on multimodality, 91–117. Amsterdam: John Benjamins.

O'Halloran, Kay L. 2004b. Visual semiosis in film. In Kay L. O'Halloran (ed.) *Multimodal discourse analysis*, 109–130. London: Continuum.

Pike, Kenneth L. 1967. *Language in relation to a unified theory of the structure of human behavior*. The Hague: Mouton.

Quirk, Randolph, Sidney Greenbaum, Geoffrey Leech & Jan Svartvik. 1985. *A Comprehensive Grammar of the English Language*. London: Longman.

Robinson, Jeffrey & Tanya Stivers. 2001. Achieving activity transitions in primary-care encounters: From history taking to physical examination. *Human Communication Research* 27(2). 253–298.

Rossano, Federico. 2012. *Gaze behavior in face-to-face interaction*. Unpublished Ph.D. dissertation, Max Planck Institute for Psycholinguistics, Nijmegen, the Netherlands.

Sacks, Harvey & Emanuel A. Schegloff. 2002 [1975]. Home Position. *Gesture* 2 (2). 133–146.

Sacks, Harvey, Emanuel A. Schegloff & Gail Jefferson. 1974. A simplest systematics for the organization of turn-taking for conversation. *Language* 50. 696–735.

Schegloff, Emanuel A. 1987. Recycled turn beginnings. In Graham Button & John R. E. Lee, (eds.) *Talk and social organization*, 70–85. Clevedon, England: Multilingual Matters.

Schenkein, Jim, (ed.), 1978. *Studies in the organization of conversational interaction*. New York: Academic Press.

Scollon, Ron. 1998. *Mediated discourse as social interaction: A study of news discourse*. London: Longman.

Scollon. Ron. 2001. Scollon Mediated discourse: The nexus of practice. London: Routledge.

Selting, Margret. 2013. Verbal, vocal, and visual practices in convertional interaction. In Cornelia Müller, Alan Cienki, Ellen Fricke, Silva H. Ladewig, David McNeill & Sedinha Teßendorf (eds.), *Body – Language – Communication. An International Handbook on Multimodality in Human Interaction (Handbooks of Linguistics and Communication Science 38.1)*, 589–609. Berlin/New York: Mouton de Gruyter.

Selting, Margret, Peter Auer, Dagmar Barth-Weingarten, Jörg Bergmann, Pia Bergmann, Karin Birkner, Elizabeth Couper-Kuhlen, Arnulf Deppermann, Peter Gilles, Susanne Günthner, Martin Hartung, Friederike Kern, Christine Mertzlufft, Christian Meyer, Miriam Morek, Frank Oberzaucher, Jörg Peters, Uta Quasthoff, Wilfried Schütte, Anja Stukenbrock, Susanne Uhmann1. 2009. Gesprächsanalytisches Transkriptionssystem 2 (GAT 2). *Gesprächsforschung-Online-Zeitschrift zur verbalen Interaktion* 10. 353–402.

Selting, Margret & Elizabeth Couper-Kuhlen. 1996. Introduction. In Margret Selting & Elizabeth Couper-Kuhlen (eds.), *Prosody in conversation: Interactional studies*, 1–10. Cambridge: Cambridge University Press.

Sidnell, Jack. 2012. Basic conversation analytic methods. In Jack Sidnell & Tanya Stivers (eds.), *The handbook of conversation analysis*, 77–99. Oxford: Wiley-Blackwell.

Stokoe, William C. 1960. *Sign Language Structure: An Outline of the Visual Communication Systems of the American Deaf*. Buffalo, NY: Det. of Anthropology and Linguistics, University of Buffalo.

Stivers, Tanya & Jack Sidnell. 2005. Introduction: Multimodal interaction. *Semiotica* 156. 1–20.

Streeck, Jürgen. 2013. Interaction and the living body. *Journal of Pragmatics* 46. 69–90.

Streeck, Jürgen, Charles Goodwin & Curtis LeBaron (eds.). 2001. *Embodied interaction: Language and body in the material world*. Cambridge: Cambridge University Press.

Tanaka, Hiroko. 1999. *Turn-taking in Japanese Conversation: A study in grammar and interaction*. Amsterdam: John Benjamins

Van Leeuwen, Theo. 2005. *Introducing social semiotics*. London/New York: Routledge.

Walker, Gareth. 2004. *The phonetic design of turn endings, beginnings, and continuations in conversation*. PhD thesis, University of York.

Walker, Gareth. 2012. Coordination and interpretation of vocal and visible resources: "Trail-off" conjunctions. *Language and Speech* 55(1). 141–163.

Weldon, Sharon-Marie, Terhi Korkiakangas, Jeff Bezemer & Roger Kneebone. 2013. Communication in the operating theatre. *British Journal of Surgery* 100. 1677–1688.

Zhang, Wei. 2012. Latching/rush-through as a turn-holding device and its functions in retrospectively oriented pre-emptive turn continuation: Findings from Mandarin conversation. *Discourse Processes* 49(3). 163–191.

Zhou Youguang. 2003. *The Historical Evolution of Chinese Languages and Scripts* (translated by Zhang, Liqing). Ohio State University National East Asian Language Resource Center. (Pathways to Advanced Skills Series, vol. 8). Colombus, Ohio: Ohio State University National East Asian Language Resource Center.

Zima, Elisabeth & Geert Brône. 2015. Cognitive Linguistics and interactional discourse: Time to enter into dialogue. *Language and Cognition* 7(4). 485–498.

Zima, Elisabeth. 2017. Multimodal constructional resemblance: The case of English circular motion constructions. In Francisco José Ruiz de Mendoza Ibáñez, Alba Luzondo Oyón & Paula Pérez Sobrino (eds). *Constructing families of constructions: Analytical perspectives and theoretical challenges*, 301–337. Amsterdam: John Benjamins.

Zima, Elisabeth & Alexander Bergs. 2017. Multimodality and Construction Grammar. *Linguistics Vanguard* 3(1), 1–9.

Part II: **Multimodal practices**

Hongyin Tao
List gestures in Mandarin conversation and their implications for understanding multimodal interaction

1 Introduction

List constructions (or lists) have long been recognized as a cross-linguistically recurrent conversational practice with various formal features and functional utilities. An example of a list construction from Jefferson (1990: 64, ex. 3) is given below:

(1) Desk: And, ih- in general what we try to do is help people figure out what the trouble is, what kind of help they need and get it for them.

While lists have been analyzed extensively (see literature review below), few have attempted to provide a working definition. Some investigators have noted that list items have formal similarities and are "notionally equivalent" (Sánchez-Ayala 2003: 337). For our purposes here, we can define a prototypical list construction as one where a set of formally similar and functionally related items are produced in adjacent conversation units (either in the same speaker turn or in adjacent turns) that fall under a broad discourse theme. Thus, in example (1), the three items, "help people figure out what the trouble is," "what kind of help they need," and "get it for them," produced by the same speaker, can be seen as closely produced and thematically related items illustrating the proposition of "what we try to do."

A Mandarin example of a list construction can be found in (2).

(2) (Two graduate students talking about the difficulties of finding jobs in desirable locations.)

1.C: .. 最近几年有的工作,[1]
Zuìjìn jǐ nián yǒu de gōngzuò,
'In recent years, jobs,

---

[1] Each punctuation line indicates roughly an intonation unit as defined in Chafe (1987, 1994) and Du Bois et al. (1993). However, in some instances longer lines are broken into multiple lines. Also, line numbering generally corresponds to intonation units; however, to save space, some IUs are lumped together under one line number. For a complete list of transcription symbols, see the Appendix.

Hongyin Tao, University of California, Los Angeles

https://doi.org/10.1515/9783110462395-004

2.　...　都是很=,
　　　　dōu shì hěn=,
　　　　almost all came from very=

3.　...　很偏远的地方.
　　　　hěn piānyuǎn de dìfāng.
　　　　very remote places. (Like)'

4.　...　Nebraska.

5.B:　...　( ) Nebras[ka].

6.C:　　　　　[Arizona].

7.B:　...　Nebraska.　　(LA)

This list (lines 4–7) contains four nominals making reference to places (including one repeated, twice, by the respondent), all in falling intonation contours, which serve to illustrate what are considered to be undesirable places with available jobs (*hěn piānyuǎn de dìfāng* 'very remote places').

Lists are noticeable due to their unique shapes and communicative potential. For example, proposals have been made to classify lists into framing and demonstrating categories (Sánchez-Ayala 2003). According to this dichotomy, framing lists serve to provide various kinds of background information for the participants to mutually identify a referent of interest or some aspect of the content of the list items (an example given by the author is one where a speaker talks about the long distance telephone company that she uses and says that it is not Company X, not Company Y, and not Company Z, but one of the little ones). Demonstrating lists (such as (1) and (2) given earlier), on the other hand, serve to provide evidence or details to support a claim and seek affiliation from the interlocutor. Another line of functional research on list constructions is reflected in discursive psychology (DP). Proponents of DP such as Edwards (1994) and Potter (1996) show that items listed under the same category in conversation are often ad hoc and are designed for the interactional task at hand. This research is intended to stand in contrast with standard cognitive psychology, which holds the view that human behavior can be analyzed as following some abstract scripts (e.g. Schank and Abelson 1977). Lists are also compared with narratives as related discourse structures since both can express multiple events and items (Fox 1987; Schffrin 1994) and can be demonstrated to be developmentally relevant in child language (Küntay 2004). Finally, in applied fields such as political discourse analysis, research has shown that lists can be mechanisms for direct interaction (such as inviting/generating applause) in political talks (Atkinson, 1984; Heritage and Greatbatch 1986); and in legal discourse analysis, studies have shown that the tripartite listing format is an effective cross-examination strategy often taken advantage of by both lawyers and witnesses (Drew 1990) and is thus recommended for professional legal rhetoric training (Boon 1999: 11–13).

More closely relevant for the present study are characterizations of demonstrable linguistic features and the interactional relevance of lists in conversation. In terms of features, researchers have described types of items that can go in a list. For example, Jefferson (1990) shows a wide range of possible materials in a list, from clausal units (as shown in (1)) to single word expressions (e.g. "Samuel just takes things casually and naturally and all that" (Jefferson 1990: ex. 23)). An especially interesting feature noted and used as a starting point by Jefferson (1990) is one of three-partedness, whereby the preferred number of items that go in a list is three (although fewer and more items are shown to occur as well). Later studies have expanded the three-partedness characterization to something larger, including the immediately prior and post environments of the main body of a list – i.e. not just the list items themselves – resulting in an expansive three-part characterization. Sánchez-Ayala (2003), for example, proposes an "onset, body, and coda" schema, where body in the middle refers to the traditional list itself, while Selting (2004, 2007)'s tripartite model identifies three major components – projecting, list, and post-detailing – to describe similar phenomena. Based on the multi-embedding and multi-component nature of lists, Knerich (2013) calls lists "preformed structures," highlighting the regularity of the formal features of list constructions.

Prosody is another area where extensive research on lists has been carried out in recent decades. Here, most of the focus has been on intonation units and prosodic patterns within and across list items, with characterizations focusing on parallel as well as variation in pitch contour, register levels, and overall (upward or downward) intonation directions (Couper-Kuhlen 1986; Sánchez-Ayala 2003; Selting, 2004, 2007). Sánchez-Ayala (2003) especially notes the importance of the intonation unit (Chafe 1987) as a way to characterize individual items and major component boundaries. Prosodic feature differentiating closed and open lists have also been proposed (Selting, 2004, 2007), where the former is said to exhibit a downward intonation trend whereas the latter does not. Selting (2004, 2007) insightfully points out that it is the prosodic similarity among list items rather than any particular prosodic pattern per se that makes lists recognized as such. In this vein, an extensive review of early literature on prosodic features of lists and a characterization of non-native English prosody in listing can be found in Ouafeu (2006).

Finally, a number of researchers highlight the integrative nature and complexity of list production, which is found to involve parallel syntax (Auer 2014), rhythm, turn taking, and other fabrics of conversation. Here it is shown that different aspects of modality as well as elements in the communicative environment can be orchestrated by multiple parties in highly organized ways to build courses of action through a list sequence (Erickson 1982, 1992). This aligns well with other conversation analytic research showing how speakers orient to lists and take advantage of their formal features as a resource for interaction (Jefferson 1990; Lerner 1994).

All of these are extremely helpful for our understanding of lists in Mandarin conversation. For example, in the Mandarin case we just saw in Extract (2), it is clear that the Mandarin extract exhibits lexico-grammatical as well as prosodic patterns of a list similar to some of those described by Sánchez-Ayala (2003) and Selting (2004, 2007), and that interlocutors' mutual orientation to a list in progress, as discussed by Jefferson (1990) and Lerner (1994), is also strongly demonstrated by the co-construction and repetition of list items by both speakers.

As rich and stimulating as the existent literature has been, however, a glaring gap in most of the current studies has been the lack of attention to bodily behavior, especially hand gestures. With the exception of Streeck and Hartge (1992), Streeck (2008), and Karlsson (2010), there is so far virtually no study showing gesture's relevance to the production of lists and the exact role it plays in the process of interaction.[2] This is somewhat surprising given that linguistic materials in lists, as will be shown later, are often fitted together with gestures. Streeck and Hartge (1992: 150–152) and Streeck (2008), in demonstrating how gesture can contextualize speech, and turn-taking in particular, briefly shows that in the Philippine language *Ilokano* a palm up gesture with left index finger pointing to the palm projects a list. In Karlsson (2010), two instances of hand gestures in Swedish conversations are analyzed. Karlsson further puts forward two types of functions found in her data: to help take back the floor in one instance and to mark contrast and the finished status of a unit in another. However, one limitation in both of these studies is that a limited number of instances are examined, so it is not immediately clear how recurrent these gestures are in list formulations and what tendencies can be seen in them. By contrast, what I call "list gestures," especially of the "composite" type (to be detailed below) in this paper are quite regularly bounded with Mandarin lists, to the extent that some of them may well be labeled emblematic (Kendon 2004) list gestures. By considering list gestures in Mandarin conversation, I aim to show that not only are list sequences common across at least some typologically different languages, but that gestures can play

---

[2] I thank Xiaoting Li for some of the references discussed here.

critical roles in shaping the form of lists and in doing various types of interactional work during the process of conversational exchanges. List gestures in Mandarin, I contend, can be taken to be a strong case for arguing that gesture is a distinct mode of interaction and that talk as social practices involves multiple modalities organized in concerted ways (Goodwin 2000, 2013; Stivers and Sidnell 2005, Schröder 2017). Finally, I will argue that it is necessary to recognize both the integration of multiple modalities as well as the unique contributions that each modality makes to everyday interaction.

2 Data and methodology

2.1 Data

Data for this study come from a corpus of video-recorded, naturally-occurring Mandarin conversations. Four sample video recordings, collected by researchers from the Universities of California, Los Angeles and Santa Barbara, are used in this study. Each of the four conversations lasts 30–60 minutes and represents casual talk between close friends whose ages range from their twenties to fifties. The conversations took place in Beijing and Seoul. Table 1 shows the basic information about the recordings.

Table 1: Description of data.

Conversation	Length	Location	No. of Spkrs	Gender	Year Recorded
Reunion	30 m	Beijing	3	3M	1996
Soccer	45 m	Beijing	3	3M	2001
Hometown	50 m	Seoul	3	3F	2008
Cards	55 m	Seoul	4	2M2F	2008

2.2 List gestures and their physical characteristics in Mandarin conversation

When viewing the Mandarin video recorded conversations, one immediately realizes that lists are frequently co-articulated with hand gestures of some sort. To give a more accurate assessment of the frequency information, I examined one of the four conversations, Hometown, which lasts slightly longer than 50 minutes,

Table 2: Gesture-marked lists in Hometown, a 50:19min. Conversation among three females.

Use of gesture	Number of Tokens	Percentage
No visible hand gestures	12	32%
With visible hand gestures	26	68%
Total	38	100%

and identified all instances of lists, with and without hand gestures. The results are shown in Table 2.

The numbers in Table 2 clearly show that lists with gesture are very common in Mandarin conversation, hence the necessity of paying more attention to gestures. Furthermore, my observation of the Mandarin data suggests that hand gestures can be classified into two broad types: composite gestures and reiterative gestures. Composite gestures are more or less fixed gestures with distinct listing qualities. In Mandarin Chinese, they are realized typically as several key kinetic components and variations, including a) an extended arm with palm up and curled (or extended) fingers, b) some motions of the fingers, typically retractions or extensions, in the extended hand, and, optionally, c) the touch or pointing of fingers from one hand to the other in some counting motion. They are called composite mainly because they involve both conventionalized physical shapes and sequences of finger action as just described while having an exposed hand gesture that more or less stays in the public interactional space throughout the production process of the list. In short, composite list gestures have a strong emblematic quality in them.

Figures 1–4 are composite list gestures produced by four different speakers from my database, which serve to illustrate the aforementioned features and their combinations.

The list gestures of the composite type seen here are deemed more or less conventionalized also because they appear very similar to a typical counting gesture, where some numbers may be involved and indexed by digits of the hand and finger movements (usually with an extended arm). Figure 5 is a snapshot of a series of counting motions involving one hand from a speaker (on the right) in the conversation Hometown, where the speaker is engaged in the act of inferring, by way of calculating, the addressee's age ("21, 22, 23, or 24") and her years at different stages of college education. That counting and listing share a certain basic shape is perhaps understandable.

Reiterative gestures, by contrast, do not have a fixed shape similar to counting and are not exhibited throughout the process of a list. Instead, reiterative gestures are a series of gestures of various types produced intermittently with

List gestures in Mandarin conversation and their implications — 71

Figure 1: List gesture (featuring a & b).

Figure 2: List gesture (featuring a & b).

Figure 3: List gesture (featuring a, b, & c).

Figure 4: List gesture (featuring a, b, & c).

different items of a list. Thus, typically a list item receives a one-time gesture (e.g. a beat gesture with hands, hands in non-beat-like motions, a pointing gesture, etc.), and when the individual item is completed, the gesture is also done, as indicated by, for example, retrieving the hand to its rest position or in a post-stroke hold (Kita 1993, Kendon 2004: 112). When the next list item comes up, the same gesture or a different type of gesture may appear with the new item and through a similar process. In other words, reiterative gestures typically manifest as the repetition of like strokes (Kendon 2004: 112) with more or less the same physical components and motion types rather than variations of them. The recurrence of parallel gesture units constitutes a visual rhythm, much like prosodic rhythm, hence a recognizable list-like discourse unit. Of course there is no guarantee that each and every one of the articulated list items will receive a gesture (stroke), let alone an identical one; variations do exist. An example of a series of reiterative gestures for different list items is given in (3).

Figure 5: A counting gesture for reference to years of age.

(3) (Speaker X in the middle recounts how one time classmates around her all fell asleep during an important lecture class.)

1. |~~~~~~~~****/****~~~~~~~ [3]   [Fs. 6 & 7][4]
X: 在那, <F旁边旁边 F>都睡下,
   Zài nà, <F **pángbiān pángbiān** F> dōu shuì xià,
   '(People) there, **(this) side, (that) side**, all fell asleep;

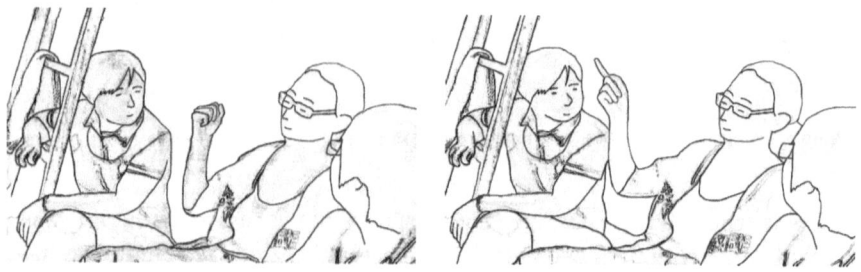

Figure 6: *Pangbian* "(this) side".   **Figure 7:** *Pangbian* "(that) side".

---

3 Gesture transcription lines are typically placed on top of the associated speech unit. In some cases where the speech unit and the gesture unit are produced by different speakers, gesture units are marked in connection with the gesturing party and with an apostrophe (') after the line number. The gesture conventions used here follow those of Kendon (2004), with the following notations: | |: gesture unit; ~~~~: preparation; ****: stroke; ; ****: post-stroke hold; -.-.-.-: recovery.

4 [F. Number] at the end of a gesture transcription line indicates the corresponding figure underneath it. The figures are intended to depict a most representative moment of the gesture phrase in question as many list gestures, especially those of the composite type, consist of a series of hand motions, the screen grabs are necessarily brief and limited in their representation of the entirety and complexity of the gestures.

2. ****-.-.-.-.| [F. 8]
    前面都睡下,
    qiánmiàn dōu shuì xià,
    in the front (they) all fell asleep;

Figure 8: *Qianbian* "in the front".

3. 就很多那样睡着的么。
    jiù hěnduō nàyàng shuìzháo de me.
    (There were) just a lot (of them) falling asleep like that.'

The gestures in Figures 6–8, though appearing as pointing, are all very quick beats, especially those in Figures 6 and 7, indicated with the fast tempo symbols <F>. After the first two beat strokes (indicated with ****) in the first line, the speaker holds up the hand (indicated with ~~~~) and then produces the third stroke in line 2. Taken all together, these three gestures make up a series of visual cues signaling a total of three items of a list.

In the single conversation sample (Hometown) where frequency information is calculated, composite gestures and reiterative gestures are found to have exactly the same frequencies of occurrence (the numbers given in Table 3 represent sets of gestures for a single list construction rather than gesture strokes, where applicable, for individual list items; and no mixing of the two types is found in the data).

Table 3: Distribution of different types of gestures in lists.

Gesture Type	Number of Tokens	Percentage
Composite gestures	13	50%
Reiterative gestures	13	50%
Total	26	100%

Given, as we saw earlier, that many recent studies have provided ample cross-linguistic evidence showing that lists are most prominently marked by lexical choice, syntactic parallelism, compatible intonation features in list items, and overall identifiable prosodic tendencies across list items and across major components, questions arise as to why gestures are just as pervasive (at least in the case of Mandarin) in face-to-face conversation. Is this simply a matter of redundancy and overt marking? Or is it for communicating different types of meaning, as many in the field of gesture studies have argued (see, e.g., Kendon 2004)? We will explore gestures' contributions to the construction of lists next.

3 Roles that gestures play in constructing list sequences

List gestures are found to serve a wide range of functions in conversation. These functions can be divided into two broad groups based on the type of gestures deployed. For composite gestures, the most common functions are to enhance the rhetorical effects of persuasion, exemplification, and clarification, which have been widely noted in previous research. Reiterative gestures, by contrast, contribute more in terms of discourse structuring, tracking, and interlocutor metainteraction (such as turn and floor management). The following sections will deal with these two broad types of gestures and their functions in turn.

3.1 Composite list gestures

3.1.1 Enhancing rhetorical effects of persuasion, clarification, and exemplification

These functions overlap with most of the major functions that have been proposed in the previous literature, e.g., framing and demonstrating (Sánchez-Ayala 2003), rhetorical use (Edwards 1994; Potter 1996), referential functions (Tao 1996: 95), and so forth, which are proposed without examining gestures. However, when gestures are taken into consideration, it can be argued that the speaker is afforded a powerful visual channel and an additional modality to exercise persuasive influence.[5] Extract (4) is an example of this type of function.

---

[5] For some different perspectives, see the papers in Cienki and Müller (2008).

(4) (Y describes a popular financial education program to R, a skeptical interlocutor.)

1. Y: ..试一下清华那个,
   shì yīxià Qīnghuá nèige,
   '(You should) try Qinghua's

2. .. FMBA。

3. R: ..F=M=BA 是什么玩意儿?
   FMBA shì shénme wányìer?
   What the heck is this FMBA thing about?

4. Y: ..金融 MBA 呀。
   jīnróng MBA ya.
   It's a finance MBA (for crying out loud).

5. R: ..唉呀=。
   āi ya=.
   (Sigh)

6. Y: ..那个可红=。
   nèigè kě hóng=.
   That's red hot.

7. ...可牛啊。
   kě niú a.
   Hot as hell.

8. ((W and F talk in kitchen, F laughs))

9. R: ..都学什么呀,   [F. 9]
   dōu xué shénme ya,
   What (do you) learn then?

10. 这玩意儿?
    zhè wányìer
    with this thing?

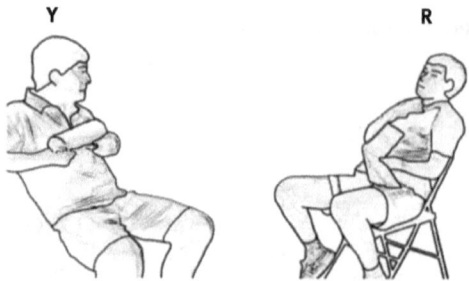

Figure 9: Posture and space formation right before the list gesture (at lines 9–10).

11. |~~*******/************/*****   [F. 10]
Y: ...从开始投..银行投资开始,
       cóng kāishǐ tóu ..yínháng tóuzī kāishǐ,
       Starting with banking investment,

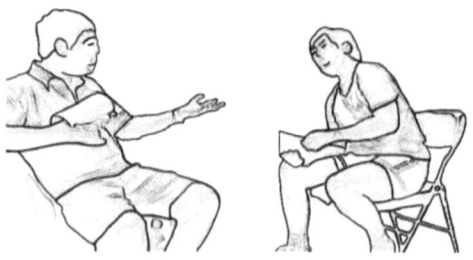

Figure 10: First list item: "Starting from banking investment". Thumb flexed inward to be in contact with the palm.

12. R: ..[嗯]。
       En.
       Okay.

13.   ~~~~~~~~
Y: ..[那个]==,
       nèige,
       then=,

14.   *******-.-.-.-   [F. 11]
       证券投资,
       zhèngquàn tóuzī,
       securities investment,

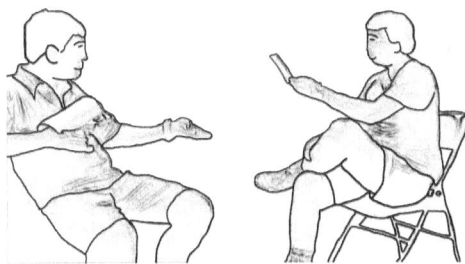

Figure 11: Second list item: "securities investment". Index finger flexed inward and on top of the curled thumb.

15.   ~~**********-.-.-.-   [F. 12]
         ...西方经济学,
         xīfāng jīngjìxué,
         Western economics.

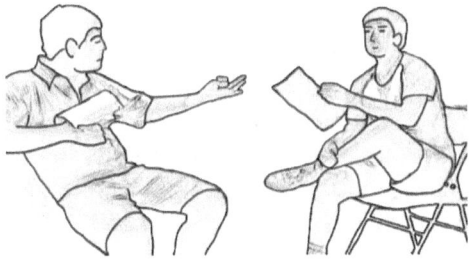

Figure 12: Third list item: "Western economics". Middle finger flexed inward to be in touch with the palm.

16.   ~~**********-.-.-.-| [F. 13]
         ..全英文授课。
         quán Yīngwén shòukè.
         Taught totally in English.

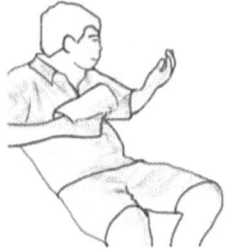

Figure 13: Fourth list item: "taught totally in English". Arm and hand extend to R and then retract to rest position. (R is blocked by the entrance of the host.)

17.   ((W enters and partially blocks the scene))

18. R: ..我操,
          wǒ cāo,
          Damn.

19.   听不懂=。
           tīng bùdǒng.
           Can't understand (a thing in English).'

In this is example, R's sarcastic inquiry at the beginning (line 3) shows that he is skeptical of the value of the financial education program that Y is recommending and planning to take. However, after R shows a cursory interest in learning more about the program (lines 9–10), Y launches into an extensive description of the program, with a number of what are presumably highlights listed in lines 11, 14, 15, and 16. Y does so not only with an enthusiastic tone of voice, whereby he raises his voice level and accentuates most of the syllables in the highlighted items, but also with his left hand extended to the space close to R (or the o-space close to R's p-space, as in Kendon's (1990) terms): each time a list item is produced, he prominently extends his left arm and hand to R, with additional finger movements (described next), holds up the arm/hand, and then retracts them to rest position. Thus for the first item, *yínháng tóuzī* 'banking investment,' as shown in Figure 10, he flexes the thumb inward to be in contact with the palm, lowers the left hand, and then holds it steady in the common space. For the second item, *zhèngquàn tóuzī* 'securities investment,' he flexes the index finger inward and rests it on top of the curled thumb (Figure 11). After another holding and retraction sequence, he produces the third item, *xīfāng jīngjìxué* 'Western economics' (Figure 12), where he flexes the middle finger inward to be in contact with the palm, again repeating the holding and retracting sequence. Finally, for the fourth item, *quán Yīngwén shòukè* 'totally taught in English' (Figure 13), he extends his arm and hand to the space close to R, with palm up and open, and retracts to the rest position to complete the gesture unit. In doing this highly coordinated complex gesture-speech sequence, he publicly demonstrates and enhances his enthusiasm toward the program being highlighted. Throughout the listing process, R, being a reluctant listener to the "sales pitch" of Y, so to speak, still tries to curb Y's enthusiasm by looking at some paper (likely the consent form that the investigator gives to him) instead of paying attention to him, yet his eye gaze orients to Y's hand movements as relevant to the interaction (as Figures 10 and 12 indicate; he is, however, blocked from being seen in Figure 13 as the host enters the scene), a fact showing that gesture impacts his attention. In this sense, we can say that list gestures provide an additional avenue, on top of prosody and syntax, for the speaker to enhance rhetorical effect – in this case, the "sales pitch" done with a selected few highlights of a program – to convince his skeptical audience.

3.1.2 Joint production with composite gestures

Given that composite gestures can help provide specific information as well as for clarification and exemplification, they can also be exploited by one speaker toward the other when the speaker seeks to solicit background information from the interlocutor. Thus, although it is typically the case that the same speaker provides the list items and gestures, there is also one case where the addressee follows along and initiates a list on behalf of the first/main speaker and thus makes it relevant for the main speaker to complete it. This is shown in Extract (5).

(5) (Discussing courses taken in an overseas college program. H (right) initiates a list on behalf of the main speaker, X (center).)

1. X: ... 语言就说学那个,
    Yǔyán jiù shuō xué nèige,
    'In language classes, (we) just learn

2.   .. 最基础的那个 a i o e, 那个--
    zuì jīchǔ de nàgè a i o e, nèige--
    the basic stuff like a, i, o, e, and so on

3.   ~~~~~********~   [F. 14]
H: 你们就光学日语?
    Nǐmen jiù **guāngxué rìyǔ**?
    You guys **just study Japanese**?

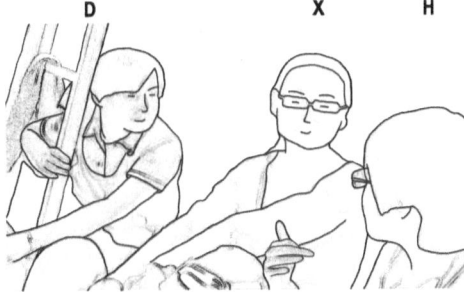

Figure 14: H's right hand raised with thumb extended outward to anticipate a list.

4.   ****   [F. 15]
          .. 还有,
          Hái yǒu,
          And?

Figure 15: H's thumb extends further and index finger extends slightly to correlate with *hái yǒu* 'and'.

5. X: (0)   政治,
              Zhèngzhì,
              Politics,
5'. H: ****   [F. 16]

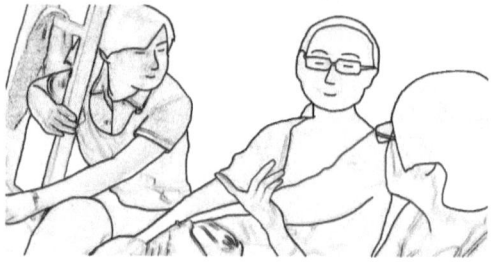

Figure 16: H's index finger extends further outward to correspond to the other speaker, X's *zhèngzhì* 'politics'.

6. X: 经济,
        jīngjì,
        economics,
6'. H: ****   [F. 17]

List gestures in Mandarin conversation and their implications — 81

Figure 17: H's middle finger extends outward to correspond to the other speaker, X's *jīngjì*, 'economics'.

7. X: 文化.
   wénhuà.
   and culture.'
7'. H: ****   [F. 18]

Figure 18: H moves her ring finger outward to correspond to the other speaker, X's *wénhuà* 'culture'.

In this segment, the main speaker X (center) is in the middle of describing what her undergraduate program requirements, including the foreign language requirement, are, H (right) provides one candidate item *nǐmen jiù guāngxué rìyǔ?* 'You guys just study Japanese?' (line 2), which is quickly followed by an additive conjunction *hái yǒu* 'and'. These two utterances in the turn (line 2) are correlated with firstly a slight outward extension of her right thumb (Figure 14) and then a full outward extension of the thumb (Figure 15), a sequence that forms a list gesture which serves to solicit (or anticipate) a list of items from X. When X follows along by producing three additional items, H extends her other fingers (index, middle, and ring fingers in Figures 16, 17, and 18 respectively) and synchronizes, at each of the listed items, her finger movements with X's utterances (lines 5–7). Thus this speech-gesture co-articulation can be said to be the result of a joint production of a list initiated by an audience member, one that is very different from the kinds of speech- and syntax-based co-constructions that have previously been discussed in the literature (e.g. Lerner 1991, Helasvou 2004).

Thus, the two sample cases discussed so far show that composite list gestures can be used by both the main speaker and the recipient to provide (or solicit) additional background information, clarification, and exemplification, and sometimes they also aid with the rhetorical effect of persuasion. Next we discuss reiterative list gestures.

3.2 Reiterative gestures highlight other important aspects of the listed items

Since reiterative gestures are not confined to a certain number of relatively stable hand forms and predictable motion patterns as composite ones are, they have the advantage of expressing other qualities that a composite gesture may not.

3.2.1 Referential function

Reiteratives can be realized as a set of well-choreographed pointing gestures, characterizing some aspects of a referent under discussion. This can be illustrated by Extract (3) above, in which some spatial references are conveyed via multiple synchronized pointing gestures. This example is expanded and reproduced below.

(3) (Speaker in the middle recounts how one time students around her all fell asleep in an important lecture class after the air conditioner was turned off.)

1. W: 专业课?
   Zhuānyèkè?
   'A major class?

2. H: 专业课。
   Zhuānyèkè.
   (Yes, it was) a major class.

3. W: 哇, 专业课都能睡。
   Wa, zhuānyèkè dōu néng shuì.
   Wow, (people) even sleep in a major class.

List gestures in Mandarin conversation and their implications —— 83

4. H: 俄罗斯学。
Èluósī xué.
(It was) Russian Studies.

5. W: 啊。
a
Yeah.

```
         |~~~~~~~****/****~~~~~~                    [Fs. 6 & 7]
```
6. H: 在那，<F旁边旁边 F>都睡下，
Zài nà, <F **pángbiān pángbiān** F> dōu shuì xià,
There, **(this) side**, **(that) side**, (people) all fell asleep;

Figure 6: *Pangbian* "(this) side".

Figure 7: *Pangbian* "(that) side".

```
7.       ****-.-.-.-.|                              [F. 8]
```
前面都睡下，
qiánmiàn dōu shuì xià,
in the front (they) all fell asleep;

Figure 8: *Qianbian* "in the front".

8. 就很多那样睡着的么。
   jiù hěnduō nàyàng shuìzháo de me.
   (There were) just a lot (of them) falling asleep like that.'

In this extract, three items indicating spatial points are articulated with gestures. With the rapid pointing gestures, synchronized with the three expressions of spatial direction, the list gives a sense of the complete environment in which the speaker was engaged in the depicted event. Note that the referential meanings of the first two spatial orientations are made clear only by the gesture, as they share an identical lexical form *pángbiān* 'side,' which does not by itself differentiate between the intended referential meanings. Another notable feature is that the first two items appear together in a single intonation unit rather than separate ones, in contrast with commonly observed patterns (Sánchez-Ayala 2003), while the last one appears in a separate intonation unit. In terms of gesture patterns, the first two are accompanied by two rapid pointing strokes while the last one is produced with single long pointing stroke. This provides further evidence supporting the role of gesture in making a viable list, for without gestures the list relation may not be as clear as it should be (we will return to this issue in the Discussion section). Note also that in this three-part list, the first two items are done both intonationally (in the same IU) and gesturally different (two rapid pointing gestures as opposed to one long stroke) from the last one, again supporting earlier observations about the uniqueness of the third item.

3.2.2 Tracking long and complicated lists

Another regular utility of flexible reiterative gestures is the provision of visual cues for structuring complex tellings and descriptions. As Jefferson (1990) and many others have shown, lists can become quite complicated, with multiple embeddings and extensive elaboration on individual components and items. Selting (2007: 501–4) shows that prosody can help the projecting of complex lists by maintaining similar phonetic/prosodic patterns across non-adjacent key elements. In my data, reiterative gestures can perform similar tasks when other kinds of resources do not necessarily project an obvious list. The following extract is an illustration.

(6) (X (center) is discussing with D (left) and H (right) her ideal boyfriend and future husband.)

1. X: 但我就觉得, .. 你找个男朋- -- 唉你就这样说, .. 两个选择在你面前。
Dàn wǒ jiù juéde, nǐ zhǎo gè nán péngyǒu, e nǐ jiù zhèyàng shuō, liǎng gè xuǎnzé zài nǐ miànqián,
'Well I feel that to look for a boyfriend, well you see, there are basically two choices in front of you:

2. |~*******-.-.-| [F. 19]
... 一个男的, 就是说那种一般稍微偏上一点,
Yígè nán de, jiùshì shuō **nà zhǒng yībān** shāowéi piān shàng yīdiǎn,
One kind of guy is like **a kind of middle**- or upper middle-class,

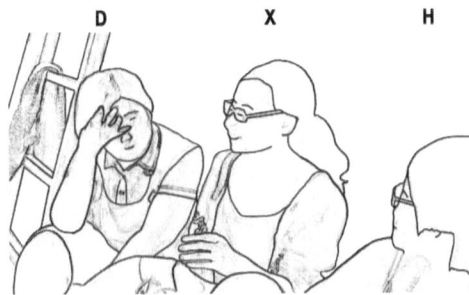

Figure 19: X's initial indication of the first choice with her left hand slightly raised.

3. 就是那种中等家庭吧, 就是说, 嗯有个房子, 不是很, 就是说有房有车, 就是很一般, 一般的车那种,
jiùshì nà zhǒng zhōngděng jiātíng ba, jiùshì shuō, en yǒu gè fángzi, búshì hěn, jiùshì shuō yǒu fáng yǒu chē, jiùshì hěn yībān, yībān de chē nà zhǒng,
just middle-class, that's to say, (he) has a house, not so much (rich), just say having a house and a car, just a regular, a regular type of car.

4. |~~*****-.-.-.-.-.-.-.-| [F. 20]
...然后这是一个男的, 但是, 他可能对你很专一呀, 不在外面乱搞那样的。
Ránhòu zhè shì yígè nán de, dànshì, tā kěnéng duì nǐ hěn zhuānyī ya, bú zài wàimiàn luàn gǎo nàyàng de.
And, this is one kind of guy, (he) is actually very devoted to you, and not sleeping around.

Figure 20: X's recap of first choice with a raised open palm of the left hand.

5. H: ...我老头啊。
   Wǒ lǎotóu a.
   Oh that sounds like my man.

6. X: .. 呵呵。
   Hēhē.
   (Laugh)

7. D: ... 我就喜欢这样的。
   Wǒ jiù xǐhuān zhèyàng de.
   That's exactly my kind of guy.

8. |~~**********-.-| [F. 21]
X: ... 一个是这样的,
   Yígè shì zhèyàng de,
   So that's the first type.

Figure 21: X again recaps the first choice, with a raised left hand and an extended index finger.

9. |~~~~~~~~~************/**-.-.****-.-.-.**-.-***.-.-| [F. 22]
X: ... 还有一个是家里面很有钱, 然后当然他也给你花钱,
       hái yǒu yígè shì **jiā lǐmiàn hěn yǒuqián**, ránhòu dāngrán tā yě gěi nǐ huā qián,
       Another type is that **(he) may have a lot of money**, and he is also generous with you with money.

Figure 22: X starts to talk about the second choice with open palm of left hand raised and then rested on her right knee.

10. |~~~~~~~********-.-.-.-.--.-.| [F. 23]
X: ...但问题是说, ...除了你以外还有别的女人。
       dàn wèntí shì shuō, **chúle nǐ yǐwài hái** yǒu bié de nǚrén.
       But the problem is, **in addition to you, he has other** women.

Figure 23: X continues to elaborate what the second choice would mean.

11. H: ...我要前一种啊。
       Wǒ yào qián yī zhǒng a
       I'll definitely want the former.

12. D:　肯定要前一种, 是女的都要前一种, 嗯。
　　　　Kěndìng yào qián yī zhǒng, shì nǚ de dōu yào qián yī zhǒng, en.
　　　　Of course you go with the first type. Any women would choose the first type, wouldn't they?'

In this excerpt, Speaker X (center) starts with an explicit expression of the two choice items (*liǎng gè xuǎnzé zài nǐ miànqián* '(there are) two choices in front of you'), which projects a (short) list to come. When the first item is briefly mentioned, the speaker uses a gesture (at line 2, Figure 19) to visually register it for the recipient to notice. Once the first item is introduced, it elicits a complex description of what types of choice it entails (line 3); and because of this complexity, the speaker gives it a quick summary in line 4, Figure 20. At this point, the two co-participants join the discussion by offering their commentaries (lines 5–7). Since this is still only one part of the two choice configuration, in line 8, Speaker X again flashes a hand gesture with a raised left hand and an extended index finger (Figure 21) to go with an interim summary (*yígè shì zhèyàng* de 'so one type is like that') and signals the incompleteness of the on-going list. After that, she immediately uses another gesture (and later a series of gestures, with open palm raised and then rested on her right knee), at line 9, Figure 22, to describe what the second choice would be like (*hái yǒu yígè shì* 'there is another type, which is...') and goes on to describe what this entails.

What we can see here is that although the overall structure of the list is technically quite simple because there are only two items involved (again for a discussion of the significance of lists with less than three items, see the Discussion section), and there are clear lexical and grammatical parallel structures (*yígè* 'one type,' *hái yǒu yígè* shì 'another one type') indexing the semi-list nature of the relevant components, the list gets complicated fairly quickly in other ways with the contents of each item elaborated, the items contrasted, and the exchange sequence extended by contributions from the other participants. Timing obviously reflects the complexity as well: from the explicit articulation of the first choice (line 2) to the completion of the discussion of the choice (line 8), 17 seconds have passed, making the parallel items rather murky. The repeated gestures – all involving the left hand – at summary points (lines 4 and 8) and at the transition point (line 8) help to create a consistent visual mark. The manual signaling of the second choice, which immediately follows the signal for the end of the first, in line 9, Figure 22, further aids with the ease of transition. Thus we can say that the list gestures are strategically placed at key points of the extended interactional sequence, serving as signposts, so to speak, to help the co-participants to track the discourse structural boundaries in a visible way. Here we can see that the gestures are especially helpful given the large amount of contributions made by the two co-participants.

3.2.3 Meta-interactional functions involving turn taking and floor holding

While the cases discussed so far may be characterized as socio-cognitively oriented, in the sense that the cognitive demand of producing and comprehending complicated list structures or simple list structures with less neatly patterned linguistic features or complex turn changes engenders the deployment of gestures, the following can be shown to be directly geared toward turn/floor management (called "meta-interaction"). In this excerpt, three male speakers are competing with different proposals as to the best courses of action to take for an educational program that some of them plan to take on. Since participants differ rather substantively in terms of their ideas and access to information, it has not been easy for them to persuade each other. In fact it has not been easy for them even to get other participants to focus their attention on the speaking parties over the relevant issues, as the interlocutors in this excerpt are long-term friends who can seemingly talk over one another without being perceived to have offended anyone. At this point, Speaker Y on the left wants the others to listen to him speak about a particular future plan.

(7) (Y, left, offers to share his education plans for the next year with W (center) and R (right).)

```
1.              |~~*************|           [F. 24]
Y:  其实我的感觉, ..听我的计划吧。
    Qíshí wǒ de gǎnjué, tīng wǒ de jìhuà ba.
    'Actually, I feel, .. just listen to my plan now.
```

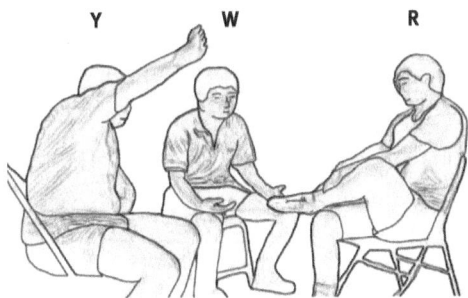

Figure 24: Y raises his right hand and asks explicitly for recipients' attention.

```
2.   |~*******|                              [F. 25]
     …首先,
       shǒuxiān,
       First of all,
```

Figure 25: Y keeps his hand and several extended fingers in the air to hold the turn/floor.

3. |~~~~~~~~~~*******| [F. 26]
    ..关于这个学..肯定要上。
    Guānyú zhège xué.. kěndìng yào shàng.
    certainly some programs have to be had.

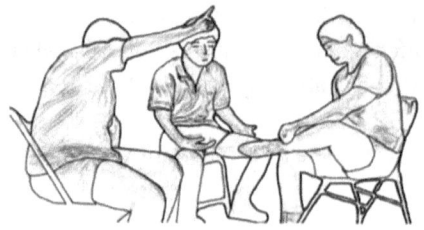

Figure 26: Y does the same kind of gesture and maintains the same holding pattern as in 25.

4. W: ..嗯。
         En.

5. R: ..嗯。
         En.

6. |~~~~~~~~~~~~~~~****| [F. 27]
Y: 第一个选择是...[PMP],
         dì yīgè xuǎnzé shì PMP,
         The first option would be PMP,

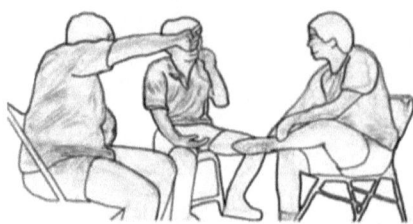

Figure 27: Y continues with his turn/floor holding gesture while uttering the first choice.

7. W: [肚子疼]。
   Dùzi téng.
   (Got a) stomachache.

8. |~~~~~~~~~~~~~~~~~~*******| [F. 28]
   Y: ...另外一个选择是这个..应用数学,
      lìngwài yī gè xuǎnzé shì zhège.. yìngyòng shùxué
      Another option is this, applied mathematics,

Figure 28: Y continues with his turn/floor holding gesture while uttering the second choice.

9. |~~~~~~~~~~~~*****| [F. 29]
   Y: ...第三个选择..FMBA。
      dì sān gè xuǎnzé..FMBA.
      The third option is FMBA.

Figure 29: Y continues with his turn/floor holding gesture while uttering the third choice.

10. R: ..太贵。
    Tài guì.
    too expensive.

11. |~********~~****| [F. 30]
   Y: 今年不成[1明年上1]。
      jīnnián bùchéng [1 míngnián shàng 1].
      If not this year [1 it must be next year 1].

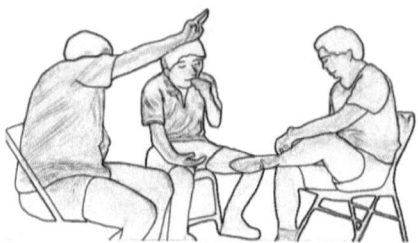

Figure 30: Y extends and retracts his hand to correlate with the two temporal expressions.

12. R: [1 经济1]-
                    Jīngjì
                    economically

13. Y: [2@@2]

14. R: [2 经济上 2]你得,
                    Jīngjì shàng nǐ déi,
                    Economically you have to

15.   你得考虑到[3X这个X3]。
                    nǐ déi kǎolǜ dào zhège.
                    You have to take into account the (economics of) this.

16. Y: [3X 今年 X3]先把钱挣上。
                    Jīnnián xiān bǎ qián zhèng shàng.
                    This year better make some money first.'

Prior to this excerpt, the three speakers are engaged in a lively discussion about the pros and cons of their respective education plans. At the beginning of this excerpt, Speaker Y literally asks the other two participants to refrain from talking and yield the floor to him. He deploys his body for this task and the ensuing list. Y's gestures are highly visible due to the raised-up and extended right arm throughout this sequence (Figures 24–30). As Y produces the multiple items (*xuǎnzé* 'choices') (lines 6, 8, and 9), he adjusts the height of the arm and moves the fingers of the exposed hand to signal the individual items, yet the arm sticks out and maintains a visibly high position throughout the extended sequence that is in progress. This way the other coparticipants have little other choice than to pay attention to what he has to say (as evidenced by their continuers in lines 4–5 and later responses in lines 10, 12, and 14–15), even though they try to escape the imposition by sometimes gazing at each other and sometimes at their own possessions. Thus the gestures here can be regarded as meta-interactionally helpful in multiple ways for speaker Y: in attempting to secure both the initial turn and the attention of the coparticipants, expressing the listed items, and maintaining the conversation floor.

4 Discussion and conclusion

Overall, the Mandarin data validate many observations made by earlier studies, including those on lexical, syntactic, and prosodic features, the uniqueness of the third (or final) part, and how interlocutors orient themselves to the production and contents of lists with various levels of cooperation. At the same time, we can also see that list gestures in the video-recorded Mandarin conversations contribute in various ways to the interactional process. While gestures can certainly be deployed to elaborate on linguistic materials, as many have pointed out, they are also shown here to be able to provide an additional dimension for speakers to operate with in interpersonal communication, and this has proven to have special utilities in comparison with other modalities.

List gestures and the sequences in which they appear also raise important theoretical and methodological questions in this area and beyond. First, there is the very issue of what constitutes a list. Although operational definitions can be attempted for methodological soundness, as I tried to do at the beginning of this paper, in reality, theoretical orientations can also constrain analyst focus. In this regard, it can be pointed out that so far the literature on list constructions almost always focuses on materials that have three parallel (morphosyntactically and prosodically observable) parts, which are no doubt the prototypical list structure based on, for example, frequency of occurrence. However, in real time interaction, speakers often use gestures to mark a list, or to make a sequence appear list-like, where linguistic structures may be too weak (or unsuitable) to establish a list (as in Extracts (3) and (6)), or the articulated items may be less than three (Extract (6)). This calls for a theoretical and methodological questioning of whether or not one should count these as lists. In this paper these are treated as lists on the grounds of speaker bodily behavior: conversation participants use similar gestures (in terms of physical shape and motion) as they do for other more visibly patterned lists. In one sense, one might say that we have expanded the notion of lists in our inquiry; in another, this is simply what the speakers do and we have failed to realize this until we began to pay attention to how they make use of gesture resources. Participants' interactional patterns seem to support our analysis. For example, in those otherwise "weak" cases analyzed, when a list is projected, recipients display their orientation to the ongoing talk as part of an (incomplete) list through withholding extended and off-topical talk. Thus in Extract (6), for example, although the recipients offered brief remarks at the end of the first item (at lines 5 and 7), they only commented extensively upon the main speaker (X) completing the two items (at line 10). The main speaker displays her orientation to the current talk as a list in progress by continuing her extended talk and by giving repeated summaries before the projected completion (i.e., the final part of the list). For this reason, Streeck and Hartge (1992) treat lists as one of the places where relevant gestures can contextualize upcoming utterances. Thus the point to take home is that a multimodal view of interaction can enable us to see properties that may otherwise have escaped our attention.

The second, and related, issue concerns the feature of three partedness. Since Jefferson (1990), the tripartite characteristic of lists has been widely noted as an important feature of lists toward which interlocutors orient. For example, it has been demonstrated that both the second item (Lerner 1994) and the third item (Jefferson 1990) have important projecting implications for turn taking and other conversational practices. It is argued that interlocutors monitor the production and completion of these items and adjust their verbal behavior accordingly. While there is no question that the tripartite characteristic, whether in the traditional narrow sense or in the newer expansive sense, is omnipresent, we also saw that with gestures deployed, some of the list materials can be fairly elaborative and the overall structure can be quite complicated. In these cases, the interactional dynamic can be quite different from relatively simple lists that are identifiable chiefly on lexical, syntactic, prosodic, and semantic grounds. Thus, we saw that in the case of Extract (6), just after the first item is produced, co-participants start to offer commentaries, though very briefly, which ends up with multiple speaker exchanges.

Third, list gestures can contribute to meta-interaction in many ways, and this raises questions about the environment and the process in which lists emerge. As we have seen in the literature review section, earlier studies tend to focus on the main body of the list (Jefferson 1990) while recent studies have expanded the scope by situating the body of the list in a larger sequence in which the list itself is deemed to occupy just one (middle) section. This is clearly an advancement in our understanding of lists in interaction, as they do not occur out of the blue but often require both an initiation process before the list and a follow-up one thereafter. However, despite the rich literature, there is still a lack of in-depth understanding of how lists emerge as a process and as an achievement. Our gesture-based analysis has hopefully begun to shed some light in this regard. For example, we saw that in extracts such as (7), speakers sometimes have to make a considerable effort to gain and retain the conversation floor in order to produce a list, in which case the visual modality may be taken advantage of and deployed for the task. We have also seen that (in Extract 5) a list can be initiated by an addressee and made relevant for the main speaker to complete it, suggesting a much more active role by the audience in list-oriented strips of talk than hitherto assumed. Although this study is nowhere near providing a fine-grained analysis of the interactional emerging process of list constructions, it does show that such an analysis cannot be done without examining the role bodily behaviors, such as hand gestures, play in it.

Finally, the gesture studies literature has extended studies on the role of gesture as a discourse framing device. For example, Kendon (1972) shows how speakers use different arms to signal different conversation topics. Kendon (2004, chpt 9) also shows how topic and comment structures are marked by different gestures, serving what he calls the parsing functions. McNeill and his colleagues have, in a series of studies (Levy and McNeill 1992; McNeill and Levy 1993; McNeill, Levy, and Duncan 2015), shown how gesture can be used to mark information status and discourse dynamism, and there is strong evidence for the correlation of gesture with discourse units (termed "catchment"). On this basis, they argue that gesture is part of the creation of higher-level discourse units and should thus be recognized as an integral part of speech communication. My analysis of gestures in the production of lists adds further evidence for the role gesture plays in creating higher-level units, albeit with a different kind of units than those researched in the aforementioned studies.

To sum up, the general conclusion to be drawn from this study is that while multimodality is an undisputed fact in human interaction, there is also conspicuous evidence demonstrating that different modalities may contribute to social interaction in unique ways due to the fluid situational needs of communication: different situations may call for the use of particular kinds of communicative resources or a special configuration of the multiple resources for interaction. Such complex relations of mutually elaborative yet independent resources present both challenges and opportunities for us to understand everyday interactional practices.

Acknowledgments

I am grateful to Kawai Chui, Xiaoting Li, Tsuyoshi Ono, and a referee for their insightful comments as well as useful reference information, which helped improve the quality of the paper substantively. Thanks also go to I-Ni Tsai and Ko Tuan Chan for help with the drawings, to Jee Won Lee and Monica Turk for some of the video data, to Susanna Karlsson for her effort in making accessible her work on Swedish, and to Elizabeth Carter for valuable editorial assistance. While working on this project, I was supported by a chair professorship at the National Taiwan Normal University, by UCLA Academic Senate Faculty Research Grants (2012–13, 2016–17), and by a U.S. Department of Education grant (CFDA 84.229, P229A0200) to the Center for Advanced Language Proficiency Education and Research, Pennsylvania State University. However, the contents of this paper do not necessarily represent the policy of the Department of Education, and you should not assume endorsement by the Federal Government. An earlier version of this paper was presented at a discourse unit symposium at the University of Helsinki, at a UCLA CA Working Group meeting, and at a colloquium in the English Department of the National Taiwan Normal University, where I received helpful comments from many members of the audiences. Any remaining shortcomings are of course entirely my own.

References

Atkinson, J. Maxwell. 1984. Public speaking and audience responses: some techniques for inviting applause. In: Atkinson, J.M. & John Heritage (eds.), *Structures of social action: Studies in conversation analysis*, 370–409. Cambridge: Cambridge University Press.

Auer, Peter. 2014. Syntactic structures and their symbiotic guests: Notes on analepsis from the perspective of on-line syntax. *Pragmatics* 24(3). 533–560.

Boon, Andy, 2nd edition, 1999. *Advocacy*. London: Cavendish Publishing Limited.

Chafe, Wallace. 1987. Cognitive constraints on information flow. In Russell Tomlin (ed.), *Coherence and grounding in discourse*, 21–51. Amsterdam: John Benjamins.

Chafe, Wallace. 1994. *Discourse, consciousness, and time: The flow and displacement of conscious experience in speaking and writing*. Chicago: University of Chicago Press.

Cienki, Alan & Cornelia Müller (eds.), *Metaphor and gesture*. Amsterdam: John Benjamins.

Couper-Kuhlen, Elizabeth. 1986. *An introduction to English prosody*. Tubingen: Niemeyer.

Drew, Paul. 1990. Strategies in the contest between lawyer and witness in cross-examination. In Judith N. Levi, Anne Graffam Walker (eds.), *Language in the judicial process*, 39–64. New York: Plenum Press.

Du Bois, John W., Stephan Schuetze-Coburn, Susanna Cumming, & Danae Paolino. 1993. Outline of discourse transcription. In Jane Edwards and Martin Lampert (eds.), *Talking data*, 45–89. Hillsdale, NJ: Lawrence Erbaum Associates.

Edwards, Derek. 1994. Scripts formulations: An analysis of event descriptions in conversation. *Journal of Language and Social Psychology* 13(3). 211–247.

Erickson, Frederick. 1982. Money tree, lasagna bush, salt and pepper: Social construction of topical cohesion in conversation among Italian-Americans. In Deborah Tannen (ed.), *Analyzing discourse*, 43–70. Washington, DC: Georgetown University Press.

Erickson, Frederick. 1992. They know all the lines: Rhythmic organization and contextualization in a conversational listing routine. In Peter Auer & Aldo Di Luzio (eds.), *The contextualization of language*, 365–397. Amsterdam: John Benjamins.

Fox, Barbara A. 1987. *Discourse structure and anaphora: Written and conversational English*. Cambridge: Cambridge University Press.

Goodwin, Charles. 2000. Action and embodiment within situated human interaction. *Journal of pragmatics* 32(10). 1489–1522.

Goodwin, Charles. 2013. The co-operative, transformative organization of human action and knowledge. *Journal of Pragmatics* 46(1). 8–23.

Helasvuo, Marja-Liisa. 2004. Shared syntax: the grammar of co-construction. *Journal of Pragmatics* 36(8). 1315–1336.

Heritage, John & David L. Greatbatch. 1986. Generating applause: A study of rhetoric and response at party political conferences. *American Journal of Sociology* 92(1). 110–157.

Jefferson, Gail. 1990. List-construction as a task and a resource. In George Psathas (ed.), *Interaction competence*, 63–92. Washington, D.C.: University Press of America.

Karlsson, Susanna. 2010. Multimodalitet i listproduktion. In Camilla Lindholm and Jan Lindström (eds.), *Språk och interaktion* 2, 141–170.

Kendon, Adam. 1972. Some relationships between body motion and speech. In A.W. Siegman & B. Pope (eds.), *Studies in dyadic communication*, 177–213. New York: Pergamon.

Kendon Adam. 1990. *Conducting interaction: Patterns of behavior in focused encounters*. Cambridge: Cambridge University Press.

Kendon, Adam. 2004. *Gesture: Visible action as utterance*. Cambridge: Cambridge University Press.

Kita, Sotaro. 1993. *Language and thought interface: A study of spontaneous gestures and Japanese mimetics*. University of Chicago dissertation.

Knerich, Heike. 2013. List structures as preformed structures – Preformed expressions within list structures. *Linguistik Online* 62, 5/2013, http://www.linguistik-online.de/62_13/knerich_a.html. (Last accessed July 17, 2016.)

Küntay, Aylin C. 2004. Lists as alternative discourse structures to narratives in preschool children's conversations. *Discourse Processes* 38(1). 95–118, DOI: 10.1207/s15326950dp3801_4

Lerner, Gene H. 1991. On the syntax of sentences-in-progress. *Language in Society* 20(3). 441–458.

Lerner, Gene H. 1994. Responsive list construction: A conversational resource for accomplishing multifaceted social action. *Journal of Language and Social Psychology* 13(1). 20–33.

Levy, Elena T., & David McNeill. 1992. Speech, gesture, and discourse. *Discourse Processes* 15(3). 277–301.

McNeill, David, & Elena T. Levy. 1993. Cohesion and discourse. *Discourse Processes*. 16(4). 363–386.

McNeill, David, Elena T. Levy, & Susan D. Duncan. 2015. Gesture in discourse. In Deborah Tannen, Heidi E. Hamilton, & Deborah Schiffrin (eds.), *The handbook of discourse analysis*, 262–289. Oxford: Blackwell Publishers. DOI: 10.1002/9781118584194.ch12

Ouafeu, Yves Talla Sando. 2006. Listing intonation in Cameroon English speech. *World Englishes* 25(3/4). 491–500.

Potter, Jonathan. 1996. *Representing reality: Discourse, rhetoric and social construction*. London: Sage.

Sánchez-Ayala, Ivo. 2003. Constructions as resources for interaction: lists in English and Spanish conversation. *Discourse Studies* 5(3). 323–349.

Schank, Roger C. & Robert Abelson. 1977. *Scripts, plans, goals and understanding*. Hillsdale, NJ: Lawrence Erlbaum.

Schiffrin, Debroah. 1994. Making a list. *Discourse Processes* 17(3). 377–406.

Schröder, Ulrike. 2017. Multimodal metaphors as cognitive pivots for the construction of cultural otherness in talk. *Intercultural Pragmatics* 14(4). 493–524.

Selting, Margret. 2004. Listen: Sequenzielle und prosodische Struktur einer kommunikativen Praktik – eine Untersuchung im Rahmen der Interaktionalen Linguistik. *Zeitschrift für Sprachwissenschaft*. 23(1). 1–46.

Selting, Margret. 2007. Lists as embedded structures and the prosody of list construction as an interactional resource. *Journal of Pragmatics* 39(3). 483–526.

Stivers, Tanya & Jack Sidnell. 2005. Introduction: Multimodal Interaction. *Semiotica* 156(1/4). 1–20.
Streeck, Jürgen. 2008. Metaphor and gesture: a view from the microanalysis of interaction. In Alan Cienki & Cornelia Müller (eds.), *Metaphor and gesture*, 289–294. Amsterdam: John Benjamins.
Streeck, Jürgen & Ulrike Hartge. 1992. Previews: Gestures at the transition place. In Peter Auer & Aldo Di Luzio (eds.), The contextualization of language, 135–157. Amsterdam: John Benjamins.
Tao, Hongyin. 1996. *Units in Mandarin conversation: Prosody, discourse, and grammar*. Amsterdam and Philadelphia: John Benjamins.

Appendix: Transcription conventions

These transcription conventions are part of Du Bois et al. (1993), with slight modifications.

UNITS
    Intonation unit   {carriage return with a punctuation mark}
    Truncated intonation unit   --
    Truncated word   -
    Speaker identity/turn start   :
    Speech overlap   [ ]
UNIT TYPES
    Final   .
    Continuing   ,
    Question   ?
    Exclamation   !
LENGTHENING
    Lengthening   =
PAUSE
    Long (more than three seconds)   ...( )
    Medium (two seconds)   ...
    Latching   (0)
LAUGHTER   @
TRANSCRIBER'S PERSPECTIVE AND NON-VERBAL ACTIONS
    Comment or non-verbal actions   (( ))
    Uncertain hearing   <X X>
    Indecipherable syllable   X

K.K. Luke and Xiaoling He
Hand gestures and emergent speakership: A study of turn competition and gesticulation in Cantonese conversation

1 Introduction

Previous video-based Conversation Analytic studies have uncovered multifarious ways in which hand gestures are used in interaction, singly or in combination with verbal utterances or other bodily visual behavior (e.g., eye gaze, body posture and orientation, and facial expression), to perform a variety of tasks, including (but not limited to) constructing turns-at-talk (Goodwin 1981, Bolden 2003), establishing reference (Levinson 2007), demonstrating procedures (Mondada 2011; Zemel, Koschman and LeBaron 2011), maintaining coherence (Chui 2009), and conducting particular kinds of communicative events, such as auctioning (Heath and Luff 2011).

The role of gesture in conversational turn-taking has also long been recognized.[1] In an early paper, Schegloff (1984) singles out gesture as the main, even only, visual conduct that is tied exclusively to speakership, i.e., only current speakers gesticulate. At the same time, he points out three major classes of exceptions where non-current speakers can be observed to gesticulate. Of these three classes of exceptions, two turn out to be accountable for by reference to the turn-taking system after all; namely, when gestures are used by non-current speakers to indicate incipient speakership, and when gestures are used by an interrupted speaker to indicate retention of her claim to speakership. These observations strongly suggest gesture's potential role in turn competition. However, this possibility was only alluded to but not commented on or further developed in Schegloff (1984).

---

[1] The contribution of gestures to turn-taking has also been studied outside of the CA tradition, most notably by Duncan and associates (e.g., Duncan 1972, Duncan and Niederehe 1974). However, as this line of research is based very much on coding and counting, rather than on close observation of gesturing in motion, its findings are not of direct relevance to our concerns in this paper.

Note: Funding for this research was awarded by Nanyang Technological University in the form of a MOE-AcR-Tier-1 grant (Ref: 2015-002-123), which is gratefully acknowledged.

K.K. Luke and Xiaoling He, Nanyang Technological University

The subject matter of the uses of hand gestures in turn-taking was taken up again in Streeck and Hartge (1992), where it is shown that a particular counting gesture is used in the Philippines by non-current speakers at pre-turn beginning position to propose turn transition and readiness to speak. More recently, Streeck (2009) reports the use of a particular gesture (Open Hand Palm Up) at turn transition points. Mondada and Oloff (2011), in a study of multimodality in their French data, give a fine-grained account of the use of hand gestures during stretches of interaction where overlapping talk occurs, and show how different degrees of 'perturbation' in speakers' use of gestures may correlate to the strength with which claims to continued speakership are made.

Li (2014) examines hand gestures, along with other bodily visual behavior, from the point of view of how they work seamlessly with Mandarin syntax and prosody in projecting turn completion. Building on Duncan's (1972, 1974) and Sacks and Schegloff's (2002) ideas about a 'home position', Li describes how "the return to rest position is observed to project the possible completion of a turn" (Li 2014: 158). In the same work Li also looks at turn competition, and observes how "the fight for the speaking turn between two speakers is embodied as the fight of their hands" (Li 2014: 169).

Given Sacks, Schegloff & Jefferson's (1974) characterization of the conversational turn-taking system and subsequent work by Goodwin and others (Goodwin 1980, 1981, 1986, 2014; Langford 1994; Arnold 2012; Berger & Rae 2012), it should come as no surprise that 'speakership', at least in the context of everyday conversation, is a highly fluid and malleable phenomenon. Speakership is never fixed or given but always in a state of flux, always 'emergent'. It is never a simple matter of 'whoever happens to be speaking' but something that is constantly being claimed, contested, and negotiated.

In investigating a set of video-recordings of naturally occurring conversations collected in Hong Kong (conducted mostly in Cantonese with an occasional mixing in of English), a number of hand gestures were identified which appear to have as their primary function the display of a person's readiness to speak and the management of turn-transitions. Due to space considerations, we will present only a small selection of these by focusing on the use of two gesture-types, and their variations, in episodes of multi-party interaction where turn competition is at issue. By closely examining the relationship between hand gestures and emergent speakership, we hope to add to our current inventory of hand gestures for turn-taking, and to advance our understanding of the variety of ways in which hand gestures can contribute to the business of turn-taking at junctures where two or more participants bid, negotiate, and compete for speakership. By describing and explicating a range of practices where hand gestures are used, by current as well as non-current speakers, in negotiating the taking of turns, we hope to show how gestures can make a critical contribution (typically in combination with verbal utterances and other bodily visual behaviors) to the local management of turn-taking in multi-party conversations.

Armed with Schegloff's notion of "incipient speaker" (Schegloff 1984), a close examination was carried out of those moments in our data where speakership appears to be either 'problematic' in some way or is 'up for grabs'. It soon became clear that, in order to cope with variations in participation framework configurations and the particular actions being implemented in a sequence, the notion of incipient speakership must be refined and further specified. The validity and insightfulness of the concept is not in question; what is being offered here is an elaboration of that concept and an account of how hand gestures can contribute to a variety of practices through which speakership may emerge from an interaction.

The data used for this study is taken from a set of video recordings of everyday conversations between family and friends obtained in Hong Kong in the mid-2000's. From a total of some five hours of recordings, a collection was made of fragments that were relevant to our interest in gesturing and overlapping talk. The data excerpts presented below are typical examples of two main kinds of gestures as found in that collection. In carrying out this research, the method of conversation analysis was used, which gives primacy to naturally occurring interactions and has as its aim the production of fine-grained analyses based on detailed, contextualized, and temporalized (i.e., moment-by-moment) observations. In matters of the forms and functions of gestures, we follow Kendon (1994, 2004), McNeill (1992, 2005) and Schegloff (1984) in recognizing the communicative value of gestures (in the context of talk). Following McNeill (2005), gestures are conceptualized in terms of the dimensions of 'iconicity', 'metaphoricity', 'deixis', 'temporal highlighting' and 'social interactivity' (See also Cienki 1998; Cienki & Muller 2008; Williams 2008). The gestures examined in this chapter are all used essentially for 'social interactivity'. For further details, readers are referred to McNeill (2005: 38–42).

2 Raising of a hand

2.1 Bidding to speak with a raised hand

One of the most common hand gestures used by non-current speakers (in multi-party talk where they have *not* been selected as next speaker), often in conjunction with the verbal production of the recognizable beginning of a new turn (i.e., the non-current speaker's new turn), to display readiness (or eagerness) to speak at the next opportunity (usually an upcoming TRP) is the raising of a hand, occasionally accompanied by a raising of the index finger. In data fragment (1), three friends, Rose, Katy and Sarah (from left to right in the line drawings below) are talking about Katy's upcoming wedding. As we join the conversation, Katy is seeking Rose's opinion on having her wedding photos taken in Sunny Bay (based on some photos of other people's weddings that Katy has seen).

(1) Price (SR_C04: 0144-0153)

```
01   Katy:  Ja|no        godou jing      le:,  |gei   leng   wo
            Sunny_Bay  there take-photo  PT   quite  pretty  PT
              |(Turns to Rose on right)         |(Smiles)
            'The photos were taken in Sunny Bay. (They look) quite pretty.'

02   Rose:  Jano?   o,  e:[e e
            Sunny_Bay?  Oh, e: e e
            'Sunny Bay? Oh, e: e e'

03   Katy:             [e: Diksilei     gobin     lo=
                        e: Disneyland  that-side   PT
                       'Where Disneyland is.'

04   Rose:  =[    (aa|ngo zi)      ]
                  oh I   know
                      |(Nods then turns head to right, away from Katy)
            'Oh I know'

05  →Sara:  =[|HEOI  JAU  GONG-GWO]  |gaacin  wo
              (s)he   has    said             price    PT
       →          |(Raises left hand with index finger pointing up)

06          |(Katy begins turning to Sara on 'heoi' [(s)he)]and
             engages her with gaze on 'gong-gwo' [said])

07                              |(Sara retracts hand as Katy engages)
            'They did mention the price, you know.'

08          ngo   m-geidak-zo:
            I     forgotten
```

09		*keoi hai: jau go package gamjoeng ge gaacin*
		(s)he EMPH has CL package like-that GEN price
		'I've forgotten (what it was). They have a package sort of price.'
10	Katy:	*hai aa? (.) daan m-zi geicin*
		yes PT but don't-know how-much
		'Yeah? But (I wonder) how much (it would cost).'

Figure 1: 'Turn-bidding' with an a raised hand and an upward-pointing index finger (From left: Rose, Katy and Sarah).

Note first the seating arrangement in this conversation. The three friends are seated in such a way that it is not possible for Katy, the one in the middle, to see both of the other two co-participants at the same time. At any one time, if she chooses to place her gaze on another co-participant, Katy simply has to make a choice: either Rose (on her right) or Sara (on her left). At the beginning of this fragment, when Katy talks about wedding photos and Sunny Bay (line 1), she is clearly talking to Rose (as opposed to Sara), as her head is turned to her right, with her gaze fixed on Rose. The mention of Sunny Bay, however, triggers a repair initiation from Rose (line 2: "Sunny Bay? ..."), whereupon Katy provides a repair (line 3: "where Disneyland is"), which in terms of content, design, and embodiment, is again addressed to Rose, who has now been selected as the next speaker, the relevant next action being to show recognition (or non-recognition) based on the additional description of "Sunny Bay".

At this very moment, however, just as Rose is about to deliver her response (line 4: "Oh I know"), Sara, sitting on the other side of Katy, makes what can only be described as a competitive attempt to come into the conversation by speaking *before* the second pair part to Katy's prior turn is delivered. In terms of participation frameworks, what Sara is doing at this point may be characterized as proposing to transform the current, ongoing participation framework, where Katy is the speaker, Rose the addressee and Sara the bystander or overhearer, to a different one, where Sara and Katy would be the interlocutors, with Rose on the sideline. Note in this regard how Sara's turn in line 5 is shaped ("THEY DID MENTION the price, you know"): it begins loudly, with a volume that is clearly higher than surrounding talk (both Katy's prior turn and Rose's more-or-less simultaneous turn)[2] and ends in an utterance particle 'wo' which is regularly used to signal epistemic primacy (Luke 1990), i.e., Sara is here volunteering a piece of relevant information (i.e., the price of a photo-shoot) which, in her estimation, is either unknown to Katy or at least not on her mind at this point in time. This combination of urgency and new (but highly relevant) information can be regarded as something of a 'justification' (or an account) that is built into her turn, which in this sense is 'self-consciously' competitive.[3] It is also interesting to see how Sara's turn competition is contextualized through an organic integration of words, prosody, gesture and body orientation, which appear to work together seamlessly. Note also how Sara's utterance in line 5 is underscored by the raising of an index finger (at a time when Katy is not even looking) (Figure 1b), kept in that position for a few moments, until Katy has turned around and moved her gaze to engage Sara (Figure 1c), and then, just at that very moment, the finger is retracted from its extended position (Figure 1d).

2.2 Bidding and holding

It seems clear in our data that the raising of a hand with an open palm at particular moments of interaction can serve essentially the same function as that of a raised finger. In the next data fragment, we present an example not only of the use of a raised hand but also the transformation of it in the course of turn competition. A transformation of the practice of 'bidding to speak next with the help of a raised

---

[2] Cf. Local and French's (1983) observations regarding the use of loudness as a prosodic accompaniment of turn-competitive incomings. Thanks to one of the reviewers for pointing this out.

[3] Sara's hand gesture here seems comparable to the finger-raising gesture used to bid for next turns in large group meetings, as reported in Ford and Stickle (2012). Thanks to one of the reviewers for pointing this out.

hand/finger' becomes relevant when the bid for the next turn is 'registered', but its execution is put on hold. Having made her bid, and having secured some form of recognition from the co-participants (in the form of an eye-gaze, for example), but for various reasons (such as running into concurrent bids from other non-current speakers) having had her bid put temporarily on hold, the bidder is now faced with the problem of what to do next; in particular, what to do with her hand gesture which has now been activated? As we shall see, one solution to this problem is to transform the ongoing gesture from a turn-bidding one to one where the hand is retracted to a half-way position by, for example, touching one's own chin or nose, and yet clearly not retracting all the way back to the home position.

We can see an example of this in data fragment (2) below. In this episode, Yan is telling her friends Tanya and Mabel about her son and daughter-in-law's choice as to which area to live in after they get married. According to Yan, the newly-weds have decided, against her good advice, to live in an area which is more 'posh' but further away from their places of work (as opposed to another area which is more modest but closer to their workplaces).

(2) Shark fin (SR-C01: 0012-0032)

```
01  Yan:   lokyu  a    sing,       ngo  zikcing  zau  heoi  matye,
            rain   PT   and-all    I    just     go   DIR   what

02          daap   diksi:  aa,    haanfaan  godi  cin      aa,
            take   taxi    PT     save      that  money    PT

03          dou    yau     zoeksou  laa:
            also   have    gained   PT
            'And when it rains, and all that, I can just go and, you know, take a
            cab, and (I would) still have gained by saving some money.'

04  Tan:   |syn          laa    [syn-
            forget-it    PT     forget-
           |(T turns away from Yan and looks into the mid-distance)
            'Forget it, forget-'

05  Yan:                 [ngodei-  ngodei  |gai             gwo  [keoi  laa
                          we       we       calculate       ASP   him   PT
                                           |(T turns gaze back at Y
                                           momentarily)
                         'We've done some calculations for them.'
```

```
06  Tan:                  [|m-gwaan-si
                           not-relevant
                          |(T turns away again and looks in M's direction)
                          'That's not the point.'

07                        [gamyeong jinggoi hai]
                          like-that  should   be
                          'That shouldn't'

08  Mab:   |[m-   m-   m-wui   aa::]
            not   not  won't   PT
           'That won't- that won't- that won't (happen).'
   →       |(M raises right hand with an open palm, stretches it
   →       into common space and waves twice as she says 'not')

09  Tan:   |m-gwaan-si    lo,   mhai   gogo   mantai
            not.relevant  PT    not    that   question
           'matter, that's not the question.'
   →       |(M keeps hand in a raised position, then moves it back
   →       to touch her own chin)

10  Mab:   |ming-m-ming     aa   Yan
            understand-or-not PT Yan
   →       |(M moves hand from chin back to common space, and
   →       waves it more vigorously while gazing at Yan)
           'Don't you understand, Yan?'
```

As mentioned above, during this part of the conversation, Yan is telling her friends about her son and daughter-in-law's choice of a new home. Just prior to the beginning of this fragment, Yan was sharing with her friends her own reservations regarding the new couple's choice of a location to rent an apartment. As we join the conversation, Yan is continuing with this account, giving another reason (to Tanya, to whom she is speaking) in support of her own preference for the couple to live nearer to their places of work, the reason being they would be able to save more money on taxi fares and traveling expenses (lines 1–3). Tanya's reaction to this – "Forget it!" (line 4), is anything but affiliative, and at the same time as Tanya is saying this, she turns her gaze away from Yan and starts looking into the mid-distance. Undeterred, Yan carries on to elaborate how she has come to that conclusion about savings by offering to detail the calculations that she has done for the newly-weds: "We've done

(2a) Tan: 'That's not the point!' (L6) (2b) Mab: 'That won't happen' (L8)
(2c) Tan: 'That shouldn't matter' (L9) (2d) Mab: 'Don't you understand, Yan?' (L10)

Figure 2: Bidding with a raised hand and holding with the hand in a tense position (touching own chin) (From left: Mabel, Yan and Tanya).

some calculations for them." (line 5). Tanya, however, remains unimpressed (and unconvinced?), as she delivers yet another dismissive response: "That's not the point" (line 6).

At this juncture, Mabel, who has to some extent been left out of the storytelling until now, decides to join in, and offers her own opinion ("That won't happen", i.e., Yan's reasoning is not going to fly with the newly-weds; line 8). As she delivers her utterance, Mabel raises her right arm with the hand in an Open Hand Palm Down configuration reaching out into the common space, or, in Kendon's (1990) terminology, the "o-space" in front of them, and then waves her hand twice (Figure 2b). Since Tanya did not select a next speaker in her just-prior TCU ("That's not the point"), and since that TCU has indeed reached a point of possible completion, it is entirely legitimate (by reference to the conversational turn-taking system (Sacks, Schegloff & Jefferson, 1974)) for Mabel to start speaking here. However, as it turns out, Tanya is not done yet. To that prior TCU is now added two more ("That shouldn't matter. That's not the question."), in quick succession (line 9), to drive home the point that she has been making, namely, that Yan's (financial) considerations are unlikely to be shared by the new couple as the decisive factor in choosing a location to live.

In view of the overlap between her own utterance and Tanya's in lines 7 and 8, Mabel stops speaking (at the end of line 8), even though her short utterance in line 8 is in a sense not complete. (It does come with what looks like a possibly complete grammatical unit, "won't happen"; nevertheless, the sense of that utterance is arguably not all that clear yet, and more talk is to be expected). Having stopped speaking, and now listening to (and monitoring) Tanya's extension and progression of her turn, Mabel starts retracting her out-stretched arm back to a position closer to herself, indeed within her own private space, or, in Kendon's (1990) terminology, "p-space", and then proceeds to touch her chin while waiting for Tanya to finish (Figure 2c). Not surprisingly, as soon as Tanya is done with her two quick, additional, TCUs (line 9), Mabel comes back into the conversation in full force, with a strong plea for Yan to show greater understanding ("Don't you understand Yan?", line 10). As Mabel is delivering this utterance, she stretches her right arm out again into o-space and waves it several times more (Figure 2d), which is of course fully in line with her newly acquired status as current speaker (in the sense of Schegloff 1984, whereby gesticulation is current speaker's prerogative).

In observing Mabel's series of hand gestures in this data fragment, one is struck by their consistency and systematicity. The out-stretched arm first reaches out into o-space to make a bid for next speakership (Figure 2b). Upon encountering competition in the course of making the bid, and having been put on the 'waiting list' (i.e., on hold), the participant sees to it that the arm stays up in a raised position (Figure 2c), and stays up there until it is time to take the next turn. A drop of the arm to a lower level or a retraction to its home position on her lap at this point in time (which Mabel is *not* doing) could be construed as relinquishing the bid to be the next speaker. This suggests that a useful distinction may be made between a 'public action' (as in turn-bidding) as opposed to a 'private action' (as in stroking one's own chin, grooming one's own hair, or bringing both hands together), in the context of turn bidding and turn competition.

3 Arm-taps

3.1 Bidding to speak next with arm-taps

Another practice which appears to have a very similar function to the upward-pointing index finger is arm-taps. This may be less 'prototypical' but no less common, and certainly no less useful. Consider data fragment (3), which occurs shortly before data fragment (1). Here, Katy is telling her friends the date of her upcoming wedding.

(3) Bridesmaids (C04: 0059-0113)

01 Sara: |Daaibaa sigaan [gaamfei   laa
           lots-of   time   lose-weight PT
           |(smiling)
           'Lots of time to lose weight!'

02 Rose: [Daanhai
                             but
                             'But'

03 Katy: (lin-)

04 Rose: ok-

05 Katy: |Dim   aa? huh huh huh huh HAH HAH HAH
           how   PT
           |(Turns from Rose to Sara with a smile on her face)
           'What? Huh huh huh HAH HAH HAH'

06 Sara: |Hehheh heh   heh   heh
           Hehheh   heh   heh   heh
           |(with gaze on Katy, sits up, leans forward and laughs)

07 Rose: Daanhai o[k-zo |lei go   jatzi hai [go   jat?
           but   ok ASP you   CL   date be that day
                            |(Katy lifts and examines the upper part of her
                                         right arm)   [
           'But your date has been fixed?'   [
                                                             [

08 Katy: [Hai aa   [
                    yes   PT   [
                    'Yes'   [
                                                             [

09 Sara: [WEI [NGO SAPJYUT
                                                   hey   I   October
                                                   JATHOU
                                                   first

→	*wui jing	zimui soeng aa*	[
→	will take bridesmaid photo PT	[
→		(taps Katy's left arm	[
	twice with the back of	[
	her right hand)	[
	'Hey October first I'll be	[
	taking bridesmaid photos.'	[
		[

10 Katy: [|*Mei aa,*
           not-yet
           >*ngo mei*
           PT   I   not

jingtung<   aa
agreed   PT
'Not yet, I haven't agreed yet'

|(Gaze first on Rose, but turns quickly to Sara in the course of her turn, while raising the index finger of her right hand in a swiping action that seems to 'pass' the utterance to Rose as she turns her gaze towards Sara)

11 Katy: *sap-jyut   [jat-hou?*
           October   first
           'First of October?'

12 Sara: [*Hai   aa,*
                       yes   PT
                       'Yes'

In response to Katy's indication of the date of her wedding (just prior to the beginning of this data fragment), Sara reacts with a tease ("(So you'll have) lots of time to lose weight!", said with a smile in line 1). Upon hearing Sara's wisecrack, Katy, who was originally looking in Rose's direction, now turns to Sara and shares a laughter with her, as she issues an 'official' note of incomprehension (using the "open-class repair initiator" *dim aa* 'What?', line 5) (Drew 1997). Meanwhile, Rose is reacting to Katy's informing very differently: with a confirmation-seeking question (first "but" in line 2, then "ok" in line 4, both of which were stalled in overlap with the other two co-participants' utterances, and finally "But your date has been fixed?" in line 7). In the course of Rose's turn (line 7), Katy once again turns her head back in Rose's direction, in readiness to respond to her question.

(3a) Sara: "Lots of time to lose weight." (L1)   (3b) Rose: "But your date has been fixed?" (L7)

(3c) Sara: "Hey October first..." (L9)   (3d) Katy: "First of October?" (L11)

Figure 3: Turn bidding with arm-taps (From left: Rose, Katy and Sara).

However, at this very moment, just before the arrival of Rose's TRP (at the end of line 7), Sara comes in, in overlap with the last two syllables of Rose's turn and in a loud voice, with an announcement: "HEY OCTOBER FIRST I'LL BE TAKING BRIDESMAID PHOTOS!" (line 9)

Three features in the design of Sara's announcement seem worth noting. First, with its placement in an early start position and its delivery in a loud voice, Sara's utterance is clearly hearable as one that is coming from a 'third party' who has not been selected as the next speaker. It is in this sense a competitive bid for speakership at a place where a special effort is required for someone other than the selected next speaker to start speaking. Second, note that Sara's utterance is begun with a disjunction ("HEY"), which of course is a display of 'sudden remembering' or 'noticing' that furnishes the speaker's action at this point with an account or a warrant (cf. Why speak now?). Finally, and this is of direct relevance to the theme of this chapter, it can be seen on the video that as she is verbalizing this utterance, Sara at the same time reaches out and gives two quick taps on Katy's left arm with the back of her right hand. (Figure 3c). By intruding into another's "private space"(Kendon 2004), the arm tap appears to carry a sense of greater urgency than the raised finger, as it serves to augment a non-selected-next-speaker's bid to transform the ongoing participation framework. (Cf. Wu 1979 where a similar use of arm-taps is reported in a Mandarin conversation.)

3.2 Re-establishing a participation framework after a temporary disruption with an arm-tap (by current speaker)

Interestingly, arm taps are used not only by non-current speakers to make a bid for speakership, they can also be used by current speakers to re-establish an ongoing participation framework after it has been (temporarily) disrupted -- a 'disruption' from the point of view of the current speaker, at any rate. In the next data fragment, which occurred some time after the talk shown in data frgment (2) above, Mabel, Yan and Tanya (from left to right in the drawings below) are having a conversation, when Yan begins to tell a story about her daughter-in-law.

(4) Complaining (SR_C01: 0155-0170)

```
01   Yan:     |Heoi  dou    tai   le   zau    cyunbou  ze, (.)
              go     reach  see   PT   then   all      I-mean
              |(Eye gaze on Tanya)

02            dou    hai   |mou  gaangaak      ge
              also   be    no    partitioning  PT
                          |(Turns to look at Mabel)

03            |dimbatzi      le,  keoi  loupo  zau    haidou (dental click)
              surprisingly   PT   his   wife   then   keep-on
              |(Turns back to look at Tanya)

04            jim-SAA::M-jim-sei  jau   [mou-  man-   ]
              complaining         and    no-   ask-
              'When they got there to see (the apartment), there was, I mean, no
              partitioning of any kind. And then his wife kept on (dental click)
              complaining, and a-, ask-'

05   Mabel:                       [|Jim-jim-jim          mee    aa?]
                                    com- com- complain   what   PT
                                  |(Leans forward with eyes on Yan)
                                  'Com- com- complaining about what?'

06   Yan:     (To Tanya)|man   keoi  lougung   wo:=
                         ask   her   husband   PT
                        'asked her husband,'
                        |(Yan does not turn to Mabel in spite of her question
                        and continues to talk to Tanya)
```

07   Tanya: (to Mabel) |=*mou   gaangaak   lo*=
                         no   partitioning PT
                       | (Tanya turns gaze from Yan to Mabel; at the same
                         time, Mabel turns gaze from Yan to Tanya)
                         'No partitioning.'

08 → Yan: =*keoi   waa   wo, |mou   fong   dim   wo?*
              she   said   PT   no   room   how   PT
    → |(gives Tanya a single tap on her arm)
             'And she said, How (can we live in an apartment) without rooms?!'

(4a) Yan: "...complaining" (L4)   (4b) Mabel: "Complaining about what?" (L5)

(4c) Tanya: "No partitioning" (L7)   (4d) Yan: "And she said, no room then how?" (L8)

Figure 4: Current speaker fending off an insertion sequence with an arm tap (From left to right: Mabel, Yan and Tanya).

In Yan's story (lines 1–4), her son and his fiancée went looking for an apartment just before they got married. In looking at a particular apartment, the couple saw that it was in fact a 'studio flat' with no partitioning in it. At this point, to Yan's "surprise" (line 3), her son's "wife" started "complaining" (line 4: *jim-saam-jim-sei*), and in complaining "a-, ask- ..." (presumably) a question However, before Yan can go on to report what question the wife was asking, Mabel comes in in overlap with Yan's latest story component to seek clarification as to what it is that the wife is complaining about (line 5: "com- com- complaining about what?"). Instead of taking a pause from the ongoing story to answer Mabel's question and in so doing completing what was looking to become an insertion sequence (that could be used to supply a piece of background information),[4] Yan keeps her gaze firmly on Tanya and continues with the next bit of her story ("(She) asked her husband," line 6). At this very moment, however, Tanya, upon seeing that Yan was not going to provide the clarification that Mabel is seeking, shifts her gaze from Yan to Mabel, and answers Mabel's question on Yan's behalf ("no partitioning", line 7), i.e., the daughter-in-law's complaint is that the apartment has no partitioning. Without turning her gaze or attention to this quick exchange between Mabel and Tanya, Yan presses on and delivers what turns out to be the story's punch line: "And she said, 'How (can we live in an apartment) without rooms?!'" (line 8).

With regard to changes and shifts in speakership, what seems to be happening in this data fragment goes something like this. As the story unfolds (lines 1–4), we see a clear participation framework forming and establishing itself, with Yan being the storyteller and Tanya the main story recipient (and Mabel something of a secondary recipient). As Yan approaches the end of the story and is getting all ready to deliver the punch line, Mabel makes a bid (in line 5) to put the story on hold for what seems like a very good reason, namely, for a clarification to be made regarding the object of the daughter-in-law's complaint (which will in all likelihood be critical to a proper understanding of the story). In one sense Mabel's question is an invitation to suspend, albeit only temporarily, the current participation framework, and bring about a "change of footing" (Goffman 1981), where Mabel is a story-recipient seeking background information from Yan the storyteller, who, if the invitation is accepted, would step out of the storytelling mode[5] temporarily into what might be described as a ground-preparation mode through which an information gap could be filled.

However, by not aligning with Mabel's action and continuing to progress the story (line 6), Yan is making it quite clear that Mabel's invitation to change footings is either not heard or not accepted. At the pace with which Yan is bringing the story to its climax, Mabel's attempt to generate a side sequence could easily have been thwarted, or, to use Jefferson's terminology, "sequentially deleted" (Jefferson 1978), if not for Tanya's 'intervention' in line 7. What Tanya does at this critical juncture turns out to be quite interesting.[6] She has, throughout the

---

[4] See Schegloff (2007) for a discussion of insertion sequences and other methods of sequence expansion.
[5] I am using 'mode' here in the sense of Goodwin's (1984) 'storytelling segment' vs 'background segment'.
[6] 'Juncture' here refers to the end of lines 4 and 5, i.e., at just the point where Mabel is asking her question about the daughter-in-law's complaint *in overlap with* Yan's display of readiness to launch into what the daughter-in-law is about to say to the husband (which promises to be the punch-line of her story).

storytelling so far, been fixing her gaze on the storyteller. Even when Mabel asks her question (in line 5), Tanya's body and head orientation remains unchanged. However, when it becomes clear that Yan is not answering Mabel's question but is going on to finish the story (line 6) in spite of Mabel's expressed inability to locate the source of the daughter-in-law's complaint, Tanya 'steps in', *in the middle of Yan's ongoing turn* ("asked her husband"; line 6), turns her gaze towards Mabel, and answers her question on Yan's behalf (line 7).[7] In doing this, Tanya is breaking away from the established *participation framework* (defined in terms of Yan's story) and moving into a different (albeit brief and temporary) framework where Mabel, as a story recipient, is seeking background information and where Tanya, as a fellow story recipient, is providing the required information on behalf of the storyteller. In building this little side sequence (together with Mabel), however, Tanya has in effect put the ongoing story on hold, and, as we shall see presently, this will mean that some effort will be needed to put the story back on track again.

For the purposes of this paper, we may focus our analysis of this fragment on the use of a single arm-tap by Yan to Tanya. In terms of its placement, the arm-tap is administered precisely at a point when Yan the storyteller has, after Mabels' brief 'interruption', re-cycled her previous turn beginning ("And she said", line 8) and readying herself for the delivery of the punchline (second part of line 8). As in the previous example, this arm-tap clearly helps to secure mutual orientation between the tapping and the tapped participants. However, in this case, the tapping is done by someone who is in a sense the current speaker and not, as in the previous case, by a non-current speaker. I said Yan is "in a sense" the current speaker because within the ongoing storytelling project she is indeed the 'current speaker'. Nevertheless, when Tanya 'intervened' to complete the Q-A sequence initiated by Mabel, and in so doing succeeded in shifting her footing from story-recipient to surrogate/assistant storyteller, within this subsidiary participation framework Tanya must be recognized as the 'current speaker'. It is within this context of the two interplaying and interconnected participation frameworks that the work of Yan's arm-tap is to be understood, i.e., as a move that is assisting Yan in her attempt to invite Tanya to return to the main project of storytelling by re-assuming her (i.e., Tanya's) role as (primary) story-recipient.

Note also that the arm-tap is timed to provide something of a punctuation between the two parts of Yan's final story component (line 8), "And she said"

---

[7] Cf. Stivers and Robinson (2006) where a preference for progressivity is reported. In our data fragment here, Tanya's answering of Mable's question, initially addressed to Yan, can be seen as 'warranted' by this preference.

(part 1, which introduces the punch line) and "No room then how?" (part 2, which constitutes the punch line). Thus, the arm-tap appears to serve three purposes at once: to re-establish the previous/main participation framework (where Yan is the storyteller), to secure attention from the main story-recipient (Tanya), and to add weight to a beat of silence that precedes the delivery of the punch line.

4 Concluding discussion

Taking Schegloff's (1984) idea of 'incipient speakership' as a starting point, this chapter examines two kinds of hand gestures that appear to have a direct bearing on turn-taking -- indeed a direct bearing on the management of turn competition in multi-party talk. Our interest is in conversational participants, who, at the time of constructing and administering these gestures, do not have the status of either 'current speaker' or 'selected next speaker'. How do they go about bidding for and securing speakership at the next opportunity? What role, if any, do these gestures play in that process? And what other functions might these same gestures serve in addition to their use as a turn-taking resource?

To this end we have examined two gesture-types in some detail – the raised hand/finger and the arm-tap. That they can be used by participants to make a bid for speakership, *and to make one in such a way as to display their orientation to their own status as non-current speaker and non-selected next speaker*, is not in question. (Note how the same gestures are never used by current speakers who continue to talk past a TRP, or by selected next speakers as they take up the next turn.)

Bidding for and securing speakership are of course two different things. The latter does not simply follow from the former. In the course of making a bid for next speakership, a participant may encounter competition, resistance, or outright disregard and neglect. As we have seen in our data, participants also have verbal and bodily-visual resources at their disposal to deal with such contingencies, including changing and transforming their just-administered gestures in response to the changing circumstances, as when Mabel keeps her hand up in the air and then turning it into a self-swipe of the chin in preparation for a well-timed comeback as soon as Tanya finishes her turn (in data fragment 2 above).

It must not be forgotten that while our focus has been on speakership and turn-taking, this does not mean that the gestures we have identified have these as their only functions. We saw how, in data fragment (4) for example, Yan's arm-tap serves also to punctuate between the introduction and the doing of the story punch line, which is of course something quite different from, and independent of, its work in the context of the transformation of participation frameworks.

The present report makes no claim at all to comprehensiveness. The modest list of practices here is certainly not exhaustive. Others have been reported in the literature, including Li's (2014) description of the 'hand-fight' (which may apply more to two-party interactions?). This chapter would have served its purpose if it succeeds in adding two more items to a growing inventory of hand gestures that can make a direct contribution to the management of emergent speakership.

References

Arnold, L. 2012. Dialogic embodied action: using gesture to organize sequence and participation in instructional interaction. *Research on Language and Social Interaction* 45(3): 269–296.

Berger, I. and Rae, J. 2012. Some uses of gestural responsive actions. *Journal of Pragmatics* 44(13): 1821–1835.

Bolden, G. 2003. Multiple modalities in collaborative turn sequences. *Gesture* 3.2: 187–212.

Chui, Kawai. 2009. Conversational coherence and gesture. *Discourse Studies* 11(6): 661–680.

Cienki, A. 1998. Metaphoric gestures and some of their relations to verbal metaphoric expressions. In J.-P. Koenig (Ed.), *Discourse and cognition: Bridging the gap*. Stanford, CA: Center for the Study of Language and Information.

Cienki, A. and Müller, C. (eds.), 2008. *Metaphor and Gesture*. Amsterdam/Philadelphia: John Benjamins.

Drew, P. 1997. Open class repair initiators in response to sequential sources of troubles in conversation. *Journal of Pragmatics* 28.1: 69–101.

Duncan, S. Jr. 1972. Some signals and rules for taking speaking turns in conversation. *Journal of Personality and Social Psychology*, 23.2:283–292.

Duncan, S. Jr. and Niederehe, G. 1974. On signalling that it's your turn to speak. *Journal of Experimental Social Psychology* 10: 234–247.

Ford, C.E. and Stickle, T. 2012. Securing recipiency in workplace meetings: multimodal practices. *Discourse Studies* 14.1: 11–30.

Goffman, E. 1981. *Forms of Talk*. Philadelphia: University of Pennsylvania Press.

Goodwin, C. 1980. Re-starts, pauses and the achievement of a state of mutual gaze at turn beginning. *Sociological Inquiry* 50: 272–302.

Goodwin, C. 1981. *Conversational Organization: Interaction between speakers and hearers*. New York: Academic Press.

Goodwin, C. 1984. Notes on story structure and the organization of participation. In M. Atkinson & J. Heritage (eds.), *Structures of Social Action*. Cambridge: Cambridge University Press. 225–246.

Goodwin, C. 1986. Gesture as a resource for the organization of mutual orientation. *Semiotica* 62(1–2): 29–49.

Goodwin, C. 2014. The intelligibility of gesture within a framework of co-operative action, In M. Seyfeddinipur & M. Gullberg (eds.), *From gesture in conversation to visible action as utterance: Essays in honor of Adam Kendon*. Amsterdam, John Benjamins Publishing Company. 199–216.

Heath, C. and Luff, P. 2011. Gesture and institutional interaction. In Streeck, Goodwin & LeBaron (eds.), pp 276–288.

Jefferson, G. 1978. "Sequential aspects of storytelling in conversation." In *Studies in the Organization of Conversational Interaction*, ed. by Schenkein, J. New York: Academic Press. 219–248.

Kendon, A. 1990. *Conducting Interaction: Patterns of behavior in focused encounters*. Cambridge: Cambridge University Press.

Kendon, A. 1994. Do gestures communicate?: A review. *Research on Language and Social Interaction* 27.3: 175–200.

Kendon, A. 2004. *Gesture: Visible Action as Utterance*. Cambridge: Cambridge University Press.

Langford, D. 1994. *Analysing talk: Investigating verbal interaction in English*. London, UK: Macmillan Press.

Li, Xiaoting. 2014. *Multimodality, Interaction and Turn-taking in Mandarin Conversation*. Amsterdam/Philadelphia: John Benjamins.

Local, J. and French, P. 1983. Turn competitive incomings. *Journal of Pragmatics* 7.1: 17–38.

Levinson, S. C. 2007. Optimizing person reference – perspectives from usage on Rossel Island. In Enfield, N.J. and Stivers, T. (eds.) *Person Reference in Interaction: Linguistic, cultural and social perspectives*, pp 29–72.

Mondada, L. and Oloff, F. 2011. "Gestures in overlap: the situated establishment of speakership". In Stam, G. and Ishino, M. (eds.) *Integrating Gestures: The interdisciplinary nature of gesture*. Amsterdam/Philadelphia: John Benjamins. 321–338.

McNeill, D. 1992. *Hand and Mind: What gestures reveal about thought*. Chicago: University of Chicago Press.

McNeill, D. 2005. *Gesture and Thought*. Chicago: University of Chicago Press.

Mondada, L. 2011. The organization of concurrent courses of action on surgical demonstrations. In Streeck, Goodwin & LeBaron (eds.). 207–226.

Sacks, H., Schegloff, E.A. and Jefferson, G. 1974. A simplest systematic for the organization of turn-taking for conversation. *Language* 50: 696–735.

Sacks, H. and Schegloff, E.A. 2002 Home position. *Gesture* 2.2: 133–146.

Schegloff, E.A. 1984. On some gestures' relation to talk. In J.M. Atkinson and J. Heritage (eds.), Structures of Social Action, pp 266–298. Cambridge: Cambridge University Press.

Schegloff, E.A. 2007. *Sequence Organization in Interaction, Vol. 1: A Primer in Conversation Analysis*. Cambridge: Cambridge University Press.

Stivers, T. and Robinson, J.D. 2006. A preference for progressivity in interaction. *Language in Society* 35.3: 367–392.

Streeck, J. 2009. *Gesturecraft: The manufacturing of meaning*. Amsterdam: John Benjamins.

Streeck, J., Goodwin, C., and LeBaron, C. (eds.), 2011. *Embodied interaction: Language and body in the material world*. Cambridge: Cambridge University Press.

Streeck J. and Hartge, U. 1992. Previews: Gestures at the transition place. In P. Auer & A. di Luzio (eds.), *The Contextualization of Language*. Amsterdam/Philadelphia: John Benjamins. 135–157.

Williams,. R.F. 2008. Gesture as a conceptual mapping tool. In Cienki and Müller (eds.) *Metaphor and Gesture*. 55–92.

Wu, R.-J. R. 1997. Transforming participation frameworks in multi-party Mandarin conversation: The use of discourse particles and body behavior. *Issues in Applied Linguistics* 8.2: 97–117.

Yang, Ping. 2011. Nonverbal aspects of turn-taking in Mandarin Chinese interaction. *Chinese Language and Discourse* 2.1: 99–130.

Zemel, A., Koschman, T., and LeBaron. 2011. Pursuing a response: prodding recognition and expertise within a surgical team. In Streeck, Goodwin & LeBaron (eds.), pp 227–243.

Kawai Chui
Grounding and gestural repetition in Chinese conversational interaction

1 Introduction

There are different lines of research on gestural communication. In the area of the production of gesture, Beattie and Shovelton (2001), among many others, examined speakers' gestures which encoded the viewpoint of a character in a cartoon stimuli (cf. Mittelberg 2017). Numerous studies investigated narrators' use of gestures to express motion based on elicited narratives (Özyürek and Kita 1999; McNeill and Duncan 2000; Kita and Özyürek 2003; Özyürek et al. 2005; Kita et al. 2007; Ortega 2017). The studies in Cienki and Müller (2008) examined the gestural representations of metaphorical concepts in a diverse range of contexts. In Parrill et al. (2013), they examined the production of motion verbs and iconic gestures after participants had read texts in the past progressive tense. Furthermore, speakers' production of gesture to express motion, metaphors, and frame knowledge in Mandarin Chinese was also investigated (Chui 2009a, 2011, 2012, 2017; Gu et al. 2017).

In the area of the comprehension of gesture, which is mainly concerned with whether and in what way gestural information would affect participants' understanding of language, Beattie and Shovelton (1999a, b) found that subjects' comprehension of the relative position and size of objects was better when speech and gestures were available in the stimuli. Hassemer and Winter's (2016) experimental findings showed that the gestural forms could affect the understanding of height gestures. Other studies provided behavioral and neurocognitive evidence for the semantic integration of gesture and speech during the comprehension of metaphor (Kelly and colleagues 2004, 2007, 2008; Bernardis and Gentilucci 2006; Holle and Gunter 2007; Özyurek et al. 2007; Wu and Coulson 2007, 2010; Cornejo et al. 2009; Kircher et al. 2009).

Rather than separating gesture production and comprehension, a different line of research considers both the speaker and the addressee in spontaneous interaction so that the use and understanding of gesture can be examined in sequential context. For instance, Bavelas et al. (1992) found that many more interactive gestures were produced in the dyad condition where two participants finished two verbal tasks together than in the alone condition where just one participant did the tasks. In another experimental study (Bavelas et al. 2002), speakers gestured more frequently and used non-redundant gestures to convey meaning

---

Kawai Chui, National Chengchi University

https://doi.org/10.1515/9783110462395-006

not found in words, when they were informed that addressees would see their videotapes. In Mandarin conversational discourse, gestures were produced to achieve coherence in successive turns when addressees conveyed understanding of gestural information (Chui 2009b).

Another important aspect of language use in spontaneous interaction is grounding (Clark and Schaefer 1987, 1989; Schober and Clark 1989; Clark and Brennan 1991; Clark 1996; Clark and Krych 2004), as the speaker and the addressee "go beyond autonomous actions and collaborate with each other moment-by-moment to try to ensure that what is said is also understood" (Schober and Clark 1989: 211). Participants continuously demonstrate their understanding to reach common ground by the use of linguistic and non-linguistic resources. Many studies have investigated grounding and non-verbal acts in experiments where participants collaborated and interacted freely to perform different tasks. For example, in a problem-solving task, Boyle et al. (1994) found that gaze could help the establishment of common ground. In Clark and Krych (2004), pairs of participants – each pair comprised of a director and a builder – engaged in the task of assembling ten Lego models. Whether the director could see the builder and whether instructions were given face-to-face or by audiotape affected the linguistic and gestural demonstration of the participants' understanding of the construction of the Lego pieces. The findings provided evidence in support of the bilateral and interactive nature of speaking, in that "[s]peakers monitor not just their own actions, but those of their addressees, taking both into account as they speak. Addressees, in turn, try to keep speakers informed of their current state of understanding" (Clark and Krych 2004: 62). Bavelas et al. (2011) studied grounding in a floor-plan design task with regard to grounding sequences and abstract deictic gestures produced by speakers. They found that the non-redundant speech-gesture combinations during speakers' presentations of information were largely understood by addressees and that most of the addressees' understanding was, in turn, acknowledged by speakers. Finally, Holler and Wilkin's (2011) study demonstrated that when participants engaged in a referential communication task and talked about a set of geometrical figures, a previous speaker's gesture would be mimicked for the establishment of common ground.

All the previous research on grounding and gesture as described above was mainly based on data from task-oriented interactions with participants being non-acquaintances. The goal of the interaction was to cooperate and finish a task. Moreover, the different nature of the tasks affected the occurrence of gestural types. The types found in Clark and Krych (2004: 72) "were taken to mean 'Do you mean this one, or like this, or here?' or 'I need more information'." Bavelas et al. (2011) only examined abstract deictic gestures that were related to a floor plan. These gestures were 'nonredundant' in the speaker's turn, "which contributed information that was missing from the words" (Bavelas et al. 2011: 54). In Holler and Wilkin (2011), deictic gestures designating spaces for referents were excluded; only iconic and metaphoric gestures conveying meaning were analyzed.

The current study investigates grounding and gesture in daily conversation, rather than in task-oriented discourse. It investigates how Mandarin speakers and addressees ground what they say by virtue of linguistic and gestural resources in grounding sequences. The investigation is crucial to the further analysis of gestural repetition, which has been shown to play a part in grounding in a referential communication task (Holler and Wilkin 2011). Gestural repetition in grounding refers to an act by which a manual configuration which has been produced by the speaker is replicated by the addressee for the same referent. Gestures of this type are called 'mimicked gestures' (cf. de Fornel 1992; Tabensky 2001; Kimbara 2006; Parrill and Kimbara 2006; Holler and Wilkin 2011; Mittelberg and Evola 2014).

The occurrence of gesture, whether repeated or not, is examined in grounding sequences in Mandarin conversations with participants knowing each other. Not only are face-to-face conversations the most fundamental type of talk-in-interaction (Sacks et al. 1974; Clark 1996; Bavelas and Chovil 2006), but also participants are free to initiate any topics of interest and develop the sequential turns in their own way without topic assignment or video stimuli. The way participants speak and gesture to demonstrate their understanding in conversational discourse is analyzed in grounding sequences (Bavelas et al. 2011), each consisting of a succession of 'information presentation', 'response' and 'acknowledgement'. Last, various types of gestures being produced during the presentation of information in the speaker's turn are analyzed.

In brief, this study aims to investigate the way speakers and addressees communicate their understanding, and the occurrence of gestural repetition in grounding.[1] Two types of grounding sequences are then identified: One type does not involve gestural repetition; in the other type, the addressee mimics the speaker's previous gesture while providing a response. It will be shown that there are different linguistic-gestural patterns of grounding in conversational discourse and that the grounding pattern with the occurrence of mimicked gestures can bear out the bilateral and interactive nature of speaking, in that addressees monitor

---

[1] In a multi-party conversation, the person who makes a response or acknowledgement may not be the addressee. The term 'participant' is thus more appropriate than 'addressee'. However, since there were just 10 cases out of all 190 grounding sequences in the database, the terms 'speaker' and 'addressee' are used here for the distinction between these two major roles in interaction.

prior speakers' gestures, take them into account as part of the turn construction, and, at the same time, inform the others about their understanding of the gestural information.

In the next section, the data for the present study is introduced. Section 3 provides the analysis of the grounding sequences without the occurrence of gestural repetition; Section 4 focuses on the grounding sequences with gestural repetition. A general discussion of the findings and conclusion are given in Section 5.

2 Data and methods

The data for this study consisted of daily face-to-face conversations among adult native speakers of Mandarin from the NCCU (National Chengchi University) Corpus of Spoken Taiwan Mandarin (Chui and Lai 2008; Chui et al. 2017). The participants were recruited to hold a conversation with their friends, family members or colleagues who knew each other well. Participants gave written consent for the data to be accessed online.[2] All of the participants were paid, and they were informed that they were participating in research on conversation, but gestures were not mentioned. For each recording, the participants chose a place where they could talk in a leisurely manner, such as a classroom, students' lounge, dorm room, or living room. They recorded themselves with a digital video camera on a tripod for approximately an hour. Participants were free to find and develop topics of common interest. One stretch of talk, at a time when the participants were comfortable in front of the camera, of about twenty to forty minutes from the total length of each talk, was then selected for transcription. In this study, the speech and the gestural data were from nine conversational extracts for a total length of about 180 minutes of talk. Six conversations comprised two participants; the rest consisted of three participants.

The identification of grounding sequences is crucial to the investigation of grounding patterns. In Clark and colleagues (Clark and Wilkes-Gibbs 1986; Clark and Schaefer 1987; Clark and Brennan 1991; Clark and Krych 2004), two phases for grounding were proposed: a 'presentation phase' on the part of the speaker, followed by an 'acceptance phase' on the part of the addressee. To include the speaker's feedback to the addressee's understanding, this study adopted the

---

[2] Permissions were obtained from all of the participants to use the audio-visual data from The NCCU Corpus of Spoken Taiwan Mandarin for research. The access date for this study was May, 2014. The data can also be accessed online at TalkBank http://talkbank.org/access/CABank/TaiwanMandarin.html.

sequence pattern consisting of three phases, as proposed by Bavelas et al. (2011: 51): "The person who is speaking at the moment *presents* some information, the addressee *responds* with an indication or display of understanding (or not), and then the speaker *acknowledges* this response by indicating that the addressee's understanding was correct (or not) [italics in original]."

Example 1 is about the change of a friend's body shape. The first phase of the grounding sequence is in line 1, where the speaker presents new information about the friend becoming fat and then thin alternately. In the second phase in line 2, the addressee responds explicitly and positively by the use of the agreement marker *duì* 'right'. After that, the speaker in the last phase in line 3 acknowledges the addressee's response implicitly by continuing the subject matter and providing some opinion on being overweight, as the addressee should have understood the information in line 1.[3]

(1) 1 Speaker: .. tā   yěshì yǒu pàng shòu pàng shòu pàng shòu.. zhèyàng
                 3SG also PRF fat thin fat thin fat thin like this
                 'She is fat, thin, fat, thin, fat, thin, like this.'
    2 Addressee: .. duì
                 right
                 'Right.'
    3 Speaker: .. kěshì qíshí   wǒ juédé pàng yě   méiyǒu shémo..
                 but   in fact 1SG think fat also NEG   what
                 yě   méiyǒu guānxì a
                 also NEG   matter PRT
                 'But, in fact, I think being fat is nothing; it does not matter.'

Several criteria were adopted for the identification of the grounding sequences used for analysis in the current study. First, for the understanding of the use of mimicked gestures, speakers' utterances without gestures in the first phase were not considered. Secondly, given that "*[t]he clause...with its crucial predicate, appears to be a unit which facilitates the monitoring of talk for social actions* [italics in original]" (Thompson and Couper-Kuhlen 2005: 485), clausal utterances in the presentation phase, each consisting of no more than one independent clause such as the one in line 1 of Example (1), were chosen. For a turn to include numerous clauses, there would be a lot more content and more than one speech-accompanying gesture, and it would be difficult to determine what information and which gesture the

---

[3] Without any linguistic expression against the response in line 2, the continuation of talk in line 3 was regarded as acceptance and categorized as 'implicit acknowledgement' in the study.

addressee was responding to. As for the turns that include no more than one independent clause, grounding could start whenever participants find it necessary to gain common ground for a piece of information, whether the clause is complete or not. Finally, in a few cases in the three-party conversations, the person who provided feedback was not the addressee, but a third participant who also took part in the interaction, received the same information and responded before the addressee did. Similarly, the speaker in the third phase in a sequence might not be the same person who had presented information in the first phase, but another participant who also received the addressee's response. Three responses from non-addressed recipients were included here without further distinction. Whether addressed and non-addressed participants would ground what they say differently awaits future research when more data are available.

Gestures in the presentation phase can be illustrated by Example 1. At the time the words *pàng* 'fat' and *shòu* 'thin' are uttered three times in the clause, the speaker's fingers of both hands at chest level extend and curl alternately three times (see the division of gesture space in McNeill 1992) for the depiction of the two conditions of the friend's body shape (Figure 1).

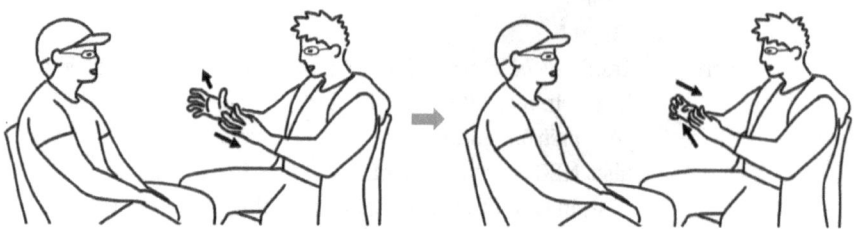

Figure 1: Gestural depiction of getting fat and thin alternately.

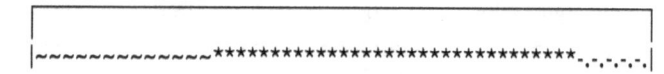

(1) 1 Speaker: .. tā yěshì yǒu pàng shòu pàng shòu pàng shòu.. zhèyàng
 3SG also PRF fat thin fat thin fat thin like this
 'She is fat, thin, fat, thin, fat, thin, like this.'

The analysis of the speech-accompanying gestures in the data started with the identification of the gestural boundaries with respect to three major phases: 'preparation', 'stroke', and 'retraction' (McNeill 1992). The preparation phase refers to "the limb mov[ing] away from its rest position to a position in gesture space where stroke begins"; the retraction phase is the "return of the hand to a rest position"; in-between is the stroke phase during which "the meaning of the gesture is expressed" (McNeill 1992: 83). While both preparation and retraction are optional, the stroke is obligatory. Next, the gestures were categorized. Based on the linguistic context and the socio-cultural knowledge about the conversational topics (Koschmann and LeBaron 2002), a manual configuration was categorized as an 'iconic gesture' depicting the meaning of a concrete idea, a 'metaphoric gesture' enacting the meaning of an abstract idea, a 'deictic gesture' – a pointing at a referent in the immediate speech environment, a 'spatial gesture' designating a space for a referent not in the speech environment, or an 'emblematic gesture' having some standard of well-formedness, like the thumbs-up gesture (McNeill 1992). Both the identification of the boundaries and the categorization of gesture are necessary for understanding whether certain types of gesture tend to occur in gestural repetition in grounding.

Two coders worked separately to identify grounding sequences in the data. They followed the selection criteria, and out of all the 4330 turns of talk, a total of 190 grounding sequences were found with consensus between the coders. They constituted the database for the investigation of the way the speaker and the addressee achieve common ground, and the way that gestural repetition is produced to reach the same goal.

For the analysis of mimicked gestures produced by the addressee, Parrill and Kimbara (2006) proposed the features of motion, hand shape, and location to determine the similarity of gestural forms depicting the same referents. Kimbara (2008), on the other hand, focused on one gesture feature – hand shape, and all of the hand shapes in her study corresponded to the signs of American Sign Language to which they most looked like. In our data, the determination of such a close resemblance was not straightforward, since most of the spontaneous gestures involve the dynamic movement of fingers, hands and arms. Instead, five gesture features were adopted: 'handedness', 'position', 'orientation', 'hand shape' and 'motion' (McNeill 1992, 2005) which sufficed to determine the similarity between gestures in the data. Moreover, following Holler and Wilkin's (2011: 139) definition that mimicked gestures are "gestures highly similar in their form *and* in the meaning they depict [italics in original]," 'form' and 'meaning' are then the two major criteria to be used to determine similarity. First, a high similarity in form is a matter of degree and mimicked gestures could be performed with "some degree of leeway...[or] in a slightly more elliptical form; that is, while the gesture may have looked more sloppy or may have been reduced by a particular semantic aspect, the general conceptualization did not change and a core aspect of the semantic representation was always retained in any gesture coded as mimicked" (Holler and Wilkin 2011: 140). The high similarity between two gestures in this study was mainly determined by rates of the congruence in the judgment of the five gesture features. Another criterion has to do with meaning, that is, whether or not a mimicked gesture, in addition to having a high similarity in form, also represents the same referent being depicted by its corresponding gesture in the prior context. The context and the content of the utterances made it clear whether the two similar gestures refer to the same referent or not. The analysis of gestural repetition in accordance with the criteria will be taken up in Section 4.

3 Grounding without gestural repetition

How do the speaker and the addressee demonstrate their understanding to reach common ground in grounding sequences in conversational interaction? Grounding sequences with and without gestural repetition were separated for tabulation. Two coders followed the criteria detailed in Section 2, and analyzed whether gestures produced by speakers in the first phase were mimicked to depict the same referents by addressees. Total agreement was reached between two coders that 173 sequences did not involve repetition with respect to both gestural forms and meaning, and 17 sequences included mimicked gestures. The way participants ground what they say in the sequences without gestural repetition is investigated here in accordance with the successive phases of 'information presentation', 'response', and 'acknowledgement'. The remaining 17 sequences will be discussed in Section 4.

3.1 Presentation of information

In the first phase of a grounding sequence, speakers present information of all kinds such as the quality of states, activities, or processes, or the characteristics of people or objects. Part of the utterance is simultaneously depicted by gesture. As shown in Example 1, the speaker's judgment on the body shape of a friend is expressed in both speech and gesture. In the data, 13 out of all the 173 grounding sequences include more than one gesture, yielding a total of 188 gestures of various kinds. The fat-thin gesture in Example 1 is metaphoric, depicting the abstract idea about the different states of the body by the use of more or less gestural spaces. An iconic gesture can be found in Example 2 about the construction of walls. The speaker presents information about having some thin wood which was adhered directly onto a cement wall. At the time he utters the verb *tiē* 'adhere', both of his hands in front of his chest go swiftly to the upper-left periphery at shoulder level to enact the concrete action of adherence (Figure 2).

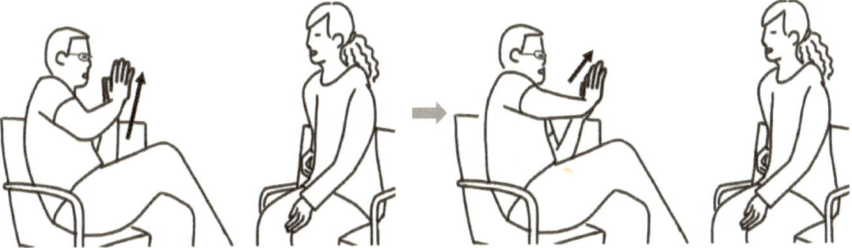

Figure 2: Gestural depiction of adherence.

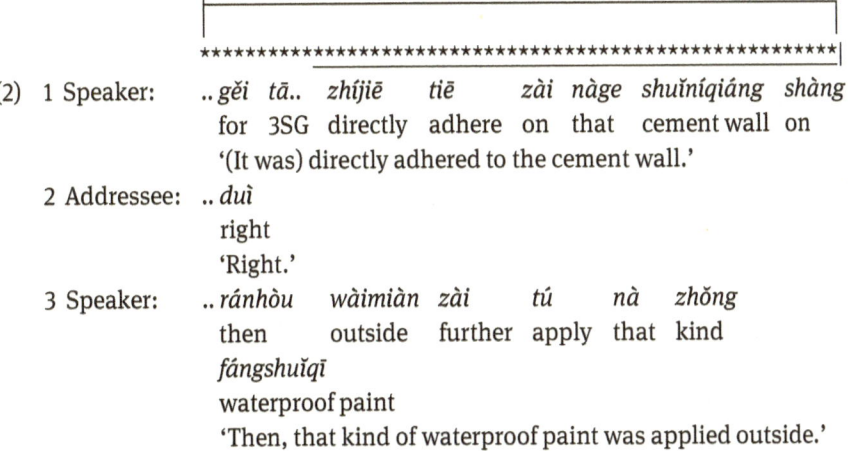

(2) 1 Speaker: *.. gěi tā.. zhíjiē tiē zài nàge shuǐníqiáng shàng*
for 3SG directly adhere on that cement wall on
'(It was) directly adhered to the cement wall.'

2 Addressee: *.. duì*
right
'Right.'

3 Speaker: *.. ránhòu wàimiàn zài tú nà zhǒng fángshuǐqī*
then outside further apply that kind waterproof paint
'Then, that kind of waterproof paint was applied outside.'

Deictic gestures, which point at referents in the immediate interactional environment, were produced by the participants to refer to themselves and associated with the pronominal *wǒmen* 'we' or *nǐ* 'you' in the data. Spatial gestures are used to locate referents at various points in the gesture space. For instance, in an utterance about growing sweet potatoes between two rows of tea plants, the speaker has his right index finger point at a space in front of him as the designated location for sweet potatoes. Finally, emblematic gestures in the data are the manual representation of numbers, negation and enumeration, such as the full extension of the index, middle and ring fingers with the others curling into the palm for the numerical *sān* 'three', or moving the hand side to side for *méiyǒu* 'not'. Despite the fact that emblematic forms are much more conventional than iconic or metaphoric gestures, all three types depict semantic information directly related to the utterances. The reliability between the two coders for the identification and categorization of gestures was 100% for iconic gestures, deictic gestures, spatial gestures and emblematic gestures, and 96% for metaphoric gestures. In the case of disagreement, data were re-analyzed and consensus was reached on 188 instances. Table 1 shows the frequency distribution of the gestural instances Representational gestures, whether iconic or metaphoric, constitute the great majority (74.4%). Moreover, 139 of the gestures (73.9%) carried new information which had not been brought up in the prior context. They mostly enacted new concepts iconically and metaphorically (83.5%, 116 out of 139), such as the adhering gesture in Example 2 and the fat-thin gesture in Example 1, respectively.

Table 1: Types of gesture and frequency distribution.

Iconic gestures	83	44.1%
Metaphoric gestures	57	30.3%
Deictic gestures	10	5.3%
Spatial gestures	21	11.2%
Emblematic gestures	17	9.1%
Total	188	100.0%

3.2 Response

After the speaker's presentation of information, the addressee makes a response to indicate whether s/he understands it or not in the next phase. Following Bavelas et al. (2011), the study categorized the feedback from the addressees into four types. The 'explicit positive' type, which demonstrates that the presented information is regarded by the addressee as unproblematic, is typically indicated by agreement markers like *duì* (Examples 1 and 2) and *he-a* 'right', markers of understanding like *o* 'I see', *mhm* or *uhuh* 'I see' or *wǒ zhīdào* 'I know', head nods, and echoic repeats of the prior speaker's words or rephrasing the speaker's idea for showing understanding or agreement, or a combination of these. The 'explicit negative' type, which demonstrates that the presented information is considered as problematic, can be indicated by the use of *méiyǒu* 'no', *búshì* 'no' or *kěshì* 'but', head shakes, negative assessments such as *hǎo qíguài* '(It is) very strange', correction, requests for clarification, or a combination of these. In a topic about providing tomatoes for committee members during an oral defense of a dissertation, the speaker in Example 3 says that it is difficult to pick tomatoes up from a plate using a fork (line 1). The addressee, in response, uses the disagreement marker *kěshì* 'but' to deny that tomatoes are very difficult to pick up, and then proposes a different idea about using hands to pick up the fruit.

(3) 1 Speaker: .. tīngshuō fānqié   hěn   nán   chā   a
                      hear   tomato   very difficult pick up with a fork PRT
                      '(I) heard that it was very difficult to pick up tomatoes with
                      a fork.'
    2 Addressee: .. kěshì tāmen kěyǐ yòng shǒu ná
                      but   3PL   can   use   hand take
                      'But they could (do it) by using their hands.'
    3 Speaker: .. tāmen búyào yòng shǒu   ná... tāmen dàgài   jiùshì
                      3PL   NEG   use   hand   take   3PL   probably just
                      jiùshì juédé shǒu zāng.. bù   xiǎng yòng shǒu ná
                      just   think hand dirty NEG want   use   hand take
                      'They did not want to pick up (the tomatoes) by hand. They
                      probably thought their hands would get dirty. (They) did
                      not want to pick up (the tomatoes) by hand.'

The third 'implicit positive' type has the addressee "[say] something that built on a presupposed understanding" (Bavelas et al. 2011: 56). The topic in Example 4 is about military service. The speaker in line 1 tells that he was a radar operator in an army troop. Based on such understanding, the addressee in line 2 continues the topic and provides new information that the speaker might also have needed to fire artillery in the army.

(4) 1 Speaker: ...wǒ shì... zài   lǐmiàn jiùshì... léidá cāozuòshǒu ma
                      1SG COP   be.at inside that is   radar operator   PRT
                      'In the troops, I was a radar operator.'
    2 Addressee: .. tā   yào   qù   dǎ   pào
                      3SG will go   fire artillery
                      'He would have fired artillery'
    3 Speaker: ... léidá cāozuòshǒu.. wǒ   yǒu qù dǎ   fēidàn
                      radar operator   1SG EXP go fire missile
                      'Radar operator...I fired missiles.'

The last type is 'moot', as the addressee utters something not overtly related to the speaker's information. Responses of this type in the data occurred when addressees tried to follow what they had brought up before the speakers' turns, once they themselves had gained the floor. In Example (5) about a hornets' nest, the speaker in line 1 mentions *fēngmìjiǔ* 'mead'. Rather than responding to *fēngmìjiǔ*, the addressee talks about having a long broomstick that could be used to get rid of a hornets' nest, an idea not completely expressed in her previous turn.

(5) 1 Speaker: ..fēngmìjiǔ
                mead
                'Mead'
    2 Addressee: @@@ wàimiàn bú   shì   yǒu   nàge...(0.7) cháng
                     outside NEG COP   there.be   that   long
                 de sào[bǎ ma]
                 DE broom QST
                 'There was a long broomstick outside, wasn't there?'
    3 Speaker: [nǐ kàn].. nǐ   mì   mìfēng   kěyǐ pào   jiǔ..
                 2SG see   2SG honey honeybee can   soak   alcohol
                 fēngcháo   kěyǐ jǐ   nàge mì   chūlái
                 honeycomb can   extract that honey   out
                 'You see, you..honey..honeybees can be soaked in alcohol;
                 honey can be extracted from honeycombs.'

Two coders analyzed the responses separately; the inter-coder reliability for the categorization of responses was 95%. Consensus was gained after re-analysis of the cases where no agreement was found in the first analysis. Table 2 indicates the frequency distribution across the four types of responses. Positive feedback constitutes a large majority (85%) and explicit responses are preferred, demonstrating that addressees, most of the time, understand the linguistic-gestural information conveyed by speakers.

Table 2: Response types and frequency distribution.

Explicit positive	119	68.8%
Explicit negative	19	11.0%
Implicit positive	28	16.2%
Moot	7	4.0%
Total	173	100.0%

3.3 Acknowledgement

The last phase in a grounding sequence is the speaker's acknowledgement to demonstrate whether the addressee's response is accepted or not. According to Bavelas et al. (2011), three types of feedback were distinguished, namely 'explicit', 'implicit', and 'other'. In 'explicit acknowledgement', the speaker reacts either positively or negatively to the addressee's understanding. The use of markers like *duì* 'right' or *o* 'I see', or *wǒ zhīdào* 'I know' demonstrates that the addressee's response is considered as unproblematic. In some instances, further information after the overt markers is provided. Explicit negative acknowledgements can be indicated by markers such as *búshì* 'no', typically followed by a correction of the addressee's information. Example 6 is about love affairs in college. The speaker in line 3 shows disagreement toward what the addressee has just said in line 2 by first uttering *méiyǒu* 'no' and then making a correction about getting to know her boyfriend at a summer camp.

(6) 1 Speaker: .. *nǐ   kàn   chényínshān   gēn   lǎoshurén   tāmen   chā*
                   2SG look Chenyinshan   and   Laoshuren   3PL   gap
                sān   jiè
                three   year of college
                'Look, there was a three-year gap between Chenyinshan and Laoshuren in college.'

   2 Addressee: .. *kěshì   tāmen   yí   rèn..   yí   rènshì   jiù   yǒu*
                   but   3PL   as   know   as   know each other   just   have
                gǎnjué ...   nǐmen   shì   xiān   rènshì   hěn   jiǔ
                feeling   2PL   COP   first know each other   very   long
                cái   nàge
                then   that
                'But they had feelings toward each other as soon as they got to know each other. You (and your boyfriend) were like that only after having known each other for a long time.'

   3 Speaker: .. *méiyǒu   rènshì   hěn   jiù   a ...   wǒ   shì*
                  NEG   know each other   very   long   PRT   1SG   COP
                shǔjià..   jiù   wǒmen   nà..   qù   dāng
                summer vacation   just   1PL   that   go   be
                dàibiǎoduì   kǒuqín   yín   de   shuéyuán
                representative team harmonica camp   DE   member
                de shíhòu..   wǒ   cái   rènshì   tā   de   a
                DE time   1SG   just   know   3SG   DE   PRT
                '(My boyfriend and I) hadn't known each other for a long time. I just got to know him when we participated in the harmonica camp as the members of a representative team during summer vacation.'

The second type is 'implicit acknowledgement', as "the speaker/gesturer's response presupposed that the addressee had understood so far" (Bavelas et al. 2011: 57). In some instances, the speaker continues talking about what has been started in his/her prior turn. In Example 1, the speaker in line 3, assuming that the addressee has understood the information presented in the prior turn and that common ground has been gained, further expresses what he thinks about people being fat. In other cases, the speaker brings up something new and different. For instance, in a topic about the growth of tea leaves, the speaker in the first phase tells that two or three tea trees, which are planted separately in the beginning, will grow together gradually. After the addressee has indicated his understanding of this point, the speaker brings up a different but related subject about the time that the leaves can be plucked off a tea tree.

Finally, the speakers' acknowledgements may not be related to the responses made by the addressees. This happens when what the speaker wants to say in the first phase is not yet finished, and the speaker attempts to finish it, regardless of the feedback from the addressee. In Example (5), the addressee in line 2 talks about a long broomstick, but the speaker in the following phase (line 3) continues the discussion on mead which has been started in the first phase in line 1. Acknowledgements of this type were categorized as 'other'.

The two coders had total consensus on the categorization of acknowledgements. According to the frequency distribution in Table 3, implicit acknowledgements are the most commonly used type of utterances made by speakers to accomplish and end grounding sequences. Among all the 135 instances of implicit acknowledgements, 86.7% (n=117) are the cases where the speaker continues what has been started in his/her prior turn; in the remaining cases, the speaker provides new information about a different subject of a talk. Concerning the explicit counterparts that total 36 instances (Table 3), positives (27 instances) outnumber negatives (9 instances) by three to one.

Table 3: Acknowledgement types and frequency distribution.

Explicit	36	20.8%
Implicit	135	78.0%
Other	2	1.2%
Total	173	100.0%

To sum up, in the process of grounding, the speaker and the addressee demonstrate their understanding of each other in order to establish common ground. A pattern of grounding is frequently used in Chinese conversational interactions. The speaker first presents information, part of which is depicted by gesture. A large majority of gestures convey new information being expressed both in words and manual configurations. Next, the addressee tends to provide a positive response to demonstrate understanding. In turn, under the assumption that the addressee does not have a problem in understanding, the speaker is inclined to express an acknowledgement to end the sequence in an implicit way by continuing the subject matter under discussion or by providing new information about a related topic. Similar results in English can be found in Bavelas et al. (2011): Addressees understood most of the presentations involving non-redundant gestures that conveyed meaning not found in words, and speakers' acknowledgements were mainly implicit. Whether such a grounding pattern is universal needs more studies across various types of discourse in different languages.

4 Gestural repetition in grounding

The previous section has shown the usual way that Mandarin speakers and addressees communicate their understanding. Then, does gestural repetition have an influence on this commonly used pattern? This question is taken up in this section. The identification and analysis of gestural repetition is first discussed, followed by the occurrence of mimicked gestures in addressee responses.

4.1 Identification of gestural repetition

After the two coders had learnt to distinguish sequences with regard to whether gestures were mimicked or not, they agreed on seventeen instances of gestural repetition. Each instance was a pair of gestures similar in form, and also the two gestures referred to the same referent. First, the similarity of forms was determined by the analysis of the gesture features. The degree of similarity between the two instances in each pair was rated on a five-point scale of agreement for each of the five features: The realization of a feature in both of the gestures of each pair was coded as 'Alike' if the coder chose 'agree' or 'strongly agree', as 'Not Alike' if the judgment was 'disagree' or 'strongly disagree', and as 'Neutral' for the choice 'neutral' on the scale. The judgment was based on the relatively objective spatio-physical manifestation of the features, and the two coders reached total agreement on their analysis.

Table 4 shows the congruence results across the five gesture features, among which total congruence was found for 'hand shape', and very high congruence for 'motion' and 'position'.

Table 4: The congruence rates across five gesture features.

	Hand shape		Motion		Position		Orientation		Handedness	
Alike	17	100%	16	94%	15	88%	14	82%	13	76%
Not alike	0	0%	1	6%	2	12%	3	18%	4	24%
Neutral	0	0%	0	0%	0	0%	0	0%	0	0%

('Alike': coders (strongly) agreed that the realization of a feature was similar between both gestures; 'Not Alike': coders (strongly) disagreed that the realization was similar between both gestures; 'Neutral': similarity or difference not noticeable)

'Motion' is the movement *per se*. The only case of incongruence occurred when the extent of the movement of the hand was not identical between the two corresponding gestures in the pair for *bǎntiáo* 'a kind of rice noodle the dough of which is made into thin sheets, which are then cut into noodles'. As shown in Example 7, the two participants talk about the characteristics of rice noodles. At the time the speaker on the left presents *bǎntiáo* in line 1, he puts the right palm flat above the left palm to depict the flatness of a layer of rice noodles, and then he moves the right hand rightward horizontally to signify the layer of the flat noodles (Figure 3a). In line 2, the addressee on the right quickly provides a negative response by the use of *luàngài* 'nonsense' followed by a rhetorical question to deny that rice noodles are layered. The addressee repeats only the right-palm-flat-above-left-palm hand shape in the center space without moving rightward for the depiction of the layer (Figure 3b).

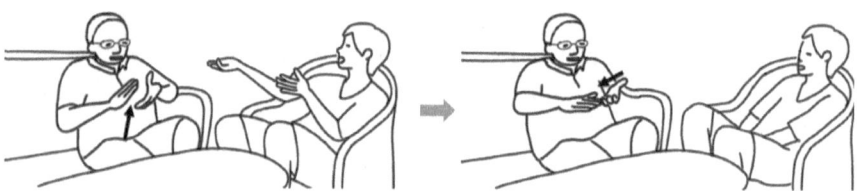

Figure 3a: Gestural depiction of rice noodles.

(7) 1 Speaker: .. *bǎntiáo shì shuō.. tā yī yī [nàge]*
rice noodles COP say 3PL follow follow that
'Rice noodles are..they follow, follow that'

2 Addressee: *[luàngài].. méiyǒu rén zuò... ni nálǐ céngjīng*
nonsense NEG people do 2SG where ever

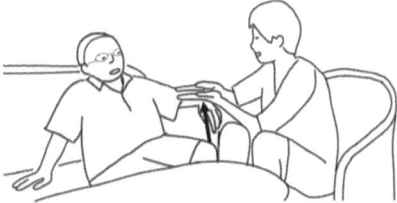

Figure 3b: Gestural repetition of rice noodles.

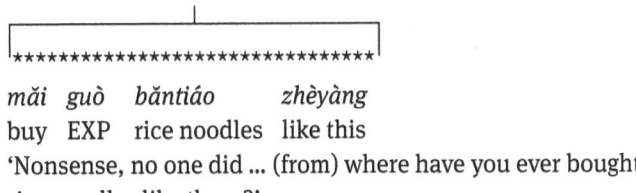

mǎi guò bǎntiáo zhèyàng
buy EXP rice noodles like this
'Nonsense, no one did ... (from) where have you ever bought rice noodles like these?'

The 'position' of gesture is another feature for which high congruence was found. The two cases of incongruence lay in inconsistency in the use of gesture space, which can be illustrated by the pair of gestures for winnowers in Example 8 (Section 4.2.). While both the speaker on the left and the addressee in the middle form a rotating hand shape with their right hand, and move the hand counter-clockwise, the speaker performs the gesture in the right periphery (Figure 4a), whereas the addressee gestures in the center space.

For the feature of 'orientation', there are three instances where there is inconsistency in the direction of the hands and fingers in the mimicry between speakers and addressees. Example 9 (Section 4.2.) is about musical instruments. To gesture *yuèqín* – an instrument which has a body with a round back and a flat top and a long neck and strings which are played with the fingers, the speaker on the right has the right hand above the left hand in front of her chest, with both hands being formed into fists, facing each other (Figure 5a). The addressee, though forming two fists in the same way, has the left hand rest on the arm of a sofa rather than under the right hand (Figure 5b).

Finally, the feature with the lowest level of congruence is 'handedness', probably because of the mirror-image effect or availability of the hands during speaking. In three cases, addressees gestured with their left hands, and not with their right hands, as the speakers had done.

Overall, 94% of all gesture pairs differed in one feature at most (nine were identical; seven differed in one feature); the remaining pair varied in two features. Moreover, the low consistency in the hand/finger orientation and handedness, but the high consistency in the other three features, did not affect the conclusion of the analysis that the two gestures were highly similar gestures for the same referent. In summary, while repetitions of gesture are never exact copies, the mimicked data found in the conversational data maintain a very high resemblance with their corresponding counterparts.

For the categorization of the mimicked gestures, total agreement was reached between the two coders: Seven are iconic gestures depicting concrete entities and actions; six are metaphoric gestures representing abstract ideas, qualities and location; four gestures are emblems depicting the act of enumeration, the state of a great extent, and the action of using a phone.

4.2 Gestural repetition in responses

In a referential communication task (Holler and Wilkin 2011), a total of 113 mimicked gestures were produced. The current study shows that in face-to-face conversation, gestural repetition is not frequent, because addressees do not necessarily mimic speakers' gestures to communicate their understanding in progress. Nevertheless, the quantitative data in Holler and Wilkin (2011) provide evidence that the use of mimicked gestures is by no means a matter of chance. In this section, the way this particular gestural act takes part in the achievement of common ground will be shown to differ from the pattern of grounding without gestural repetition.

First, for all of the instances of gestural repetition in the data, their first occurrence in the speaker's turn depicts new information. The only exception is the enumeration gesture the speaker produced to present three items of clothing which had just been mentioned in the preceding context. Thus, in comparison to the gestures in the sequences without repetition, the proportion of newness in a gesture is much higher when gestural repetition occurs (94.1%, 16 out of the total 17). Grounding new information is imperative; the lack of understanding would affect the establishment of common ground, without which communication could be hindered.

Then, how can grounding be accomplished when addressees mimic speakers' gestures for the same new referents? As shown in Section 3, the usual way for the addressee to show his/her understanding of the information presented by the speaker is to respond positively (85%, Table 2); negative responses are a minority (11%, Table 2). Explicit positive responses were also found along with gestural repetition in the data, as illustrated in Example 8 about winnowing grains of rice. While the participants are talking about agricultural tools in the past, the speaker in line 1 first presents the new referent *fēnggǔ* 'winnower' and depicts the rotation of the machine in gesture, by moving the right hand clockwise in a big circle at the right side of the body three times (Figure 4a). The addressee in line 2 responds explicitly and positively with *he-a* 'right', and simultaneously replicates the rotating gesture in the same way, though on a smaller scale – moving the right hand in the center space only twice and in smaller circles (Figure 4b).

Figure 4a: Gestural depiction of a winnower.

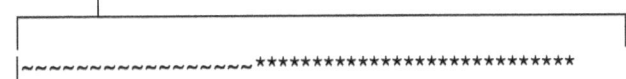

(8) 1 Speaker: .. *jiùshì yǒu nàge fēnggǔ a [jīqì la]*
that is there.be that winnower PRT machine PRF
'That is, there was a winnower, a machine.'

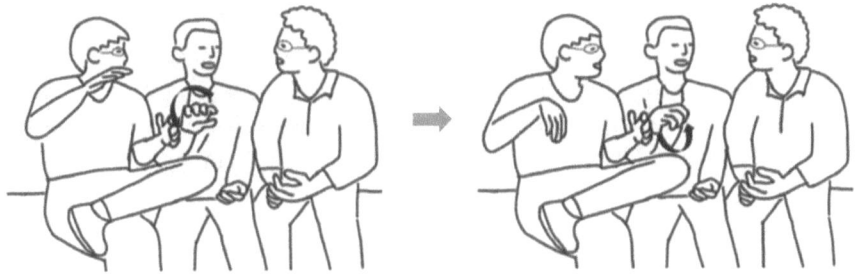

Figure 4b: Gestural repetition of a winnower.

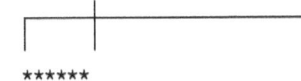

2 Addressee: .. *[he a]*
right PRT
'Right.'

3 Speaker: .. *shèbèi duó zhíqián a*
equipment much valuable PRT
'(The) equipment was very valuable.'

In the data, however, gestural repetition occurs much more frequently when the addressee responds negatively (47.1%, Table 5) due to disagreement or a lack of clarity.

Table 5: Response types in gestural repetition and frequency distribution.

Explicit positive	3	17.6%
Explicit negative	8	47.1%
Implicit positive	6	35.3%
Total	17	100.0%

The talk in Example 9 is about the kind of musical instrument that is played by a character in a movie. The speaker uses a general term *yuèqì* 'musical instrument' in speech (line 1) but gestures the particular kind of instrument that requires the use of a bow to play: During the pause after the classifier *zhǒng* 'kind', the speaker's right hand goes up to shoulder level with the fingers curled into a fist as if holding a bow; the left hand rises to waist level, also with fingers curled into a fist as if holding the lower part of the instrument. Then, at the time *yuèqì* is uttered, the right hand moves horizontally to the left one time to enact the playing of a string instrument that requires the use of a bow (Figure 5a). The addressee holds a contrary opinion about the referent *yuèqì* in regard to the instrument played in the movie, the explicit disagreement marker *méiyǒu* 'no' is used at the beginning of his turn in line 2, followed by a correction that it is the type that is played with the fingers, as represented in speech by *yuèqín* 'plucked lute with a wooden body'. Intriguingly, instead of enacting *yuèqín*, which is played with the fingers, the addressee mimics the speaker's gesture in detail (Figure 5b): The fingers of the addressee's right hand form a fist like holding a bow, and the right hand moves in the same leftward direction to enact the idea of playing music with a bow.

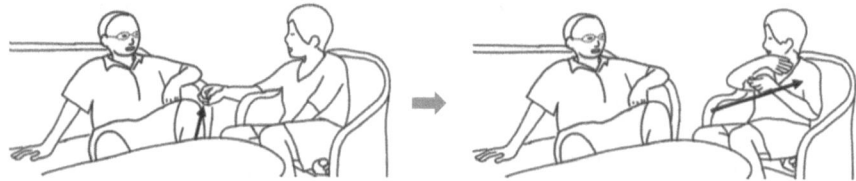

Figure 5a: Gestural depiction of a musical instrument with a bow.

```
                                            |~~*****************-.-.|
(9) 1 Speaker:  .. màobó    shì   nà    zhǒng... zhuānyiè    de   nà    zhǒng...
                   Maobo    COP   that  kind     professional DE  that  kind
                yuèqì              de    ..nǐ    zhīdào   ma..   suǒyǐ
                musical instrument DE    2SG     know     QST    so
                'Maobo (used) that kind of professional musical instrument,
                you know. So'
```

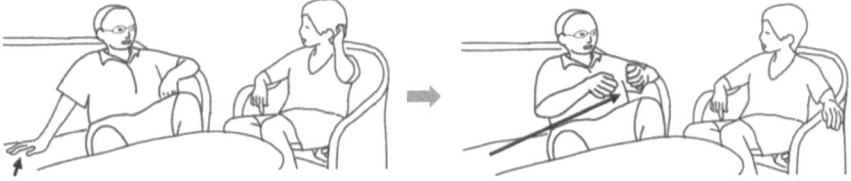

Figure 5b: Gestural repetition of a musical instrument with a bow.

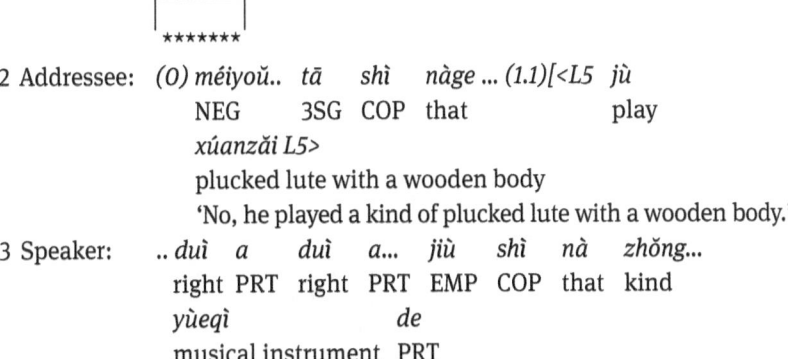

```
2 Addressee:  (O) méiyǒu.. tā    shì   nàge ... (1.1)[<L5  jù
              NEG        3SG    COP   that              play
              xúanzǎi L5>
              plucked lute with a wooden body
              'No, he played a kind of plucked lute with a wooden body.'
3 Speaker:    .. duì    a     duì    a...  jiù   shì   nà    zhǒng...
              right   PRT   right   PRT   EMP   COP   that   kind
              yùeqì            de
              musical instrument   PRT
              'Right, right. It's that kind of musical instrument.'
```

For the remaining implicit responses, their low occurrence in the sequences without gestural repetition (16.2%, Table 2) is contrary to their relatively higher occurrence when addressees repeat speakers' gestures and continue to talk about what has been under discussion (35.3%, Table 5). The topic in Example 10 is about the speaker, *Jiapei*, whose father considered that her voice and speaking manner when talking on the phone were too different from her usual style, and *Jiapei* thought that her father was going to snatch the phone from her and tell the person on the other end of the line about the speaker's usual way of speaking. What the speaker utters in line 1 is what she thinks that her father might have said about her usual speaking style, and, at the same time, she produces a conventional hand-held-telephone gesture, extending the thumb and little finger while holding the three middle fingers curled, with the thumb held near the ear and the little finger pointing at the mouth (Figure 6a). In line 2, the addressee shows her understanding of the speaker's quoted speech by using the same hand-held-telephone gesture (Figure 6b) and continuing the quoted speech about what *Jiapei's* father also might have said on the phone. In line 3, the speaker acknowledges the addressee's response and provides more information about the father's reaction.

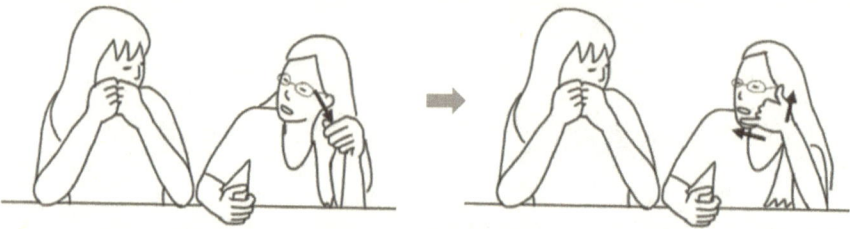

Figure 6a: Gestural depiction of holding a hand-held telephone.

```
                |~~~~~~~~~~~~~~~~~~~~~***********************************|
(10) 1 Speaker: .. tā    cāo        xiǎng bǎ  diànhuà  qiǎngguòlái shuō..
                3SG  very much  want  BA   phone    snatch.come say
                tā    de  shēngyīn
                3SG   DE  voice
                ****************************************************
                bú   shì  zhèyàng.. tā   bú   shì  zhèyàngzhi de rén
                NEG  COP  like this 3SG  NEG  COP  like this  DE person
```

'He wanted to snatch the phone away very much and say, "Her voice is not like this. She is not this kind of person."'

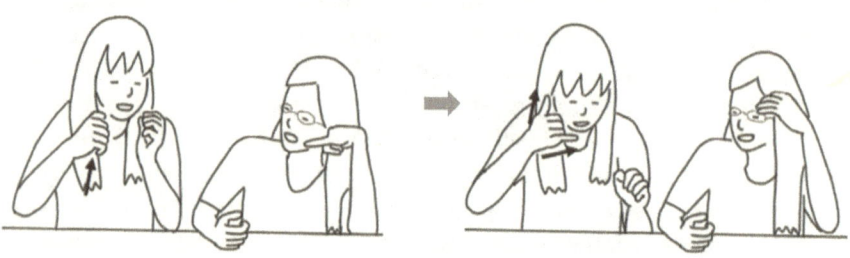

Figure 6b: Gestural repetition of holding a hand-held telephone.

```
              ***********************************************~.~.|
2 Addressee: .. nà    bú   shì   jiāpèi  a
               that   NEG  COP   Jiapei  PRT
```

'That is not Jiapei.'

3 Speaker: .. hòulái   wǒ   xiǎng shuō ... yǒu   yì   tōng   dǎ
            later   1SG   think say   there.be one   CL   call
            gěi   lǎoshī   ei..   hòulái tā   shuō.. háihǎo   wǒ
            for   teacher PRT   later   3SG   say   fortunate 1SG
            méiyǒu   bǎ   diànhuà   qiǎngguòlái
            NEG   BA   phone   snatch.come
            'Later, I said, "I was making a phone call to my teacher."
            Then he said, "Fortunately, I didn't snatch away the
            phone."'

In addition to the proportion of new information and of response types, the last difference between grounding with and without gestural repetition lies in the kind of information conveyed in addressees' turns. Of all of the 173 addressee responses without mimicked gestures, the majority (57.2%) are simply markers indicating (dis)agreement, awareness and support (93 instances), mere head nods (5 instances) and repetition of the speaker's words (1 instance). However, responses of this type, like the mere use of 'right' in Example 8, are a minority in gestural repetition (2 instances, 11.8%). Addressees also tend to bring up new information about the subject of a talk, along with the manual repetition, such as information about the right kind of musical instrument being played in the movie in Example 9, or further ideas about the father's reaction to his daughter's unusual manner of talking on the phone in Example 10.

The discussion above clearly demonstrates that "participants work together in determining the course of each utterance. They rely not only on each other's vocal signals, but on each other's gestural signals" (Clark and Krych 2004: 79). There can be various ways speakers can use to incorporate manual signals in the process of grounding. In Clark and Krych (2004: 79), participants in the Lego task-based communication relied on "exhibiting, poising, pointing at, and placing physical objects, nodding and shaking heads, and directing eye gaze, and on other mutually visible events" to show understanding thus far. Bavelas et al. (2011), on the other hand, found that speakers produced non-redundant abstract deictic gestures in a floor-plan design task. Common ground could also be obtained by the use of iconic and metaphoric mimicked gestures as participants grounded referents of geometrical figures in Holler and Wilkin (2011). The present study, in the context of everyday conversation, found that, besides representational gestures, emblematic gestures could also be mimicked in grounding. All were elaborate re-productions of speakers' gestures presented in the first phase. Most importantly, the way mimicked gestures occurred in grounding to display understanding is not in line with the usual way of grounding without gestural repetition.

This section has shown that addressees usually express their understanding by repeating a gesture produced by the speakers in the prior turn and by providing explicit responses. Gestural repetition is thus visible evidence of the addressee's understanding of what has been presented in gesture by the speaker. In most cases (15 out of the total 17), a mimicked gesture also functions as a semantic foundation shared by the speaker and the addressee, upon which further information is simultaneously conveyed in the same turn, as illustrated by the responses in line 2 in Examples 8 and 9. Given the *principle of least joint effort* that participants "should exploit that combination of vocal and gestural actions they judge will take the least joint effort [to accomplish a task]" (Clark and Krych 2004:64; also see Clark and Wilkes-Gibbs 1986; Clark and Schaefer 1987; Clark and Brennan 1991; Clark 1996), such division of effort between the linguistic and gestural modalities in grounding is efficient to facilitate the simultaneous realization of the visible expression of mutual knowledge in gesture and new meaning in speech within the same clause. With the gestural manifestation of common ground, what is further uttered in the turn can be readily understood.

5 General discussion and conclusion

In grounding, participants collaborate moment-by-moment to establish mutual understanding in progress. The present study distinguished two types of grounding sequences and found two correspondingly different patterns of grounding in Mandarin conversational discourse. In the first type, without the occurrence of gestural repetition, addressees habitually manifest their understanding of the information presented by speakers by offering positive responses, most usually in an explicit way. In turn, speakers largely express implicit acknowledgements. However, in the second type of sequence, where gestural repetition occurs, a different pattern of grounding was found in addressee responses and speaker acknowledgements. First, no matter whether the addressee agrees or disagrees with what the speaker has uttered, the addressees mimic the prior gestures of the speakers', to express their understanding of the meaning of the speaker in an explicit way, and, most of the time, also provide further information about the subject matter under discussion. In the following phase, the speakers' acknowledgements are essentially explicit. Such a cross-modal grounding strategy to repeat the speaker's gesture to demonstrate understanding visibly while providing new information is efficient to establish common ground and convey new information within a clausal unit. Finally, not only can the use of the second type of gestural repetition serve to demonstrate understanding along with speech in a way different from the way without gestural repetition, but also the occurrence of mimicked gestures in the second type provides evidence for the bilateral and interactive nature of speaking. First, the bilateral process in Clark and Krych (2004) was supported by the experiment that manipulated the visibility of participants and workspaces when participants built Lego models. They found that speakers, in addition to monitoring their own speech, also monitored addressees for understanding. Multi-modal resources, including speech, pointing, eye gaze, head nods and head shakes, were used to communicate their understanding in progress; responses from addressees were often provided. Besides grounding, many other aspects of speech communication resulting from the joint collaboration between the speaker and the addressee, such as the construction of turn units, also require the participants to monitor each other (see the review in Clark and Krych 2004). In brief, the major characteristics of speaking as a bilateral process lie in participants' monitoring each other for the construction of utterance, and addressees informing speakers about their state of understanding. In the current study, gestural repetition is a distinct type of evidence from naturally-occurring conversations, in that not only do addressees monitor speakers' gestures, they also take them into account and incorporate the gestures in turn construction. Last, the occurrence of a mimicked gesture resulting from the addressee's monitoring of the speaker's gesture also informs the speaker about the addressee's understanding. In the future, it is hoped that more mimicked gestures will be available to understand whether other types of gestures, like deictic and spatial gestures which do not carry substantive semantic information, also play a part in grounding.

Appendix 1: Speech and gesture transcription conventions

Transcription of speech
[ ]	speech overlap
...(N)	long pause
...	medium pause
..	short pause
@	laugh
<L5 L5>	switching from Taiwan Mandarin to Taiwan Southern Min

Transcription of gesture

Kendon's (2004) transcription conventions for gesture were adopted.

| | gesture phrase boundaries
~ ~ ~   preparation phase
~ ~ ~   pre-stroke hold
****   stroke phase
****   post-stroke hold
-.-.-   recovery phase
/   gesture phase boundaries

Appendix 2: Abbreviations of linguistic terms

1PL	first person plural
1SG	first person singular
2PL	second person plural
2SG	second person singular
3PL	third person plural
3SG	third person singular
BA	morpheme *ba*
CL	classifier
COP	copula verb
DE	morpheme *de*
EMP	emphatic morpheme
EXP	experiential morpheme
NEG	negative morpheme
PRT	discourse particle
QST	question morpheme

References

Bavelas, Janet B., Christine Kenwood, Trudy Johnson & Bruce Phillips. 2002. An experimental study of when and how speakers use gestures to communicate. *Gesture* 2(1). 1–17.

Bavelas, Janet B. & N. Chovil. 2006. Hand gestures and facial displays as part of language use in face-to-face dialogue. In Valerie L. Manusov & Miles L. Patterson (eds.), *Handbook of nonverbal communication*, 97–115. Thousand Oaks, CA: Sage.

Bavelas, Janet B., Jennifer Gerwing, Meredith Allison & Chantelle Sutton. 2011. Dyadic evidence for grounding with abstract deictic gestures. In Gale Stam & Mika Ishino (eds.), *Integrating gestures: The interdisciplinary na&ture of gesture*, 49–60. Amsterdam: Benjamins.

Bavelas, Janet B., Nicole Chovil Douglas A. Lawrie & Allan Wade. 1992. Interactive gestures. *Discourse Processes* 15. 469–489.

Beattie, Geoffrey & Heather Shovelton. 1999a. Do iconic hand gestures really contribute anything to the semantic information conveyed by speech? An experimental investigation. *Semiotica* 123. 1–30.

Beattie, Geoffrey & Heather Shovelton. 1999b. Mapping the range of information contained in the iconic hand gestures that accompany spontaneous speech. *Journal of Language and Social Psychology* 18. 438–462.

Beattie, Geoffrey & Heather Shovelton. 2001. An experimental investigation of the role of different types of iconic gesture in communication: A semantic feature approach. *Gesture* 1. 129–149.

Bernardis, Paolo & Maurizio Gentilucci. 2006. Speech and gesture share the same communication system. *Neuropsychologia* 44. 178–190.

Boyle, Elizabeth A., Anne H. Anderson & Alison Newlands. 1994. The effects of visibility on dialogue and performance in a cooperative problem solving task. *Language and Speech* 37(1). 1–20.

Chui, Kawai. 2009a. Linguistic and imagistic representations of motion events. *Journal of Pragmatics* 41(9). 1767–1777.

Chui, Kawai. 2009b. Conversational coherence and gesture. *Discourse Studies* 11(6). 661–680.

Chui, Kawai. 2011. Conceptual metaphors in gesture. *Cognitive Linguistics* 22(3). 437–458.

Chui, Kawai. 2012. Gestural manifestation of knowledge in conceptual frames. *Discourse Processes* 49(8). 599–621.

Chui, Kawai. 2017. Entity metaphor, object gesture, and context of use'. *Metaphor & Symbol* 32. 30–51.

Chui, Kawai & Huei-Ling Lai. 2008. The NCCU Corpus of Spoken Chinese: Mandarin, Hakka, and Southern Min. *Taiwan Journal of Linguistics* 6(2). 119–144.

Chui, Kawai, Huei-Ling Lai & Hui-Chen Chan. 2017. Taiwan spoken Chinese corpus. In R. Sybesma (ed.), *Encyclopedia of Chinese language and linguistics*, 257–259. Boston, MA: Brill.

Cienki, Alan & Cornelia Müller (eds.). 2008. *Metaphor and gesture*. Amsterdam: John Benjamins.

Clark, Herbert H. 1996. *Using language*. Cambridge: Cambridge University Press.

Clark, Herbert H. & Deanna Wilkes-Gibbs. 1986. Referring as a collaborative process. *Cognition* 22. 1–39.

Clark, Herbert H. & Edward F. Schaefer. 1987. Collaborating on contributions to conversation. *Language and Cognitive Processes* 2. 19–41.

Clark, Herbert H. & Edward F. Schaefer. 1989. Contributing to discourse. *Cognitive Science* 13. 259–294.

Clark, Herbert H. & Meredyth A. Krych. 2004. Speaking while monitoring addressees for understanding. *Journal of Memory and Language* 50(1). 62–81.

Clark, Herbert H. & Susan E. Brennan. 1991. Grounding in communication. In Lauren B. Resnick, John M. Levine & Stephanie D. Teasley (eds.), *Perspectives on socially shared cognition*, 127–149. Washington: APA Books.

Cornejo, Carlos, Franco Simonetti, Agustín Ibáñez, Nerea Aldunate, Francisco Ceric, Vladimir López & Rafael E. Núñez. 2009. Gesture and metaphor comprehension: Electrophysiological evidence of cross-modal coordination by audiovisual stimulation. *Brain and cognition* 70(1). 42–52.

de Fornel, Michel. 1992. The return gesture: Some remarks on context, inference, and iconic gesture. In Peter Auer & Aldo Di Luzio (eds.), *The contexualisation of language*, 159–176. Amsterdam: John Benjamins.

Gu, Yan, Lisette Mol, Marieke Hoetjes & Marc Swerts. 2017. Conceptual and lexical effects on gestures: the case of vertical spatial metaphors for time in Chinese. *Language, cognition and neuroscience* Volume 32. 1048–1063.

Hassemer, Julius & Bodo Winter. 2016. Producing and perceiving gestures conveying height or shape. *Gesture* 15(3). 404–424.

Holle, Henning & Thomas C. Gunter. 2007. The role of iconic gestures in speech disambiguation: ERP evidence. *Journal of Cognitive Neuroscience* 19(7). 1175–1192.

Holler, Judith & Katie Wilkin. 2011. Co-speech gesture mimicry in the process of collaborative referring during face-to-face dialogue. *Journal of Nonverbal Behavior* 35. 133–153.

Kelly, Spencer D., Corinne Kravitz & Michael Hopkins. 2004. Neural correlates of bimodal speech and gesture comprehension. *Brain and language* 89(1). 253–260.

Kelly, Spencer D., Sarah Ward, Peter Creigh & James Bartolotti. 2007. An intentional stance modulates the integration of gesture and speech during comprehension. *Brain and Language* 101. 222–233.

Kelly, Spencer D., Sarah M. Manning & Sabrina Rodak. 2008. Gesture gives a hand to language and learning: Perspectives from cognitive neuroscience, developmental psychology and education. *Language and Linguistics Compass* 2. 569–588.

Kendon, Adam. 2004. *Gesture: Visible actions as utterance*. Cambridge: Cambridge University Press.

Kimbara, Irene. 2006. On gestural mimicry. *Gesture* 6(1). 39–61.

Kimbara, Irene. 2008. Gesture form convergence in joint description. *Journal of Nonverbal Behavior* 32(2). 123–131.

Kircher, Tilo, Benjamin Straube, Dirk Leube, Susanne Weis, Olga Sachs, Klaus Willmes, Kerstin Konrad & Antonia Green. 2009. Neural interaction of speech and gesture: differential activations of metaphoric co-verbal gestures. *Neuropsychologia* 47(1). 169–179.

Kita, Sotaro & Asli Özyürek. 2003. What does cross-linguistic variation in semantic coordination of speech and gesture reveal? Evidence for an interface representation of spatial thinking and speaking. *Journal of Memory and Language* 48. 16–32.

Kita, Sotaro, Asli Özyürek, Shanley Allen, Amanda Brown, Reyhan Furman & Tomoko Ishizuka. 2007. Relations between syntactic encoding and co-speech gestures: Implications for a model of speech and gesture production. *Journal of Language and Cognitive Processes* 22. 1212–1236.

Koschmann, Timothy & Curtis LeBaron. 2002. Learner articulation as interactional achievement: Studying the conversation of gesture. *Cognition and Instruction* 20(2). 249–282.

McNeill, David. 1992. *Hand and mind: What gestures reveal about thought*. Chicago: University of Chicago Press.

McNeill, David. 2005. *Gesture and thought*. Chicago: University of Chicago Press.

McNeill, David & Susan D. Duncan. 2000. Growth points in thinking-for-speaking. In David McNeill (ed.), *Language and gesture*, 141–161. Cambridge: Cambridge University Press.

Mittelberg, Irene & Vito Evola. 2014. Iconic and representational gestures. In Cornelia Müller, Alan Cienki, Ellen Fricke, Silva Ladewig, David McNeill & Sedinha Tessendorf (eds.),

Body – language – communication: An international handbook on multimodality in human interaction, 1732–1746. Berlin: De Gruyter Mouton.

Mittelberg, Irene. 2017. Experiencing and construing spatial artifacts from within: Simulated artifact immersion as a multimodal viewpoint strategy. *Cognitive Linguistics* 28(3): 381–415.

Ortega S.A.N. 2017. *Comprehending and speaking about motion in L2 Spanish: A Case of implicit learning in Anglophones*. London: Palgrave Macmillan.

Özyürek, Asli & Sotaro Kita (1999). Expressing manner and path in English and Turkish: Differences in speech, gesture, and conceptualization. In Martin Hahn & Scott C. Stoness (eds.), *Proceedings of the twenty first annual conference of the cognitive science society*, 507–512. Mahwah, NJ: Lawrence Erlbaum Associates Inc.

Özyurek, Asli, Roel M. Willems, Sotaro Kita & Peter Hagoort. 2007. On-line integration of semantic information from speech and gesture: Insights from event-related brain potentials. *Journal of Cognitive Neuroscience* 19. 605–616.

Özyürek, Asli, Sotaro Kita, Shanley Allen, Reyhan Furman & Amanda Brown. 2005. How does linguistic framing of events influence co-speech gestures? Insights from cross-linguistic variations and similarities. *Gesture* 5. 215–237.

Parrill, Fey & Irene Kimbara. 2006. Seeing and hearing double: The influence of mimicry in speech and gesture and observers. *Journal of Nonverbal Behavior* 30 (4). 157–166.

Parrill, Fey, Benjamin Bergen & Patricia Lichtenstein. 2013. Grammatical aspect in multimodal language production: Using gesture to reveal event representations. *Cognitive Linguistics* 24(1). 135–158.

Sacks, Harvey, Emanuel A. Schegloff & Gail Jefferson. 1974. A simplest systematics for the organization of turn-taking for conversation. *Language* 50(4). 696–735.

Schober, Michael F. & Herbert H. Clark. 1989. Understanding by addressees and overhearers. *Cognitive Psychology* 21. 211–232.

Stivers, Tanya, N. J. Enfield, Penelope Brown, Christina Englert, Makoto Hayashi, Trine Heinemann, Gertie Hoymann, Federico Rossano, Jan Peter De Ruiter, Kyung-Eun Yoon & Stephen C. Levinson. 2009. Universals and cultural variation in turn-taking in conversation. *Proceedings of the National Academy of Sciences of the United States of America* 106 (26). 10587–10592.

Tabensky, Alexis. 2001. Gesture and speech rephrasings in conversation. *Gesture* 1(2). 213–236.

Thompson, Sandra A. & Elizabeth Couper-Kuhlen. 2005. The clause as a locus of grammar and interaction. *Discourse Studies* 7. 481–505.

Wu, Y.C. & Seana Coulson. 2007. Iconic gestures prime related concepts: An ERP study. *Psychonomic Bulletin & Review* 14. 57–63.

Wu, Y.C. & Seana Coulson. 2010. Gestures modulate speech processing early in an utterance. *Neuroreport* 21 (7). 522–526.

Tomoko Endo
Embodying stance: *wo juede* 'I feel/think' and gaze

1 Introduction

Stance-taking is a ubiquitous phenomenon in human interaction. It is rare for people to merely transmit objective information; rather, they share their experiences, values, and affections, and this can be the ultimate goal of their interaction. As Du Bois (2007: 139) puts it, stance-taking is "one of the most important things that we do with words". Sharing the same values is a crucial factor for the establishment and sustainment of communities, and this sharing and negotiation of values is done both in public opinion statements and in daily conversation.

Various linguistic devices can be used as resources for stance-taking. For example, in written and spoken English, the following five grammatical categories are identified as contributing to stance-taking: stance adverbials, stance complement clauses, modals and semi-modals, stance nouns and prepositional phrases, and premodifying stance adverbs (Biber et al. 1999). In languages such as Japanese and Mandarin Chinese, the category of sentence-final particle, such as *a* and *o* in Mandarin Chinese or *ne* and *yo* in Japanese, should also be regarded as a grammatical device for stance-taking (Hayano 2013; Morita 2005; Wu 2004). Interjections such as *eh* in Japanese or *oh* in English also display the speaker's stance (Hayashi 2009; Heritage 1984a, 2002). Constructions with a subject and a complement-taking predicate such as the English *I think* are commonly observed as fixed expressions in languages with the basic word order of SVO (Kärkkäinen 2003; Nuyts 2001; Thompson 2002; Thompson and Mulac 1991; see also Helasvuo 2014 for Finnish counterparts). *Wo juede* 'I think' in Mandarin conversation, which is the target of analysis in this paper, is one of those constructions. As shown in the example below, *wo juede* 'I think' is used to mark that the speaker is telling his or her personal opinion about a topic.

(1) na   wo   juede zhe   zhong fang-   zhiliao   fangfa   dai
    then   1SG   feel   this   kind   metho-   treatment   method   need
    gaijin   a.
    improvement   FP
    'Then I think this kind of metho- treatment method needs to be improved.'

Tomoko Endo, Seikei University

https://doi.org/10.1515/9783110462395-007

Here, *wo juede* 'I think' marks that the statement *zhe zhong fang- zhiliao fangfa dai gaijin a* 'This kind of metho- treatment method needs to be improved' is the speaker's opinion, rather than an objective fact. Since *wo juede* marks the speaker's attitude towards what he or she is saying in terms of the credibility or information source, *wo juede* works as an epistemic stance marker, which is functionally roughly equivalent to *I think* in American English conversation (cf. Kärkkäinen 2003; Thompson 2002; Thompson and Mulac 1991).

In this paper, I analyze the participants' visual and verbal practices in interaction, focusing on the co-occurrence of the epistemic marker *wo juede* 'I think/feel' and gaze. This is because, as the data shows, gaze is the most relevant visual practice concurrent with *wo juede*. Example (1) can be rewritten with an indication of gaze shift, as shown below. At the beginning of the utterance, Wei and Xun have mutual gaze, but as Wei says *wo juede zhe zhong* 'I think this kind', she looks away. In the middle of the utterance, she does not look at Xun; towards the end of the utterance, she looks at Xun again. See Appendix C for the symbols.

(1') ((1) with gaze symbols)
    Wei: na |**wo juede** zhe zhong| fang- zhiliao fangfa haiyou |dai gaijin| a.
              'Then I think this kind of meth- treatment method needs to be improved.'
    WeiG X::|,,,,,,,,,,,,,,,,,,,,,,,,,,|_____|,,,,,,,,,,,,|X::
    XunG W:|-----------------------|----------------------- |-------------|::::

The aim of this paper is to show that the visual behavior of gaze shift and the linguistic behavior of producing *wo juede* cooperate to perform actions and display the speaker's stance in interactions. The paper also proposes a new kind of stance, namely, participation stance.

2 Background

2.1 Stance

Participants take stances on various elements of interaction, such as the topic, the previous speaker's evaluation, or the content of the utterance that they are producing.[1] When a participant makes an evaluation about something, she or he is taking

---

[1] Various kinds of classifications of stance have been proposed as a great number of studies in stance-taking accumulate from fields such as sociolinguistics, interactional linguistics, linguistic

an evaluative stance.² For example, by producing the utterance *This is beautiful*, the speaker makes the positive evaluation *beautiful* about the target *this*. When a participant takes an evaluative stance, it becomes relevant for other participants to agree or disagree with it (Sacks [1973] 1987; Pomerantz 1984; Du Bois 2007). That is, it is naturally expected that other participants should take a position toward the evaluated object, and by doing so take a position toward the participant who has already made his or her position public. The stance toward the other participant is called the (dis)affiliative stance, or the stance of (dis)affiliation.³ While a stance of (dis)affiliation can be expressed by overt expressions such as *I agree* or *I disagree* (cf. Du Bois 2007), it can also be expressed by taking another evaluative stance, after an assessment is made by another participant. That is, if Speaker A says *This is beautiful* and Speaker B then says *This is gorgeous*, Speaker B conveys not only his or her evaluative stance toward the topic, but also their affiliative stance toward Speaker A's stance (cf. Pomerantz 1984).

Epistemic stance is generally characterized as the speaker's indication of his or her stance toward how he or she knows or has come to know the information that he or she is conveying.⁴ Participants may take an epistemic stance merely because

---

anthropology, and conversation analysis (see papers collected in Englebretson 2007 and Jaffe 2009). For example, Biber et al. (1999), in a descriptive work about English grammar based on spoken and written data, classify stance into three types: epistemic stance, attitudinal stance, and style of speaking stance. On the other hand, Du Bois (2007), emphasizing the importance of the interactional aspects of language use but still focusing on linguistic forms, names four categories: evaluation, epistemic, alignment, and affective. Further, Goodwin (2007) investigates the multimodal realization of stance in daily activities and proposes five categories: instrumental, epistemic, cooperative, moral, and affective. Although these classifications have some overlap, none are identical, their differences reflecting the different orientations of the studies.

2 Other terms, such as assessment (Pomerantz 1984) and appraisal (Martin 2000), are used to refer to the same phenomenon (see Jaffe 2009 for a summary of terms related to evaluative stance).

3 Note that the terminology regarding notions such as agreement, disagreement, alignment, and affiliation is quite complex. For example, the same kind of notion is called aligning in Du Bois (2007) and alignment in Goodwin (1981, 2007) and Morita (2005). In contrast, Stivers (2008) makes a distinction between affiliation and aligning, defining the former as a social/interactional display of endorsement of another's stance and to the latter as a speaker's structural treatment of the activity in progress in conversation. Following Stivers, in this paper I use the terms *affiliative* and *disaffiliative stance* to refer to a participant's stance in agreement or disagreement with another's stance (see Lindström and Sorjonen 2013 for a further discussion on the terms).

4 In linguistics, this kind of notion is traditionally called evidential or epistemic modality (Chafe and Nichols 1986; Palmer 2001; Nuyts 2001). In conversation analysis, terms such as epistemic stance and epistemic primacy are commonly used to refer to the speaker's relative degree of confidence in his or her knowledge or its source (Stivers, Modada, and Steensig 2011: 9). While epistemic modality in linguistics refers to the semantic and syntactic features of particular linguistic items (Lyons 1977; Palmer 2001), studies on epistemic stance in conversation

they are not certain about the truth-value of the proposition that they are communicating, but it is also common that participants take an epistemic stance with interactional motivations. For example, in American English *I think* can be used as a resource for mitigating disagreement (Kärkkäinen 2003). In Mandarin, *wo juede* can be used in similar environments (Endo 2010, 2013; Lim 2009). In other words, in taking an evaluative stance, especially when a speaker is taking a disaffiliative stance in the second position of an assessment sequence, the speaker often takes an epistemic stance as well, to mitigate the conflict with the other participant.

In addition to evaluative, affiliative, and epistemic stance, I propose a new type of stance: participation stance. By participation stance, I mean the participant's stance toward participation, especially speakership. As shown by the seminal work of Sacks, Schegloff, and Jefferson (1974), in principle one person speaks at a time in talk-in-interaction. At the end of a turn, determining the next speaker becomes an issue for the participants, which is when techniques for turn allocation come into play. Sometimes the current speaker selects the next speaker; other times, the next speaker self-selects. Stivers (2008) argued that participants in conversation show their alignment with the ongoing project of selecting the next speaker in the moment. Their orientation toward speakership plays an important role in the progress and organization of conversation. Participants' orientation toward speakership is also a stance that they express during conversation; I call this kind of stance *participation stance*.[5] The four types of stances are summarized in Table 1.

In section 5, I show that *wo juede*, whose meaning consists in marking the speaker's epistemic stance, is also used to take a stance of (dis)affiliation and participation. I argue that participants make use of both the linguistic resource *wo juede* and the visual behavior of gaze when they are conveying opinions that conflict with those of the previous speaker and/or when they are selecting the next speaker.

2.2 Gaze

Among various visual resources in interaction, gaze has been attracting attention from researchers as gaze is considered to be the cue of attention (Frischen

---

analysis focus on the social and interactional practices of participants in conversation (Heritage 2012; Hayano 2013).

5 Participants in conversation can become a speaker by saying anything. The act of speaking itself thus can be the display of participation stance. In that sense, participation stance differs from other types of stance. However, some linguistic and non-linguistic behaviors can work as markers of participation stance. As I argue in this paper, *wo juede* is one of such resources for taking participation stance.

Table 1: Types of stance.

Stance type	Target	Content
Evaluative stance	Topic of talk (object, person, etc.)	Positive or negative assessment
Epistemic stance	Proposition	Degree of certainty in or commitment toward the truth-value of the proposition, source of information
(Dis)affiliative stance	Stance taken by other participant(s)	Affiliative (agreeing) or disaffiliative
Participation stance	Speakership	Who is to be the next speaker

et al. 2007; Simon et al. 2015). In studies based on actual interaction, gaze has been analyzed mostly in terms of turn organization. For example, Kendon (1967) examined the gaze patterns in face-to-face interaction and found that gaze can be used as a monitoring device and has a turn regulatory function; that is, from the gaze of the recipient, the speaker knows whether the recipient is ready for turn-taking. Similarly, Goodwin (1981) showed that restarts in conversation may be triggered by the recipients' gaze. That is, the speakers do not start talking substantially until the recipients look at them; mutual gaze between participants may thus serve as an indication that the recipients are ready to listen (also see Rossano 2013; Rossano et al. 2009; Stivers et al. 2009).

Recently, gaze has been discussed in terms of playing an important role in taking an evaluative stance, in addition to facilitating turn organization. Haddington (2006) argued that three types of gaze, namely looking together at an assessable, looking at each other, and looking away, are relevant to various aspects of stance-taking, such as establishing joint attention toward an object to be assessed and indicating a convergent or divergent evaluative stance. The data in this paper confirm Haddington's observation that looking away is indicative of a divergent evaluative stance. Further, I will argue that looking away from one participant can be followed by looking at another participant; such a shift of gaze may indicate the current speaker selecting the next speaker, which is a manifestation of what I call participation stance.

3 Mandarin *wo juede* 'I think'

The phrase *wo juede* consists of the first person pronoun *wo* 'I' and the cognition verb *juede* 'to think/feel'. The verb *juede* is a complement-taking predicate that takes a clausal complement as its object. Because Mandarin is an SVO language like English, the canonical order of *wo juede* and its complement clause is [*wo juede* + complement clause], as in the following example.

(2) **wo juede** ta hen piaoliang.
 1SG feel/think 3SG very pretty
 '**I think** she is pretty.'

The phrase *wo juede* is so frequent a combination that it has become a fixed expression. Mandarin *wo juede* is analogous to *I think* in American English, which is highly frequent in conversation and fixed as an epistemic stance marker (Thompson 2002; Kärkkäinen 2003). Like *I think*, *wo juede* has flexibility in its position in a clause. In addition to its canonical position, i.e., before the complement as in (2), it can also be used in the middle of a clause as in (3) or at the end of a clause as in (4).

(3) ta, **wo juede,** hen piaoliang.
 3SG 1SG feel/think very pretty
 'She, **I think**, is pretty.'

(4) ta hen piaoliang **wo juede**.
 3SG very pretty 1SG think/feel
 'She is pretty, **I think**.'

The fact that *wo juede* can be used in the post-posed position as in (4) is often cited as evidence that *wo juede* is grammaticalized as an epistemic pragmatic marker (Fang 2005; Huang 2003).

When *wo juede* is used in its canonical position, it is often in the initial or very close to the initial position of a turn. In (5), *wo juede* in line 05 is very close to the initial position of the turn, only preceded by the conjunction *danshi* 'but', and in line 21, *wo juede* is indeed in the initial position of the turn.

(5) [snowfall]
01 Li: suoyi- (.) tebie da de xue de shihou wo- wo- wo
 so especially big PCL snow PCL time 1SG 1SG 1SG
 meiyou kanjianguo.
 NEG see-EXP
 'So ... when it snowed especially heavily, I did not see (the snow).'

02 Ming: h aiya tai yihan le.
 INJ too pity PCL
 'Oh, that's a pity.'

03 Li: dui   ya.   danshi wo   faxian [jinnian
          right PCL   but   1SG find   [this.year
          'Yeah. But I found this year'

04 Ming: [wushi nian yi yu de daxue ni dou
                                       mei kanshang.
                                       [fifty year one meet PCL big.
                                       snow 2SG all NEG see
                                       'You didn't get to see the once-
                                       in-50-years big snowfall.'

05 Li: danshi **wo juede**   zhe ge   bu   shi (.) wushi nian yi
          but   1SG   feel/think this CL   NEG COP   fifty year one
          yu   de   wenti.
          meet PCL   matter
          'But **I think** this is not a matter of once in 50 years.'

06 Ming: shenme wenti? huh
          what   matter
          '(Then) what kind of matter (is it)? (laughter)'

     ((10 lines omitted regarding a slip of the tongue made by Li))

17 Li: suoyi wo   xiangxin jinnian   haishi hui zhemeyang de huh.
          so   1SG believe   this.year still   can this.way   PCL
          'So I believe this year will be the same.'

18 Ming: shi   ma.
          COP   Q
          'Really?'

19 Li: en.
          INJ
          'mm hm'

20 Ming: yinggai mei name rongyi de   ba.
          should   NEG that easy   PCL FP
          '(It) shouldn't be that easy.'

21	Li:	**wo**	**juede**	yinggai	haishi	zheyangzi	de. huh huh huh
		1SG	feel/think	must	still	this.way	PCL

'I think (it) should be the same. (laughter)'

Researchers have pointed out that, when *wo juede* is used in the turn-initial position, it often precedes disagreement (Endo 2010, 2013; Lim 2009).

When *wo juede* is used in the post-posed position as in (4), it can serve as the end of the whole turn. In the example below, *wo juede* is used at the end of a turn, and a speaker transition occurs smoothly.

(6) [college reunion]

01	Li:	en:	keneng	daxue	dongxuehui,		
		INJ	maybe	college	reunion		

02		bu	hui	meinian	dou	zhaokai	**wo**	**juede**.
		NEG	can	every.year	all	hold	1SG	feel/think

'Um, maybe college reunions won't be held annually **I think**.'

03	Ming:	bu	keneng:
		NEG	possible

'(It's) impossible.'

In this example, *wo juede* epistemically qualifies the speaker's opinion, thereby soliciting agreement from the other participant (Endo 2013).

Based on a quantitative analysis, Endo (2010) argued that *wo juede* is most likely to be in the turn-final position when it is in the clause-final position, as opposed to other clause positions. In her data, approximately 60% of tokens of *wo juede* in clause-final positions were also in the turn-final position; that is, more than half of the clause-final *wo juede* serve as the end of a turn. In contrast, tokens of *wo juede* used in clause-initial or clause-medial positions tend to also be used in turn-initial or turn-medial positions; only 15% of tokens of *wo juede* in clause-initial positions and 22% of tokens in clause-medial positions are found in the turn-final position.

The turn-initial and turn-final positions are highly important for interaction, as those positions are close to the transition relevance place (TRP; Sacks, Schegloff, and Jefferson 1974), where a speaker transition is at issue. As previous studies on gaze have suggested (Kendon 1967; Goodwin 1981), participants in conversation behave in particular ways at such positions. Therefore, in the following analysis, I focus on cases in which *wo juede* is used in the turn-initial and turn-final positions.

My research questions are as follows. How do participants in conversation display their stance, whether evaluative, epistemic, (dis)affiliative, or participation, with their linguistic and non-linguistic behavior? In particular, when producing the epistemic stance marker *wo juede*, what kind of visual movement co-occurs with the use of this linguistic item? Through the examination of vocal and visual stance-taking behaviors, I investigate the interplay between epistemic, (dis)affiliative, and participation stance.

4 Data and methodology

The data for this paper are taken from a collection of videotaped casual face-to-face conversations between native speakers of Mandarin Chinese recorded in Beijing. The participants were college students, graduate students, or young teachers; two to three persons formed a single group. Most participants were female, but there were two male groups. The participants were instructed to talk freely during the recording. Fifteen groups participated in the recording, and the total duration of the recordings is approximately thirteen hours. For this paper, I selected three excerpts from two conversations in the database.

The framework adopted for the purposes of this paper is Interactional Linguistics (Ford, Fox, and Thompson 2002; Ochs, Schegloff, and Thompson 1996; Selting and Couper-Kuhlen 2001; Thompson et al. 2015). Incorporating the methodology developed in the field of conversation analysis (Sidnell and Stivers 2013), interactional linguistics investigates talk-in-interaction from a micro-analytic perspective. The aim of interactional linguistics is to discover the reflexive relationship between grammar and interaction. Focusing on the linguistic item *wo juede* and the visual behaviors that accompany its production, this paper examines how this item is utilized in interaction, especially in stance-taking. The transcription system used in this paper is based on Jefferson (2004), with some modifications. See Appendix for details.

5 Analysis

In this section, I examine three excerpts that contain five tokens of *wo juede*. I argue that the speakers' gaze expresses the (dis)affiliation and participation stances that the speakers are taking while using the epistemic stance marker *wo juede*. Specifically, the disaffiliation and participation stances are observed to be expressed through the visual behavior in conjunction with the use of *wo juede*.

5.1 *Wo juede* in the turn-initial position

Let us first examine a case with an instance of turn-initial *wo juede*. Excerpt (7) demonstrates that a speaker displays a stance of disaffiliation through visual and vocal behaviors, that is, by looking away from the interlocutor while simultaneously saying *wo juede*. This excerpt is taken from a conversation between graduate students in different fields. Prior to the excerpt, Xun, who majors in developmental psychology, explained that one of her colleagues did an experiment that took forty hours per week for twenty weeks. Hearing that, Wei, who majors in engineering, says *ershi ge xiaoshi* 'twenty hours' (line 09), probably confusing the numbers of hours and weeks. Xun immediately corrects Wei by saying that twenty hours is of no use (line 10). Surprised, Wei then repeats *meiyou yong* 'of no use', adding the final particle *a* (line 12), which can be heard as a pre-misalignment (Wu 2004), and then starts her turn by saying *na wo juede* 'then I think' (line 14). Before Wei states the substantial part of her opinion, however, Xun starts explaining why twenty hours is not enough for the study (lines 13, 15, and 16). After Xun's explanation, Wei restates her opinion that such a treatment method needs to be improved (line 18).

```
(7) [treatment_method]
09   Wei:     ershi    ge    xiaoshi.=
              twenty   CL    hour
              'Twenty hours.'

10   Xun:     =ershi   ge    xiaoshi   meiyou   yong.
              twenty   CL    hours     NEG      use
              'Twenty hours is of no use.'

11            (0.4)

12   Wei:     meiyou   yong   a?
              NEG      use    FP
              'Of no use?'

13   Xun:     dui.    [zhe    shi.
              right   [this   COP
              'Right. This is'

14   Wei: →           [na,    na    wo     juede   XX
                      [then   then  1SG    think   XX
                      'Then, then I think'
```

| 15 | Xun: | jiushi ershi ge xiaoshi gen ling de (.)
just twenty CL hour with zero POS
chabie bu da.
difference NEG big
'That is, the difference between twenty hours and zero is not big' |

| 16 | | jiushi - (.) [meiyou tai da de chabie.
just [NEG too big POS difference
'That is, there is no significant difference.' |

| 17 | Wei: | [n n
['uh huh' |

| 18 | Wei: → | na **wo juede** zhe zhong fang- zhiliao fangfa
then 1SG think this kind method- treatment method
haiyou dai gaijin a.
still wait improvement FP
'Then I think this kind of meth- treatment method needs to be improved.' |

| 19 | Xun: | huh huh |

When Wei's first attempt to take a turn at line 14 fails, perhaps due to the overlap with Xun, Wei yields the speakership and waits until Xun finishes her explanation. When Wei restarts her turn in line 18, she uses the same expression she tried to use in line 14, *na wo juede* 'then I think'. In other words, she recycles the turn-beginning. It has been argued that the turn-beginning is a very important position because the speaker may determine the turn shape and/or the action performed by the turn (Sacks, Schegloff, and Jefferson 1974; Schegloff 1987, 1996; Lerner 1996; Heritage 1984a, 2002). Thus, the recycling of *wo juede* here seems to be highly relevant to what Wei is going to do on her turn.

This recycling of a turn-initial *na wo juede* indicates mitigation of disagreement, which is frequently observed as the function of *wo juede* in the turn-initial position (Endo 2010). Wei's claim is that the kind of treatment needs to be improved, implying that the present method is imperfect, which is obviously a negative assessment of the method. Although Xun is not the primary investigator in the experiment, nor is she overtly making assessments of it, denying the effectiveness of the design of the experiment can be taken as an offence to her, as she has been explaining this experiment as an example of the work done in her department. The negative implication of Wei's opinion is mitigated by the use of the epistemic stance marker *wo juede*, as it marks that the opinion is personal and subjective rather than objectively true.

Wei's production of *wo juede* is accompanied by a gaze shift. While Xun explains that twenty hours is of no use, shaking her head horizontally, Xun and Wei have mutual gaze (line 10, Figure 1). When Wei tries to start her turn by saying *na wo juede* (line 14), she frowns and shifts her gaze away from Xun (Figure 2). As Xun takes the floor and continues her explanation, Wei stops frowning and recovers a mutual gaze with Xun (line 15, Figure 3). In her second attempt to present her opinion (line 18, Figure 4), Wei shifts her gaze away from Xun and looks down, just as she did the first time. At the end of her turn, as she says *haiyou dai gaijin a* 'still needs improvement' (line 18), Wei shifts her gaze back to Xun (Figure 5). In this example, we clearly see that Wei looks away from Xun both times she says *wo juede* (Figures 2 and 4).

```
10   Xun:    =ershi ge xiaoshi meiyou yong.
             'Twenty hours is of no use'
     XunG    W:::::::::::::::::::::::::::::::::::
     XunB    ((shake head horizontally))
     WeiG    X:::::::::::::::::::::::::::::::::::
```

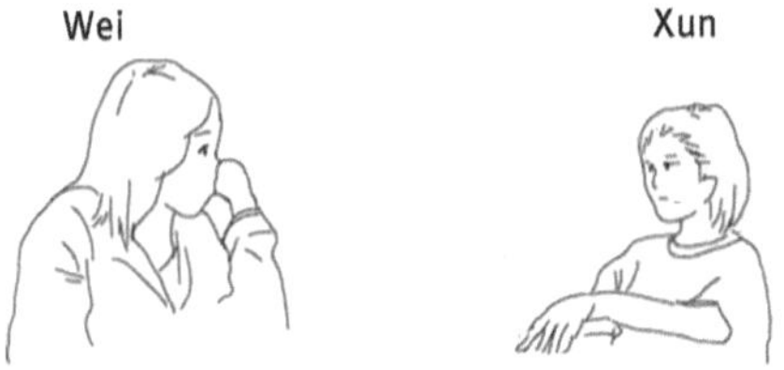

Figure 1: Xun and Wei's mutual gaze throughout line 10.

```
11              | (0.4) |
     XunG    W:::::::::::
     WeiG    X:::::::::::

12   Wei:    meiyou |yong a?
             'Of no use?'
     XunG    W:::::::::|:::::::::::
     WeiG    X:::::::::|:::::::::::
     WeiB              |((turns face even more closely to Xun))

13   Xun:    |dui. |[zhe shi- (.) ershi ge xiaoshi
             'Right. This is, (.) twenty hours'
     XunG    |W::::|----------------------------------
     XunB    |((nods))
```

14 Wei: → [na, na **wo juede** XX
              'Then, then I think'
    WeiG |X:::|,,,_____
    WeiB |((puts left hand to face))

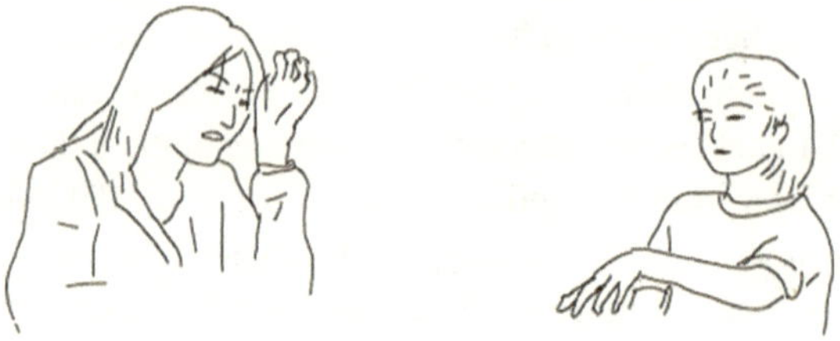

Figure 2: Wei frowns and shifts her gaze away when saying *na wo juede* 'then I think' in line 14.

15 Xun: gen ling de |(.) chabie bu da.
              'and zero... the difference is not big'
    XunG W:-----------|:::::::::::::::::::::
    WeiG ,,,,,,,,,,,,,, |X:::::::::::::::::::

Figure 3: Mutual gaze recovered as Xun explains in line 15.

16 jiushi – (.) [meiyou tai da de chabie.
      'That is, there is no significant difference'

17 Wei: [n n
              'uh huh'
    XunG W:::
    WeiG X:::

18 Wei: → na |wo juede zhe zhong| fang- zhiliao fangfa haiyou |dai gaijin| a.
              'Then I think this kind of meth- treatment method needs to be
              improved.'
    WeiG X:::|,,,,,,,,,,,,,,,,,,,,,, |_____|,,,,,,,,,,, |X::::
    XunG W::|------------------------ |------------------------|----------- |::::::

Figure 4: Wei looks down as she says *na wo juede* 'then I think' in line 18.

Figure 5: Wei looks at Xun saying *haiyou dai gaijin a* 'needs to be improved' in line 18.

Here, we can see that the production of *wo juede* and gaze shift occur at the same time. The recycling of *wo juede* and gaze shift seems to indicate that their co-occurrence is not a coincidence. In conjunction with the epistemic stance marker *wo juede*, gaze shift seems to be expressing the participation stance of the speaker. As Kendon (1967) pointed out, speakers tend to look away at the beginning of a turn. Looking away from Xun suggests the change of Wei's participation role from listener to speaker; the gaze shift thus displays participation stance.

It should also be noted that, in this case, looking away might be an indication of the speaker's disaffiliative stance. As is discussed above, Wei is making a negative assessment on the topic. Although she resumes mutual gaze with Xun at the end of her turn, she does not look at Xun when she starts verbalizing her criticism of the treatment method. Looking away may embody some kind of distance-keeping on the side of the speaker; moreover, in this case, being critical about the method described by Xun can also be Wei's motivation for the gaze shift.

In excerpt (8), one participant, Ying, is complaining about her nanny's dish being too tasteless (lines 1 to 3). In the omitted lines 4 to 13, she says that the nanny does not add much spices, salt, or sugar, and that her dish is therefore tasteless. Hearing that, the other participant, Tao, says that dishes will be sweet if no salt is added (lines 14 and 15). In response to this, Ying produces the agreement token *dui* 'right' and continues to talk about the nanny's dish (line 16). Then, a third participant, Mei, cuts in to give her opinion that eating light-taste food is relatively good (line 17). Ying then complains again by saying that every dish that the nanny makes is light-taste and very hard to eat (lines 18 and 19).

(8) [nanny's dish]

```
01  Ying:   na     baomu  zuofan   (0.5)  wo    juede   queshi  you    wenti.
            that   nanny  cook.food       1SG   think   surely  have   problem
            'That nanny's cooking, I think surely has a problem.'

02          zuo (.)  xian    bu    xian,   dan    bu    dan,   la     bu    la,
            make     salty   NEG   salty   light  NEG   light  spicy  NEG   spicy
            tian    bu    tian,
            sweet   NEG   sweet
            'not salty, not light-taste, not spicy, not sweet,'

03          aiyo  huh  huh  huh   ke     nanshou      lo.
            INJ                   EMP    hard.accept  FP
            'Oh, (it's) pretty hard to accept.'

            ((10 lines omitted about the nanny's not using much salt or
            seasonings))

14  Tao:    ruguo  zuo    cai    bu    fang   yidianr-  fang   yan    te
            if     make   dish   NEG   put    a.little  put    salt   special
            shao    de    ne    na    jiu-   neige-
            little  PCL   FP    then  just   that
            'If (one) doesn't add salt when (one) cooks, or add salt only a little,
            then'

15          neige  cai    jiu    fa       tian.
            that   dish   just   become   sweet
            'that dish will be sweet.'

16  Ying:   dui.    ta    zuo    de    cai-=
            right   3SG   make   POS   dish
            'Right. The dish she cooks-'
```

17	Mei:	=danshi **wo juede** chi qingdan yidianr (>hui bu hui<)
		but 1SG think eat light-taste a.little can NEG can
		bijiao hao ba.
		compare good FP
		'But I think eating light-taste food is relatively good, isn't it.'

18	Ying:	ta de cai dou shi ^qingdan de.
		3SG POS dish all COP light-taste FP
		'Every dish she makes is light-taste.'

19		→ ke nanchi le **wo juede**.
		EMP hard.to.eat PFV 1SG think
		'(It's) pretty hard to eat I think.'

20	Tao:	tai qingdan yidian you ye meiyou, ren chi de
		too light-tase a.little oil also NEG person eat PCL
		meiyou you=
		NEG oil
		'(If a dish is) too bland with no oil, (if) what people eat does not contain oil'

21	Mei:	=bu shi you de wenti. ta shuo de shi
		NEG COP oil POS problem 3SG say POS COP
		qingdan [neizhong
		light [that.kind
		'It's not a matter of oil. What she said is light-tasted, that kind.'

22	Ying:	[qingdan
		[light-tase
		'light-tasted'

Ying is taking a strongly negative stance toward the assessable, i.e., the dish the nanny cooks (lines 1 to 3). Generally, taking an evaluative stance makes the agreement or disagreement relevant in the subsequent turn (Sacks 1987; Pomerantz 1984). However, as the other participants in this excerpt have never had the dish, it is hard for them to agree or disagree with Ying's stance. What they can do is make an assessment from a different perspective (Goodwin and Goodwin 1987: 26–27), so they give their opinions about light-taste food in general. Tao speculates that a dish without salt will be sweet, implying that the dish would not be tasteless (line 15), and Mei takes a positive stance toward light-taste dishes (line 17). Here, Mei is disaffiliating with Ying's negative evaluation of light-taste food. In her turn, *wo juede* 'I think' is used to mitigate the conflicting opinions.

In conversations between more than two participants, the question of who will be the next speaker is far more complicated than it is in conversations between only two participants. Since Ying is the one who has been complaining about the nanny's dish, she becomes the primary recipient when Tao and Mei give their opinions about light-taste dishes. This participation framework is observed in their bodily behaviors as well. As Tao develops her turn in lines 14 and 15, she does not look at Mei or Ying, but at the end of the turn, she looks at Ying. Tao's face and gaze direction, coupled with the content of her utterance, indicate that her turn should be understood as primarily directed to Ying, after which Ying becomes the next speaker.

```
14    Tao:    ruguo zuo cai bu fang yidianr- fang yan te shao de ne na jiu- neige-
              'If (one) doesn't add salt when (one) cooks, or add salt only a little,
              then'
      TaoG    _____
      YingG   T--------------------------------------------------------
      MeiG    T--------------------------------------------------------

15            neige cai jiu | fa tian|.
              'that dish will be sweet.'

16    Ying:                           |dui. ta zuo| de cai-|
                                      'Right. The dish she cooks-'
      TaoG    _____|,,,,,,,Y:|  |Y:----------|--------|
      YingG   T----------|------:::|  |T:,,,,,,,,, M|::::::::|
      MeiG    T----------|--------|   |T-----------|--------|
```

Responding to Tao, Ying says *dui* 'right' and continues to talk more about the nanny's dish in line 16 (Figure 6). However, Mei cuts in, and Ying yields the speakership to Mei.

When Mei says *danshi wo juede*, her gaze is directed at Tao. Mei shifts her gaze to Ying at the end of the turn as she says *bijiao hao ba* 'relatively good, isn't it'. The sentence-final particle *ba* functions to solicit agreement from the recipient (Li and Thompson 1981). In the moment Mei says *ba*, her gaze is fixed on Ying, which suggests that Mei is soliciting agreement from Ying.

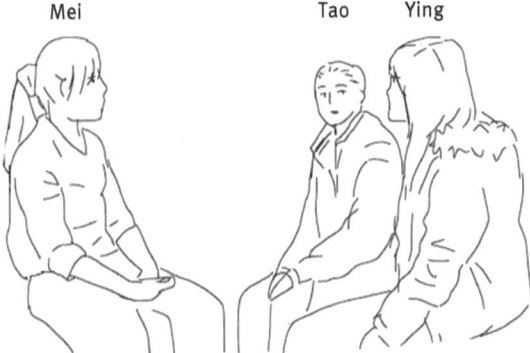

Figure 6: Ying shifts her gaze to Mei in line 16.

```
17   Mei:    =danshi wo juede |chi qingdan yidianr bu hui |bijiao |hao ba.|
             'But I think eating light-taste food is relatively good, isn't it.'
     MeiG    T::::::::::::::::::: |:::::::::::::::::::::::::::::::::|,,,,,,Y|::::::::::|
     TaoG    Y,,,,,,,,,,,,,,,,,,,,,M|:::::::::::::::::::::::::::::::::|--------|----------|
     YingG   M-------------------- |---------------------------------|--------|::::::::::|
```

The reason why Mei is not looking at Ying when Mei says *danshi wo juede* 'but I think' can be understood by considering the stance Mei is taking. Because Mei is making a positive evaluation about light-taste food, she is disaffiliative with Ying's negative stance toward light-taste food. Her disaffiliative stance is reflected in her avoiding achieving mutual gaze at the beginning of her turn. In this instance, the use of *wo juede* in a turn-initial position is associated with the visual behavior of not maintaining mutual gaze. This synchronization is not surprising because both of these behaviors, *wo juede* as a linguistic item and the absence of mutual gaze, serve as resources for displaying a disaffiliative stance.

In this section, two cases of *wo juede* in a turn-initial position and their accompanying gaze shifts were analyzed. In those cases, the speakers of *wo juede* expressed opinions that conflicted with another participant's opinion, and the gaze shift embodied the participation stance and disaffiliative stance of the speaker. The speaker's epistemic stance was displayed through the meaning of the epistemic stance marker *wo juede*. The speaker displayed her participation stance by starting a new turn using said marker in conjunction with a gaze shift. The whole turn conveys a speaker's evaluative stance about a topic; and, if it is in conflict with another speaker's, it also conveys the speaker's disaffiliative stance. It is in this way that the different kinds of stance are interrelated.

5.2 *Wo juede* in the turn-final position

As briefly noted in section 2, *wo juede* can be used at the end of a clause. Although the frequency of use in this position is far lower than in the clause-initial position,[6] *wo juede* in the sentence-final position is well established (Fang 2005; Huang 2003) and has its own characteristics. In this section, I analyze a case of sentence-final *wo juede* that is also in the turn-final position.

The token of *wo juede* in line 19 in Excerpt 8 is used at the end of the speaker's turn. When Ying produces the first turn construction unit (TCU), *ta de cai dou shi qingdan de* 'Every dish she makes is light-taste', she is looking at the previous speaker Mei, and they have mutual gaze. Tao looks at Ying toward the end of line 18 (Figure 7). Ying then speaks the negative assessment *ke nanchi le* 'pretty hard to eat', shifting her gaze from Mei to Tao. Ying adds *wo juede* 'I think' at the end of the TCU, while keeping her gaze on Tao (Figure 8).

```
18   Ying:    ta de cai dou shi| ^qingdan de.|
              'Every dish she makes is light-taste.'

19                                          | ke nanchi | le wo juede.
                                              '(It's) pretty hard to eat I think.'
    YingG    M:::::::::::::::::::|::::::::::::::::: |::::::: |,,,,,,,,,,,,,T|:::::::::::::::::::
    TaoG     M--------------------|,,,,,,,,,,,,,,,,Y|--------|---------------|:::::::::::::::::
    MeiG     Y:::::::::::::::::::|:::::::::::::::::|--------|---------------|------------------
```

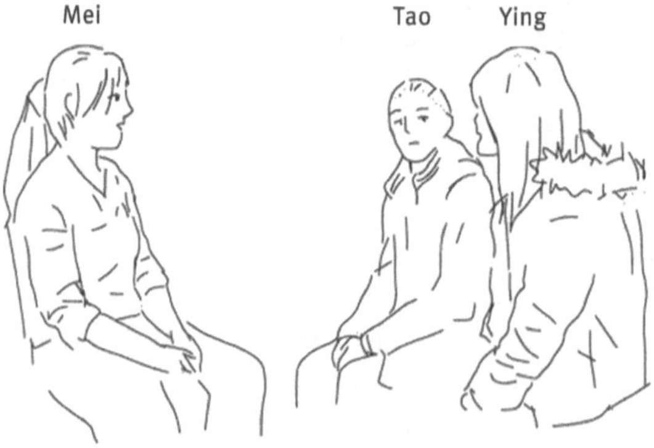

Figure 7: Ying starts her turn in line 18 looking at Mei.

---

6 In Endo (2010), 84.7% of all *wo juede* tokens in a corpus are in clause-initial or near clause-initial positions (only preceded by a conjunction), 6.9% are in clause-medial positions, and 6.4% in clause-final positions.

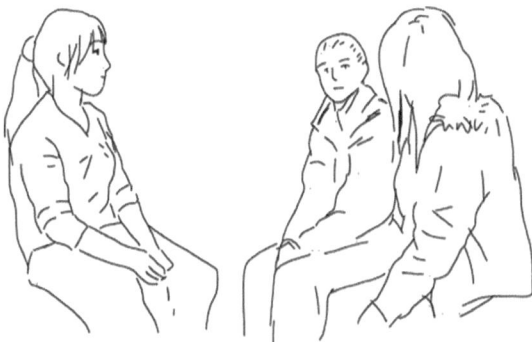

Figure 8: Ying looks at Tao at the end of line 19.

Ying's shift of gaze from Mei to Tao is accompanied by her production of *wo juede* at the final position. This co-occurrence seems to be motivated by two related factors. First, Ying and Mei are expressing conflicting opinions on the topic. The assessment in Ying's turn, *nanchi* 'hard to eat' (line 19), contrasts with that in Mei's, *hao* 'good' (line 17). Ying is taking a disaffiliative stance with respect to Mei, which is embodied by her shifting her gaze away from Mei. Secondly, Ying is selecting Tao as the next speaker by looking at her. Because it has already been made clear that Mei will not agree with Ying, Ying can only count on Tao for support. Thus, it may be the case that Ying is seeking affiliation from Tao via the gaze shift (cf. Tao 1999). In this way, *wo juede* 'I think' in the final position and gaze shift are used as resources for managing the speaker's stance of disaffiliation and for facilitating turn organization.

The token of *wo juede* in line 17 examined in the previous section and the one in line 19 examined above differ in their position in the turns. This difference has a significant implication for interaction. *Wo juede* in a turn-initial position projects that the speaker is going to state her opinion, which is often disaffiliative with another participant's stance; *wo juede* serves as a marker of mitigation in this case (Endo 2010; Lim 2009). In the turn-final position, on the other hand, the speaker's opinion has already been stated, so no projection is made by *wo juede*. Instead, *wo juede* in this position signals that the speaker is finished, which makes it relevant for other participants to take the turn.

By looking at a particular co-participant, the current speaker may indicate that she or he is selecting that participant as the next speaker. With a token of *wo juede* in the turn-final position, this selection becomes more salient. Using turn-final *wo juede* and gaze, the current speaker takes a participation stance, indexing that (i) she or he is not going to keep the floor any longer and that (ii) she or he is selecting another participant as the next speaker.

Used with *wo juede*, gaze shift also plays a role in expressing a disaffiliative stance. In Excerpt (8), Ying and Mei are having conflicting opinions. When they take disaffiliative stances toward each other, they look at the third participant, Tao. Looking at Tao seems to be a way to avoid looking at the participant who they are disaffiliating with, and to seek affiliation from Tao, whose evaluative stance toward the topic is yet to be revealed.

One final example of *wo juede* in the turn-final position is examined below. Unlike in the cases examined earlier in this paper, there is no clear conflict of opinions between the participants. This excerpt shows that *wo juede* can be produced after a transition relevance place, functioning to recomplete an extended turn, accompanied by the bodily behavior of gaze to select the next speaker. In this sense, the epistemic stance marker *wo juede* serves mostly to show the participation stance of the speaker.

In this excerpt, the same participants as in the previous example are talking about food issues in China in relation to the Olympic Games that were going to be held in Beijing in the year 2008. Prior to the excerpt, Mei said that foreign athletes might want to bring their own chefs. Ying in line 02 asks what the other participants think the athletes will do if they want to eat Chinese dumplings but their chefs are not able to make them. After laughing for a while, Mei answers by saying that the chefs will make baked goods anyway (line 06), and explains how to make bagels (detailed steps in her explanation are omitted in the excerpt). Her explanation comes to its end in line 14 when she says *ranhou jiu ge kaoxiang li kao le* 'then put into an oven and bake'. She then says *a:::* 'oh' and makes an evaluative comment that the procedure is very simple, simpler than making Chinese buns (line 15). This comment is delivered with a final, falling intonation. Although Mei's explanation has finished, neither of the other participants takes a turn. After 0.5 seconds of silence, Mei adds *wo juede* 'I think'. Still, nobody starts talking. After another 0.5 seconds of silence, Mei starts to add something by saying *danshi* 'but' (line 19), but Ying starts telling a story at the same time (line 20).

(9) [bagel]
01 Ying: *gangcai   shuo   ta   yao   jiushi   na   ge   waiguoren*
           just.now   say   3SG   want   just   that   CL   foreigner
           yundonyuan   yao   dai   chushi,
           athlete   want   bring chef
           'You just said that they want, that is, foreign athletes want to bring their chef,'

02		ta	dailai	le	xiang	chi	zhongguo	de	jiaozi,	na
		3SG	bring	PFV	want	eat	China	POS	dumpling	then
		bu	hui	zuo	zenme	ban	hh	huh	huh	
		NEG	can	make	how	do				

'What if they want to eat Chinese dumplings but the chefs can't make them'

03	Tao:	[hhhhhh
04	Mei:	[hhhhhh

04 (1.0)

05	Ying:	wo	juede-=
		1SG	think

'I think'

06	Mei:	=fanzheng	tamen	zuo	na	xie	kao	de	dongxi.
		anyway	3PL	make	that	CL	bake	POS	thing

'They will cook those baked stuff anyway.'

((7 lines omitted, Mei explains how to make a bagel))

14	Mei:	ranhou	jiu	ge	kaoxiang	li		kao	le.
		then	just	put	oven		inside	bake	PFV

'Then put (it) into an oven and bake.'

15		a::::.	hen-	feichang	jiandan.	bi	zheng	mantou
		INJ	very	extremely	simple	than	steam	bun
		jiandan	duo	le.				
		simple	much	PFV				

'Oh! It's so simple. Much simpler than steaming a Chinese bun.'

16 (0.5)

17	→	**wo**	**juede**.
		1SG	think

'I think'

18 (0.5)

19 Mei: [*danshi*
              [but
              'but'

20 Ying: [*wo   XX neige:: (.)   zhishi,   hen-   hen   zao   hen   zao*
              [1SG   XX   INJ   only   very   very   early very   early
              yiqian   jiushi,   wo   tingshuo yi   ge   gushi.
              before   just   1SG   hear   one CL   story
              'I XX well, just, long time ago, I heard a story.'

21   *jiushi   na   waiguo   de,   jiushi   neige   ren,   gang*
              just   that   foreign.country   POS   just   that   person just
              kaishi   de   shihou,
              start   POS   time
              'That is, in a foreign country, a man, when he just started,'

22   *bu   zhidao   nei   ge   jiaozi   shi   zenme   zuo,*
              NEG   know   that   CL   dumpling   COP   how   make
              'did not know how to make dumplings'

23   *bu   zhidao   nei   ge   xian   shi   zenme zai   limian   de.*
              NEG   know   that   CL   filling   COP   how   at   inside   PCL
              'did not know how the filling gets inside'

The story that Ying starts telling in line 20 is about a man who did not know how to make dumplings. In this context, the question she asked in line 02 turns out to be a preface to this story, rather than a genuine question. However, at the point when line 02 was uttered, this purpose of the question was not clear to Mei and Tao. Mei treated the question as a request for information, so she responded by stating her opinion that the foreign chefs would make baked goods and started explaining how to make bagels (line 06). Her explanation was very long and detailed, and when it was done (line 15), it was not clear to Tao and Ying what would be the relevant next action. For the 0.5 pause in line 16, none of Tao or Ying took turn. The pause can be taken as these particpants' display of hesitation to be the next speaker.

The use of *wo juede* 'I think' in line 17 functions as a *recompleter* (Sacks, Schegloff, and Jefferson 1974: 718; Ford and Thompson 1996; Ford, Fox, and Thompson 2002); that is, *wo juede* is used to cue a response from the recipients after the turn has arrived at a possible completion point. The assessment that making bagels is easier than making Chinese buns becomes easier for the other participant to agree with after it is epistemically downgraded with *wo juede*. At the same time, by adding *wo juede*, Mei emphasizes that her turn has come to an end. *Wo juede* is semantically superfluous in that it is clear to the participants that Mei has been talking about what she thinks. In addition, from a syntactic point of view, nothing further can be further added after the *wo juede*. The post-posed *wo juede* after a pause thus serves as a device to recomplete an extended turn.

The visual behavior of the speaker enhances the turn-recompleting function of the final *wo juede* and facilitates a speaker transition. As is shown in the transcript below, when Mei says that making bagels is simple (line 15), she is looking at Tao. As Mei is sitting on the left side, her body faces both Ying and Tao. Toward the end of the utterance, Mei's gaze is directed at Tao. When she says *wo juede* after a 0.5-second silence (lines 16–17), she looks at Ying (line 18). This shift of gaze from Tao to Ying indicates that Mei is specifically selecting Ying as the next speaker. There are two reasons for this selection of the next speaker. First, it may be reasonable to select Tao as the next speaker because she had not spoken while Ying and Mei talked in the previous turns. In fact, Mei's face was directed at Tao instead of Ying at the end of line 15, but Tao did not take the next turn. Secondly, it was Ying who asked a question at first in lines 01 and 02. As Mei's extended turn started as a response to Ying's question, it is relevant for Ying to take the next turn. Thus, both Tao and Ying are eligible for the next speakership. As Tao does not take the turn, Mei's gaze shifts fvrom Tao to Ying.

```
15   Mei:   hen- feichang jiandan. bi zheng mantou| jiandan duo le.|
            'It's so simple. Much simpler than steaming a Chinese bun.'
     MeiG   T/Y:::::::::::::::::::::::::::::::::::::::::: |T:::::::::::::::::: |
     TaoG   M::::::::::::::::::::::::::::::::::::::::::::: |::::::::::::::::::::::|
     YingG  M::::::::::::::::::::::::::::::::::::::::::::: |---------------------|

16              (0.5) |

17              |wo juede.|
                'I think'

18                         | (0.5)    |
     MeiG   T:::::::::|,,,,,,,,,Y::::|::::::::::--|
     TaoG   M:::::::::|--------------|------------|
     YingG  M--------|---------::::::|:::::::,,,T|
```

As Ying starts talking, she directs her gaze at Tao (line 20, Figure 9). Tao then immediately looks at Ying, and Ying continues her story.

```
19   Mei:    [danshi
             but
     MeiG    Y--------|-------------|---------|----------------------------------|:::::::::::::::::
             
20   Ying:   [wo XX |neige:: (.)| zhishi,|he- hen zao hen zao yiqian| jiushi, wo
             tingshuo yi ge gushi.
             'I XX well, just, long time ago, I heard a story'
     YingG   T--------|------::::::::|::::::::::|,,,,,,,,,,,,,,,,,,,,,,,,,,,,,,|T/M :::::::::::::
     TaoG    M,,,,,,,,,|,,,,,,Y:::::|::::::::|:::::::::::::::::::::::::::::|:::::::::::::::::
```

Figure 9: Ying looks at Tao, starting her story (line 20).

This example demonstrates that a final *wo juede* can be used as a recompleter, accompanied in this case by a gaze shift. It should also be pointed out that *wo juede* and gaze shift work differently. A final *wo juede* downgrades the preceding assessment by marking it as the speaker's personal opinion, signals the end of the turn, and invites input from other participants; a gaze shift, on the other hand, serves to select the next speaker. With such a division of labor, linguistic and non-linguistic resources together contribute to the formation of interaction. Note again that *wo juede* by itself does not indicate that the speaker is selecting the next speaker; it does not convey a message such as 'what do you think' in the same way as tag questions such as *shi bu shi* 'isn't it?', *dui bu dui* 'isn't it right?', *shi ba* 'right?', or *dui ba* 'right?'. What the speaker uses *wo juede* for here is to mark the end of her turn. As the turn has reached its completion in every possible sense, syntactically, prosodically, and pragmatically, marking the end of the turn again at line 17 serves to emphasize that the turn is genuinely over. Here, the speaker is expressing her participation stance in the sense that her role as the speaker is finished and she is ready to yield the speakership to other participants. By shifting her gaze from one participant to another, she selects the next speaker. The shift of gaze that accompanies *wo juede* in this way is a manifestation of the speaker's participation stance.

6 Discussion and conclusion

This paper focused on how producing the epistemic stance marker *wo juede* in the initial and final positions of a turn in conjunction with a speaker's bodily behavior functions to facilitate stance expression and turn organization. It was shown that, using these resources, speakers take two kinds of stance, one of (dis)affiliation and one of participation. The speakers were found to look away from participants with conflicting opinions, and toward participants who they wished to select as the next speaker. While the position of a linguistic item in a sequence is always important for understanding its function, it is especially important in the case of participation stance. Next-speaker selection becomes more relevant in a turn-final position than in other positions. It is when a turn comes to its end that the question of who will become the next speaker becomes an issue for the participants.

Though this paper focused mostly on the interactional aspect of the use of *wo juede*, its semantic features should not be ignored. In fact, the type of stance that speakers take using *wo juede* is to some extent determined by the semantic features of *wo juede*. That is, the epistemic stance marker consists of *wo* 'I' and *juede* 'to feel/think', and the meaning of the whole phrase that derives from the meanings of these components is crucial for the function of the marker *wo juede*. The meaning that this expression denotes, 'I feel/think', is highly subjective in that it refers to the speaker's mind. By attributing one's opinion to one's subjective and personal domain using *wo juede* 'I feel/think', it becomes easier for a speaker to state an opinion that conflicts with what has been said by their interlocutors. In this way, the (dis)affiliative stance that the speakers take using *wo juede* has its basis in the semantics of the marker.

The semantic features of *wo juede* 'I think' are also relevant to its function in the selection of the next speaker when it is used at the end of a turn. Marking that what has been said belongs to the speaker's mind makes it relevant for another participant to take the next turn to state his or her opinion in return (cf.

Pomerantz 1980). The function of *wo juede* in showing the speaker's participation stance is thus linked with the token's semantic features, generally associated with the epistemic stance.

In this paper, I showed how the linguistic item *wo juede* and the bodily behavior of gaze shift work together, arguing that they serve as resources for stance-taking and turn regulation in interaction. Natural conversations are full of such cooperation between different modalities of communication. For a more complete understanding of stance-taking, it is necessary to investigate even more verbal and non-verbal behaviors involved in human interaction.

Appendix A: Symbols used in transcript

,	continuing intonation
.	terminal intonation
[ ]	overlapping speech
X	uncertain hearing
^	stressed syllable
:	lengthening
(.)	micro pause
(2.1)	long pause and its length in seconds
-	truncated speech
=	latching (no gap after the previous turn)
huh	laughter or laughing quality
h	hearable exhalation
°	soft voice

Appendix B: Abbreviations in glosses

CL	classifier
COP	copula
FP	final particle
INJ	interjection
NEG	negation
PCL	particle
PFV	perfective
POS	possessive
Q	question particle

1SG	first-person singular
3SG	third-person singular
3PL	third-person plural

Appendix C: Annotation of gaze direction

_____	not directed at any participant
X-------	directed at a participant whose name starts with X, but not mutual
X:::::::	mutual gaze with a participant whose name starts with X
X/Y----	gaze directed at two participants whose names start with X and Y
X/Y::::	mutual gaze with two participants whose names start with X and Y
,,,,,,,,,,,	transition period

Acknowledgments
This work is supported by JSPS (Japan Society for the Promotion of Sciences) Grant-in-Aid for Scientific Research #21-3926, "Stance expressions and syntactic status of complements in Mandarin conversation" and Grant-in-Aid for Scientific Research #25-40090, "Pursuing response in Child-caregiver interaction".

References

Biber, Douglas, Stig Johansson, Geoffrey Leech, Susan Conrad & Edward Finegan. 1999. *Longman grammar of spoken and written English*. London: Longman.
Chafe, Wallace & Johanna Nichols (eds.). 1986. *Evidentiality: The linguistic coding of epistemology*. Norwood: Ablex.
Du Bois, John. 2007. The stance triangle. In Robert Englebretson (ed.), *Stancetaking in discourse*, 139–182. Amsterdam/Philadelphia: John Benjamins.
Endo, Tomoko. 2010. Epistemic stance marker as a disagreement preface: *Wo juede* 'I feel/think' in Mandarin conversation in response to assessments. *Kyoto University Linguistic Research* 29. 43–76.
Endo, Tomoko. 2013. Epistemic stance in Mandarin conversation: The positions and functions of *wo juede* 'I feel/think'. In Yuling Pan & Daniel Kádár (eds.), *Chinese discourse and interaction: Theory and practice*, 12–34. London: Equinox.
Englebretson, Robert (ed.). 2007. *Stancetaking in discourse*. Amsterdam/Philadelphia: John Benjamins.
Fang, Mei. 2005. Lunzheng yi weibin dongci de xiuhua – cong weibin dongci dao yuyong biaoji [Grammaticalization of epistemic-evidential complement-taking verbs]. *Zhongguo Yuwen [Chinese Language]* 6. 495–507.
Ford, Cecilia & Sandra Thompson. 1996. Interactional units in conversation: Syntactic, intonational, and pragmatic resources for the management of turns. In Elinor Ochs,

Emanuel A. Schegloff & Sandra A. Thompson (eds.), *Interaction and grammar*, 135–184. Cambridge: Cambridge University Press.

Ford, Cecilia, Barbara Fox & Sandra Thompson (eds.). 2002. *The language of turn and sequence*. Oxford: Oxford University Press.

Ford, Cecilia, Barbara Fox & Sandra Thompson. 2002. Constituency and the grammar of turn increments. In Cecilia E. Ford, Barbara A. Fox & Sandra A. Thompson (eds.), *The language of turn and sequence*, 14–38. Oxford: Oxford University Press.

Frischen, Alexandra, Andrew P. Bayliss & Steven P. Tipper. 2007. Gaze cueing of attention: Visual attention, social cognition, and individual differences. *Psychological Bulletin*. 133(4): 694–724. doi: 10.1037/0033-2909.133.4.694

Goodwin, Charles. 1981. *Conversational organization: Interaction between speakers and hearers*. New York: Academic Press.

Goodwin, Charles. 2007. Participation, stance and affect in the organization of activities. *Discourse & Society* 18(1). 53–73.

Goodwin, Charles & Goodwin, Majorie Harness. 1987. Concurrent operations on talk: notes on the interactive organization of assessments. *IPrA Papers in Pragmatics* 1(1): 1–55.

Haddington, Pentti. 2006. The organization of gaze and assessments as resources for stance taking. *Text and Talk* 26. 281–328.

Hayashi, Makoto. 2009. Marking a 'noticing of departure' in talk: *Eh*-prefaced turns in Japanese conversation. *Journal of Pragmatics* 41. 2100–2129.

Hayano, Kaoru. 2013. Claiming epistemic primacy: *Yo*-marked assessments in Japanese. In Tanya Stivers, Lorenza Modada & Jakob Steensig (eds.), *The morality of knowledge in conversation*, 58–81. Cambridge: Cambridge University Press.

Helasvuo, Marja-Liisa. 2014. Agreement or crystallization: Patterns of 1st and 2nd person subjects and verbs of cognition in Finnish conversational interaction. *Journal of Pragmatics* 63. 63–78.

Heritage, John. 1984a. A change-of-state token and aspects of its sequential placement. In John Maxwell Atkinson & John Heritage (eds.), *Structures of social action*, 299–345. Cambridge: Cambridge University Press.

Heritage, John. 1984b. *Garfinkel and ethnomethodology*. Cambridge: Polity Press.

Heritage, John. 2002. *Oh*-prefaced responses to assessments: A method of modifying agreement/disagreement. In Cecilia E. Ford, Barbara A. Fox & Sandra A. Thompson (eds.), *The language of turn and sequence*, 96–224. Oxford: Oxford University Press.

Heritage, John. 2012. The epistemic engine: Sequence organization and territories of knowledge. *Research on Language & Social Interaction* 45(1). 30–52.

Huang, Shuanfan. 2003. Doubts about complementation: A functionalist analysis. *Language and Linguistics* 4(2). 429–455.

Jaffe, Alexandra (ed.). 2009. *Stance: Sociolinguistic perspectives*. Oxford: Oxford University Press.

Jefferson, Gail. 2004. Glossary of transcript symbols with an introduction. In Gene H. Lerner (ed.), *Conversation analysis: Studies from the first generation*, 13–31. Amsterdam/Philadelphia: John Benjamins.

Kärkkäinen, Elise. 2003. *Epistemic stance in English conversation: A description of its interactional functions, with a focus on* I think. Amsterdam/Philadelphia: John Benjamins.

Kendon, Adam. 1967. Some functions of gaze-direction in social interaction. *Acta Psychologica* 26. 22–63.

Lerner, Gene. 1996. On the "semi-permeable" character of grammatical units in conversation: Conditional entry into the turn space of another speaker. In Elinor Ochs, Emanuel A. Schegloff & Sandra A. Thompson (eds.), *Interaction and grammar*, 238–271. Cambridge: Cambridge University Press.

Li, Charles N. & Sandra A. Thompson. 1981. *Mandarin Chinese: A functional reference grammar*. Berkeley/Los Angeles: University of California Press.

Lim, Ni-Eng. 2009. Stance-taking with *Wo juede* in conversational Chinese. In Yun Xiao (ed.), *The 21st North American Conference on Chinese Linguistics* 2, 323–340. Smithfield, Rhode Island: Bryant University.

Lindström, Anna & Marja-Leena Sorjonen. 2013. Affiliation in conversation. In Jack Sidnell & Tanya Stivers (eds.), *The handbook of conversation analysis*. West Sussex: Wiley-Blackwell.

Lyons, John. 1977. *Semantics*, vol. 3. Cambridge: Cambridge University Press.

Martin, James. 2000. Beyond exchange: Appraisal systems in English. In Susan Hunston & Geoff Thompson (eds.), *Evaluation in text: Authorial stance and the construction of discourse*, 142–175. New York: Oxford University Press.

Morita, Emi. 2005. *Negotiation of contingent talk: The Japanese interactional particles ne and sa*. Amsterdam: John Benjamins.

Nuyts, Jan. 2001. *Epistemic modality, language, and conceptualization: A cognitive-pragmatic perspective*. Amsterdam/Philadelphia: John Benjamins.

Ochs, Elinor, Schegloff, Emanuel A. & Thompson, Sandra A. (eds.). 1996. *Interaction and grammar*. Cambridge: Cambridge University Press.

Palmer, Frank. 2001. *Mood and modality*, 2nd edn. Cambridge: Cambridge University Press.

Pomerantz, Anita. 1980. Telling my side: 'Limited access' as a 'fishing device'. *Sociological Inquiry* 50. 186–191.

Pomerantz, Anita. 1984. Agreeing and disagreeing with assessments: Some features found in preferred/dispreferred turn shapes. In John Maxwell Atkinson & John Heritage (eds.), *Structures of social action: Studies in conversation analysis*, 57–101. Cambridge: Cambridge University Press.

Rossano, Federico. 2013. Gaze in conversation. In Jack Sidnell & Tanya Stivers (eds.), *The Handbook of Conversation Analysis*. 308–349. Hoboken: Wiley-Blackwell.

Rossano, Federico, Penelope Brown, and Stephen C. Levinson. 2009. Gaze, questioning, and culture. In Jack Sidnell (ed.), *Conversation Analysis: Comparative Perspectives*, 187–249. Cambridge: Cambridge University Press.

Sacks, Harvey. 1987 [1973]. On the preferences for agreement and contiguity in sequences in conversation. In Graham Button & John R. E. Lee, (eds.), *Talk and social organization*, 54–69. Philadelphia: Multilingual Matters.

Sacks, Harvey, Emanuel A. Schegloff & Gail Jefferson. 1974. A simplest systematics for the organization for turn-taking in conversation. *Language* 50(4). 696–735.

Schegloff, Emanuel A. 1987. Recycled turn beginnings: A precise repair mechanism in conversation's turn-taking organization. In Graham Button & John R. E. Lee (eds.), *Talk and social organization*, 70–85. Clevedon: Multilingual Matters.

Scheglogg, Emanuel A. 1996. Turn organization: one intersection of grammar and interaction. In Ochs et al. (eds.), *Interaction and grammar*, pp.52–133. Cambridge: Cambridge University Press.

Selting, Margret & Couper-Kuhlen, Elizabeth (eds.). 2001. *Studies in Interactional Linguistics*. Amsterdam: John Benjamins.

Sidnell, Jack & Stivers, Tanya (eds.). 2013. *The handbook of Conversation Analysis*. Malden: Wiley-Blackwell.

Simon, Ho, Tom Foulsham, Alan Kingstone. 2015. Speaking and listening with the eyes: Gaze signaling during dyadic interactions. *PLoS ONE* 10(8): e0136905. https://doi.org/10.1371/journal.pone.0136905

Stivers, Tanya. 2008. Stance, alignment, and affiliation during storytelling: When nodding is a token of affiliation. *Research on Language & Social Interaction* 41(1). 31–57.

Stivers, Tanya, NJ Enfield, Penelope Brown, Christina Englert, Makoto Hayashi, Trine Heinemann, Gertie Hoymann, Federico Rossano, Jan Peter de Ruiter, Kyung-Eun Yoon & Stephen C. Levinson. 2009. Universals and cultural variation in turn-taking in conversation. *Proceedings of the National Academy of Sciences of the United States of America* 106(26): 10587–10592. doi: https://doi.org/10.1073/pnas.0903616106

Stivers, Tanya, Lorenza Modada & Jakob Steensig. 2011. Knowledge, morality and affiliation in social interaction. In Tanya Stivers, Lorenza Modada & Jakob Steensig (eds.), *The morality of knowledge in conversation*, 3–24. Cambridge: Cambridge University Press.

Tao, Hongyin. 1999. Body movement and participant alignment in Mandarin conversational interaction. *CLS* 35: 125–139.

Thompson, Sandra A. 2002. "Object complements" and conversation: Towards a realistic account. *Studies in Language* 26(1). 125–164.

Thompson, Sandra A. & Anthony Mulac. 1991. A quantitative perspective on the grammaticization of epistemic parentheticals in English. In Elizabeth C. Traugott & Bernd Heine (eds.), *Approaches to grammaticalization*, vol. 2, 237–251. Amsterdam: John Benjamins.

Thompson, Sandra A., Barbara A. Fox, & Elizabeth Couper-Kuhlen. 2015. *Grammar in Everyday Talk: Building Responsive Actions*. Cambridge: Cambridge University Press.

Wu, Ruey-Jiuan Regina. 2004. *Stance in talk: A conversation analysis of Mandarin final particles*. Amsterdam/Philadelphia: John Benjamins.

Part III: **Multimodal organization of talk and interaction**

Xiaoting Li
Multimodal turn construction in Mandarin conversation – Verbal, vocal, and visual practices in the construction of sytactically incomplete turns

1 Introduction

One important feature of the organization of talk-in-interaction is that overwhelmingly one party talks at a time (Sacks, Schegloff and Jefferson 1974). Two issues are central for the routine achievement of the "one speaker at a time" or smooth turn transition between speakers. The first issue is when the current speaker may (or may not) end his/her turn, and the other is who will speak next. A substantial body of work has shown that and how multimodal resources such as syntax, prosody, and body movement are relevant to the projection of possible turn completion (Sacks, Schegloff and Jefferson 1974; Auer 2009; Selting 1996, 2000; Local and Kelly 1986; Walker 2004; X. Li 2014; Duncan 1972, 1974;) or continuation of the current speaker's turn (Schegloff 1982, 1998; Ford, Thompson and Drake 2012). Further, these multimodal resources usually work in a convergent manner in the projection of possible turn completion (Ford and Thompson, 1996). However, they may also create potentially divergent trajectories (Schegloff 1996; X. Li 2014). Along this line of inquiry, the present study investigates a particular type of divergence in projecting possible turn completion in Mandarin conversation where a turn is incomplete in its syntactic structure, but interactionally complete in and through its prosodic and visual features as well as in the action it performs. Excerpt (1) exemplifies the type of syntactically incomplete turns under investigation.

In this excerpt, Cai (female) tells Yun (female) how one of her female friends got a positioin in an oil company in Canada. She strongly implies that her friend seems to have been a "diversity hire",[1] because that friend is not particularly

---

[1] "Diversity hire" refers to the employment of a person because his/her personal traits such as gender, age, ethnic and/or cultural background add diversity to a workplace. Here, Cai's friend who is a young Chinese female would arguably add diversity to the Canadian oil company.

Xiaoting Li, University of Alberta

https://doi.org/10.1515/9783110462395-008

outstanding (line 01). The target syntactically incomplete turn is Yun's response at line 06.

(1) Employment equality

```
01   Cai:    suoyi wo neige pengyou dangshi ta   tiaojian      ye MEI you
             so   we  that.CL friend  then    3SG qualification also NEG have
             tebie        youxiu   me.
             especially   excellent PRT
             'So that friend of mine, her qualification wasn't particularly
             outstanding.'

02   Cai:    ranhou ge fangmian: jiu shi chengji bijiao hao.
             then   every aspect just be grade relatively good
             'It was just that her grades were pretty good.'

03   Cai:    jiu  bei?  yixiazi    jiu bei    shunli    de luqu le;
             just PASS immediately just PASS smoothly CSC admit CRS
             '(So she) was, immediately was hired.'

04   Cai:    [suoyi.
             [so
             'So...'

05   Yun:    [zhe ye zhengchang;
             [this also normal
             'This is normal.'

06 →Yun:     yinwei tamen zheibian nüquan yundong     bi    zhongguo? (1.1)
             because they  this.CL feminist movement compare China
             jiu   shi;
             just  be
             'Because their feminist movement compared to China is...'

07   Cai:    DUI.
             right
             'Right.'
```

At line 06, Yun begins to provide an account for her evaluative comment on Cai's report *zhe ye zhengchang* 'this is normal' (line 05) by comparing the level of the feminist movement in Canada and in China. This turn is syntactically incomplete since in the comparative construction, and particularly the final adjective, is not verbalized. However, Cai's immediate next-turn response at line 07 with no gap or overlap with Yun's SIT displays that she orients to Yun's SIT as unproblematic and interactionally complete. When the syntactic structure constituting the turn is incomplete, there must be other resources that allow projection of possible turn completion to be made from the talk. This study examines how multimodal resources such as prosody, bodily-visual behavior, and sequential position interact with (incomplete) syntax in the projection of possible turn completion. How do multimodal resources work together in accomplishing the action initiated through a syntactically incomplete turn (SIT)? A fuller account of this excerpt, and particularly the interplay of multimodal resources in the construction of the SIT, will be provided in Section 4.

Two notions are relevant to the multimodal construction of SITs, and thus should be discussed first: multimodal turn construction and SITs.

2 Multimodal turn construction

In talk-in-interaction, the opportunities for people to participate in conversation are not random, but are distributed in an orderly fashion. One key issue for participation in the turn-taking system is to anticipate the transition relevance places (TRPs) to begin one's talk or to pass up the opportunity to talk. Speakers can and routinely do talk in such a way as to allow the projection of possible turn completion and TRPs (Sacks, Schegloff and Jefferson 1974; Duncan 1972, 1974; Selting 1996, 2000; X. Li 2014).

In their seminal work on turn-taking, Sacks, Schegloff and Jefferson (1974) propose that the projectability of the trajectories of certain syntactic units is crucial to the projection and prediction of possible turn completion. Auer (2005, 2009) also argues that projection is a fundamental feature of syntax which makes it usable as a means to project the trajectory of turns and to signal possible turn completion. CA-informed phoneticians and scholars on interactional prosody have enhanced our understanding of the role of phonetics/prosody in the construction of turns and projection of TRPs (Local, Kelly and Wells 1986; Wells and Macfarlane 1998; Selting 1996, 2000; Schegloff 1998; Ogden 2001, 2004). Local, Wells and Sebba (1985) and Local, Kelly and Wells (1986) report that sets of phonetic features such as slowing down of tempo and pitch step up or pitch drop seem to relate to possible turn completion in London Jamaican and Tyneside English. Schegloff (1996, 1998) and Wells and Macfarlane (1998) show how pitch peak or final major accent may project possible turn completion. Based on Finnish conversational data, Ogden (2001, 2004) observes that voice quality such as creaky voice may also be relevant to possible turn completion and turn transition.

Instead of focusing on specific sets of turn-ending phonetic features, Selting (1996, 2000) argues that in German conversation, the overall prosodic contour constituted by both the pitch peak and its subsequent syllables with various pitch movements is used to locally configure and indicate the possible turn completion. Further, discussing the interplay of syntax and prosody in turn construction, she proposes that syntactic structure is used for "far-reaching projection" while prosody is for local configuration and projection. Ford and Thompson (1996) underline the necessity of taking into account of not only syntax, but also intonation and "pragmatics" (conversational action) in studying turn construction. They observe that turn transition usually occurs at the convergence of syntactic, intonational, and pragmatic completion in English conversation. The function of body movement in turn construction and projection has been addressed as early as the 1970s by Duncan and his collaborators (Duncan 1972, 1974; Duncan and Niederehe 1974; Duncan and Fiske 1977). Duncan (1972, 1974) describes how the termination of gesticulation and relaxation of a tensed hand position can be visual signs for turn completion. An interactional account of the interplay of syntax, prosody, and body movement in turn construction is provided by Ford, Fox and Thompson (1996), who show that syntax, prosody, bodily behavior such as gesture and gaze, and social action are integral to turn construction. Li (2014) systematically explores the interplay of syntax, prosody, body movement, and pragmatic resources (i.e., social action) in the construction of turns in Mandarin conversation. She observes that syntax, prosody, and social action are relevant to the indication of possible turn completion; body movement, when appearing, may converge or diverge with syntax and prosody in foreshadowing the possible turn completion.

This research on multimodal resources in turn-taking puts turn construction at the center of the inquiry. There is another line of research that has addressed multimodal resources in turn construction as situated in and occasioned by different conversational activities in different types of interactions. For example, Mondada (2007) demonstrates that pointing gesture can be used to project possible turn completion at work meetings, among its other features and functions (Kita, 2003). Heath and Luff (2013) shows how gesture and gaze are deployed by auctioneers to manage turns and participation in particular activities in auctions.

It can be seen from the previous research that our knowledge about turn construction has progressed significantly in the past decades, from the understanding of the role of syntax, to prosody, body movement, social action, and the import of different types of activities. Many previous studies have demonstrated that multimodal resources such as syntax, prosody, gaze body movement, and action work together in projecting possible turn completion (Ford and Thompson 1996; Ford, Fox and Thompson 1996; X. Li 2014) and managing joint attention (Goodwin 2003; Frischen, Bayliss and Tipper 2007). However, turn completion and transition is contingent and interactionally achieved, and each modality has its own organization (Stivers and Sidnell 2005). Sometimes the projected trajectories of different resources may be in conflict with each other. This paper explores the conflicting trajectories between incomplete syntactic structure on the one hand, and completion-implicative prosodic and visual features and social action on the other.

3 Syntactically incomplete turns

SITs are those turns constituted by an incomplete syntactic construction (as is projected by the syntactic schema in a language), which may or may not be completed by bodily-visual behaviors. They reveal the contingent, interactive, and multimodal nature of naturally occurring interaction, and thus have become the focus of research in conversation analysis, interactional linguistics, research in multimodality and embodied interaction, and construction grammar (see Zima 2017).

SITs have been mainly studied in two types of interactional settings: interaction in educational settings (such as teacher-student classroom and tutoring interaction), and interaction in everyday settings. In educational interaction, SITs are often designed to be syntactically incomplete, and deployed as a practice to achieve specific pedagogical purposes. For example, syntactically incomplete TCUs can be a format that teachers use to provide opportunities for student participation in classroom (Lerner 1995). In one-on-one second language writing conferences, teachers are documented to use syntactically incomplete utterances to elicit students' self-correction (Koshik 2002).[2] In dance class instruction, teachers routinely produce interactional units consisting of an incomplete syntactic construction and a bodily demonstration (Keevallik 2013). In everyday interaction, SITs seem to be deployed to deal with problematic and sensitive matters and to perform interactionally inappropriate actions. Olsher (2004) examines the 'embodied completion' of syntactically incomplete TCU where a

---

[2] Gestures can also be used a practice to guide the conceptualization process in instructional interactions (Williams 2007).

speaker initiates a TCU with talk and brings it to a completion through embodied action such as gesture. The syntactically incomplete TCUs seem to be used to invite recipients to explicitly address a problem in the ongoing interaction (Olsher 2004: 225). Chevalier and Clift (2008) document that turns can be designed to be syntactically incomplete to perform socially delicate actions such as last-minute changes disruptive to the maintenance of social solidarity (Chevalier and Clift 2008:1744). Thus, SITs afford a resource to put something interactionally delicate on the record without verbalizing it (Chevalier and Clift 2008:1746). Li (2016) observes that some SITs are used to accomplish socially and interactionally inappropriate actions and display sensitivity to the recipients' disengagement from the ongoing talk and participation framework.

This research on SITs in both educational and everyday settings reveals that these utterances are designed to be syntactically incomplete and are deployed as a practice to achieve particular pedagogical and interactional tasks. Their syntactically incomplete form is constitutive of the actions that these turns perform in specific situational and sequential environments.

Building on the previous research, the current study focuses on the projectability of syntax and bodily-visual conduct, as well as prosody and sequential position, for the projection of possible completion of SITs. The data show clearly that prosody, bodily-visual conduct and sequential position may indicate possible turn completion, although the syntax may be normatively incomplete. The action performed by SITs is usually projectable and recognizable due to its sequential position in a course of actions, as is evidenced by the recipients' 'appropriate' responses, displaying a clear understanding of the action. An examination of the SITs in the data shows that bodily-visual conduct seems to interact with syntax in turn construction in at least two ways: 1) it may visually represent the referential meaning of the "missing" element in the syntactic structure; and 2) it may project possible turn completion by indicating the possible boundaries of interactional units. Section 4 provides detailed accounts of the first type of interaction between talk and the body, while Section 5 examines the second.

4 Embodied completion of syntactically incomplete turns

Awareness of the role of bodily-visual behavior in the syntax of conversation is not new (e.g., Slama-Cazacu 1976). But the systematic study of their interaction is a rather recent endeavor (see Ford, Thompson and Drake 2012; Keevallik 2010,

2013; X. Li 2014). In my everyday Mandarin conversational data, a speaker may cease to talk before the projected syntactic completion of his/her turn, which is then completed through bodily-visual behavior. That is, the bodily-visual behavior functions as a replacement for the obligatory element of the syntactic unit of a turn. The recipient orients to the turn constructed by the verbal-visual 'hybrid construction' as possibly complete. The interplay of the lexico-syntactic, prosodic, bodily-visual, and sequential features (among other multimodal features) in the construction of turns and the projection of possible turn completion is exemplified in Excerpts (2) and (3).

Excerpt (1) above is taken from Excerpt (2) where Yun (female) and Cai (female) contrast the employment equality policy in Canada and China. Cai tells Yun about how one of her female friends who is allegedly 'not very outstanding' (line 18) got a job at an oil engineering company in Canada possibly as a "diversity" hire (lines 1–6, 17–20). The target multimodal turn construction is at line 23.

(2) Employment equality

```
01   Cai:   yinwei wo you yige pengyou.
            because I have one.CL friend
            'Because I have a friend.'

02   Cai:   jiushi ta zai  yige shiyou(-) neizhong leixing de(.) qiye gongzuo ma.
            just be 3SG at one.CL oil that kind ASSC enterprise work PRT
            'She works at an oil that kind of company.'

03   Cai:   gong::cheng lei de qiye.
            engineering type ASSC enterprise
            'engineering company.'

04   Cai:   ranhou ta [men dangshi danwei;
            then   th[ey      then company
            'Then her company...'

05   Yun:             [<<all> wo juede> zheizhong shi
                      [       I think   this kind  be
                      'I think this is...'

06   Cai:   JIU yao zhao yige       [nü de.
            just want hire one.CL [female
            'just wanted to hire a woman.'
```

07 Yun: [guoqi shi guoqi cai you zheizhong.
                [state-owned enterprise be state-owned
                enterprise only have this kind
                'Only (Chinese) state-owned enterprise has this
                kind (of situation).'

08 Cai: jiu jianada de.
           just Canada ASSC
           '(It's a) Canadian company.'

09 Yun: ou (-) jianada ya.
           ou Canada PRT
           'Ou, it's Canada.'

10 Cai: zai jia- wo shuode shi waiguode.
           at Ca- I say NOM be foreign ASSC
           'In Ca- I meant foreign companies.'

11 Yun: na yaoshi zhongguo ne.
           that if China PRT
           'Then, what if it's in China?'

12 Cai: zhongguo jiu bu cunzai le.
           China just NEG exist CRS
           'It doesn't exist in China.'

13 Cai: zhongguo wo xian:(-) bu shuo.
           China I first NEG say
           'I'm not talking about China now.'

14 Cai: jiu shi shuo zai zhege difang.
           just be say at this.CL place
           'I'm just talking about here.'

15 Cai: yinwei nei nei ci taolun jiu shi jianada me.
           because that that time discuss just be Canada PRT
           'Because what we discussed that time was Canada.'

16 Yun: ou.
           ou
           'Ou.'

17 Cai: *ranhou ta jiu shi xiang zhao yige nüxing de yuangong;*
          then 3SG just be want hire one.CL female ASSC employee
          'Then they just wanted to hire a female employee.'

18 Cai: *suoyi wo neige pengyou dangshi ta tiaojian ye MEI you tebie youxiu me.*
          so we that.CL friend then 3SG qualification also NEG have especially excellent PRT
          'So that friend of mine, her qualifications weren't particularly outstanding.'

19 Cai: *ranhou ge fangmian: jiu shi chengji bijiao hao.*
          then every aspect just be grade relatively good
          'It was just that her grades were pretty good.'

20 Cai: *jiu bei? yixiazi jiu bei shunli de luqu le;*
          just BEI immediately just BEI smoothly CSC admit CRS
          '(So she) was, immediately was hired.'

21 Cai: [*suoyi.*
          [so
          ['So...'

22 Yun: [*zhe ye zhengchang;*
          [this also normal
          'This is normal.'

Figure 1: Yun's (right) gesture at *jiushi* at line 23.

Figure 2: Yun's (right) body position after *jiushi* at line 23.

23 →Yun: *yinwei tamen zheibian nüquan yundong bi zhongguo? (1.1)*
          because they this.CL feminist movement compare China
          jiu shi;
          just be
          'Because their feminist movement compared to China is...'

24 Cai: DUI.
           right
           'Right.'

25 Yun: yishi hui gao   [henduo.
           awareness will high [much more
           '(Their feminist) awareness is a lot higher.'

26 Cai: [suoyi.
                               [so
                               'So...'

27 Yun: erqie tamen you zhuanmen de shenme;
           further they have special ASSC what
           'Also, they have special things like...'

Cai's telling about her female friend's employment by a Canadian oil company comes to a possible closure at line 21 indicated by the sequence-closure-implicative discourse marker *suoyi* (Fang 2000: 464). Overlapping with Cai's completion-implicative *suoyi*, Yun gives her assessment of Cai's report *zhe ye zhengchang* 'that's normal' (line 22), which disaffiliates with Cai's stance towards the event. Cai seems to treat how her female friend got hired (lines 18–20) as something controversial and worth reporting, but Yun considers it rather "normal" (line 22). Yun continues to provide accounts for her disaffiliative assessment, comparing the feminist movement in Canada and China (line 23). The target turn at line 23 is constructed by an incomplete syntactic structure and an iconic gesture visually representing the final "missing" syntactic element.

At line 23, Yun produces a comparison structure comparing the feminist movement in Canada and in China (Li and Thompson 1981). After *bi zhongguo* 'compare to China...', Yun produces a 1.1-second "holding silence" (Local and Kelly 1986), indicated by the initial glottal closure and subsequent glottal release and inbreath (Figure 3). The pause and the pause filler *jiushi* 'just be' (Zhang and Gao 2012) are displays of Yun's trouble in verbalizing the final degree adjective of dimension in the comparison structure. However, the verbally unproduced adjective is visually displayed through Yun's gesture. Concurrent with *jiushi*, Yun moves her left hand up palm facing down, and produces a stroke at the highest point (Figure 1). This is an iconic gesture visibly representing the referential meaning of the ADJ that has not been verbalized in the syntactic structure, i.e., "high" (see McNeill 1985 and Schegloff 1984 for iconic gestures and their temporal relation with their 'lexical affiliates'). At the end of *jiushi*, Yun moves

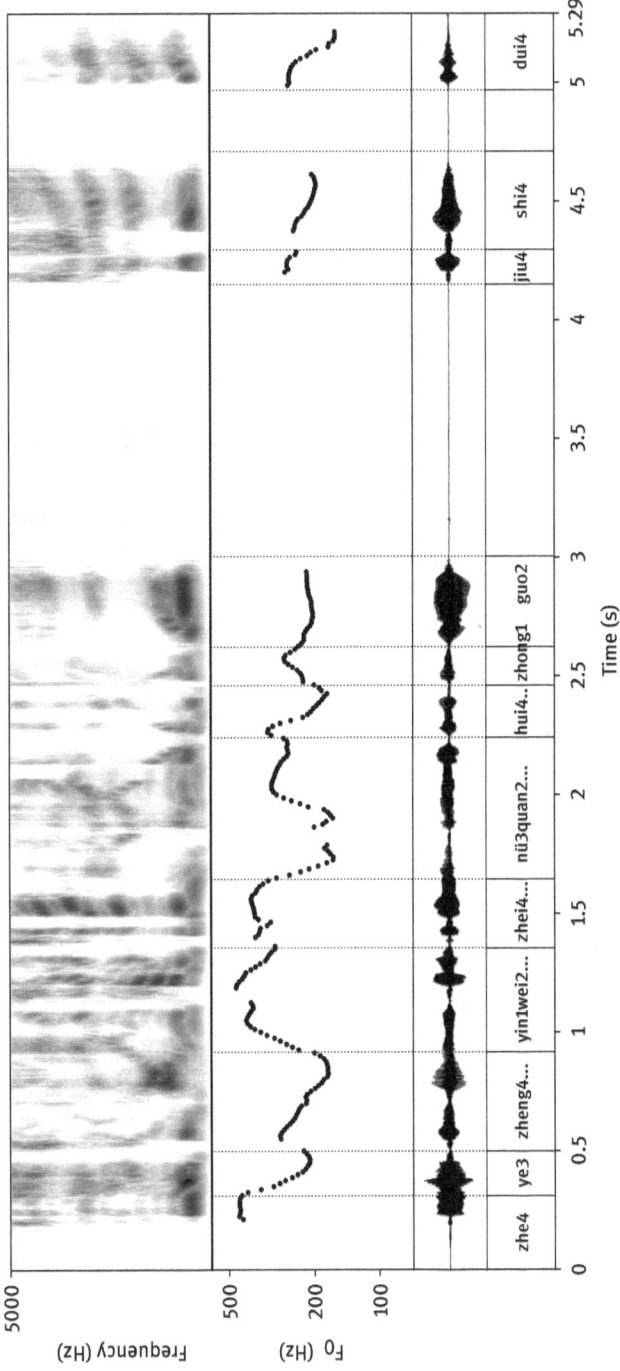

Figure 3: Pitch trace (dotted line), spectrogram and waveform of lines 22 to 24 in Excerpt (2).

her left hand back to home position on her lap (Figure 2). That Yun ends her turn upon the retraction of her gesture and Cai starts her next-turn response (line 24) immediately after Yun's gesture provides evidence that both interactants orient to the syntactically incomplete turn as interactionally complete.

It should be noted that the verbal and visual practices occur simultaneously. Yun's iconic gesture is produced simultaneously with her verbal pause filler *jiushi* (line 23), displaying the next item due, i.e., the final degree adjective, before its actual production. The iconic gesture preceding its speech affiliates (Schegloff 1984) and the concurrent speech disfluencies (i.e., the 'holding' pause and lexical pause filler) provide the co-participant an opportunity to not only recognize the possible turn completion, but also participate in the current activity by displaying her (dis)affiliation with Yun's assessment of feminism in Canada and in China. Cai's accented agreement token *dui* 'right' at line 24 indicates that she not only recognizes the possible completion of Yun's prior SIT, but also that she affiliates with Yun's stance. In this excerpt, Yun's gesture and talk mutually elaborate each other in the co-organization of the current action and activity.

The multimodal construction of a turn and co-organization of an action through both verbal and visual practices is also seen in Excerpt (3). In this interaction, Fen (female), Bai (female), and Lan (male) are doctoral students at the same program. Fen and Lan are second-year students, and Bai is in her first year. Fen and Lan are explaining to Bai about the different requirements and expectations of doctoral dissertations in China and abroad. Prior to this sequence, Fen and Lan expressed their stance that writing a doctoral dissertation in other countries is to demonstrate one's research ability, and thus it is not expected to be very innovative. Fen and Lan provide detailed accounts in support of their stance at lines 1–11.

(3) Requirements on doctoral dissertations

01 Fen: jiushishuo ta   haoxiang jiu kan ni zhege(.)zhengge yanjiu guocheng a;
           just.to.say 3SG seem just look your this.CL entire research process PRT
           'That is to say, they'll just look at your entire research process,'

02 Fen: sheji de shi bu shi yanjin na.
           design CSC be NEG be tight PRT
           '(to see) if it's tight.'

03 Bai: en.
           mm
           'Mm.'

04 Fen: nide yanjiu fangfa [shi bu shi HUI ya;]
           your research method [be NEG be understand PRT]
           'and if you understand the research method.'

05 Lan: [dui dui dui CHENGxuxing de ha.]
                               [right right right procedural ASSC PRT]
                               'right right right. In terms of research procedure,'

06 Lan: [nei ge dou hui.]
           that CL all can.
           'you can do all of it.'

07 Fen: [jiu xiang shi Yu] Yu Dilun jiu shuo jiu shi yi zhong training.
           [just like be (NAME)]   just say just be one CL training
           'It's just like what Yu Dilun's said; it's just a type of training.'

08 Fen: jiushi kan ni hui le   [jiu xing le;]
           just be see you understand PRT [just OK PRT]
           'It's OK as long as (they) see you know how to do research.'

09 Lan: [en en en.]
                               [mm mm mm]
                               'Mm, mm, mm.'

10 Lan: [ranhou bingqie]
           [then moreover]
           'Also,...'

Figure 4: Fen's (left) head position at *zhiyu* at line 11.

Figure 5: Fen's (left) head position at *zhege* at line 11.

```
                Head shake<--------- ---------->  <-- --><-- -->              <-- -->
11 → Fen:    [zhiyu  ni   zhege dongxi] benshen <<creaky>sha de>.
             [as.to your this.CL thing] -self  something like that
             'As for things like your research (finding) itself...'

12   Bai:    boshi lunwen ma
             doctoral dissertation Q
             '(For) doctoral dissertation?'

13   Lan:    !A!:(.)dui.=
             a right
             'Yeah Right.'

14   Fen:    =<<f>HAOjige> dou zheyang;
             great many.CL all like this
             'Many dissertations are like that.'

15   Fen:    guowai ZHEN shi zheyang de.
             abroad REALLY be like this PRT
             'It's really like this abroad.'
```

Here, Fen maintains that faculty in other countries are concerned about whether the research process and method are sound and tight in a doctoral dissertation (lines 1–2, and 4), and whether one knows how to do research. Fen then uses the conjunction *zhiyu* 'as for' (line 11) to switch the topic from the research method to research findings (B. Li 2012). As a topic-change marker, *zhiyu* 'as for' may contrast the subsequent topic with the preceding one in terms of their importance, and thus the *zhiyu*-prefaced topic is usually followed by negative markers diminishing its importance in contrast to the former (B. Li 2012:59). This conjunction *zhiyu* is employed by Fen as a resource to project the incipient negative comment on the importance of research findings in contrast to research method in a doctoral dissertation. This projected negation is also visually displayed through Fen's head shakes (Kendon 2002). Concurrent with *zhiyu* at line 11, Fen begins to shake her head four times with the first one of the largest amplitude (Figures 4 and 5). Here, the lexical device *zhiyu* and the concurrent head shakes are deployed as multimodal resources to build and interpret the action-in-progress, i.e., a contrasting negative stance on the importance of research findings in a dissertation.

However, in addition to building and recognizing the action performed, participants are still faced with the task of projecting and predicting the possible turn completion. The syntactic construction at line 11 is the topic component in a topic-comment structure (Li and Thompson 1981; Tao 1996), as indicated by the topic (change) marker *zhiyu* 'as for'. The construction *shade* 'things like that' is the colloquial form of *shenme de* (Lü 1985:127), which marks the end of a non-exhaustive list. After one list item *ni zhege dongxi benshen* 'your thing itself', *shade* is used to mark it as part of a non-exhaustive list as well as the completion of the list (Chao 1968; Lü 1985; Dong 1998). The prosodic features of *shade* also indicate non-holding and possible completion of the turn (X. Li 2014). The pitch register of the two syllables *shade* drops to the bottom of the speaker's pitch range after the preceding accented syllable *shen* (Figure 6), and *shade* is also produced with creaky voice. Drop in pitch register after accented syllables and creaky voice are prosodic features relevant to possible turn completion (X. Li 2014; Ogden 2001). As mentioned earlier, the comment in the topic-comment structure is projectable through Fen's verbal (lexical) and visual practices (head shakes). Bai's repair initiation at line 12 does not seem to involve an understanding problem of the verbally unproduced comment component in Fen's turn at line 11. Rather, Fen and Lan both treat it as Bai's doubt about Fen's previous statement about the low expectation on the research finding: Lan uses marked extra stress on her response *A* 'yeah' (line 13) and Fen uses emphatic adverbs *HAOjige* 'great number of', *dou* 'all' (line 14), and *ZHEN* 'really' (line 15) to emphasize her affiliation. with Bai's candidate response in their responses. That Bai launches her turn immediately after the completion of Fen's utterance at line 11 provides evidence that she orients to Fen's SIT as interactionally complete.

At line 11, the (incomplete) syntactic structure and head shake displaying Fen's stance towards the topic (i.e., research findings expected in a doctoral dissertation), and the completion-implicative prosody are deployed as resources to furnish Bai with an opportunity to display her understanding and (dis)affiliation with Fen's conveyed stance. Unlike Cai's affiliative response in Excerpt (2), Bai displays her doubts about Fen's prior statement by initiating a repair at line 12. Here, lexico-syntax, prosody, and visual behavior work together in the construction of Fen's turn and the organization of participation in the current activity.

In the preceding examples, the syntactic structure of the speaker's turn is incomplete, and the turn is constructed through both the (incomplete) verbal construction and visual behavior. The visual behavior seems to function as a replacement of the obligatory element (an assessment in Excerpt (2) and a Comment in Excerpt (3)) in the syntactic structure projected by the syntactic construction. However, the actions performed through the SITs are clearly completed through the use of multimodal resources, as is shown by the behavior of the participants themselves.

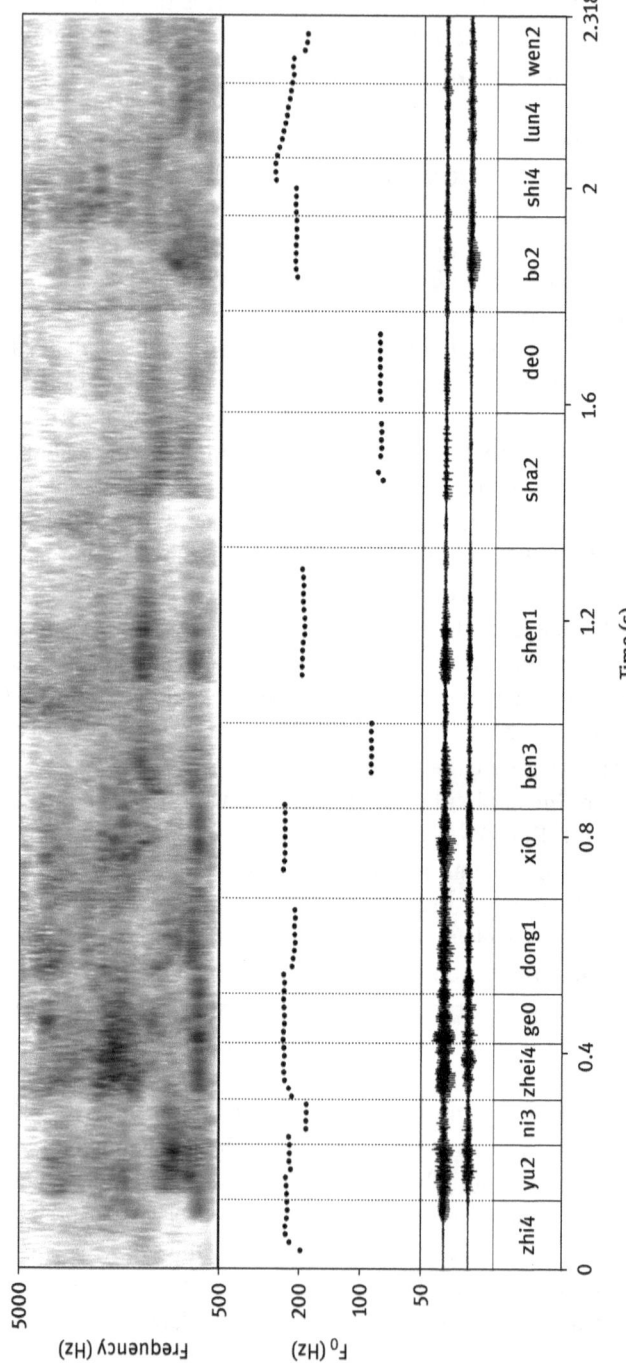

Figure 6: Pitch trace (dotted line), spectrogram and waveform of lines 11 to 12 in Excerpt (3).

In the previous two data excerpts, we can see that visual and verbal behaviors have different organization, which work together to construct turns and accomplish actions in a mutually elaborative manner. For example, iconic gesture and head shake can precede their 'speech affiliates', and therefore project the incipient turn elements before their possible verbalization. In this way, they function as early visible displays of the ensuing obligatory elements in the syntactic structure and the speaker's evaluative stance, and thereby allow and indeed invite the recipients to participate in the current activity before the verbal completion of the turn. That the recipients initiate their turns immediately after the completion of the gesture and head shakes (and before the projected syntactic completion of the turn) provides evidence that they orient to these visual behaviors as relevant to the possible completion of the turns and the action performed.

5 Multimodal resources in the projection of possible completion of SITs

The previous section has demonstrated one type of multimodal construction of SITs, in which a turn (and action) may be initiated by a syntactic construction and completed by visual behavior. This section explores another type of multimodal construction of SITs. In these cases, a turn is syntactically incomplete, but other multimodal resources such as prosody, visual behavior and its sequential position indicate its possible completion without standing in for an element in the projected syntactic structure. The sequential environment of this type of SIT and its multimodal construction are exemplified by Excerpts (4) and (5).

Excerpt (4) is taken from the same interaction as Excerpt (2). In this excerpt, Cai and Yun, two female graduate students, are discussing the preference for boys over girls by Canadian families. Prior to this excerpt, Cai has reported that about 58% Canadian families prefer boys over girls. She then comments that after her initial surprise, this percentage is actually not very high and rather "normal", considering the balance of 50/50 between boys and girls. The excerpt begins with Yun's elaborate accounts for her doubts about Cai's comment.

(4) Boy or girl

01 Yun: *danshi guanjian de   wenti   shi.*
          but   key ASSC question   be
          'But the key thing is,'

02 Yun: *shi baifenzhi wushiba de bili cezhong yu nansheng;*
           be percent fifty-eight ASSC percentage emphasize on boy
           '58% (of the people) prefer boys.'

03 Yun: *shengxia baifenzhi sishier de bili ta mei shuo ta pianxiang nansheng haishi nü.*
           rest percent forty-two ASSC percentage 3SG NO say 3SG bias towards boy or girl
           'It's not mentioned if the rest of the 42% (of the people) prefer boys or girls.'

04 Yun: *ruguo ni shi wushiba cezhong nansheng;*
           if you be fifty-eight emphasize boy
           'If 58% prefer boys,'

05 Yun: *sishier cezhong nüsheng;*
           forty-two prefer girl
           'and 42% prefer girls,'

06 Yun: *na zheige bili shi pingheng de.*
           that this.CL percentage be balanced NOM
           'then the percentage is balanced.'

07 Yun: *danshi shi(-) wushiba shi nansheng;*
           but be fifty-eight be boy
           'But 58% prefer boys,'

08 Yun: *sishier limian keneng baifenzhi ershi baifenzhi sanshi shi (.) neutral de guanxi.*
           forty-two in maybe percent twenty percent thirty be neutral ASSC relationship
           '(and) among the 42%, there may be 20–30% people who don't have a preference.'

09 Yun: *ranhou shengxia baifenzhi SHIji cai shi pianxiang nüsheng;*
           then rest percent more than ten just be prefer girl
           'so the people who prefer girls are only some ten percent.'

10   Yun: na:(-) bili jiu bu pingheng le.=
            that percentage just NEG balanced CRS
            'Then the percentage is not balanced.'

11   Yun: =ni yaoshi baifenzhi wushiba gen baifenzhi SHIer erSHI bi.
            you if percent fifty-eight with percent twelve twenty compare
            'If you compare 58% with 12% or 20%,

Head   < / >
Gesture |~~~~~~~~~****~~~~****-.-.|
12 → Yun: NA: zheige bili   bu jiu.
            that this.CL ratio NEG. just
            'then the percentage is just...'

13   Cai: ou::.
            ou
            'Ou.'

14   Cai: dan ta meiyou::.
            but 3SG NEG have
            'But it didn't,'

15   Cai: ta meiyou shuo houmian de neixie shi cezhong yu shenme de.
            3SG NEG have say after NOM those be prefer on what NOM
            'it didn't say what the rest prefer.'

Here, Yun expresses her doubts about Cai's comment that the number of 58% Canadian families preferring boys is not very high, because Yun thinks what the figure means is actually rather equivocal (lines 01–03). The syntactic structure of the last TCU in Yun's turn at line 12 is incomplete, but the two participants both orient to it as interactionally complete, as is evidenced by Yun's turn yielding and Cai's immediate turn initiation at the end of line 12.

The projection and recognition of possible turn completion at line 12 is accomplished through the working together of lexico-syntactic, prosodic, bodily-visual, and sequential features. Sequentially, line 12 is part of Yun's multi-TCU turn that accounts for her disaffiliation with Cai's stance. It is a partial repetition of the TCU at line 10. The repetition of the just-prior TCU at

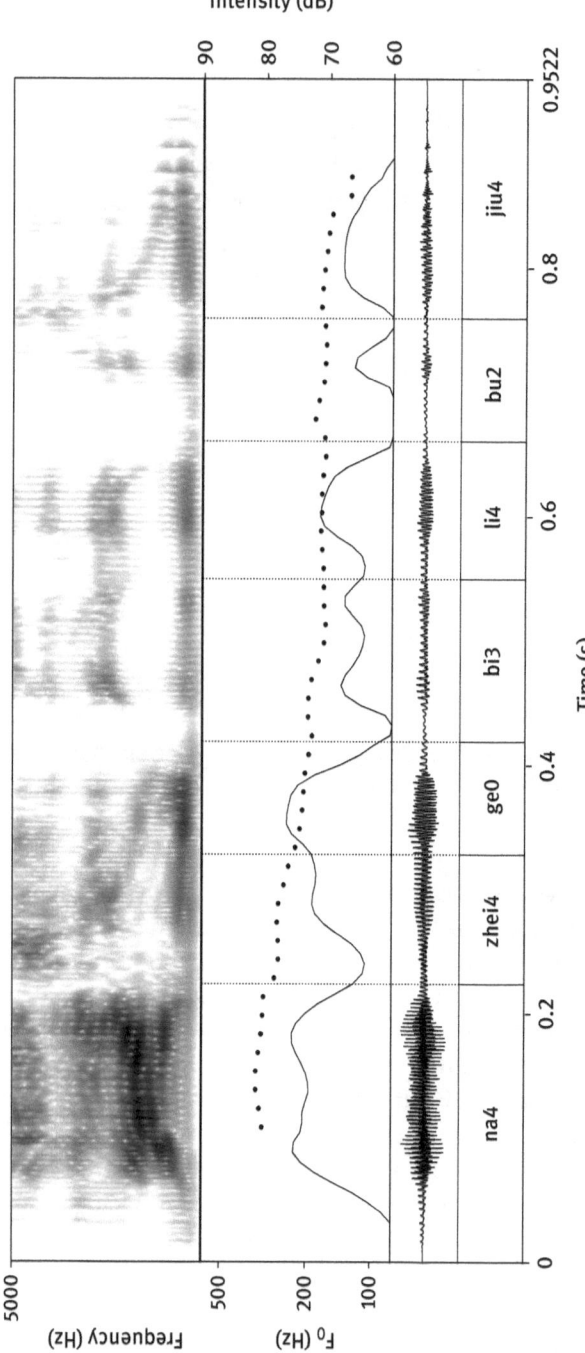

Figure 7: Pitch trace (dotted line), intensity (solid line), spectrogram and waveform of line 12 in Excerpt (4).

line 12 indicates that the speaker is not able or willing to expand the turn (Svennevig 2000: 190). It is designed to ostensively close the current multi-TCU turn which has not been concluded in the prior TCU at line 10: After presenting two opposite interpretations of the statistics (one being "balanced" (line 06), the other "unbalanced" (line 10)), Yun's extended turn comes to a possible completion at the end of line 10. However, Yun's TCU in line 10 is followed by a latched utterance at line 11; prosodically Yun uses continuous articulation, which indicates a rush-through (Schegloff 1982). By talking past a possible turn completion point, Yun contingently extends her turn and reiterates the ground for her opposing opinion (lines 11–12). By repeating most of line 10 immediately after the turn extension, and thereby "repositioning" a just-prior TCU, the syntactically incomplete utterance at line 12 seems to be a technique to end her extended turn here and now (Wong 2000). The syntactic incompleteness seems to be deployed as a practice to accomplish the task of ending her turn without being viewed as repeating herself and non-informative after the turn continuation.

Lexico-syntactically, lines 11 and 12 form a conditional clause *yaoshi...(bu) jiu...* 'if...then...' in Mandarin (Xing 2001). The adverb *bujiu* 'then just' (literally 'negator+just') (line 12) not only precedes a conclusion based on the previous conditional clause (Lü 1980), but also indicates the speaker's negative evaluative and/or affective stance (Shi 2003). Although the syntactic structure of the clause at line 12 is not complete, the conclusion after *bujiu* is obvious and projectable by the trajectory of the lexico-syntactic structure as well as the repetition of the TCU at line 10. The local prosodic and visual features at the end of line 12 indicate possible turn completion, despite its syntactic incompleteness.

Prosodically, at line 12, *na* 'that/then' is the possible last TRP-projecting accent (as is indicated by the long duration, high pitch register and loudness in Figure 8). *Bujiu* occurs after this accent and is produced with low pitch movement and decreased loudness. In particular, the syllable *jiu* is lengthened, produced with an open configuration of vocal tract (i.e., no glottal or supra-glottal closure) and creaky voice (Figure 7), which are the prosodic features relevant to possible turn completion (X. Li 2014; Walker 2004; Ogden 2001).

Yun's bodily-visual behaviors at the end of line 12 also signal possible turn completion and turn transition. Concurrent with the syllable *bu*, Yun starts to move her hands apart and turns her palm upwards. At *jiu*, Yun's hands are wide apart in front of her chest with the palm open and facing up (Figure 8). This type of Palm Up Open Hand (PUOH) gesture is documented as a visual display of possible turn completion, i.e., the speaker's "giving" or "offering" the turn to the recipient (Müller 2004; Streeck 2007, 2009). Concurrent with *jiu* and the PUOH

Figure 8: Yun's (right) gesture at *bujiu* at line 12.

gesture, Yun also tilts her head to the right (Figure 8).³ Head tilts are reported to display one's attention to something and/or affirmation (De Jorio 2000:97). The co-occurrence of the head tilt with *jiu*, the (possible) last syllable at line 12, together with the TRP-projecting PUOH gesture, can be argued to visually cue the recipient for uptake. That Cai starts her next-turn response (line 13) immediately upon the retraction of Yun's gesture and head tilt shows that she orients to Yun's bodily behaviors as relevant to possible turn completion.

The previous fine-grained multimodal analysis of line 12 shows that although Yun's turn is syntactically incomplete, it is designed to be, and is treated as, interactionally complete. The sequential position of the TCU, the lexical and prosodic features of *bujiu* at the end of line 12, and the concurrent gesture and head tilt work together as an ensemble to project the possible completion of the turn. Excerpt (4) shows that, unlike Excerpts (2) and (3), the gesture and head tilt in this excerpt do not function as elements in the projected syntactic structure, but rather serve (together with other multimodal practices) to manage turns at talk.

This use of visual behavior in turn organization is also observed in Excerpt (5). In this interaction, Hai (male) and Yin (female) are telling Qin (male) and Lei (male) about a kayaking trip that they took together. At the beginning of this excerpt, Hai describes the mountain and waterfalls where he and Yin did kayaking.

(5) (TO_HLQY_09_waterfall)

01 Hai: *ranhou neige shan;*
          then that.CL mountain
          'Then that mountain'

---

3 Head tilt refers to a movement in which the head leans right or left while the face remains oriented forward (McClave et al. 2007:355).

02 Hai: *yinwei ta neige;*
          because 3SG that.CL
          'because that...'

03 Hai: *pubu   dou hen   zhai;*
          waterfall all very narrow
          'The waterfalls were all very narrow.'

04 Hai: *jiu shi shanjIAN qishi shi.*
          just be creek   actually be
          '(They were) actually creeks.'

05 Yin: *dui.*
          right
          'Right.'

Figure 9: Hai's (right) body position at *podu* at line 06.

Figure 10: Hai's (right) body position at the end of line 06.

06→Hai: *ranhou(.)ranhou you youxie podu ranhou you yixie zheige;*
         then   then have a bit slope then have some this.CL
         'Then, (they) were a little bit steep, and a little bit...'

07 Qin: *=shanjian shi shenme yisi.*
          creek   be what   meaning
          'What does creek mean?'

At line 01, Hai halts his projected telling about the mountain where he and Yin went kayaking, and provides background information about the waterfalls in the mountain through the use of *yinwei* (line 02). One function of *yinwei* is reported to precede parenthetical sequences inserted in the middle of a TCU, introducing background information relevant to the ongoing turn (Li and Luo forthcoming). After Hai's inserted background information about the waterfalls (lines 03–04) and Yin's confirmation (line 05), the parenthetical sequence comes to a possible closure. At line 06, Hai deploys *ranhou* as a lexical device to return to the projected "host TCU" at line 01 (Lu 2009:42). The "pre-insert part of the host TCU" is the topic component (*neige shan* 'that mountain') and the "post-insert part of the host TCU" (*you xie podu* 'has some slope') is the comment component in the topic-comment structure (Li and Thompson 1981). After returning to and completing the host TCU, Hai's turn comes to a possible completion at *podu* 'slope' at line 06. However, he continues his articulation and talks past this possible turn completion point to the next TCU with no discernable break between them. The latched TCU *ranhou you yixie zheige* 'then has some this...' is also a partial repeat of the prior TCU *ranhou you yixie podu* 'then has some slope' (line 06).

The lexico-syntactic feature of the end of line 06 seems to diverge from its prosodic, visual, and pragmatic features in the projection of possible turn completion. In the partial repeat at line 06, the obligatory head noun is absent from the NP structure *yixie*+N ('some'+N). The final proximal demonstrative *zheige* 'this' is used as a discourse marker that can hold the turn while searching for the next word due (Liu 2009:93). The quantifier *yixie* in the NP and the demonstrative *zheige* strongly projects that the turn-so-far is incomplete and a noun is incipient. However, the prosodic and visual features indicate that the turn is possibly complete: the low pitch of *zheige*, the lengthening of *ge*, and the open configuration of vocal tract in the production of *ge*. In the middle of line 06, Hai leans forward towards the table and moves his hands up in front of his face depicting the slope of the mountain (Figure 9). At the end of line 06, Hai starts to move his hands back and leans back, with his hands and upper body both returning to home position at the syllable *ge* (Figure 10). The lean and retraction of hand to home position visually display Hai's orientation to his extended turn as possibly complete (X. Li 2013), providing evidence that despite its syntactic incompleteness, the turn is designed to be, and treated as, interactionally complete, as shown by Qin's turn initiation immediately after *zheige* at line 07.

Here, the partial repeat of the immediately prior TCU at line 06 shows that Hai is not contributing any new information to the progress of the turn. However, that he has just preemptively talked past a possible turn completion point at the end of the first TCU and extended his turn into this TCU projects turn continuation and signals that more talk on this matter is under way. At this particular sequentially immediate subsequent position, the syntactically incomplete repeat (i.e., with only the final projectable item absent) signals non-continuation of the talk, yet without being held accountable for repeating himself and expanding the turn with no new information. So the incomplete syntactic structure and the completion-implicative prosodic and visual features of the TCU seem to be designed as such by the speaker and are fitted into the sequential environment and interactional contingency that emerge in the temporally unfolding interaction.

The previous two excerpts have demonstrated a turn format where syntactically incomplete utterances may occur. If the speaker pre-emptively continues his/her turn through latching and rush-through[4] and repeats the just-prior TCU in the latched utterance, this utterance may be syntactically incomplete but prosodically, visually, and interactionally complete. The data show that the divergence of multimodal practices in the construction of these syntactically incomplete utterances is not random but is intricately designed for their sequential environments and the unique interactional tasks they accomplish.

6 Concluding discussions

Through the turn taking system, interactants manage transfer of speakership in conversation. However, turn transition is not pre-determined, but contingently and interactively organized. Although smooth turn transition usually takes places at the convergence of syntactic, intonational, and pragmatic completion (Ford and Thompson 1996), it may also occur when one or more resources diverge from others in turn projection. This study examines the divergence between syntax and other multimodal resources in the construction of turns in Mandarin conversation. In particular, this article focuses on how interactants deploy multimodal resources to manage the possible completion of SITs and turn transition. It has been shown that a variety of multimodal resources are available to interactants to indicate and recognize the possible completion of SITs. Further, verbal and visual resources seem to work together in the construction of SITs in two ways. A turn may be initiated by an incomplete syntactic structure, and completed by bodily-visual conduct. That is, the bodily-visual conduct visibly realizes the syntactic component that is "missing" from the syntactic structure. Alternatively, a turn may be constituted by an incomplete syntactic structure, and bodily-visual conduct may signal possible turn completion rather than serving any role in the incomplete syntactic structure. In the first type of interaction

---

4 See Zhang (2012) for a conceptual distinction between latching and rush-through in Mandarin conversation. In this study, they are both considered as practices for pre-emptive turn continuation.

between (incomplete) syntax and other multimodal resources, certain final elements of a syntactic structure (such as the gradient adjective in Excerpt 2 and the Comment component in Excerpt 3) may not be verbalized, but are produced visually. Here, the communicative meaning of a turn is fully produced through the working together of verbal and visual practices. Prosodic features such as glottal release or an open configuration of vocal tract (Excerpt 2) and creaky voice (Excerpt 3) usually signal possible turn completion at the end of the SITs. In the second type of multimodal construction of SITs, bodily-visual behavior may not embody the "missing" elements in a syntactic structure, but rather is primarily used to visibly indicate the possible completion of a SIT. A PUOH gesture, head tilt, or return of hands and leaning back to home position seem to project possible turn completion in SITs. Similar completion-implicative prosodic features of final lengthening, open configuration of vocal tract, and creaky voice are also observed in these SITs (Excerpts 4 and 5). The sequential position of a syntactic incomplete TCUs as a (partial) repetition of and subsequent to just-prior TCUs in the same turn also serves as a resource to project and predict possible turn completion. Here, the type of interactional work done by the bodily-visual conduct differs from that in the first type in that it *indicates* the possible completion of a turn rather than *completing* it.

Although the aforementioned multimodal resources work together as an ensemble to build turns and actions, each modality as a semiotic system has its own organization. For example, syntax and body movement[5] both create recognizable trajectories. Syntactic schemas in a language can foreshadow the type of items that may be due next and in the near future (Auer 2005, 2009). Body movement has a recognizable excursion: departing from a position of relaxation or 'home position' and often returning to the same 'rest position' or 'home position' (Kendon 2004:111). This formal organization of body movement is called a 'preparation-stroke-retraction' gesture unit by Kendon (2004) and 'home-away-home' by Sacks and Schegloff (2002[1975]). This feature of projectability of syntax and body movement means that interactants can use the recognizable trajectories of syntax and body movement to project and predict where a turn is heading and its possible completion. However, the two modalities work in different ways. When

---

[5] The body movements that involve change of space and/or orientation of (parts of) the body such as hand movement, torso movement, head movement etc., arguably all have recognizable trajectories, i.e., they return to where they depart (Kendon 2004; Sacks & Schegloff 2002 [1975]). Gaze seems to be an exception, because when not accompanied by head movement, gaze shift does not seem to involve noticeable change of position and/or orientation of the body; that is, there does seem to be a position of relaxation in gaze shift and thus there is no 'home position' for gaze to return to (Rossano 2012).

the syntactic structure of a turn is incomplete, the returning home of gesticulation and torso movement (e.g., in Excerpt 5) may serve as a visible cue signaling its possible turn completion.

Finally, the projection and recognition of the possible completion of an SIT and any turn in general is closely related to its sequential position and the action it accomplishes. For example, the placement of a syntactically incomplete TCU as a (partial) repeat immediately after a transition-relevant just-prior TCU seems to halt and conclude the turn. The completion of the SIT is projectable and understandable with reference to this particular placement of the syntactically incomplete TCU relative to its preceding TCU and the interactional work it accomplishes.

This study has investigated the complex work being done in and through the multimodal resources of syntax, prosody, bodily-visual behavior, and sequential position in the construction of SITs in Mandarin conversation. As our knowledge of turn construction in Mandarin and particularly multimodal turn construction in Mandarin is still in its early stages, it is hoped that this study will prompt more research on multimodal analysis of Mandarin interaction in the near future.

Appendix

Transcription conventions

The transcription system used for vocal elements in this chapter is GAT 2 (Selting et al., 2009). The following is an abbreviated version adapted from Selting et al. (2009) with a few small modifications.

[ ]	overlap
=	latching
(.)	micro-pause
(-), (--), (---)	short, middle or long pauses of ca. 0.2–0.8 seconds, up to ca. 1 second
(1.0)	pauses of 1.0 second
hehehe	short and syllable-like laughter
((laughing))	description of laughter
:, : :,:::	lengthening of ca. 0.2–0.8 seconds, up to ca. 1 second
ʔ	glottal stop
((cough))	paralinguistic and non-linguistic actions
(XX)	presumed wording

(( ))	omission of text
<<creaky>XX>	creaky voice
→	specific line in the transcript which is referred to in the text
?	final pitch movements: high rise
,	final pitch movements: mid-rise
-	final pitch movements: level pitch
;	final pitch movements: mid-fall
.	final pitch movements: low fall

For a TCU separated in two lines, the final pitch movement is not notated at the end of the first line.

ACcent	primary, or main accent
!AC!cent	extra strong accent
<<p> >	piano, soft

The transcription system used for body movements in this chapter can be found below. The transcription system used for gaze and gesture can also be found in Goodwin (1981), Heath (1986) and Kendon (2004).

~	preparation of gesticulation
*	stroke of gesticulation
*	holding of stroke
*	superimposed beat
-.	recovery of gesticulation
|	boundary of gesture unit
<----->	head shake
< / >	rightward head tilt
......	a series of dots represent movement
------	close dashes indicate the holding of the body movements
away	gaze away
at	gaze at

Glossing conventions

3SG	third person singular
ASP	aspectual marker
ASSC	associative (de)
CL	classifier
CRS	currently relevant state (le)
CSC	complex stative construction (de)

DUR	durative aspect (zhe, zai)
INT	interjections in speech
NEG	negatives (bu)
NOM	nominalizer
PASS	a passive marker (bei, gei)
PFV	perfective aspect (le)
POSS	possessive (de)
PROG	progressive (zai)
PRT	particle
Q	question marker (ma)

References

Auer, Peter. 2005. Projection in interaction and projection in grammar. *Text* 25(1). 7–36.
Auer, Peter. 2009. On-line syntax: Thoughts on the temporality of spoken language. *Language Sciences* 31(1). 1–13.
Chao, Yuen-Ren. 1968. *A grammar of spoken Chinese*. Berkeley: University of California Press.
Chevalier, Fabienne and Rebecca Clift. 2008. Unfinished Turns in French Conversation: Projectability, Syntax and Action. *Journal of Pragmatics* 40(10). 1731–52.
De Jorio, Andrea. Adam Kendon (transl. and eds.). 2000. *Gesture in Naples and gesture in classical antiquity*. Bloomington: Indiana University Press.
Dong, Xiaomin. 1998. Shuo X shenmede. [On "X shenme de" construction]. *Hanyu xuexi [Chinese Language Learning]* 105. 13–15.
Duncan, Starkey Jr. 1972. Some signals and rules for talking speaking turns in conversation. *Journal of Personality and Social Psychology* 23(2). 283–292.
Duncan, Starkey Jr. 1974. On the structure of speaker-auditor interaction during speaking turns. *Language in Society* 3(2).161–180.
Duncan, Starkey Jr. & Donald W. Fiske. 1977. *Face-to-face interaction: research, methods, and theory*. New York: Wiley.
Duncan, Starkey Jr. & George Niederehe. 1974. On signalling that it's your turn to speak. *Journal of Experimental Social Psychology* 10.234–247.
Fang, Mei. 2000. Ziran kouyuzhong ruohua lianci de huayupiaoji gongneng [Reduced conjunctions as discourse markers]. *Zhongguo Yuwen* 2000(5). 459–70.
Ford, Cecilia E., Fox, Barbara A. & Sandra A. Thompson. 1996. Practices in the construction of turns: The 'TCU' revisited. *Pragmatics* 6. 427–454.
Ford, Cecilia E. & Sandra A. Thompson. 1996. Interactional units in conversation: Syntactic, intonational, and pragmatic resources for the projection of turn completion. In Ochs, Elinor, Emanuel A. Schegloff, E. A. & Sandra A. Thompson. (eds.), *Grammar and interaction*, 134–184. Cambridge: Cambridge University Press.
Ford, Cecelia, Sandra A. Thompson & Veronika Drake. 2012. Bodily-visual practices and turn continuation." *Discourse Processes* 49(3–4). 192–212.
Frischen A, Bayliss AP, Tipper SP. Gaze cueing of attention: visual attention, social cognition, and individual differences. Psychol Bull 2007;133:694–724.

Goodwin, Charles. 1981. *Conversational organization: interaction between speakers and hearers*. New York, NY.: Academic Press.

Goodwin, Charles. 2003. Pointing as situated practice. In Satori Kita (ed.), *Pointing: Where Language, Culture, and Cognition Meet*, 217–242. Mahwah, NJ: Lawrence Erlbaum.

Heath, Christian C. 1986. *Body movement and speech in medical interaction*. Cambridge: Cambridge University Press.

Heath, Christian & Paul Luff. 2013. Embodied action and organisational interaction: Establishing contract on the strike of a hammer. *Journal of Pragmatics* 46(1). 24–38.

Keevallik, Leelo. 2010. Bodily quoting in dance correction. *Research on Language and Social Interaction* 43(4). 1–26.

Keevallik, Leelo. 2013. The interdependence of bodily demonstrations and clausal syntax. *Research on Language and Social Interaction* 46 (1). 1–21.

Kendon, Adam. 2002. Some uses of the head shake. *Gesture* 2 (2). 147–182.

Kendon, Adam. 2004. *Gesture: Visible action as utterance*. Cambridge: Cambridge University Press.

Kita, Sotaro. Interplay of Gaze, Hand,Torso Orientation, and Languagein PointingSotaro Kita APA (American Psychological Assoc.) Kita, S. (2003). Pointing: Where Language, Culture, and Cognition Meet. Mahwah, N.J.: Psychology Press. MLA (Modern Language Assoc.) Kita, Sotaro. Pointing: Where Language, Culture, and Cognition Meet. Psychology Press, 2003. EBSCOhost.

Koshik, Irene. 2002. Designedly incomplete utterances: A pedagogical practice for eliciting knowledge displays in error correction sequences. *Research on Language and Social Interaction* 35. 277–309.

Lerner, Gene H. 1995. Turn design and the organization of participation in instructional activities. *Discourse Processes* 19. 111–131.

Li, Bingzhen. 2012. zhiyu de huayu gongneng [The Discourse Function of "Zhiyu"]. *Hanyu Xuexi [Chinese Language Learning]*. 2012(5). 53–61.

Li, Charles & Sandra A. Thompson. 1981. *Mandarin Chinese: A functional reference grammar*. Berkeley: University of California Press.

Li, Xiaoting. 2013. Language and the body in the construction of units in Mandarin face-to-face interaction. In Szczepek Reed, Beatrice & Geoffrey Raymond (eds.), *Units of Talk – Units of Action*, 343–375. Amsterdam: Benjamins.

Li, Xiaoting. 2014. *Multimodality, interaction and turn-taking in Mandarin conversation*. Amsterdam: Benjamins.

Li, Xiaoting & Jie Luo. Forthcoming. Interactional-discourse functions of *yinwei* in Mandarin conversation. In Yun Xiao, Linda Tsung & Zhuo Jing-Schmidt (eds.), *Current Studies in Chinese Language and Discourse*. Amsterdam: Benjamins.

Liu, Liyan. 2009. Zuowei huayu biaoji de "zheige" he "neige" [On "this" and "that" as discourse markers]. *Yuyan Jiaoxue yu yanjiu [Language Teaching and Research]* 2009(1). 89–96.

Local, John & John Kelly. 1986. Projection and 'silences': Notes on phonetic and conversational structure. *Human Studies* 9.185–204.

Local, John, John Kelly & Bill Wells. 1986. Towards a phonology of conversation: Turn-taking in Tyneside English. *Journal of Pragmatics* 22(2). 411–437.

Local, John, Bill Wells & Mark Sebba. 1985. Phonology for conversation: Phonetic aspects of turn-delimitation in London Jamaican. *Journal of Pragmatics* 9. 309–330.

Lu, Ping. 2009. "Ranhou" yuyong tanxi. [A pragmatic analysis of "ranhou"]. *Xiandai yuwen [Modern Chinese]* 2009(7). 40–42.

Lü, Shuxiang. 1985. *Jindai hanyu zhidaici. [Modern Chinese demonstrative pronouns]*. Shanghai: Xuelin Chubanshe.
Lü, Shuxiang. 1980. *Xiandai Hanyu babai ci [Eight hundred words of modern Chinese]*. Beijing: Shangwu Yinshuguan.
McClave, Evelyn Z., Helen Kim, Rita Tamer & Milo Mileff. 2007. Head movements in the context of speech in Arabic, Bulgarian, Korean, and African-American Vernacular English. *Gesture* 7(3). 343–390.
McNeill, David. 1985. So you think gestures are nonverbal? *Psychological Review* 92(3).350–371.
Mondada, Lorenza. 2007. Multimodal resources for turn-taking: Pointing and the emergence of possible next speakers. *Discourse Studies* 9(2). 194–225.
Müller, Cornelia. 2004. Forms and uses of the palm-up open hand: A case of a gesture family? In Müller, Cornelia. & Roland Posner (eds.), *The semantics and pragmatics of everyday gestures*, 234–256. Berlin: Weidler.
Ogden, Richard. 2001. Turn-holding, turn-yielding and laryngeal activity in Finnish talk-in-interaction. *Journal of the International Phonetics Association* 31. 139–152.
Ogden, Richard. 2004. Non-modal voice quality and turn-taking in Finnish. In Couper-Kuhlen, Elizabeth & Cecilia E. Ford (eds.), *Sound patterns in interaction*, 29–62. Amsterdam/ Philadelphia: John Benjamins.
Olsher, David. 2004. Talk and gesture: The embodied completion of sequential actions in spoken interaction. In Gardner, Rod & Johannes Wagner (eds.), *Second Language Conversations*, 221– 45. London: Continuum.
Rossano, Federico. 2012. Gaze in social interaction. In Sidnell, Jack & Tanya Stivers (eds.), *Handbook of conversation analysis*, 308–329. Malden, MA: Wiley-Blackwell.
Sacks, Harvey & Emanuel A. Schegloff. 2002 [1975]. Home position. *Gesture* 2(2). 133–146.
Sacks, Harvey, Emanuel A. Schegloff & Gail Jefferson. 1974. A simplest systematics for the organization of turn-taking for conversation. *Language* 50.696–735.
Schegloff, Emanuel A. 1982. Discourse as an interactional achievement: Some uses of 'uh huh' and other things that come between sentences. In Tannen, Deborah. (ed.), *Analyzing discourse: Text and talk*. Georgetown University Round Table on Languages and Linguistics, 71–93. Washington, DC: Georgetown University Press.
Schegloff, Emanuel A. 1984. On some gestures' relation to talk. In Atkinson, J. M Maxwell & John Heritage (eds.), *Structures of social action: studies in conversation analysis*, 266–296. Cambridge: Cambridge University Press.
Schegloff, Emanuel A. 1996. Turn organization: One intersection of grammar and interaction. In Ochs, Elinor, Emanuel A. Schegloff, E. A. & Sandra A. Thompson. (eds.), *Grammar and interaction*, 52–133. Cambridge: Cambridge University Press.
Schegloff, Emanuel A. 1998. Reflections on studying prosody in talk-in-interaction. *Language and Speech* 4. 235–263.
Selting, Margret. 1996. On the interplay of syntax and prosody in the constitution of turn-constructional units and turns in conversation. *Pragmatics* 6.357–388.
Selting, Margret. 2000. The construction of units in conversational talk. *Language in Society* 29. 477–517.
Selting, Margret, Peter Auer, Dagmar Barth-Weingarten, Jörg Bergmann, Pia Bergmann, Karin Birkner, Elizabeth Couper-Kuhlen, Arnulf Deppermann, Peter Gilles, Susanne Günthner, Martin Hartung, Friederike Kern, Christine Mertzlufft, Christian Meyer, Miriam Morek, Frank Oberzaucher, Jörg Peters, Uta Quasthoff, Wilfried Schütte, Anja Stukenbrock,

Susanne Uhmann1. 2009. "Gesprächsanalytisches Transkriptionssystem 2 (GAT 2) ". Gesprächsforschung-Online- Zeitschrift zur verbalen Interaktion 10. 353–402.

Shi, Jinsheng. 2003. Yuqi fuci de fanwei, leibie he gongxian shunxu [On the scope, types, and order of sequential use of modal adverbs]. *Zhongguo yuwen* 292. 17–31.

Slama-Cazacu, Tatiana. 1976. Nonverbal components in message sequence: Mixed syntax. In W. McCormack, William C. & Stephen A. Wurm (eds.), *Language and man: Anthropological issues*, 217–227. The Hague: Mouton.

Stivers, Tanya & Jack Sidnell. 2005. Introduction: Multimodal interaction. *Semiotica* 156(1/4).1–20.

Streeck, Jürgen. 2009. *Gesturecraft: The manu-facture of meaning*. Amsterdam: Benjamins.

Svennevig, Jan. 2000. *Getting acquainted in conversation*. Amsterdam: Benjamins.

Tanaka, Hiroko. 1999. *Turn-taking in Japanese conversation: A study in grammar and interaction*. Amsterdam: Benjamins.

Walker, Gareth. 2004. *The phonetic design of turn endings, beginnings, and continuations in conversation*. Unpublished PhD Dissertation, University of York.

Williams, Robert F. 2008. Gesture as a conceptual mapping tool. In Alan Cienki & Cornelia Müller (eds.), *Metaphor and Gesture*, 55–92. Amsterdam: Benjamins.

Wong, Jean. 2000. Repetition in conversation: A look at "first and second sayings". *Research on Language and Social Interaction* 33(4). 407–424.

Xing, Fuyi. 2001. *Hanyu fuju yanjiu [A study of Chinese complex sentences]*. Beijing: Commercial Publishing House.

Zhang, Wei. 2012. Latching/rush-through as a turn-holding device and its functions in retrospectively oriented pre-emptive turn continuation: Findings from Mandarin conversation. *Discourse Processes* 49(3–4). 163–191.

Zhang, Wei & Gao Hua. 2012. Ziran huihua zhong "jiushi" de huayu gongneng yu yufahua yanjiu [Functions of "Jiushi" in Everyday Conversation and Its Grammaticalization.]. *Yuyan jiaoxue yu yanjiu [Language Teaching and Research]* 2012(1).91–98.

Zima, Elisabeth. 2017. Multimodal constructional resemblance: The case of English circular motion constructions. In Francisco José Ruiz de Mendoza Ibáñez, Alba Luzondo Oyón & Paula Pérez Sobrino (eds). *Constructing families of constructions: Analytical perspectives and theoretical challenges*, 301–337. Amsterdam: John Benjamins.

Ni-Eng Lim
On co-operative modalities in the formulation of Mandarin Chinese turn-continuations

1 Introduction

There is now clear recognition that natural face-to-face interaction is essentially multimodal. Starting from the mid-1970s, the Goodwins (C. Goodwin 1979, 1980, 1981, 2003, 2007; M.H. Goodwin 1980) have consistently shown how gaze, as well as the rich semiotic structures of our material environment,[1] are vital for participation in social interaction. Streeck's work on gestures (1992, 1993, 1994, 2009) also brings into focus how gestures within embodied interaction are regularly coordinated as legitimate communicative devices in tandem with gaze and utterances, and can make projections of talk and action. In the professional workplace, Heath (1986), Heath and Luff (1992), Heath et al. (2002) and Mondada (2006, 2007, 2011) demonstrate how publicly available cultural objects (such as computers and maps) and embodied practices are finely coordinated to build interactional actions and achieve intersubjectivity in collaborative activities (Forceville & Urios-Aparisi 2009; Nuñez, Edwards & Matos 1999; Hidalgo-Downing & Mujic 2013).

But even in a singular modality, it can be seen that there exist multiple channels within that modality that can function as discrete semiotic resources. For instance, the visuospatial modality can be said to include channels such as gestures, facial expressions and body postures (Cienki 1998; Cienki & Müller 2008; Kappelhoff and Müller 2011, McNeill 2013; Hassemer & Winter 2016). Stiver and

---

[1] By semiotic structure of our material environment, we refer to how our physical context, and the material things that exist within this environment, provides the necessary resources for speakers to utilize when structuring their talk. For instance, when issuing a command to "Go there!", the speaker may point at a particular direction. For adequate understanding of such a vocal command, a participant in the conversation may have to look at the speaker's gaze to establish himself as the proper recipient, use the pointing finger as a deictic tool, as well as locate an actual and viable physical destination in the general direction of the point. But the environment also includes the non-physical, such as what has been said before (c.f. sequential organization) or our socio-cultural understanding of situations, which are also integral to understanding others' talk as well as formulating our own turns-at-talk. In this sense then, what is available in our environment provides as well as restricts how we may be able to structure our talk. C. Goodwin (personal communication) likens this to be like a web of semiotic resources that speakers pluck from the immediate and situated environment to build actions.

Ni-Eng Lim, Nanyang Technological University

https://doi.org/10.1515/9783110462395-009

Sidnell (2005) have also referred lexico-syntax and prosody as two channels in the vocal modality, each of which can perform distinct communicative functions. But others have simply referred to these channels as modalities themselves, such as Selting (2013) who take syntax, prosody and bodily-visual conducts to be part of the verbal, vocal and visual modalities, or Ford, Thompson, and Drake (2012) referring to any sort of bodily-visual behaviors as modalities. Here, we take multimodality broadly and simply to mean the various forms or ways in which information is encoded, and how action is formed through multiple semiotic resources, hence viewing these semiotic resources as modalities in and of themselves.

An important observation in face-to-face interaction is that various modalities are observed to be working in a highly integrated manner. Take for instance, the classic conversation analytic (CA) issue of how interactants are able to precisely time the start of their talk immediately after the end of the last turn. Various studies have all pointed out that *syntax*, *prosody*, *pragmatics* and *bodily-visual behaviors* work together to cue recipient of possible completion point of a turn, such that a next speaker can begin his/her turn with minimal gap (Sack, Schegloff, and Jefferson 1974; Oreström 1983; Wilson and Zimmerman 1986; Local and Kelly 1986; Ford, Fox, and Thompson 1996; Schegloff 1996; Ford and Thompson 1996; Fox 2001; Hayashi 2005; Mori and Hayashi 2006; Local and Walker 2012; Keevallik 2013; Li 2014). However, as noted by Stivers and Sidnell (2005) in their introduction to a special volume on multimodal interaction, *"relatively little is understood about how these two channels* (prosodic and lexico-syntactic) *work together"* (Stivers and Sidnell 2005: 4), and that *"(i)f we are to move towards a theory of social interaction, we will need to understand not only how the vocal modality works but how the different channels and modalities work together as well as the mechanics that underlie such co-operation"* (Stivers and Sidnell 2005: 15). This paper represents an effort towards furthering such an understanding by looking at a less explored sort of turn construction practice, that of extending a unit of talk within the turn after it has been marked as possibly complete by the speaker (or termed *turn-continuations*), and how different modalities may work cooperatively to such "continuations".

In this report, I turn towards Mandarin Chinese (henceforth Chinese) interaction, and argue that such Chinese turn-continuations are also essentially multimodal (see also Ford, Thompson, and Drake 2012), but more importantly, how such interplay of modalities are organized in a structured and cooperative manner. Specifically, the crafting of further talk as "continuations", as opposed to simply being a new turn-constructional unit (TCU), requires a complex (re)configuration between the syntax of Chinese grammar and its prosodic delivery. This is most persuasively demonstrated via two contrasting features of Chinese turn-continuations: (1) the interplay between syntactically discontinuous constituents after possible completion, and the combination of prosodic cues (i.e. rush-throughs, lack of pitch reset, and declining intonation contour) that nonetheless marks it as "continuing"; and (2) the proliferation of syntactically continuous constituents as turn-continuation in cases where further talk comes after clear prosodic disjunction (such as a gap of silence, or after talk-by-others).

2 Cross-linguistic construction of turn-continuations

What exactly are turn-continuations? And how are they recognized by interlocutors of a particular language? In a nutshell, turn-continuations are units of talk that speakers "append" after the possible completion point of a TCU, that is not a new TCU in itself, but analyzably part of, and modifies, the just preceding utterance in some way. In their seminal paper on turn-taking, Sacks, Schegloff, and Jefferson (1974) establish that turns are incrementally built out of successions of TCUs, where "each TCU is recognizable as a coherent and self-contained utterance, recognizable in context as being 'possibly complete'" (Clayman 2013: 51)[2]. By this, it means that a turn of talk may end after just a single TCU, or the speaker may build the turn using multiple TCUs. Regardless, the end of each TCU represents an opportunity for a next speaker to begin his/her turn, or when there is a lack of uptake, for the current speaker to issue another TCU. Thus the end of a TCU is also termed a transition-relevance place (henceforth TRP), where a change of turn becomes relevant. However, besides a next speaker beginning a new turn or the current speaker starting a new TCU, another possibility at TRP is the current speaker (or other co-participants) *fashions further talk as continuing from the preceding TCU* (i.e. turn-continuation).

In English, these "further talk" have been found to be most frequently administered by added units that syntactically "continues" the prior talk (Couper-Kuhlen and Ono 2007), thus the term *increments* first posited by Schegloff (2016) to

---

[2] Though Sacks, Schegloff, and Jefferson (1974) (henceforth SSJ) has indicated that unit types (i.e. TCUs) in English "include sentential, clausal, phrasal, and lexical constructions (SSJ 1974: 702)", this does not mean that TCUs are unilaterally defined through syntax as sentences, clauses, phrases and lexical items. This is because a core purpose of identifying turn-constructional units (TCUs) is to locate spaces within an utterance where a turn may have ended and a next speaker can come in. While syntactic completion (thereby making the unit seem coherent and self-contained) is one core indicator of such completion, SSJ also emphasize the importance of 'sound production (i.e. phonology, intonation etc.)' (SSJ 1974: 721) to how recipients monitor for possible completion, thereby making the operational definition of TCU more holistic.

describe one type of *post-possible completion* that constitute extensions to a TCU.³ Take for instance, Bee's account of her grandmother's medical condition in a telephone conversation where she produces not once, but twice, continuations after points of possible completion (Schegloff 2016: 240).

(1) Bee: Becuz they're gonna do the operation on the teeuh duct.
    f[fi: rs]t. Before they c'n do t[he cata] ract]s.
    Ava: [Mm-hm,]   [Right.] Yeah,]

A point of possible completion is projected right after "teeuh duct", given that the turn-so-far is prosodically, grammatically and pragmatically complete. Such completion is also evidenced by the next speaker, having parsed the turn-in-progress, decidedly starts to talk after "teeuh duct" (indicated by the overlap brackets in "*f[fi:rs]t*"), and thereby overlapping with Bee's further talk. Our interest, however, is the manner in which Bee produces further talk after TCU's possible completion and at TRP. Here Bee twice produces further talk by adding "first" and then "before they can do the cataracts" which are analyzably continuations of the preceding TCU-so-far (also known as the *host-TCU*), and in effect, re-completes the TCU in progress. Here, the label *turn-continuations* will be adopted in place of *increments* to generically reference all types of "continuations".

There are a variety of reasons why speakers produce "continuations". One recurrent formulation is that turn-continuations are often deployed to pursue lack of recipient's uptake (Heath 1984; Pomerantz 1984; Ford, Fox, and Thompson 2002). Schegloff (2016) demonstrates that other possibilities include intensifying an action, or termed *up-ing the ante* (Schegloff 2016: 243), backing down, projecting a telling, or even to convert inter-turn (or TCU) gap into intra-turn pause to eliminate possible negative resonances (Schegloff 2016: 244). How turn-continuations are formulated can be linked to its interactive function. As Schegloff (2016) suggested, the positioning of turn-continuation within transition space (i.e. TRP), whether in the "next beat", "post gap" or even "post-other-talk", is consequential in terms of what the turn-continuation is doing interactionally. However, the delivery of Chinese turn-continuations via multiple semiotic resources is the focus here, and a detailed explication of what they may be doing within interactional talk is beyond the scope of this paper.

---

3 Schegloff (1996: 90) acknowledges another type of post-possible completion that "do not represent extensions of the prior talk, but rather retrospective or retroactive alignments towards it", termed '*post-completion stance markers*'. However, how these two types defer from each other (or if they defer at all) is debatable.

What is exemplified in Bee's successive turn-continuations shown in (1), is that syntactic continuity may be the modality that English speakers frequently, and perhaps most naturally, draw upon to denote turn-continuations. However, it has been found that there is a range of other linguistic (and non-linguistic) resources (i.e. different modalities) with which different languages can choreograph further talk in contrastive ways, yet similarly conveying a sense of "continuation" from a host-TCU (Couper-Kuhlen and Ono 2007; Luke and Zhang 2007; Ford, Thompson, and Drake 2012). Cross-linguistic typological analysis has shown that different forms of turn-continuations do exist in other languages, and that the recognition of turn-continuations should be language-dependent, as "different languages provide different lexical, grammatical and prosodic resources for continuing turns at talk" (Vorreiter 2003: 4). That is to say, the narrow definition of *"increments"* (i.e. syntactically continuous segments after possible completion) is the result of an English language bias (Vorreiter 2003; Auer 2007; Couper-Kuhlen and Ono 2007). After comparing English, German and Japanese conversational data, Couper-Kuhlen and Ono (2007) proposes a schema for distinguishing different forms of turn-continuations[4] based on their syntactic, semantic and prosodic "relatedness" to the possibly complete prior talk. Although there is a body of literature on turn-continuations in Chinese, these studies by Chinese researchers (Lu 1980, Zhang 2001, Liang 2005, Zhou 2010) have almost exclusively been syntactically framed as "post-positioned elements" in the sentence (易位句 *yiwei ju*), and focuses on their information structure or phonological features. Valuable exceptions are Luke (2000, 2005) that takes talk-in-interaction as the starting point. Luke and Zhang (2007), using Chinese conversational data, also outline a schema where four interlocking strands may be used to identify *"increments"*, namely: syntactic continuity vs. discontinuity, main vs. subordinate intonation, retrospective vs. prospective orientation, and information focus vs. non-focus. A natural extension of this understanding is that practices of turn-continuation is language-specific, and the types of modalities employed to do "continuation" would "have to take into account, not only prosody and semantics, but also action structure and pragmatics at large" (Auer 2007: 657). It is argued that syntactic continuity as a resource to denote turn-continuations is relatively limited in Chinese due to its default syntactic order, where various forms of adverbials and modifiers can only grammatically appear **before** the head verb, adjective or nominal constituent. As such, it is unsurprising that the majority of Chinese turn-continuations are not necessarily syntactically fitted materials. How then do Chinese speakers formulate and recognize additional

---

4 In their paper, turn-continuations refers to the broad range of units of "further talk" that could occur after possible completion of a TCU, even including new TCUs.

talk at TRP, such that co-participants to the conversation understand them to be "continuations", or be a part of, what has previously been a possibly complete TCU?

In the following sections, while I will be showing examples of Chinese turn-continuations. It is not the intention of this report to provide a typology or categorical list of how turn-continuations may be done,[5] instead the aim is to illustrate how different modalities may be enlisted to index continuation in a structured, organized and co-operative manner.

3 Data

The data exemplified in this paper comes from both audio and video recordings of unscripted conversational Mandarin Chinese. Approximately 8 hours of video recordings, consisting of 15 sessions of two- or three-party face-to-face conversations, were collected from two sources. The first source of data consists of 11 video recordings of two-party face-to-face conversation in a recording studio. The participants were mostly Mainland Chinese graduate students, from various regions of China, all studying at a university in Hong Kong. Regardless of their diverse regional background, all the participants are native speakers of Mandarin Chinese. With only an instruction to engage in casual conversation, the participants were filmed doing unscripted Chinese conversation. The second source of data consists of 4 video recordings of three-party face-to-face conversation. Again, selected participants were Mainland Chinese graduate students from different regions of China, studying in a university in Singapore, and have native proficiency in Mandarin Chinese. The setting is largely lunchtime conversation, where the three participants were seated around a table having a casual conversation. A third source of data used to amass our collection of Chinese turn-continuations consists of 4 hours of audio recordings from 8 telephone conversations, primarily between two native speakers of Mandarin Chinese from Mainland China. These conversations were culled randomly from the CallFriend Mandarin Chinese-Mainland Dialect Corpus (www.talkbank.org), provided by the Linguistic Data Consortium (LDC) of the University of Pennsylvania. This corpus originally consisted of 60 unscripted telephone conversations, where Mainland Chinese graduate students in a U.S. university would call their family members back home. The decision to collect from both video and audio sources of data stems from how the presence (or the absence) of bodily-visual conducts may potentially contribute to the analysis of turn-continuations.

---

[5] For a more thorough typological description of Chinese turn-continuations, interested readers may refer to Lim (2014).

The above 3 sources add up to approximately 12 hours of conversational data, forming our core corpus of data from which a collection of turn-continuations were identified and analyzed. The interactions in the collection were then transcribed based on the transcription system developed by Jefferson (2004). I have chosen to present my Chinese data in four lines transcripts. For each example, the first line contains standard Chinese orthography, with gross prosodic features marked using the Jefferson transcription system (See Appendix A for transcription conventions). A second line is followed where the Chinese utterances are romanized according to the Pinyin system and italicized. The Pinyin romanization are phonograms which allows for a more detailed marking of the prosodic features in the data, also using the Jefferson transcription system. Immediately following the Pinyin transcription, morpheme-by-morpheme glosses are provided in the third line (see Appendix B for abbreviation of linguistic components). In the fourth and last line, English translations of the Chinese are presented within single parenthesis. Finally, arrows (→) after the line numbers on the left side of the transcription point to focal TCUs or turns in the transcript.

4 Multi-modalities in constructing Chinese turn-continuations

Just as upcoming TRP in Chinese conversations may be projected via an amalgam of syntactic, prosodic, pragmatic and non-vocal features,[6] how further talk is marked as not something "new", but "continuing" from what has just been completed, can also be accomplished through multiple modalities. However, how different modalities are calibrated in any particular turn-continuation can defer case-by-case. Nonetheless there are statistically more dominant types of Chinese turn-continuations than others, whose features we will now describe.

4.1 Prosodic features of syntactically discontinuous turn-continuations

The predominant type of turn-continuations in our Chinese data are instances where the appended talk cannot be seen as being "syntactically fitted" with the

---

6 See Li (2014) for a detailed account of TRP projection and turn-taking in Chinese conversations.

just prior TCU (also see Lim 2014). This is, of course, in opposition to what Schegloff (2016) suggested, that is, continuation is done "most robustly by making it grammatically fitted to, or symbiotic with, that prior TCU, and, in particular, to its end (Schegloff 2016: 241)". One crucial reason for this "syntactic discontinuity" is that adverbials of various sorts (e.g. to clarify time, location and topic; to qualify stances; to inject subjectivity) turns out to be a highly productive class of word(s) that Chinese speakers often append as "continuations".[7] A few examples are given below:

Ex.(2a) Singular Adverbs (NTU-1 [41:12-41:19])

Lin: 现在   没了   吧.   **好像.**
      xianzai mei-le   ba.   **haoxiang.**
      now   NEG-CMP   SFP.   **seem.**
      'Not anymore now. (it) seems.'

Ex.(2b) Prepositional Phrases (Graduate Dilemma [21:38-21:43])

Matt: 不   冷   啊.   在   这边.
      bu   leng   a.   **zai**   **zhebian.**
      NEG   cold   SFP.   **at**   **DEM-side**
      'It's not cold. over here.'

Ex.(2c) Adverbial Conjuncts (Graduate Dilemma [22:52-23:44])

Matt: 你-   啊   你-   比   我   早   一   年   买.
      n-   a   ni-   bi   wo   zao   yi   nian   mai.
      2SG INJ 2SG   compare   1SG   early   one   year   buy.
      <↓而且   是.
      <↓erqie   shi.
      <↓furthermore   COP
      'y- oh you bought it a year earlier than me. ↓as well.'

---

[7] The semantics of adverbials seem to be most suited to accomplish the sort of interactional work that TCU-continuations do (i.e. retroactive modification of the just completed turn), and thus also seem to be the most prolific unit of TCU-continuations in other languages as well (Couper-Kuhlen and Ono 2007).

Ex.(2d)   Adverbial Disjuncts (NTU-2 [39:57])

Tao: 现在   哪里   看   啊.   ↓请   问.
        xianzai nali   kan   a.   ↓qing   **wen.**
        now   where-LOC   see   Q.   ↓**please ask.**
        'Where to find that out. <u>if I may ask</u>.'

In the "normative" syntax of Chinese, various forms of adverbials (e.g. disjuncts, prepositional phrases, relative clauses) and other modifiers are usually placed *before (or to the left of)* the head verbal, adjective, or nominal element (i.e. right-headed syntax).[8] For instance, the examples from Ex.(2a) to (2d) would normatively be *haoxiang xianzai mei-le ba, zai zhebian bu leng a, erqie shi ni bi wo zao yi nian mai* and *qing wen xianzai nali kan a* respectively, where the adverbials *haoxiang* 'seem', *zai zhebian* 'at this side', *erqie shi* 'furthermore' and *qing wen* 'please ask' would come before the main predicate. Therefore appending adverbials (as a turn-continuation) after a possibly complete predicate in Chinese often results in it being "grammatically unfitted" with the prior (Luke and Zhang 2007). In contrast, English syntax allows adverbials and prepositional phrases to be appended grammatically right after a just-completed sentence (i.e. *left-headed syntax*); take for instance, Bee's consecutive TCU-continuations of "*first*" (time adverbial) and "*before they can do the cataracts*" (prepositional phrase) in (1). An important implication of this is that, due to the linguistic typology of Chinese grammar, it is often not possible for Chinese speakers doing turn-continuations to index "continuation" using syntax as a modality. Yet, Chinese speakers clearly do, and in fact frequently, break such syntactic "decorum" by extending a TCU with adverbials, or other kinds of syntactically discontinuous constituents.

Despite syntactic discontinuity, Chinese speakers are nonetheless able to index turn-continuations by producing the appended element with certain prosodic features, contextualizing it as "continuing" from the prior and not something new. To illustrate the role of prosody in indicating turn-continuation in Chinese, a TCU that comes to possible completion, and is subsequently appended with a turn-continuation, is shown in line 04 of Ex.(3). In a telephone conversation between two friends, Faye comments on the inconsequentiality of being a second author of an academic paper in her school at line 04. Our focal TCU is the second TCU of this turn.

---

8 Li and Thompson (1981: 172-183) and Lu (1999: 18-19). The acceptability of placing certain adverbials (such as locative prepositional phrases) before or after the head element can be fuzzy in natural talk-in-interaction (Li and Thompson 1981: 397-413).

Ex.(3) Graduate Dilemma [9:21-9:26]

```
03  Matt:  诶:.    好歹       试      一下      啊.
           ei:.    hao-dai   shi    yi-xia    a.
           INJ.    good-bad  try    one-CLF   INJ
           'Oh... But (you) should try nonetheless.'

04 →  Faye: 没用.       我们    那儿    第:   第    二    作者      都    不
            meiyong.   women  naer   di:   di   er   zuozhe   dou   bu
            NEG-use.   1PL    DEM    rank  rank two  author   all   NEG
            算.     <↓现在.
            suan.  <↓xianzai.
            count. <↓now.
            'It's useless. Over here a second author is not even counted. now.'

05          (.)

06  Matt:  是     吗.
           shi   ma.
           COP   Q
           'Is that so?'
```

In the second TCU of line 04, after *women naer di: di er zuozhe dou bu suan* 'Over here a second author is not even counted' comes to a possible turn completion, the speaker Faye rushes through (denoted by the "less than" symbol [<]) to produce a single lexical word *xianzai* 'now' before the onset of any speaker transition. As a time adverbial, *xianzai* cannot be seen as grammatically fitted with the prior, yet several features of this appended item marks it as being a "continuation" rather than a new TCU in and of itself. It is first noted that the end of *xianzai* constitutes another hearable prosodic completion due to its terminal falling intonation, thereby signaling the formulation of *xianzai* as the next unit of talk after *women naer di: di er zuozhe dou bu suan*. However, within this sequential context, this new material cannot be adequately understood without recourse to the just-prior TCU (i.e. host-TCU); namely *xianzai* 'now' only makes sense when treated as a time adverbial restricting the scope of the clause '*a second author is not even counted*'. In other words, although a time word such as *xianzai* may suffice as an independent TCU in certain sequential environments, within this context, it is necessarily retrospectively-oriented and dependent upon its host-TCU for semantic and pragmatic completeness. However, as we now know, by taking *xianzai* as a time adverbial placed at the end of the utterance to modify the host-TCU, there is a

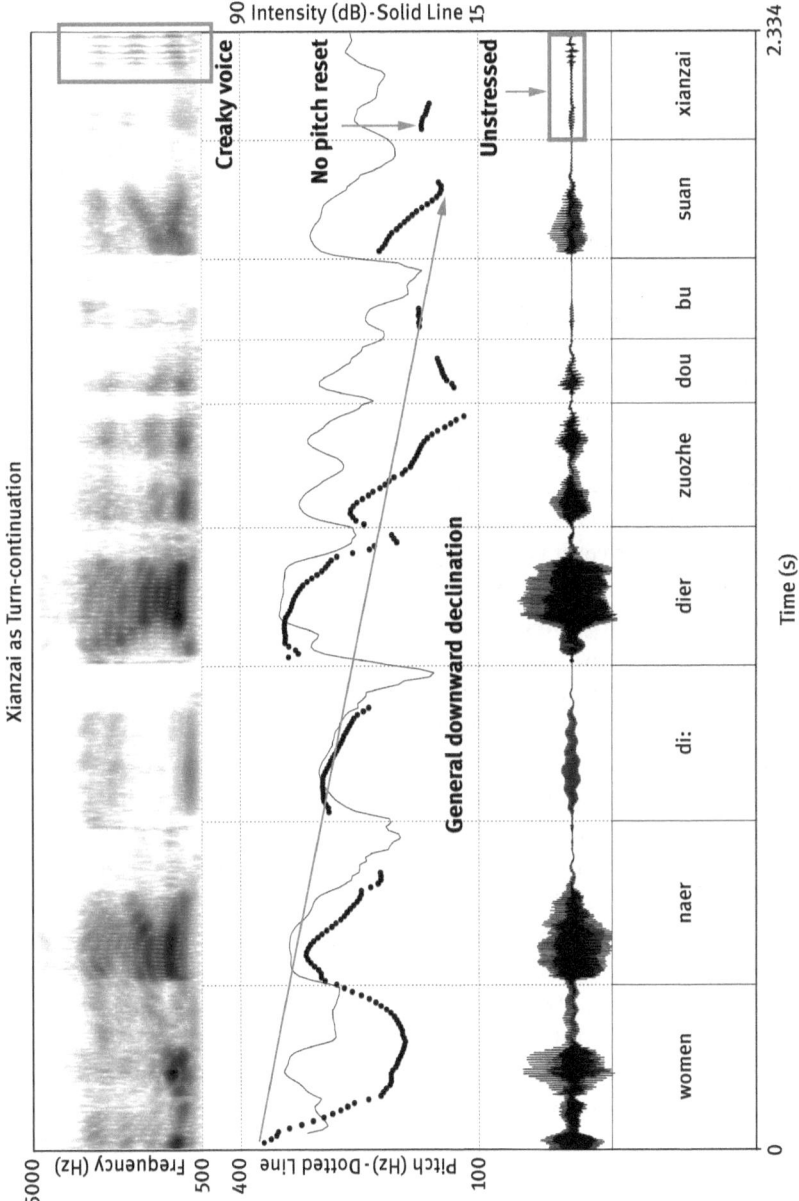

Figure 1: Acoustic analysis of line 04 in Ex.(3).

marked syntactic discontinuity (Luke and Zhang 2007: 609–610) between *women naer di: di er zuozhe dou bu suan* and *xianzai*. As mentioned, the "normative" syntactic position of time adverbial in a Chinese clause is before the main verb. The point here is that the appended constituent of *xianzai*, as with many other frequent adverbial turn-continuations in Chinese, cannot be seen as "syntactically" continuing from the just-completed TCU.

Consequently, an alternative modality, namely prosody, is provided by the speaker for recognition of a syntactically discontinuous Chinese turn-continuation. Figure (1) is produced below with a focus on *xianzai* to illustrate how some of its prosodic qualities contribute to a reading of "continuation". The 4-tiered graph (Figure 1) below is produced using the speech analysis software Praat (Boersma & Weenink 2016), providing the spectrogram, pitch trace (dotted line) and intensity (solid line), waveform, and a Pinyin transcription of the utterance. Subsequent acoustic graphs are shown in a similar fashion.

As can be seen, the production of *xianzai* is marked by a cluster of prosodic features which marks it as a "continuation". The first would be the *lack of pitch reset* at the start of articulating *xianzai*, otherwise typically seen on the onset of new TCUs (Du Bois et al. 1993: 47). The initial syllable of new TCUs typically achieves a pitch peak that is contrastively higher than at the end of the last syllable in the preceding TCU. As a TCU progresses, its overall pitch contour can be seen to decline over the projected length of the TCU, such that a declination trend can be perceived (otherwise known as a declination unit [henceforth DU]).[9] This declination of pitch is perceivable despite pitch fluctuations along the overall intonation contour of the TCU caused by individual syllabic tonal contours, or other intonational modifications denoting stances such as attitudes/emotions. Here, although a possible turn completion point has been reached at *suan* (exhibiting not only "turn-final" pitch characteristics, but also marked by the temporal extension on *suan*), the pitch trace in Figure 1 shows that the pitch onset of *xianzai* (at a peak of 166 Hz), is actually lower than the preceding syllable *suan* (at a peak of 223 Hz). Compare this with how the same speaker, Faye, begins her TCU with *women*, produced at a peak of 370 Hz. Also, the elongated syllable *suan* declines to a minimum pitch of 147 Hz around its end, which is also not much lower than the pitch peak of 166 Hz at the beginning of *xianzai*. In fact, taken in its entirety, the intonation contour of the host-TCU together with its turn-continuation *xianzai* can be seen to follow a downward declination trend, resembling a single DU.

---

9 Schuetzu-Coburn (1991); Du Bois et al. (1993); Tao (1996). Tao (1996: 48) defines DU as *"a general declination trend (slope) describing the gradual fall in F_0 (fundamental frequency) over time during a period of speech"*

Another phonetic characteristic of *xianzai* is that it is perceived to be *unstressed* (Figure 1). First of all, *xianzai* is produced with an extremely low pitch and becomes "creaky voice" (Figure 1). Also, *xianzai* is articulated with a *lower intensity* (i.e. loudness) than most other syllables in its host-TCU (Figure 1). These two prosodic features are part of what was figuratively termed *"subordinate intonation"* by Luke and Zhang (2007: 610–611), suggested to be an amalgamation of prosodic features which recipients orient to in recognizing upcoming Chinese turn-continuations.

A final notable phonetic feature of *xianzai* is that it is heard to be produced quickly after the closing of the prior syllable *suan*, or termed *"latching"* where there is no hearable beat of silence between two parts of a turn by the same speaker (Zhang 2012: 170). This is indicated with a "less than" symbol (<) before *xianzai* in Ex.(1). By latching onto the last syllable of the just-completed preceding TCU, the next bit of talk (i.e. turn-continuation) thereby minimizes the gap between turn-continuation and host-TCU. One obvious result of a "latched" production is that the current speaker is more likely to be able to implement a turn-continuation without having to compete with the onset of talk by next speaker.

While the lack of pitch reset, together with unstressed and latched production are common prosodic/phonetic features of syntactically discontinuous Chinese turn-continuations, this is not always the case. There are other variants of prosodic production on appended units of talk that can similarly be heard as "continuing" from the prior despite syntactic discontinuity. One such method is to have the turn-continuation produced as prosodically non-disjunctive (i.e. through-produced) from the host-TCU. This means that the syntactically discontinuous element and host-TCU is "in maximally close temporal proximity to each other", and exhibits some similar features to "continuous voicing" (see Local & Walker 2004: 1394–1396). This is illustrated in Ex.(4) below, which shows a short segment from a sequence where Faye is complaining to Matt about a friend's difficult request. Earlier in the talk, Faye informs about the friend's request to locate an academic article in an unfamiliar field, and her lack of success in the attempt. As such, Faye has been feeling uneasy about returning the friend's call, and Matt begins to console her at line 19.

Ex.(4) Graduate Dilemma [19:31-19:37]

19 Matt: [那: 又- 又 不是 说 有- 有 什么 东西
ne:i yo- you bushi shuo yo- you shenme dongxi
DM also also NEG-COP say have have what thing
可以 告诉
keyi gaosu
can tell
'Then- it's not as if there's something you can tell'

```
20          他    呀.   [反正         也     没    东西.
            ta    ya.   [fanzheng    ye     mei   dongxi.
            3SG   SFP.  anyway       also   NEG   thing
            'him.       There's nothing (to say) anyway.'

21 → Faye:        [对     >因为<       查         不着        关键        是.
                  [dui    >yinwei<    cha        bu-zhao    guanjian    shi.
                  yes     >because<   check      NEG-CTP    critical    COP.
                  'yea. Because (I) couldn't find it, that's the critical point.'

22          <我     不     知道      [  哪:   ]   查       下去.
            wo     bu     zhidao    [  na:   ]   cha      xia-qu.
            1SG    NEG    know         where      check    down-go
            'I don't know where else to look (for it).'

23   Matt:                          [  对 啊.  ]
                                    [  dui a.  ]
                                       right SFP
                                       'yeah.'
```

The focus is at line 21, where Faye says *cha bu-zhao guanjian shi* 'The point is that I can't find it'. The constituent of interest is a compound of two lexical items *guanjian shi*, literally 'the critical point is…', produced at the end of the utterance. Firstly, *guanjian shi* is an adverbial disjunct, whose function is to frame some propositional content as being "the main point", and hence is by itself semantically dependent. Secondly, in normative syntax, *guanjian shi* should occur before the propositional content it frames. Therefore, if the proposition it modifies is *cha bu-zhao* 'can't find it', then the speaker's production of *guanjian shi* is retrospectively oriented (Luke and Zhang 2007: 611–612) and syntactically discontinuous. While it is also positionally possible that *guanjian shi* may be produced to frame the upcoming talk instead of the preceding one (meaning *guanjian shi* is produced to frame *wo bu zhidao na: cha xia-qu* 'I don't know where else to look for it') (line 22), such a reading is prosodically impossible for the recipient. Figure 2 below provides an acoustic analysis of line 21 in Ex.(4).

Though syntactically and pragmatically complete, not only does *cha bu-zhao* end with a rising pitch movement, but its pitch contour continues seamlessly into *guanjian shi*. Though "continuous voicing" (Local & Walker 2004: 1394–1396) into the beginning of *guan* does not seem possible due to the initial voiceless consonant [g], there is still audibly a sustained voicing on the last vowel [u] of *zhao* right into the beginning of *guan*, resulting in very little pause between

On co-operative modalities in the formulation of Mandarin Chinese — 227

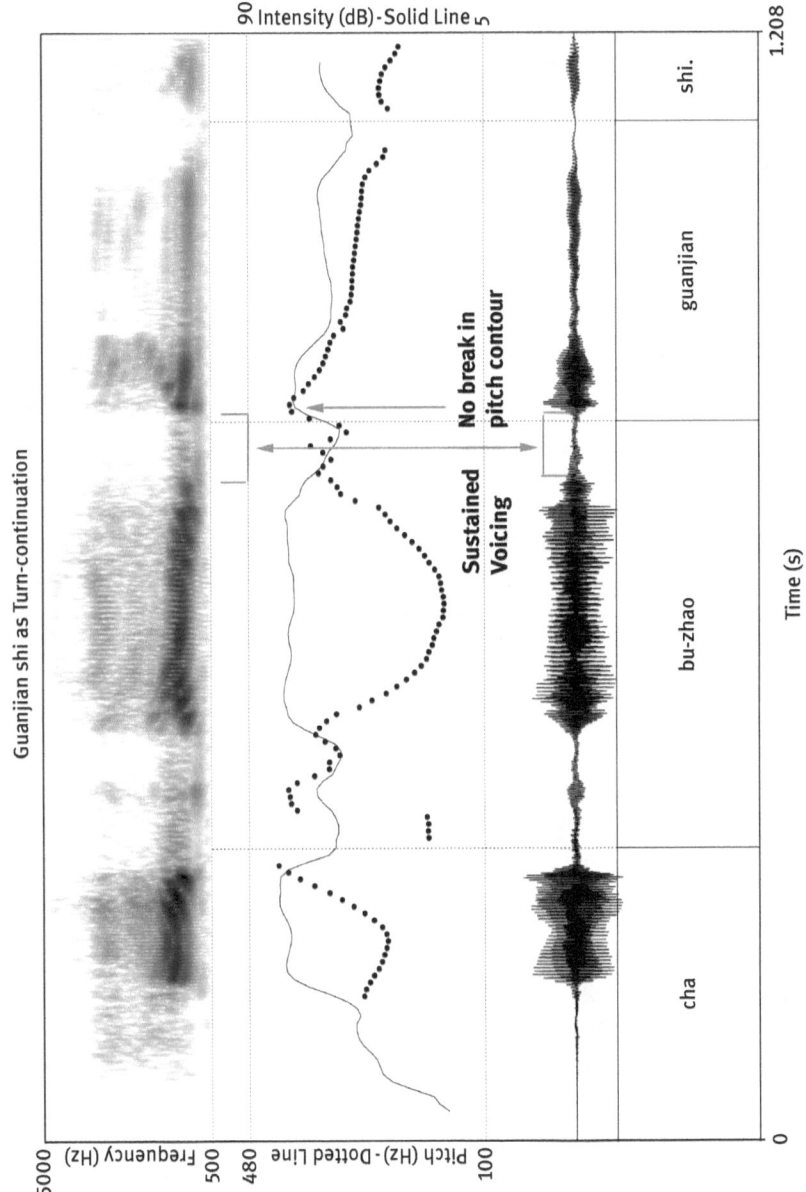

Figure 2: Acoustic analysis of line 21 in Ex.(4).

the two syllable. This is indicated by the bracketed areas on the spectrogram and speech waveform in Figure 2. In other words, *guanjian shi* is a syntactically discontinuous constituent that is heard as being "through-produced" from the end of *cha bu-zhao* without any form of prosodic break. Therefore, the recipient, through parsing the moment-by-moment talk, will first interpret that *cha bu-zhao* has not actually come to possible completion, and thereby anticipate further talk (i.e. *guanjian shi*) to be part of this TCU. In contrast, a point of possible TCU completion (and TRP) actually occurs after the next bit of talk in *guanjian shi*, indexed by its falling intonation and the temporally extended *shi*. This is further evidenced by Matt's slightly late turn transition at line 23 (*dui a* 'yeah'), running into overlap with Faye's next TCU *wo bu zhidao na: cha xia-qu*. Hence, it is clear to the recipient that *guanjian shi* has been designed to be part of *cha bu-zhao* as a single TCU.

The prosodic profile of *guanjian shi* here is somewhat different from *xianzai* in Ex.(3). Firstly, as opposed to *xianzai* whose intensity is lower than the rest of its host-TCU, the intensity on *guanjian shi*, peaking at 74 dB, is quite comparable to its prior units where intensity peaked on *cha* and *zhao* at 79 dB and 77 dB respectively. Also, whereas there is a clear point of completion at the end of *suan* before *xianzai* is "latched" onto it, the production of *guanjian shi* is "through-produced" without a discernable break in the talk, much akin to a "rush-through".[10] Although the prosodic profile of *guanjian shi* is different from *xianzai*, the point here is that it is still a syntactically discontinuous element from the prior that is prosodically marked as a 'continuation', by virtue of being "through-produced".

A third variant of prosodic production that marks "continuation" is shown in Ex.(5) below. A bit before the start of the example, Faye was enquiring about the status of Matt's wife, and whether she was pursuing a master's or doctoral program. Line 17 in the transcript begins after Matt confirms his wife as a master's student.

Ex.(5) Graduate Dilemma [00:17-00:24]

17 Faye: hhh 那   快   啦   哦?
           hhh na   kuai la   o?
           hhh DM   fast SFP   SFP
           'It should be soon then?'

---

10 Different from the typical description of a *rush-through* though, the just prior syllable before completion here (i.e. *zhao*) is not compressed, but in fact temporally extended. For a concise discussion on the difference between *latching* and *rush-through*, see Zhang (2012: 169–172).

18	Matt:	呃::	但愿	如此		吧.			
		e::	danyuan	ruci		ba.			
		AGR	hopefully	resemble.this		SFP			
		'Yeah. Hopefully that's the case.'							

19   (.)

20 →	Faye:	z-	是	几	年	呢.	<大概.	(.)	两	年.
		z-	shi	ji	nian	ne.	<***dagai.***	(.)	liang	nian.
			COP	how.many	year	SFP.	<**approximately.**	(.)	two	year.
		'How many years should it be.					approximately.		Two years?'	

21   (0.4)

22	Matt:	应该	两	年	吧.
		yinggai	liang	nian	ba.
		should	two	year	SFP
		'Should be about two years.'			

At focal line 20, Faye starts something but immediately abandons that initial formulation, adopting instead a straightforward interrogative *shi ji nian ne* 'How many years should it be', sequentially understandable to mean how much time would it take to graduate from the master's program (pursued by Matt's wife). Audibly, the intonation of this TCU follows a general downwards declination cline, but ends with a slightly higher pitched syllable in *ne* (see Figure 3 below). Furthermore, the TCU ends with a sentence final particle *ne*, indexing strong syntactic closure, and hence marks a possible completion. A single adverb *dagai* 'approximately' then latches on to the end of the host-TCU, itself coming to a possible completion with a downward intonation contour. Similar to *guanjian shi* in Ex.(4), *dagai* 'approximately' is an adverb whose meaning is semantically dependent to some form of verbal element. Also similar is that positionally, *dagai* 'approximately' can either modify the next bit of talk *liang nian* 'two years' as a grammatically fitted constituent (line 20); or retroactively modify the earlier *shi ji nian ne* 'How many years should it be' as a syntactically discontinuous turn-continuation. But again, this is made unambiguous through prosodic cues, which only allows a reading of *dagai* as continuing from the prior unit, despite its syntactic discontinuity.

Different from *guanjian shi*, however, is that *dagai* is not "through-produced" but is latched onto *ne* (again indicated by the "less than" symbol [<]) after the clear possible completion of the prior unit. The phonetic features of *dagai* are illustrated in Figure 3 below.

230 — Ni-Eng Lim

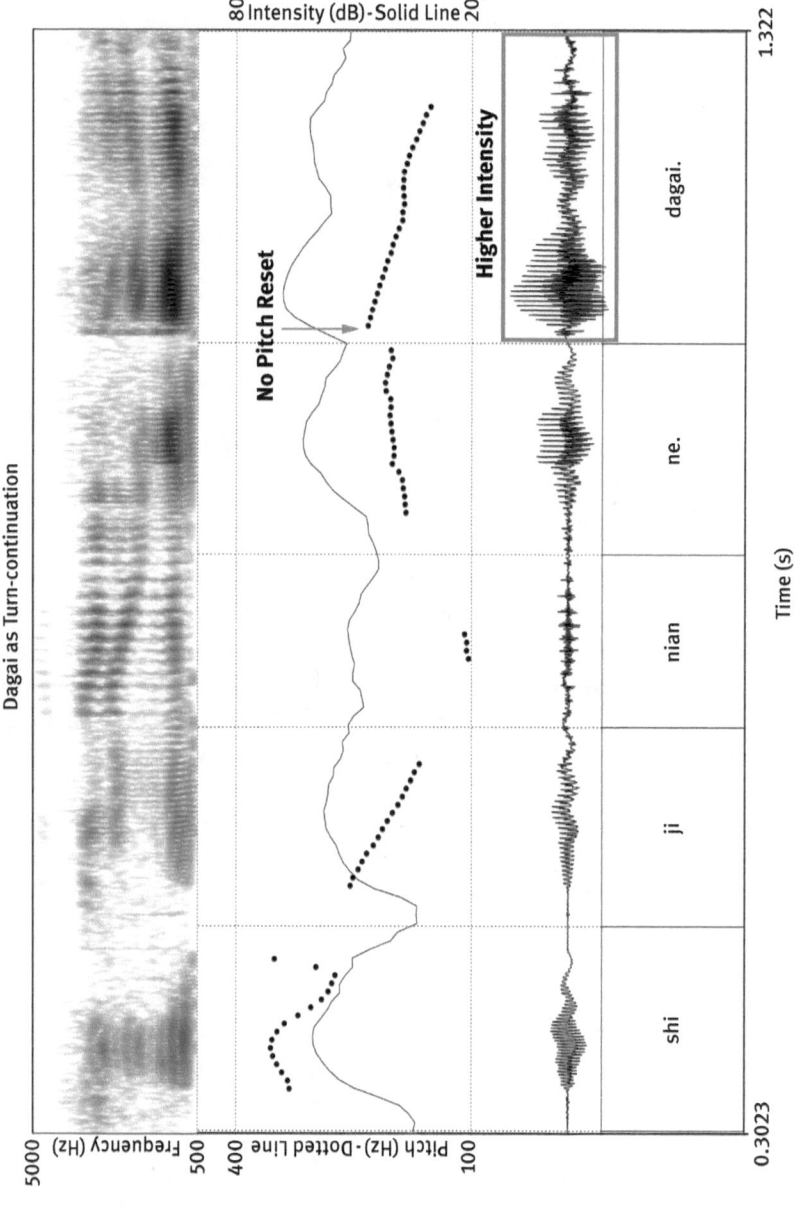

Figure 3: Acoustic analysis of line 20 for Ex.(5).

As seen in Figure 3, though *dagai* is produced at an intensity (peaking at 68 dB on the first syllable *da*) higher than *shi ji nian ne* (where each syllable peaked at 60 dB, 58 dB, 52 dB and 63 dB respectively), it does not start off at a significantly higher pitch level than the end of the preceding TCU (i.e. *lack of pitch reset*). The peak pitch of *dagai* (at 231 Hz) though slightly higher than the peak pitch of *ne* (at 211 Hz), is still significantly lower than the beginning of the turn at *shi* (which peaked at 356 Hz). Furthermore, other prosodic indicators are sufficiently present to mark *dagai* as a bona fide turn-continuation. Firstly, the terminal intonation on *dagai* followed by a micro-pause before *liang nian* 'two years' strongly signal that it has come to possible completion, and not part of what is to follow. Secondly, the latching of *dagai* and its lack of pitch reset, still allows for the reading of a retrospectively oriented turn-continuation that "continues" from the prior though being a synthetically discontinuous constituent.

From Ex.(3) to Ex.(5), it can be seen that the use of prosody to index some elements as "continuing" in syntactically discontinuous Chinese turn-continuations is not strictly confined to specific prosodic parameters, but can be molded by the speaker to fit the situated context of talk. Nonetheless, what the above three extracts exemplify is that forms of prosody that clearly subjugates the appended constituent to its prior, is quite a ubiquitous feature in Chinese turn-continuations which are frequently syntactically discontinuous. In other words, for syntactically discontinuous Chinese turn-continuations, the modality of prosody is often seen to "operate" upon the appended element when the right-headed syntax of Chinese makes it difficult for "continuation" to be marked by the modality of syntax. It is also interesting that while most Chinese turn-continuations do have certain prosodic features in common (such as the lack of pitch reset, or having the turn-continuation and host-TCU produced to be maximally close to each other),[11] speakers do not orient to strictly marking all turn-continuations with such features as if it is a fundamental or defining criterion for doing "continuation" in Chinese. There are in fact cases where the appended constituents do not have any form of prosodic "continuation" at all, but are nonetheless analyzable as turn-continuations due to other semiotic resources, such as its sequential or grammatical context. This suggests that a speaker's main concern when producing turn-continuations is to retroactively add meaningful bits of talk using whatever configuration of linguistic (or para-linguistic) modality that may signal it as further talk that continues from what has just preceded, rather than to follow some *a priori* structure. In the examples that we have just examined, this configuration involves the precise albeit flexible interplay between modalities of syntax and prosody. In other words,

---

[11] Such as latching or being "through-produced".

while the right-headed syntax of Chinese has *ab initio* led to usages of adverbials as turn-continuations to be syntactically discontinuous, Chinese speakers are routinely seen to utilize various forms of prosodic production to strengthen a reading of "continuing" from the prior. Hence, in a sense, it is the normative grammar of Chinese (i.e. right-headed syntax) that has led to speakers' use of alternate modalities to signal interactional intent (i.e. continuation from the prior).

4.2 Syntactic features of prosodically disjunctive turn-continuations

From the previous sections, it is clear that prosody has been "recruited" as another modality by Chinese interlocutors to both index and recognize turn-continuations. Specifically, Chinese adverbials appended after possible completion are often marked with some form of "continuing" prosodic features, that characterize them as turn-continuations despite their syntactic discontinuity. One common feature is to have these units latched-on to the just-prior possibly complete TCU, minimizing the gap between host-TCU and turn-continuation, and thereby signaling their status as "belonging" to the prior. However, in certain interactional contexts, speakers may realize the need to add further talk only after a noticeable gap has occurred after possible completion. Indeed, the very occurrence of a gap in turn-transition could prompt speakers to pursue a relevant uptake from recipients by adding further talk, in effect providing another opportunity for turn-transition by re-completing the TCU. In other cases, further talk may be triggered by recipient's talk after possible completion, resulting in a turn-continuation separated by the recipient's turn at talk. As mentioned, these forms of turn-continuations have been labelled as "post-gap" or "post-other-talk" by Schegloff (2016).

Regardless, a clear consequence of producing "post-gap" or "post-other-talk" turn-continuations is their ostensible disjunction in prosodic production from its host-TCU. In other words, just as syntactic discontinuity is seen as a barrier towards recognizing turn-continuation, it is also difficult to see how a prosodically disjunctive unit can be part of a prior TCU. Yet, it is found that a majority of these prosodically disjunctive units are quite easily recognizable as turn-continuations in Chinese conversation. One reason for this is, of course, that many of these prosodically disjunctive units can still be produced with other prosodic features of "subordinate intonation" despite having a noticeable gap with the preceding TCU. But more interestingly, a majority of these prosodically disjunctive turn-continuations have been linearly appended to the prior TCU in a syntactically coherent way, thereby strongly marking them as "continuing". Significantly, in our collection of Chinese turn-continuations that are syntactically continuous, about 70% were instances where the appended unit was produced either after a gap of silence, or after talk-by-others; making it apparent that there is a correlation between the use of syntactically continuous turn-continuations and "continuing" utterances after clear breakages in the flow of talk.[12]

Naturally, for this to be a systematic practice, there must exist a sizable number of structural/grammatical environments in Chinese which *provide for* certain constituents or phrases produced after possible completion to be construed as syntactically continuous. Just as adverbials (and certain other constituents) appended after possible completion are seen to be syntactically discontinuous in a right-headed syntax language; there also has to be some constructions in Chinese where an utterance can first be seen to be syntactically complete, and then further talk still viably analyzed as being syntactically continuous. It is *through* these distinctive Chinese grammatical structures or constructions that various forms of prosodically disjunctive turn-continuation can still be construed as "grammatically fitted", and thereby "continuing" from the prior. In this section, we will illustrate with four examples how Chinese speakers, though producing prosodically disjunctive turn-continuations, can nonetheless utilize certain grammatical structures to index continuity. As the focus here is on relevant grammatical structures in the Chinese language and not on the prosodic profile of the turn-continuation, detailed phonetic description of the appended constituent and corresponding Praat graphs will not be provided.

4.2.1 Serial verb construction

One syntactic environment of Chinese where prosodically disjunctive turn-continuations can frequently be produced in a syntactically continuous manner is the serial verb construction, where clausal phrases (VPs) may be structurally stringed together without the need for conjunctions (Li and Thompson 1981: 594–622). Additionally, Chinese is also commonly known as a "pro-drop" language, where the subject noun phrase (NP_s) of a clausal sentence may be "dropped" or omitted provided that it can be found, traced and understood from the preceding context. Schematically the construction is seen as:

$$\{ NP_{s_1} + VP_1 + ((NP_{s_2}).VP_2) + ((NP_{s_3}).VP_3)... + ((NP_{sn}).VP_n) \}$$

---

[12] Naturally, a more equitable way of doing this quantification would be to see how many prosodically disjunctive TCU-continuations are, in fact, syntactically continuous.

Given that follow-up clauses in Chinese (that have a clear referent in its earlier discourse) need not begin overtly with a subject NP, pronoun or a dummy subject; adjacently placed clauses are structurally more amenable to be seen as syntactically continuous from the preceding TCU, via the serial verb construction framework. Ex.(6) below exemplifies such an instance of a prosodically disjunctive turn-continuation that is, nonetheless, syntactically continuous.

Ex.(6) ES-M-01 [10:39-10:43]

```
01  Chen:    他    喜欢     上学             哦.=
             ta    xihuan   shangxue        o.=
             2SG   like     attend-school   SFP
             'He likes to go to school, huh?'

02  Lian:    =喜欢.
             =xihuan.
             like
             'He really likes it.'

03           (.)

04  Chen:    学校     肯定      有      很      多      小      朋友.
             xuexiao  kending  you     hen     duo     xiao    pengyou.
             school   sure     have    very    many    small   friend.
             'There must be a lot of children in the school.'

05           (0.3)

06 → Chen:   跟       [他     玩儿.]
             gen      [ta     wanr.]
             follow   3SG    play.
             'to play with him.'

07  Lian:            [好      玩儿.]
                     [hao     wanr.]
                     good    play
                     'It's fun (for him).'
```

In Ex.(6), two graduate students in a university, Chen and Lian, are chatting about their respective children. At one point, Lian starts a story on how her son has been unwell and absent from school for the past few days; but felt much better that morning and proactively requested to go to school. One interactional issue here is that Lian begins her telling without clearly prefacing the point of her story, leaving for her recipient, Chen, to make her own inferences. At line 01 of the extract, Chen then picks up on the child's proclivity for attending school, and requests verification from Lian by saying *ta xihuan shang xue o* 'he likes to go to school, huh?'. This is met with agreement almost immediately and most emphatically by Lian in line 02, but receives no further elaboration on possible reasons for the child's enthusiasm in going to school. In line 04, Chen adds that *xuexiao kending you hen duo xiao pengyou* 'there must be a lot of children in the school', which can sequentially be seen as proposing a candidate reason. This is however, in contrast to line 01, met with a 0.3 second gap of silence in line 05. Possibly to clarify what she meant by 'lot of children in school' as a reason, Chen then further appends a verbal clause *gen ta wanr* 'to play with him' in focal line 06, as a turn-continuation from line 04. With the gap of silence in line 05, this is an instance of a "post-gap" turn-continuation, where the production of further talk is done in a prosodically disjunctive manner. However, by producing the prepositional phrase *gen ta* 'with him' followed by the verb *wanr* 'play', Chen has added another verbal clause (VP) that can be seen to be a resultant predicate that stems from the first verbal clause (i.e. there must be a lot of children in the school), thereby instantiating the structure of a Chinese serial verb constructions, and syntactic contiguity between the host-TCU (*xuexiao kending you hen duo xiao pengyou*) and turn-continuation (*gen ta wanr*).

4.2.2 Topic-comment structure

Another common syntactic environment where prosodically disjunctive turn-continuations can be produced as grammatically fitted constituents is immediately after nominal phrases that can act as topics for further comments. The topic-comment structure is argued to be the default sentence structure in Chinese, and hence Chinese is deemed a *topic-prominent* language (Li and Thompson 1976; Li and Thompson 1981: 85–102). A "topic" in this structure is independent of the syntactic category of subject or object. By this, it means that any nominal constituent in the "topic" position (i.e. utterance-initial) can be followed by a "comment" (usually a clause, or a full clause with its own subject) that treats the nominal constituent as its subject, object or any other relevant nominal arguments. In other words, the topic-comment structure is a valid syntactic structure in Chinese where the semantic relations between the "topic" constituent and the "comment" constituent can be very loosely defined. A schematic representation of the topic-comment construction is given below:

{ TOPIC_Nominal Phrase + (COMMENT_Clausal Phrase) }

Given that Chinese is an isolating language, a topic is without morphosyntactic markings, and its topical status must be inferable from the discourse situation. This means that any TCU made up by a nominal phrase is amenable to be retroactively "made into" a topic with further talk that comments on the nominal phrase relevantly as a topic. Hence, a clausal "continuation" of this type, though prosodically disjunctive, can still be seen as syntactically continuous under the topic-comment structure of Chinese. An instance of such a turn-continuation is illustrated in Ex.(7) below. The interlocutors in this extract are again Chen and Lian. This time, they are having a discussion on the best time in the year to have a baby, such that (s)he would be able to enroll into the primary school system of mainland China at the youngest age possible. The dilemma here is: if the child does not reach the biological age of six by the final date for primary school admission (even if it is just by a day), he or she will not be allowed to enroll till the next academic year.

Ex.(7) ES-M-01 [13:13-13:25]

```
01    Chen:   那      这么      说     小孩     几         月       份
              na      zheme    shuo   xiaohai  ji         yue      fen
              DM      this.way say    children how.many   month    CLF
              出生           比较      好      呢?
              chusheng      bijiao    hao     ne?
              born          compare   good    SFP
              'If that's the case, when will you say is a better month to give
              birth to a child?'

02    Lian:   .hhhh

03            (.)

04    Lian:   [uh:    <几         月       份      出生         啊:       ]:>.
              [uh:    <ji         yue      fen    chusheng     a:        ]:>.
                      how.many    month    CLF    born                   SFP
              'Mmm... with regards to which month would be better...'
```

05	Chen:	[如果 说 想- 小孩儿 就是 说 六 岁.]
		[ruguo shuo xiang- xiaohair jiushi shuo liu shui.]
		if say think children that.is say six age.
		'If we wanted to... for children... I'mean, to be six years old?'

06		(0.4)

07	Chen:	九 月 份 以后?
		jiu yue fen yihou?
		nine month CLF after
		'(Maybe) after September?'

08		(0.5)

09 →	Chen:	出生 好 一些.
		chusheng hao yi-xie.
		birth good a-bit.
		'(as the) better (time) to give birth.'

10		(1.3)

11	Lian:	((contemplative tone)) <九 月 [份>.]
		((contemplative tone)) <*jiu yue* [*fen*>.]
		<nine month CLF>.
		'September...'

12	Chen:	[或者 是]:: 就是 说:::
		[*huozhe shi*]:: *jiushi shu:::o*
		or COP that.is say
		'or maybe... I'mean...'

13		(0.5)

14	Lian:	对. 九 月 份:. <我 觉得 是 九 月
		dui. jiu yue fen:. <*wo juede shi jiu yue*
		Yes. nine month CLF. <1SG think COP nine month
		份 左右
		*fen zuo*you
		CLF left-right
		'Yes. September. I think it's around September'

15	好像	比较::	比较	好.
	haoxiang	bijia::o	bijiao	hao.
	seems	compare	compare	good.

'that seems to be better.'

Before the extract, the interlocutors have agreed that it is best for a child to enter into the formal education system earlier than later. Hence the month in which a child is born becomes a relevant point of discussion, as this will directly affect his/her ability to enroll as one of the youngest six-year-old in a cohort. Ex.(7) begins with Chen positing the question on the best month for a child to be born, given the school admission policy in China. After Chen initiates the question in line 01, the recipient (Lian) finds it difficult to provide an accurate assessment, possibly due to the various complex issues in determining the "best" month for a child to be born. This is seen from line 02 to line 13 in the extract, where Lian first audibly produces a lengthened in-breath, best described as the sort of response cry when one is thrown into a quandary, and then repeats part of her interlocutor's question in line 04 (*ji yue fen chusheng a*: 'with regards to which month would be better...') and line 11 (<*jiu yue fen*> 'September...'), or mutters inaudibly to herself in between. Seeing Lian's dilemma in coming up with an answer, Chen attempts to "trouble-shoot" and clarifies her question, first at line 05 with the turn *ruguo shuo xiang- xiaohai jiushi shuo liu shui* 'If we wanted to... for children... I'mean, to be six years old?'. As it turns out, this attempt at clarifying what it means by "best" month (such that the child turns six and is still within the school registration period) in line 01 runs into overlap with Lian's repeat at line 04, and is further met with more gaps in line 06. Seeing that attempts at clarifying the question in line 05 did not yield an answer, Chen changes tack and moves into a new action by proposing *jiu yue fen yihou?* 'After September?' as a candidate solution with try-marked prosody in focal line 07. With no forthcoming acknowledgement in line 08 occupied by a gap of half a second, she further pursues the missing verification with a "post-gap" turn-continuation *chu-sheng hao yi-xie* 'better to give birth' in line 09, thereby retroactively transforming *jiu yue fen yihou?* 'After September?' into a host-TCU. Again, though being prosodically disjunctive, the turn-continuation is marked by the modality of syntax as "continuing" from the prior. With the earlier time period *jiu yue fen yihou* in line 07 as the topic, *chu-sheng hao yi-xie* then comments upon it as a verbal clause, utilizing the topic-comment structure common in Chinese.

4.2.3 Unexpressed nominal argument structure

Yet another environment where prosodically disjunctive turn-continuations can appear to be syntactically continuous is in a clause where the nominal argument

(NP$_o$) is "dropped" or missing. Two features of the Chinese language contribute to this possibility: the first is the pro-drop tendencies of Chinese where either the nominal subject or object may be left unexpressed when the referent can be deduced from prior discourse (Li and Thompson 1981: 657–676); the second is, of course, the SVO typology of Chinese where the object argument naturally comes at the end an utterance, resulting in syntactic continuity when a nominal object is appended after possible completion of an object-less clause. This is represented in the schema below.

$$\{ NP_s + VP + (NP_o) \}$$

However, a more common form of nominal-object type turn-continuations is usually seen after a possibly complete nominalizer-DE construction (Li and Thompson 1981: 575–593). The nominalizer-DE refers to the grammatical particle placed after some attributive or possessive elements, such that the entire construction constitutes a nominal used as grammatical subject, object or other arguments. This, however, means that the formulation of nominalizer-DE construction may be seen as the omission of the head noun on the right in a right-headed syntax language (e.g. Chinese). Schematically speaking, this is seen as:

{Attributive/Possessive Modifier + DE + (Head Noun)}$_{\text{Nominal Subject/Object/Other Arguments}}$

Therefore, when used as a nominal argument placed after a verb in a SVO language, the end of a nominalizer-DE construction may be a possible completion point of the utterance; and furthermore, allows for the syntactically continuous appendage of the unexpressed head noun as a turn-continuation. Ex.(8) below illustrates an example where the prosodically disjunctive turn-continuation can be syntactically seen as part of a nominalizer-DE construction.

Before the extract begins, Deng has been chiding Cai (Deng and Cai are both female students in the University of Hong Kong (HKU)) for not accepting her previous invitations to a night club with a group of friends. Cai defends herself by asking if the outing had to take place so late into the night, and also conveys her lack of understanding (perhaps even apprehension) on the activities that goes on in the night club. Deng then responds by saying night clubs only opens at around 9 p.m. at night, and that they are simply there to drink, dance, listen to music and "to look at guys". Cai awkwardly laughs at this response, and probes if Deng goes out with an all-girls group. Deng then empathetically confirms that it is indeed an all-girls group. The extract begins with Cai further enquiring if the girls Deng went out with were all from Hong Kong. Orientating to the possibility that the profile of this group of friends is going to significantly impact on whether Cai would join the group for future outings, Deng proactively endeavors to provide more information on this group in the sequence below.

Ex.(8) ES-M-07 [19:41-19:55]

```
01  Cai:     [你      上次              跟]   你    去    他    是-    都    是    (.)
             [ni      shang-ci         gen]  ni    qu    ta    shi-   dou   shi   (.)
             2SG     previous-CLF     with  2SG   go    3SG   COP-   all   COP   (.)
             香港              的.
             xianggang       de.
             NM              GEN.
             'When you went last time, he… they were all Hong Kong-ers?'

02           (0.3)

03  Deng:   >没    [有<.   <上次      ]    我    没    去.
            >mei   [you<.  <shang-ci ]    wo    mei   qu.
            NEG    have   previous-CLF   1SG   NEG   go.
            'No. I didn't go the last time round.'

04  Cai:           [     °香港-°      ]
                   [     °xianggan-° ]
                         NM
                   'Hong Kong…'

05  Cai:    啊     你     没有       去     啊.=
            a      ni     meiyou    qu    a.=
            INJ   2SG    NEG-have  go    SFP.=
            'Oh! You didn't go.'

06  Deng:   =就是:::   (0.3)  上次::          但是:     他们
            =jiushi:::  (0.3)  shang-ci::      danshi:   tamen
            DM          (0.3)  previous-CLF    but        3PL
            有:::   五     个      人        去     啦:.
            you:::  wu    ge      ren       qu    la:.
            have    five  CLF    person    go    SFP.
            'I mean…       Last time…     but they had five people that went.'

07           (0.4)
```

```
08    Cai:    °>这么     多<°.
              °>zheme   duo<°.
              >so       many<.
              'That many?'

09            (0.5)

10    Deng:   都      是:-   对.
              dou    shi:-  dui.
              all    COP    right
              'they're all... yeah.'

11            (.)

12    Deng:   呃-     都     是     港大      的.
              e-     dou    shi    gangda    de.
              AGR-   all    COP    NM        GEN.
              'Uh-hmm... they're all from the University of Hong Kong.'

13            (0.4)

14 →  Deng:   °女[生°.   ]
              °nu[sheng°.]
              female.
              '(and all) female students.'
```

After Cai initiates another enquiry on the profile of the group ('they were all Hong Kong-ers?') at line 01, a 0.3 second gap ensues in line 02. Deng then reveals at line 03 that she did not actually participate in the last outing. At line 06, Deng further conveys that five individuals from the all-girls group participated in the last outing. Following another 0.4 second gap in line 07, Cai receives this information with an unenthusiastic and softly produced *zheme duo* 'that many?' in line 08, perhaps hinting that strength in numbers did not particularly appeal to her as a pull-factor towards joining the group. This was possibly picked up by Deng as well, as another gap in the talk prefacing "disalignment" ensues in line 09, before she attempts to formulate another piece of information at line 10. Here, Deng begins with *dou shi* 'they're all' before cutting herself off to produce an agreement *dui* 'yeah', ostensibly in response *zheme duo* 'that many?' in line 08. She re-starts at line 12 again with our focal host-TCU *e- dou shi gangda de* 'Uh-hmm... they're all from the University of Hong Kong', harking back to Cai's initial question at line 01. When this was again met with more gaps of silence in line 13, Deng re-introduces the gender profile of the group in the form of a nominal phrase turn-continuation *nu sheng* 'female students'. Note that this appended constituent is done after a noticeable gap of silence, and hence in a prosodically disjunctive manner. Yet as the prior utterance in line 12 ended with a nominalizer-DE construction (*dou shi gangda de* 'all from the University of Hong Kong-DE'), the addition of an appropriate nominal argument (*nu sheng* 'female students') in line 14 thereby renders the turn-continuation as grammatically fitted, where *gangda* 'University of Hong Kong' before the *de* particle is retroactively turned into the attributive element of *nu sheng* 'female students'.

An interesting observation pertaining to the nominal-object type of turn-continuations is that *it is exactly the right-headed syntax of Chinese that has allowed syntactic continuity* when an unexpressed nominal argument is added retroactively, or when the appended head noun takes the previous nominalizer-DE construction to be its modifier. In a sense, although right-headed syntax has *ab initio* led to most adverbial turn-continuations to be syntactically discontinuous, given other structural norms such as the "pro-drop" status of nominal arguments, "right-headedness" can also provide the grammatical environment for other sorts of syntactic continuous turn-continuations to appear.

4.2.4 Verb-resultative complement construction

A final syntactic environment we want to highlight where prosodically disjunctive turn-continuations can be appended in a syntactically continuous manner is as a complement that modifies the prior verb. While most verbal complements in Chinese appear to the left of the verbal phrase (e.g. adverbials denoting time, place and manner), in a verb-resultative complement construction (Li and Thompson 1973), the resultative complement is positioned to the right of the verbal constituent, denoting some sort of state that is the result of the action of the verb. The schematic structure of the verb-resultative construction is provided below.

$$\{ NP_s + VP + (Resultative\ Complement) \}$$

Hence, in certain situations where the TCU comes to possible completion after a verb, Chinese speakers will then have the option to produce turn-continuations as syntactically continuous post-verbal complements. This is illustrated in our final example below, which also shows the resultative complement added as a "post-other-talk" type of prosodically disjunctive turn-continuation.

Ex.(9) below is a video recording of three Ph.D. students (Jie, Wei and Tao) having a snack and chatting around a table. Before the start of our example, Jie laments about the difficulty in finding *yangrou* 'mutton' in school, a red meat frequently eaten in North China. Wei then recommends an Indian food stall in the canteen that does sell mutton. This seems to peak Jie's interest as she continues to ask Wei about the pricing and portion given. However, as the conversation progresses, Jie does not appear to show enthusiasm in accepting Wei's recommendation after it was revealed that the mutton is cooked in curry. The extract shown begins with line 12, where Tao joins in to collaboratively persuade Jie on the merits of the Indian food stall.

Ex.(9) NTU-2 [0:37-1:00]

```
12   Tao:    [这边      它    的::   印度]   (sss-)  菜     还     不    错
             [zhebian   ta    de::   yindu]  (sss-)  cai    hai    bu    cuo
             DEM-side   3SG   GEN    Indian          dish   still  NEG   wrong
             啦.         其实.
             la.        qishi.
             SFP.       actually.
             'The Indian food there is not bad... actually.'

13   Wei:    是      啊.=
             shi    a.=
             COP    SFP.=
             'Yeah.'

14   Tao:    =canteen B    也     就      那个.      hh    不过       我们      因为
             =canteen B    ye     jiu     nage.     hh    buguo     women    yinwei
             NM            also   only    DEM-CLF.        but       1PL      because
             'And that the only place in Canteen B with... It's just that we're'

15           很      少       吃     印[度     的      东西. ]
             han    shao    chi    yin[du   de      dongxi.]
             very   little   eat    Indian   GEN    thing.
             'not accustomed to having Indian food.'

16   Wei:                          [对              对 ] [ 对.    ]
                                   [dui            dui] [ dui.   ]
                                   right           right  right
                                   'yea            yea    yes'
```

17 Jie: [不   是.   ]
                                                     [bu   shi.]
                                                     NEG COP.
                                                     'It's not that.'

18   那个   印度   的   那个   咖哩   我: <不   能   吃::>.
          nage   yindu   de   nage   kali   wo: <bu   neng   chi::>.
          DEM-CLF   Indian   GEN   DEM-CLF curry   1SG: <NEG   can   eat>
          'It's that curry, Indian curry exactly, that I'm unable to eat.'

19 Wei: 为什么   呢.
          weishenme   ne.
          why   SFP
          'why?'

20   (.)

21 Wei: [哈.]
          [ha.]
             Q
          'huh?'

22 → Jie: [多.]   就是   它   [味道   很]   重.
          [**duo.**] jiushi   ta   [weidao   hen]   zhong.
          much.   DM   3SG   smell   very   heavy.
          'much.   It's just the flavor is too strong.'

Up till line 12 in the sequence, it is clear that both Wei and Tao have, in a sense, collaboratively offered a recommendation to Jie with little indication of recipient's acceptance, leading Tao to postulate unfamiliarity with Indian food in lines 14–15 as a possible reason for rejecting their recommendation. It is towards this postulation that Jie overtly rejects at line 17, before stating her specific misgivings. At line 18, Jie points out that it is specifically Indian curry that she has difficulties with in *na ge yindu de na ge kali wo: <bu neng chi::>* 'It's that curry, Indian curry exactly, that I'm unable to eat'. The end of this TCU is clearly taken as a TRP, as Wei jumps in the next turn questioning at line 19, and pursues this again at line 21 with a shorter question particle which runs into overlap with line 22. After talk by others, the focal turn-continuation in this example then occurs in the third subsequent turn at the beginning of line 22, simply with *duo* 'much/many', an adverbial adjunct that qualifies *chi* 'eat' in line 18. What is notable in this example, similar to other prosodically disjunctive turn-continuations in this section, is its position. Specifically, this turn-continuation was not produced immediately after possible completion (next beat), or after some noticeable silence (post-gap), but after speaker transition (post-other-talk). Furthermore, the occurrence of *duo* 'much' after *chi* 'eat' is also arguably "grammatically fitted" in normative Chinese syntax, presenting itself as a syntactically continuous resultative complement to the prior verb, as in *wo bu neng chi-duo* 'I can't eat much'. Effectively, by extending *wo bu neng chi* 'I'm unable to eat' at line 18 to *wo bu neng chi-duo* 'I'm unable to eat much' by line 22, Jie has mitigated from a total inability to eat Indian curry to a partial one of having limited ability to stomach the dish, thereby downgrading her initial strong stance of rejection to one of partial acceptance, noticeably after requests for justification were issued by Wei in lines 19 and 21.

Interestingly, besides syntactically "continuing" with the resultative complement *duo*, Jie further provides an additional visuospatial cue to mark this appended element as an "afterthought" type of turn-continuation, namely her shift in gaze.[13] From the video recording, this bodily-visual evidence further indicates that the addition of *duo* was produced as a process prompted by, or addressed to, talk by others. At possible turn completion by Jie at line 18 and throughout Wei's turn at line 19, Jie's gaze was firmly fixed towards Wei, reifying Wei as the main recipient of her talk (see Figure 4a).

Figure 4a: Jie's gaze on Wei during production of host-TCU at lines 18–19 in Ex.(9).

---

13 Ford, Thompson, and Drake (2012) demonstrates how bodily-visual practices can by themselves act as turn-continuations. Here, I am drawing attention to how Jie's bodily-visual behavior works to elaborate the accompanying talk as a turn-continuation, much like how syntax and prosody can also work to index continuation.

Figure 4b: Jie's contemplative gaze while producing the turn-continuation "*duo*" at line 22 in Ex.(9).

But immediately after Wei's question at line 19 and in the midst of the micropause at line 20, Jie retracts her gaze from Wei and rolls her eyes to her left, characterizable as a "contemplative" look (see Figure 4b) while producing the turn-continuation *duo*.

In so far as Wei's *weishenme ne* 'why' at line 19 is a targeted response to Jie's rejection of Indian curry with *wo bu neng chi* 'I'm unable to eat' at line 18, then the subsequent backing down with a syntactically continuous resultative complement *duo*, concurrently executed with Jie's upward contemplative gaze into space, constitute a fully embodied enactment of the further talk (i.e. *duo*) as an "afterthought" that is prompted by Wei's questioning. Ex.(9) hence demonstrates a process where the turn-continuation is visibly done as an appended element addressed to the contingencies presented after talk-by-others.

The four examples in this section illustrates situated contexts where the addition of further talk were prompted by recipient's lack of uptake (displayed through occurrences of gaps of silence) or intervening talk by others (be it to clarify the prior unit in Ex.(6), pursue verification or response in Ex.(7) and Ex.(8), or to downgrade stance in Ex.(9)), thereby resulting in prosodic separation between the host-TCU and its turn-continuation. While such turn-continuations may not be prosodically "continuous", it is shown that Chinese speakers have, as a recourse, various grammatical structures in the Chinese language (e.g. serial verb construction, topic-comment structure, verb-resultative complement etc.) where appending certain constituents can be deemed syntactically continuous after a possible completion point. For Ex.(9), the bodily-visual modality (i.e. shift in gaze) was also at play in marking turn-continuation. In other words, though prosodic disjunction may act as an impediment towards recognition of some units as "continuing" from the prior, syntax can then be called upon to rectify such units as bona fide turn-continuations. Crucially, as mentioned, a good majority of syntactically continuous turn-continuations in our data are in fact instances where further talk was appended "post-gap" or "post-other-talk", suggesting that there may be *some form of compensatory mechanism where syntactic contiguity is enlisted to index an additional sense of "continuation" when progressivity has been lost due to prosodic disjunction.*

5 Some final thoughts

One of the central questions set in this volume is to understand the relationship between grammar and multimodality in natural talk-in-interaction. However, if by grammar, we mean an array of notions such as grammatical classes and their syntactic distribution, then it bears to remember that grammar itself is simply one of many semiotic resources that can be employed to constitute interactional practices. By taking modality to mean any system of semiotic resource that indexes a certain type of information (e.g. prosody, syntax, pragmatic or bodily-visual), then it is clear that multimodality figures significantly in the interactional practice of "continuing" past a possible completion point for Chinese speakers.

Cross-linguistically, a recurrent finding is that modalities of syntax, prosody and pragmatics (and sometimes bodily-visual behaviors) all have to be analyzably coming to an end for TRP to be maximally recognized (Ford and Thompson 1996; Tanaka 1999; Hayashi 2005; Mori and Hayashi 2006; Local and Walker 2012; Keevallik 2013; Li 2014). This also holds true for Chinese conversations. However, when it comes to constructing Chinese turn-continuations, modalities can, and often are, at odds with each other in terms of indexing some unit of talk as "continuing" from the prior. Yet, what is interesting is not that they are at odds, but that one semiotic resource can in fact be used by speakers to rectify another to achieve the intended interactional goal. On one end, though the right-headed syntax of Chinese has engendered forms of adverbial (a highly productive class for achieving the interactional functions of turn-continuations) to be syntactically discontinuous after possible completion, speakers have operated upon their prosodic delivery to sustain a reading of continuation. When the appendage of turn-continuations motivated by gaps in talk or talk-by-others has necessarily led to prosodic disjunction, Chinese speakers have also frequently exploited grammatical structures to impose syntactic continuity. It is this finely coordinated use of multiple semiotic resources that we see as modalities not only cooperating but adaptively *co-operating* upon one another.

Goodwin (2014) and Kendon (2009) have consistently argued that human actions, including language, do not operate as isolated systems or modalities, but is constructed by bringing together different meaning-making modalities in a co-operative manner. Goodwin (2013) further described such co-operative modalities using the metaphor of lamination, where different semiotic fields are organized as layers of diverse resources. In his words, actions are built "by combining diverse resources (e.g., language structure, categories, prosody, postural configurations, the embodied displays of a hearer, tools, etc.) to perform both simultaneous and sequential transformative operations on a local, public semiotic substrate" (Goodwin 2013: 21). While traditional construal of multimodality has often treated different modalities either as self-sufficient, or working together as cumulatively 'layered' but semiotically discrete signs; the (re)configuration between syntax and prosody in the construction of Chinese turn-continuations has shown how multimodality in natural interaction is in fact a highly integrated gestalt, where co-operative modalities are being combined in a structured and organized manner that both constrain and mutually elaborate each other.

Appendix I: Transcription conventions

[or [ ]	overlapping or simultaneous talk
=	a "latch" sign, that is, the second speaker follows the first with no discernible silence between them. When the latch sign is between utterances by the same speaker, it indicates that the speaker's talk is continuous even though there is another speaker in between.
(0.5)	length of silence between utterances in tenths of seconds
(.)	micropause
?	rising intonation, not necessarily a question
,	continuing intonation
¿	the inverted question indicates a rise stronger than a comma but weaker than a question mark
!	exclamatory intonation
-	a cut-off or self-interruption
<	the less than symbol indicates that the immediately following talk is "jump-started," i.e., sounds as if it starts with a rush

> <	the combination of "more than" and "less than" symbols indicates that the talk between them is compressed or rushed.
< >	markedly slowed or drawn out, compared to the surrounding talk
°	following talk is markedly quiet or soft
↑↓	mark sharper rises or falls in pitch
:::	indicates prolongation or stretching of the preceding sound (the more colons the longer the stretching)
_:	Inflected falling intonation contour
:_	Inflected rising intonation contour
hhh	exhalation, hearble aspiration, or laughter, the more "h"s, the more aspiration
(hhh)	laughter inside the boundaries of a word
.hhh	inhalation
Wo(h)d	plosive aspiration within a word, which may result from breathiness, crying, or laughter
word	Underlining indicates some form of stress or emphasis
WOrd	especially loud talk
(word)	uncertainty on the transcriber's part
( )	something is said, but unable to do minimal deciphering
(( ))	transcriber's description of event

Appendix II: Abbreviations in Chinese gloss

1/2/3 SG	first/second/third person singular	DM	Discourse marker
1/2/3 PL	first/second/third person plural	EXP	Experiential aspect marker
AGR	Agreement Particle	GEN	Genitive Case Marker
BA	the *ba* transitivity marker	INJ	Interjection
BEI	the *bei* (and *gei*) 'passive' marker	LOC	Locative Complement
CFM	Confirmation Particle	NEG	Negator
CLF	Classifier	NM	Proper Name
CMP	Completion aspect marker	PCM	Potential Complementizer
COM	Verb complement	Q	Question Particle
COP	Copula	SFP	Sentence Final Particle
CRS	Current relevant state Particle	SIP	Sentence Initial Particle
CTP	Continuous aspect marker	TP	Topic Marker
DEM	Demonstrative		

Acknowledgments

This chapter is based on the research done for my yet unpublished dissertation. I thank the editors for the very detailed and insightful comments which has helped me a great deal in thinking through the phonetic and prosodic presentation and descriptions of turn-continuations. All remaining deficiencies are mine solely.

References

Auer, Peter. 2007. Why are increments such elusive objects? An afterthought. *Pragmatics* 17(4), 647–658.
Boersma, Paul & David Weenink. 2016. Praat: doing phonetics by computer [Computer program]. Version 6.0.22. http://www.praat.org/
Chao, Yuan-Ren. 1968. *A grammar of spoken Chinese*. Berkeley: University of California Press.
Cienki, Alan. (1998). Metaphoric gestures and some of their relations to verbal metaphoric expressions. In J-P. Koenig (ed.), *Discourse and cognition: Bridging the gap*, 189–204. Stanford, CA: Center for the Study of Language and Information.
Cienki, Alan & Müller, Cornelia. 2008. Metaphor, gesture, and thought. In Raymond W. Gibbs Jr (ed.), *The Cambridge handbook of metaphor and thought*, 483–501. Cambridge: Cambridge University Press.
Clayman, Steven. 2013. Turn-constructional units and the transition-relevance place. In Jack Sidnell & Tanya Stivers (eds.), *Handbook of Conversation Analysis*, 150–166. Malden, MA: Wiley-Blackwell.
Couper-Kuhlen, Elizabeth & Tsuyoshi Ono. 2007. 'Incrementing' in conversation. A comparison of practices in English, German and Japanese. *Pragmatics* 17(4), 513–552.
Deppermann, Arnulf. 2013. Multimodal interaction from a conversation analytic perspective. *Journal of Pragmatics* 46, 1–7.
Du Bois, John W., Stephan Schuetze-Coburn, Susanna Cumming & Danae Paolino. 1993. Outline of Discourse Transciption. In Jane A. Edwards & Martin D. Lampert (Eds.), *Talking Data: Transcription and coding methods for discourse research*, 45–89. Hillsdale, NJ: Lawrence Erlbaum Associates.
Forceville, Charles & Urios-Aparisi, Eduardo (eds.). 2009. *Multimodal Metaphor*. New York/Berlin: Mouton de Gruyter.
Ford, Cecilia E. & Sandra A. Thompson. 1996. Interactional units in conversation: Syntactic, intonational, and pragmatic resources for the management of turns. In Elinor Ochs, Emanuel A. Schegloff & Sandra A. Thompson (Eds.), *Interaction and grammar*, 134–184. Cambridge: Cambridge University Press.
Ford, Cecilia E., Barbara A. Fox & Sandra A. Thompson. 1996. Practices in the construction of turns: The "TCU" revisited. *Pragmatics* 6, 427–454.
Ford, Cecilia E., Barbara A. Fox & Sandra A. Thompson. 2002. Constituency and the grammar of turn increments. In Cecilia E. Ford, Barbara A. Fox & Sandra A. Thompson (Eds.), *The language of turn and sequence*, 14–38. New York: Oxford University Press.
Ford, Cecilia E., Sandra A. Thompson & Veronika Drake. 2012. Bodily-visual practices and turn continuation. *Discourse Process* 49(3–4), 192–212.

Fox, Barbara A. 2001. An exploration of prosody and turn projection in English conversation. In Margret Selting & Elizabeth Couper-Kuhlen (Eds.), *Studies in Interactional Linguistics*, 287–315. Amsterdam: John Benjamins Publishing Company.

Goodwin, Charles. 1979. The Interactive Construction of a Sentence in Natural Conversation. In George Psathas (Ed.), *Everyday Language: Studies in Ethnomethodology*, 97–118. New York: Irvington Publishers.

Goodwin, Charles. 1980. Restarts, pauses, and the achievement of mutual gaze at turn-beginning. *Sociological Inquiry* 50 (3/4), 272–302.

Goodwin, Charles. 1981. *Conversational organization: Interaction between speakers and hearers*. New York: Academic Press.

Goodwin, Charles. 2000. Action and embodiment within situated human interaction. *Journal of Pragmatics* 32, 1489–1522.

Goodwin, Charles. 2003. Pointing as situated practice. In Sotaro Kita (Ed.), *Pointing: Where Language, Culture and Cognition Meet*, 217–241. Mahwah, NJ: Lawrence Erlbaum.

Goodwin, Charles. 2007. Environmentally coupled gestures. In Susan D. Duncan, Justine Cassell & Elena T. Levy (Eds.), *Gesture and the Dynamic Dimensions of Language*, 195–212. Amsterdam: John Benjamins.

Goodwin, Charles. 2013. The co-operative, transformative organization of human action and knowledge. *Journal of Pragmatics* 46, 8–23.

Goodwin, Charles. 2014. The intelligibility of gesture within a framework of co-operative action. In Mandana Seyfeddinipur & Marianne Gullbert (Eds.), *Gesture in Conversation to Visible Action in Utterance*, 199–216. Amsterdam: John Benjamins.

Goodwin, Charles, & Marjorie H. Goodwin. 1987. Concurrent Operations on Talk: Notes on the Interactive Organization of Assesments. *Papers in Pragmatics* 1(1), 1–54.

Goodwin, Charles, & Marjorie H. Goodwin. 1992. Assessments and the construction of context. In Alessandro Duranti & Charles Goodwin (Eds.), *Rethinking context: Language as an interactive phenomenon*, 147–190. Cambridge: Cambridge University Press.

Goodwin, Marjorie H. 1980. Processes of mutual monitoring implicated in the production of description sequences. *Sociological inquiry* 50(3–4), 303–317.

Hassemer, Julius & Winter, Bodo. 2016. Producing and perceiving gestures conveying height or shape. *Gesture* 15(3), 404–424.

Hayashi, Makoto. 2003. Language and the body as resources for collaborative action: A study of word searches in Japanese conversation. *Research on Language and Social Interaction* 36(2), 109–141.

Hayashi, Makoto. 2005. Joint turn construction through language and the body: Notes on embodiment in coordinated participation in situated activities. *Semiotica* 156, 21–53.

Heath, Christian. 1984. Talk and recipiency: Sequential organization in speech and body movement. In J. Maxwell Atkinson & John Heritage (Eds.), *Structures of social action: Studies in conversation analysis*, 247–265. Cambridge: Cambridge University Press.

Heath, Christian. 1986. *Body Movement and Speech in Medical Interaction*. Cambridge University Press.

Heath, Christian & Paul Luff. 1992. Collaboration and control. Crisis management and multimedia technology in London Underground line control rooms. *Computer Supported Cooperative Work* 1, 69–94.

Heath, Christian, Marcus S. Svensson, Jon Hindmarsh, Paul Luff & Dirk vom Lehn. 2002. Configuring awareness. *Computer Supported Cooperative Work* 11 (3/4), 317–347.

Hidalgo-Downing, Laura & Mujic, Blanca Kraljevic (eds.). 2013. *Metaphorical creativity across modes*. Special issue of Metaphor and the Social World 3(2). Amsterdam: John Benjamins

Jefferson, Gail. 2004. Glossary of transcript symbols with an introduction. In Gene Lerner (Ed.), *Conversation Analysis: Studies from the first generation*, 13–31. Amsterdam: John Benjamin.

Kappelhoff, Hermann & Müller, Cornelia. 2011. Embodied meaning construction. Multimodal metaphor and expressive movement in speech, gesture, and feature film. *Metaphor and the Social World* 1(2), 121–153.

Keevallik, Leelo. 2013. The interdependence of bodily demonstrations and clausal syntax. *Research on Language & Social Interaction* 46, 1–21.

Kendon, Adam. 2009. Language's matrix. *Gesture* 9, 355–372. DOI: 10.1075/gest. 9.3.05ken

Levelt, Willem J. M. 1989. *Speaking: From intention to articulation*. Cambridge, MA: MIT press.

Levinson, Stephen C. 1983. *Pragmatics*. Cambridge: Cambridge University Press.

Li, Charles N. & Sandra A. Thompson. 1976. Subject and Topic: A New Typology of Language. In Charles N. Li (Ed.), *Subject and Topic*, 457–461. London/New York: Academic Press.

Li, Charles N. & Sandra A. Thompson. 1981. *Mandarin Chinese: A Functional Reference Grammar*. Berkeley & Los Angeles: University of California Press.

Li, Xiaoting. 2014. *Multimodality, interaction and turn-taking in Mandarin conversation*. Amsterdam: John Benjamins.

Liang, Yuan. 2005. 语序和信息结构：对粤语易位句的语用分析 *Yuxu he xinxi jiegou: Dui yueyu yiwei ju de yuyong fenxi*.《中国语文》*Zhongguo Yuwen* 306(3), 239–253.

Lim, Ni-Eng. 2014. *Retroactive Operations: On 'increments' in Mandarin Chinese conversation*. Los Angeles, CA: University of California, Los Angeles, dissertation.

Local, John & John Kelly. 1986. Projection and 'silences': Notes on phonetic and conversational structure. *Human studies* 9(2), 185–204.

Local, John, & Gareth Walker. 2004. Abrupt-joins as a resource for the production of multi-unit, multi-action turns. *Journal of Pragmatics* 36(8), 1375–1403.

Local, John, & Gareth Walker. 2012. How phonetic features project more talk. *Journal of the International Phonetic Association* 42(3), 255–280.

Lu, Jianming. 1980. 汉语口语句法里的易位现象 *Hanyu kouyu jufa li de yiwei xianxiang*.《中国语文》*Zhongguo Yuwen* 154(4), 28–41.

Lu, Shuxiang. (Ed.). 1999. *Xiandai hanyu babai ci* (Modern Chinese: 800 Words (Revised Edition)). Beijing: The Commercial Press.

Luke, Kang-Kwong. 2000. 句子成分的后置与话轮交替机制中的话轮后续手段 *Juzi chengfen de houzhi yu hualun jiaoti jizhi zhong de hualun houxu shouduan*.《中国语文》*Zhongguo Yuwen* (4), 303–310.

Luke, Kang-Kwong. 2005. 说延伸句 *Shuo yanshen ju*. In Institute of Linguistics, Chinese Academy of Social Sciences (Ed.),《庆祝《中国语文》创刊50周年学术论文集》*Qingzhu "Zhongguo Yuwen" chuangkan wushi zhounian xueshu lunwen ji*, 39–48. Beijing: Commercial Press.

Luke, Kang-Kwong & Zhang, Wei. 2007. Retrospective turn continuations in Mandarin Chinese conversation. *Pragmatics* 17(4), 605–635.

McNeill, David. 2013. Gesture as a window onto mind and brain, and the relationship to linguistic relativity and ontogenesis. In Cornelia Müller, Alan Cienki, Ellen Fricke, Silvia Ladewig, David McNeill & Sedinha Teßendorf (eds.), *Body – language – communication*.

An international handbook on multimodality in human interaction. Volume 1, 28–54. Berlin & Boston: De Gruyter Mouton.

Mondada, Lorenza. 2006. Participants' online analysis and multimodal practices: projecting the end of the turn and the closing of the sequence. *Discourse Studies* 8, 117–129.

Mondada, Lorenza. 2007. Multimodal resources for turn-taking: pointing and the emergence of possible next speakers. *Discourse Studies* 9(2), 195–226.

Mondada, Lorenza. 2011. The organization of concurrent courses of action in surgical demonstrations. In: Jürgen Streeck, Charles Goodwin, & Curtis D. LeBaron (Eds.), *Embodied Interaction, Language and Body in the Material World*, 207–226. Cambridge: Cambridge University Press.

Mori, Junko & Makoto Hayashi. 2006. The achievement of intersubjectivity through embodied completions: A study of interactions between first and second language speakers. *Applied Linguistics* 27: 195–219.

Nuñez, Rafael E., Edwards, Laurie D. & Matos, Joao Filipe. 1999. Embodied cognition as grounding for situatedness and context in mathematics education. *Educational Studies in Mathematics* 39 (1–3), 45–65.

Oreström, Bengt. 1983. *Turn-taking in English conversation*. Lund Studies in English 66. Lund: CWK Gleerup.

Pomerantz, Anita M. 1984. Pursuing a response. In J. Maxwell Atkinson & John Heritage (Eds.), *Structures of social action: studies in conversation analysis*, 152–164. Cambridge: Cambridge University Press.

Sacks, Harvey, Emanuel A. Schegloff & Gail Jefferson. 1974. A simplest systematics for the organization of turn-taking for conversation. *Language*, 696–735.

Schegloff, Emanuel A. 1996. Turn organization: One intersection of grammar and interaction. In Emanuel A. Schegloff, Elinor Ochs & Sandra A. Thompson (Eds.), *Interaction and grammar*, 52–133. New York: Cambridge University Press.

Schegloff, Emanuel A. 2016. Increments. In Jeffrey Robinson (Ed.), *Accountability in Social Interaction*, 237–263. New York: Oxford University Press.

Schuetze-Coburn, Stephan, Marian Shapley & Elizabeth G. Weber. 1991. Units of intonation in discourse: A comparison of acoustic and auditory analyses. *Language and Speech* 34(2), 207–234.

Selting, Margret. 2013. Verbal, vocal, and visual practices in conversational interaction. In Cornelia Müller et al. (Eds.), *Body-Language-Communication. An International Handbook on Multimodality in Human Interaction* (vol. 1), 589–609. Berlin: de Gruyter.

Stivers, Tanya & Jack Sidnell. 2005. Introduction: Multimodal Interaction. *Semiotica* 156(1/4), 1–20.

Streeck, Jürgen & Ulrike Hartge. 1992. Previews: Gestures at the Transition Place. In Peter Auer & Aldo Di Luzio (eds.), *The contextualization of language*, 135–158. Amsterdam: John Benjamins.

Streeck, Jürgen. 1993. Gesture as communication. I: Its coordination with gaze and speech. *Communication Monographs* 60, 275–299.

Streeck, Jürgen. 1994. Gesture as communication II: The audience as co-author. *Research on Language and Social Interaction* 27(3), 239–267.

Streeck, Jürgen. 2009. Forward-gesturing. *Discourse Processes* 4 (2/3), 161–179.

Tanaka, Hiroko. 1999. Grammar and Social Interaction in Japanese and Anglo-American English: The Display of Context, Social Identity and Social Relation. *Human Studies* 22(2/4), 363–395.

Tao, Hongyin. 1996. *Units in mandarin conversation: prosody, discourse, and grammar*. Amsterdam: John Benjamins Publishing Company.

Thompson, Sandra A. 1973. Resultative verb compounds in Mandarin Chinese: A case for lexical rules. *Language*, 361–379.

Vorreiter, Susanne. 2003. Turn continuations: Towards a cross-linguistic classification. In *List No. 39, Interaction and linguistic structures*.

Walker, Gareth. 2004. On some interactional and phonetic properties of increments to turns in talk-in-interaction. In Elizabeth Couper-Kuhlen & Cecilia E. Ford (eds.), *Sound Patterns in Interaction*, 147–169. Amsterdam: John Benjamins.

Walker, Gareth. 2012. The phonetic constitution of a turn-holding practice: Rush-throughs in English talk-in-interaction. In Dagmar Barth-Weingarten & Elisabeth Reber (eds.), Prosody in Interaction, 51–72. Amsterdam: John Benjamins.

Wilson, Thomas P., & Don H. Zimmerman. 1986. The structure of silence between turns in two-party conversation. *Discourse Processes* 9(4), 375–-390.

Zhang, Chunyan. 2001. 易位句中的语音问题 *Yiwei ju zhong de yuyin wenti*. 《汉语学习》 *Hanyu Xuexi* (4), 23–28.

Zhang, Wei. 2012. Latching/Rush-through as a turn-holding device and its functions in retrospectively oriented pre-emptive turn continuation: Findings from Mandarin conversation. *Discourse Processes* 49, 163–191.

Zhou, Shihong. 2010. 从信息结构角度看汉语口语中的 "主谓倒装句" *Cong xinxi jiegou jiaodu kan hanyu kouyu zhong de "zhuwei daozhuang ju"*. 《汉语学习》 *Hanyu Xuexi* (3), 28–36.

Liang Tao
Self-repair in Mandarin Chinese: The multimodality of conversation

This study reports findings from an initial exploration of the interplay of multimodality and repair in Beijing Mandarin. The multimodal resources used in repair that are explored in this study include phonology or phonotactics, lexico-syntactic choice, pragmatics as well as bodily-visual practices (Ford, Thompson, and Drake 2012; Fox 2002).

Repair constitutes an important part of the social organization of conversation (e.g., Sacks, Schegloff, and Gail 1974). The phenomenon has received increasing attention as scholars study the interactional needs of human communication (Levelt 1983, 1989; Levelt and Cutler 1983; Fox, Hayashi, and Jasperson 1996; Fox et al. 2009; Schegloff, Jefferson, and Sacks 1977; Schegloff 2013; Tao 1995, 2010; Tao, Fox, and Gomez de Garcia 1999; Wouk 2005).

Repair is highly patterned, and the practice occurs with some basic mechanisms (Schegloff et al. 1977; Schegloff 2013; Sidnell 2009). This study focuses on the practice of recycling or repetition in same-turn self-initiated self-repair during interactive communication. The basic mechanisms of repair occur cross-linguistically (Fox et al. 1996; Fox et al. 2009). In addition, there are language specific mechanisms as well, which may be constrained by the linguistic, pragmatic, social, and cultural foundations available in individual languages. The present study extends the cross-linguistic discussion of self-repair mechanisms (Fox et al. 2009) by offering further insights into some specific multimodal practices in Chinese conversations, including lexico-syntax, phonology, and embodied practice as reflected in the instances of self-repair. The study complements previous findings on conversational repair in general, and on the study of Mandarin interactions in particular. The phenomenon of repair may also assist the exploration of the relationship between cognitive processes of language and grammar (Fox 2007).

Liang Tao, Ohio University

1 Repair in Mandarin face-to-face conversation

1.1 Repair

One organization of conversation is a turn-taking system in which participants take turns speaking (Sacks 1992; Sacks et al. 1974). Schegloff (1979) proposes that during conversations, speakers may be stuck at a spot without knowing how to continue with the utterance. They may have uttered an inappropriate lexical item or expression, or may find that the utterance projected may elicit pre-disagreement indicators from the hearer. In such cases speakers may suspend the smooth progressivity of the talk to deal with ostensible problems in speaking, hearing, or understanding. A repair may be initiated by the speaker of the "trouble source" in the same turn (same-turn self-repair) or it may be done by someone else. Studies find that even when a repair is initiated by others, self-repair still prevails (Schegloff et al. 1977). In same-turn self-repair (henceforth just, repair) speakers may "stop an utterance in progress and then abort, recast or redo that utterance" (Fox et al. 2009: 60). The initiation of such repair often involves certain linguistic behaviors such as cut-offs, sound stretches, stress, pauses, etc., before the repair. Bodily-visual practices such as gaze shifts, head and hand movements, nodding, and so forth may also co-occur with repair (Ford et al. 2012). The following is an example of a self-initiated self-repair.

(1)   ... 获过   金- (.)   全国   金奖[1]
       Huo51 guo   ***jin55***[2] (.)[3]   *quan35guo35*   *jin55jiang214*
       obtain-Asp   gold-   whole-nation   gold medal
       '(She) once won a gold- national gold medal'.
       (Bejing_04 Dec. Kids)[4]

---

[1] The two characters/syllable *jin55jiang214* 'gold medal' is a compound word (words with two or more characters/syllables), based on the book by Research Team on the Lexicon of Common Words in Contemporary Chinese (2008). This book was specially commissioned by the Chinese Ministry of Education. It took a team of Chinese lexicographers ten years to complete; therefore the 'common words' (56,008 total) from this book serve as an important source for the study of Chinese lexicon.
[2] The numerals after each syllable indicate the four Chinese tones, each with two digits indicating pitch contours. One digit after a syllable indicates a cut-off of the tone. See Section 3, for detailed explanation of Chinese tones.
[3] Repair initiation: boldface. Repair proper: underline. See Appendix for transcription notations.
[4] The descriptions inside the parentheses (Beijing ...) indicate the data source where the example was extracted.

This example illustrates a typical repair sequence, i.e., a cut-off and a short pause at the repair initiation, and the repair proper (the part that is repaired), which involves an addition and recycling of the nominal 'gold medal'; thus the repair expanded the noun phrase (Schegloff 1979). "Lexical selection is shaped by features of interactional context" (Stivers and Sidnell 2005: 2–3) as well as culturally deemed appropriate (Stivers et al. 2009). In this example, the speaker, an elementary school girl, was introducing her teachers after a special performance. This utterance was about her music teacher. The girl was trying to boast the vocal talent of this teacher by claiming that the teacher had won a gold medal. Right before the repair initiation the girl must have realized that a 'gold medal' at the national level would be more impressive to the hearer than just a 'gold medal'. This mental process must have happened while the noun 'gold medal' was being produced (Levelt 1983; Menn 2017). As a result, the speaker made a cut-off at the first syllable of the word 'gold medal'. After a very brief pause, she added 'national', then repeated/recycled the nominal 'gold medal'. The cut-off is manifested by both the tone and the short pause. The pause signaled the end of the lexical item *jin 55* 'gold' with the second syllable of this compound word being cut off. The tone remained at a high pitch instead of moving a bit lower in preparation for its following lower pitch in the second syllable of the compound word.

One important issue to note is that the speaker utilized Chinese grammatical patterns to conduct the repair. Specifically, in Chinese, noun modifications always precede the noun. In this repair, once the noun is uttered, it has to be stopped and recycled by adding the modifier first.

The practice of repair reflects speakers' mental processes during language production, processes that are deeply rooted in the interactional pressure of conversations (Ford and Fox 1996). This part is further illustrated in Section 4.4 below. The cognitive processes of speech production stipulate that the production undergoes several levels in the brain (Levelt 1989; Levelt, Roelofs, and Meyer 1999). The same can be said about the effect of co-speech or coverbal gestures, which activate brain areas that deal specifically with language in comprehension (Joue et al. 2018; Kok and Cienki 2014; Wolf et al. 2017). From formulation of a projected message to activation of lexical items, association of semantic features and syntactic roles of the lexical items, to phonological encoding and final utterance, the procedure is incremental in that production begins before planning of an utterance is completed. Production is constantly monitored and repair is performed whenever speakers detect the necessity for the utterance to be better understood. For example, in (1) at the utterance of *jin55* 'gold', the speaker must have realized that a gold medal at the national level is much more impressive to the hearer than just a gold medal; therefore, she stopped production of the second part of the compound word and added the modifier 'national'. This example illustrates that repair may be self-initiated but it is hearer-oriented (Ford and Fox 1996). Repair analyses in this study take into consideration these human cognitive processes while focusing on the multimodal nature of repair situated in the interactive communication.

A repair in conversation does not always involve hearable errors or mistakes that require correction. Therefore, the term "repair", rather than "correction" is used to capture the more general domain of such phenomenon (Fox et al. 1996; Schegloff et al. 1977). Repair is often carried out with the mechanisms such as recycling, replacement, or restructuring of an utterance (see examples (2) an (3)), (Gomez de Garcia 1994, 1995; Lee 2010; Tao 1995), although not all repair attempts may be successful. Previous studies examined repair in Chinese from several aspects, for instance: syntax and repair (Chui 1996; Tao 1995), turn-organization and interaction in repair (Chui 1996; Luke and Zhang 2010; Wu 2006, 2009; Zhang 1998), utterance-prosody in repair (Chen 2011), and tone-related repair (Tao et al. 1999). Those studies focus on the general practice of repair mechanisms (Tao 1995; Zhang 1998) that have been observed in conversations of typologically diversified languages such as English and Kickapoo (a Native American language of the Algonquian language family, Gomez de Garcia 1994, 1995; Schegloff et al. 1977), or they focus on some specific mechanisms unique to Mandarin (Chen 2011; Chui 1996; Tao 1995; Tao et al. 1999, etc.). A recent cross-linguistic study on site of initiation of simple repair (recycling and replacement of a word or two, or a very short phrase such as a preposition phrase) during same-turn self-repair (Fox et al. 2009) offered invaluable insights into the commonalities of simple repair practices, and on specific characteristics of individual languages such as Chinese. The present study complements previous studies by offering further insight into the multimodal aspects of repair in Chinese. It follows the comparative study of Fox et al. (2009), and extends the findings from that study to offer discussions and explanations of some fundamental constraints that condition repair mechanisms in Mandarin, as well as some embodied repair practices in the language.

In this study, all instances of repair involve at least two stages, repair initiation, and repair proper. Repair initiation is done either by a cut-off of a syllable or part of a compound word (words with two or more characters/syllables, see Section 3 below), a short pause, some place holder syllables (See section 4.2), or an immediate recycling of the word at the trouble source. The repair proper is almost always done with some type of recycling of the word at repair initiation, with possible additional information, and/or replacing the word at repair initiation. Detailed discussions are presented in Section 4.

1.2 Cross-linguistic study on the site of initiation in same-turn self-repair

Fox et al. (2009) have compared seven typologically unrelated languages (including: Bikol (Austronesian, spoken in the Philippines), Sochiapam Chinantec (a tone language of the Oto-Manguean family of Mexico), English, Finnish, Indonesian, Japanese, and Mandarin Chinese).

They examine the site of initiation in repair during recycling and replacement of a word, as a simple repair.[5] Their data include 250 instances of repair from six languages, and 500 instances from English. All data came from audio or video recorded spontaneous conversations. This comparative study brings out special characteristics that speakers of each language utilize for the same practice. Following is an example of simple repair from Mandarin Chinese, which involves recycling of single-syllable words.

(2) 阿靓   在在   国际上   还   还
     A55jing51 **zai51** zai51 guo35ji51 shang51 **hai35** hai35
     A   at   at   inter-nation on   still   still
     有点儿   名气。
     you35 diar21 ming35qi.
     possess bit   fame
     'Ajing (a restaurant) is to some extent a bit well-known internationally'.
     (Bejing_98 p.46)

Translated verbatim (2) means: 'Ajing in in the international realm still still possesses a bit fame'. There are two recycling repairs here. The first one is initiated on the coverb[6] *zai51* 'at/in/on', and the second one is initiated at the adverb *hai35* 'also/still/yet'. In both instances the word was recycled or repeated right after repair initiation. Both repaired and recycled words were pronounced fully. Unlike (1) that appeared to have an obvious motivation for the repair, in (2) there is no clear reason for the repair except for probably the fact that the speaker was trying to formulate a proper description while producing the utterance.

Next is an instance of repair that involves a simple replacement of numerals.

---

5 The study examined simple recycling and simple replacement repair. Example (1) is not a "simple recycling" repair because it involves addition of a lexical item in the repair.
6 See Section 3, Chinese Grammar, for explanation of the coverbs.

(3) 在那儿   当了 (0.2)   五个月 (0.3)   两个月   翻译
    *Zai51 ner51 dang55le:: (0.2) **wu21'ə yue51**: (0.3) liang21'ə yue51 fan55yi51-*
    at   there act:as-Asp   five Cl month   two Cl month interpreter
    'There (I) worked as an interpreter for five month – two months'.
    (Beijing 87_p.59)

In this example, words of the same parts of speech were replaced. The speaker first said 'five months', and after a short pause, the numeral 'five' was replaced by 'two' and the whole noun phrase 'X month' was recycled. Notice that the first person pronoun 'I' was omitted, an instance of zero anaphor, which is a common practice in Chinese discourse.

The first finding of Fox et al. (2009) brings out one common practice for the simple repair: all seven languages appear to prefer recycling (115–162 instances from each of the seven languages) to replacement (16–46 instances). In the Mandarin Chinese data, the instances of recycling are over three times more than those with replacement. So the commonality is that speakers of these languages tend to recycle an utterance or morpheme in the self-repair practice.

Secondly, extending from Schegloff (1979), Fox et al. (2009: 66) examine two sites of repair initiation: post-beginning (repair initiated during or right after the first sound, e.g., *sh-*) and pre-completion (repair initiated just before the last sound) of a morpheme.

Going back to Example (1), it presents an instance of repair that was initiated at the pre-completion site – "*jin55-*" the tone of the first syllable of the word *jin55jiang214* 'gold medal' was almost completely uttered before the cut-off occurred.

The post-beginning site of repair initiation (e.g., *b-*, Example (11) below) usually does not offer enough information for the hearer to guess what the originally intended word is going to be; thus the utterance is unrecognizable. The pre-completion site, on the other hand, may offer enough phonological information for the hearer to identify the intended word. As it turns out, most of these languages favor the pre-completion site (the only exception is Finnish, which leans slightly toward the post-beginning site for repair initiations). Their findings certainly supported Schegloff's (1979) proposal on the site of repair initiation in English: 72% of all simple replacement repair and 53% of all simple recycling repair initiated from the pre-completion site. However, the phenomenon is by no means universal because repair initiations do not seem to come mainly from these two sites in all languages.

As Fox et al. (2009: 71) point out, the majority of the simple repair initiations occur in the final segment, not before it. This is certainly true of Mandarin (as well as Indonesian, Bikol, and Sochiapam Chinantec), which has very few post-beginning repair initiations (4% and 6% for simple recycling and replacement repair, respectively), and a relatively more instances in the pre-completion site for repair initiations (29% and 17% for simple recycling and replacement repair, respectively). The majority of the simple repair as analyzed is initiated after the word had been completely uttered in Mandarin (and Sochiapam Chinantec, also a tone language). This site of repair initiation results in a fully recognizable word being produced before a simple repair is initiated.

Interestingly, Mandarin and Sochiapam Chinantec, two unrelated tone languages, both have the majority of repair initiations after the final segment of a morpheme has been uttered, hence recognizable, and they both lean toward repair initiation on monosyllabic words. Furthermore, Mandarin also keeps this practice when a repair initiation is on a dual-syllabic word (so does Indonesian), although the general tendency in Mandarin repair is on monosyllabic words. Furthermore, repair initiations in Mandarin fall equally on function and content words. These practices certainly are not observed equally in the other languages. For instance, in Example (2), the first repair initiation is on a function word *zai51* 'at/in'; whereas in (1) and (3), the initiation is on content words.

In summary, Fox et al. (2009) conclude that Mandarin tends to initiate a simple repair (for both recycling and replacement of a word) at the site after the last segment (sound) is produced, thus the overwhelming majority of the repair initiations produce a recognizable morpheme/word.[7] With this practice, multisyllable compound words are also produced as recognizable words. This is true for some other languages included in the analyses. Fox et al. (2009: 100) propose a possible explanation to this preference: late decisions to initiate a repair. The monosyllablic words would offer one "discourse beat" of delay, usually enough time for the speaker to search for the right word. A discourse beat is defined as a short delay, possibly a syllable or so (Schegloff 2000b: 19). In (2), the speaker recycled two single-syllable words, probably to give himself enough time to search for the right expressions for the utterance.

The rest of this chapter is organized as follows. Section 2 introduces the data used in this study. Section 3 provides a brief introduction to Chinese grammar that concerns the repair practice in this study. Section 4 provides detailed examinations of instances of repair from the data, and offers some possible explanations to each of the four interrelated multi-model practices of repair. Section 5 concludes the study with some suggestions for extension of this study.

---

7 This discussion involves both phonology (syllables, etc.) and words (recognizable by meaning). The recognizable part could be a word if it is a single character/syllable word. If it is part of a multi-character word, then this part could be a morpheme, part of a word. Over 94% of Chinese words are formed by two or more characters. See Section 3 below.

2 The data

The data for this study come from audio- (about two hours) and video-taped (about eight hours) naturally occurring face-to-face Mandarin Chinese conversations by native Beijing Mandarin speakers, including but not limited to the data that were used in previous studies (Fox et al. 2009; Tao et al. 1999; Tao 1995).

The analyses of the data include instances of repair that involve both simple recycling (see (2)), which is a repetition of the same morpheme, word, or phrase from where a repair is initiated, and instances of recycling with the addition and/or deletion of part of the initiated elements (see (1)). The study proposes that while recycling may offer an extra "discourse beat" or two (Fox, et al. 2009; Schegloff 2000b) for the speaker to search for the right expression (Fox et al. 2009), an addition or deletion to the recycled element may reflect speakers' simultaneous self-monitoring of their utterances (Levelt 1983) based on the immediate interactional needs. Therefore, recycling plus addition or deletion does not just offer a discourse beat to offer some extra time for speakers to conduct word search, but it also leads to possible replacement or even re-structuring of the utterance. This last part is illustrated in example (10) below.

Most of the data presented here are instances of recycling in same-turn self-repair that have no hearable errors.

3 Mandarin Chinese grammar

This section introduces the part of Chinese grammar that pertains to the repair practice in this study, starting from phonemes, tones, prosody to morphology, and syntactic patterns in conversational discourse.

The minimal word (词 *ci35*) in Chinese is a single syllable, in the form of (C)(G)V(X) (Lin 2011: 430) where C= consonant, G=glide, V=vowel or syllabic consonant, and X=V or C (Lin 2011: 430). X can only be one of two nasals n/ŋ. A syllable may contain a minimum of one nucleus (vowel). It is realized in writing by one character. Mandarin phonotactics is set up to produce a CV as the basic sound unit, which has posted a constraint that may have an impact on the characteristics of repair initiations in Mandarin, as illustrated in Section 4.3.

Spoken Beijing Mandarin has one specific feature that the examples keep intact. When a syllable is inside a multi-syllable unit (which forms a prosodic unit,[8]

---

[8] It is also called an intonation unit. In Mandarin Chinese such a unit does not have to be a multi-syllable word or a grammatical phrase. It is often marked by an intonation contour with

Chafe 1994), the onset of the internal syllable tends to be turned into a 'voiced continuant', leaving the retroflex /zh, ch, sh/ into /r/, and the palatal /j, q, x/ into /I/ (Chao 1968: 37). The former is also described as lenition of retroflex obstruent initials (Zhang 2005). This practice is transcribed as 'x'', indicating that the onset was not fully pronounced. Furthermore, such voiced continuants can turn syllabic to be fused with the vowel. In this case no vowel is indicated after it. Sometimes the onset is completely eliminated, which is indicated as ''x^9''.

Mandarin Chinese is a tonal language with four lexical tones. Every stressed syllable has a designated tone that differentiates meaning. Chinese has contour tones with both pitch register and change/movement. Using numbers 1 – 5 to represent pitch values from low '1' to high '5' (Chao 1968: 25–26[10]; Li and Thompson 1981: 8), the following illustrates the pitch fluctuations that form the four tones:

(4) First tone: 55   High level
    Second tone: 35   High rising
    Third tone: 214 Dipping/falling-rising
    Fourth tone: 51   High falling

In the high level tone 55, the pitch register of the syllable remains at level 5 throughout. In the high-rising tone 35, the pitch starts mid, and then rises high to level 5. In dipping or falling-rising tone 214, the pitch begins at a relatively low level 2, then moves down to level 1, and finally rises to level 4. With the high falling tone 51, the pitch starts high at level 5 and falls sharply down to level 1. In addition, there is a 5th tone, a neutral tone, which is a short pitch register on an unstressed syllable. In the data of this article, if a syllable is followed by one digit instead of two, it indicates the duration of the vowel and the tone in this syllable is shortened, usually due to a cut-off. If a syllable does not have a numerical digit, it indicates an unstressed syllable.

The four tones are not always produced in the citation forms in connected speech. Speakers follow a set of tone sandhi rules (Tao et al. 1999). The following is one set of such tone sandhi rules that are relevant to this study. The examples listed below are hypothetical.

'fused' phonological features. Repeated usage of such units may lead to language change (Bybee 2006; Tao 2006).

9 Here are three such instances in the data from Examples (10) and (11): *dao51r'35'ou5* 'when time comes'; *nei51j'iao41* 'that was-called'.

10 Chao (1968) based all his discussions on spoken Beijing Mandarin. But the tone descriptions represent standard Mandarin Chinese as well (Lin 2011).

(5) a. When followed by a syllable with any tone other than the dipping tone, the dipping tone 214 changes into a low tone 21. e.g., *hao214* 'good' → *hao21 ren35* 'good person'
   b. When followed by a syllable with a dipping tone, the first dipping tone changes into a high rising tone 35.   e.g., *hao214* 'good' →   *hao35 ma214* 'good horse'

In natural speech, tone sandhi rules are strictly followed as part of Mandarin Chinese phonotactics. A wrong sandhi in an utterance may disrupt intonation flow, often causing a recycling repair (Tao et al. 1999).

A Chinese word may contain a single syllable, represented in writing by one character, but the majority of contemporary Chinese words are compounds with two or more syllables. According to the *Lexicon of Common Words in Contemporary Chinese* (Research Team on the Lexicon of Common Words in Contemporary Chinese [henceforth just, Lexicon] 2008)), about 94% of commonly used words are compounds with two or more syllables, and two-syllable words constitute about 72%. This information is also important in Mandarin repair practice, further discussed in Section 4.1.

The syntactic structure of Chinese is basically SVO: Subject–Verb–Object. Noun modifications always precede the noun (see (1)) and adverbs always precede the verb. Naturally prepositional phrases always occur before the main verb. Most of the prepositions are considered coverbs due to their dual nature of both verb and preposition[11] (Tao 2011). The language allows other word orders for pragmatic needs, which Chao (1968) proposed as inverted sentences and subject/object inversions.[12] Reference presentation in discourse contains abundant zero anaphora; therefore the grammatical subject and/or object may not be present when the referents may be inferred through context (Tao 1996, 2001), especially during face-to-face conversations.

---

[11] Chinese also has postpositions but no instance of repair has been found on these elements in the data, since it occurs at the end of a phrase (See example (10)).
[12] Here is an actual utterance by a native Mandarin Chinese speaker, in the VSO order. The grammatical subject and object seem to be added as an afterthought because the question particle normally occurs at the end of a sentence.
  上   完了吗,   你,   厕所?
  Shang51 wan35le ma, ni21, ce51suo214
  Go   finish-Asp Q 2sg   restroom = finished? You, restroom?
  Are you done using the restroom?

4 Same-turn self-repair in Mandarin Chinese

This section discusses two types of repair practices in Mandarin Chinese. The first part discusses the correlation of Mandarin phonotactics and repair initiations (sections 4.1–3). The second part discusses some possible causes of repair from the interactive nature of conversation (section 4.4). This part incorporates discussions of embodiment of repair in interaction. It has been well documented that interaction often involves bodily-visual behaviors in addition to utterances (Ford et al. 2012), which include, for instance, vocal hesitations, gaze, head turn, nod, and hand gestures as an integral part of conversation (Cienki and Müller 2008; Ford et al. 2012; Fox 2002; Goldin-Meadow and Wagner 2013; Kendon 2004; Ragsdale and Sylvia 1982; Schegloff 1984).

4.1 Lexico-syntactic tendencies and Mandarin Chinese repair initiation: single-syllable

It has been observed cross-linguistically that "syntax and same-turn self-repair are interdependent and co-organizing, each requiring the other as part of its operation" (Fox et al. 1996: 186). Repair cannot exist without syntax, since syntax organizes linguistic elements through which talk is constructed, and without talk, there can be no repair (Schegloff 1979: 262). Repair operates within the grammar and discourse patterns of language.

The first observation of this study is that Fox et al. propose (2009) that it is *no accident* that repair initiation in Mandarin Chinese tends to fall on single-syllable words. Currently, the majority of Chinese words are compounds with two or more syllables, and single-syllable words only constitute about 6% of the 56,008 most commonly used words (Lexicon 2008). However, among the first 100 high frequency words, single-syllable words constitute about 82% (Lexicon 2008)! This skewed distribution suggests that single-syllable words have significantly higher usage frequency than compound words do.

In Mandarin Chinese grammar, noun modifications always precede the noun, and adverbs almost always precede the verb. Therefore, adjectives and adverbials often become the site of initiation, presumably because they are at the beginning of an NP or VP. Furthermore, coverb phrases always precede the main verb, so coverbs may also constitute a preferred site of repair initiation. This tendency is purely observational, but the practice can be commonly observed in the data. In the following examples, repair initiations in (6a) (c.f. (2)) fall on the coverb *zai51* 'in/at' and the adverb *hai35* 'still/also/somewhat'. In (6b) repair initiation falls on the numeral, the first syllable of the NP.

(6) a. 阿靓　　　　在在　　国际上　　　　还　　还　　有
A55jing51 **zai51** <u>zai51</u> guo35ji51 shang51 **hai35** <u>hai35</u> you35
A　　　　 at　　at　　inter-nation on　　still　　still　　possess
点儿　名气。
diar21 ming35qi.
bit fame
'Ajing (a restaurant) is to some extent a bit well-known internationally'.
(Bejing_98 p.46)

b. 1) B: 拿　　什么　　撬啊?
Na35 [shen35me qiao51 a?]
Take what pry-open Q

2) A: 说是一分钟　　　　之内　　把　你
[Shuo5'r yi51 fen55'ong5] zh'r55nei51 ba35 n'21
Say be one-minute within BA 2sg

3) → 六　　六　　把　　锁　　全　　撬开
liu53- <u>liu51</u> ba35 suo21 quan35 qiao51 kai55.
six six Cl lock all pry-open

1) B: 'Use [what to pry-open (the locks)]?'
2) A: '(He) [said that within one minute] (he can) get
3) all six locks of yours pried-open'.
(Beijing04_July_end, p. 2).

Example (6b) came from a conversation about crime issues in Beijing. B was reiterating a thief boasting about their special capabilities to break open any locks on a bike or a car. At line 3, the numeral 'six' starts the NP 'six locks'. The recycling repair could be triggered by the overlap earlier in the utterance, reflecting a possible broken train of thought[13] and a "delayed" repair.

---

[13] There are several instances of similar "delayed" repair in the data, in which repair initiations were not aligned with the overlap but came out after the overlapping section. This correlation needs further study to confirm.

4.2 Lexico-syntactic tendencies and Mandarin Chinese repair initiation: dual-syllables

Recycling also appears to cover two-syllable units, units within one prosodic contour with a pitch drop. The term "unit" is used because the dual-syllable covers three possible word combinations: first, a compound word with two syllables (hence two characters in writing); second, a short phrase such as a demonstrative plus a classifier, grammatical subject plus part of the predicate, or a verb plus its modifier (e.g., an adverb or a complement); and third, dual-syllables that form neither a grammatical phrase nor a word. For instance, the unit at repair initiation could be a coverb plus part of its object (see example (10) below).

This practice is in line with the claim that Chinese words follow a dual-syllabic prosodic domain, and the dual-syllable may be an intermediate category between words and phrases (Feng 2001, 2009). Given the three possible syllable-combinations at a repair, "unit" could be the best cover term for it. Studies find that readers tend to partition sentences into two-character units (Li, Rayner, and Cave 2009; Li, Gu, Liu, and Rayner 2013). This practice makes perfect sense considering that the majority of Chinese words are dual-syllable compounds (about 72%, Lexicon 2008), and so Chinese speakers favor dual-syllables in word formation (Feng 2009). In Chinese repair, there are some highly frequently used dual-syllable phrases that probably have developed into the function of place-holders during word-search (Fox 2007; Hayashi 2003). They are often recycled, probably to extend the speaker's turn while the speaker conducts word search. The following are two such filler words that speakers often use in the data. They are both uttered within the same prosodic contour with fused phonological features (e.g., sh → /r/, and /g/ turns into a glide; Chao 1968). Notice that it is common practice cross-linguistically to use the distal demonstrative pronoun as "prospective indexicals" during word search (Hayashi 2003: 134).

(7) Filler words as place-holders for word search or repair initiation
   a. 就是
      jiu51shi
      exact-be (emphatic 'be')

   b. 那个
      nei51ge
      that-Classifier

If used as syntactic expressions, (7a) contains an adverb and the verb 'to be', and it should connect two nominal expressions for emphatic confirmation, and

(7b), the distal demonstrative pronoun plus the most frequently used classifier *ge*, should precede an NP that the classifier *ge* is paired with. The classifier *ge51* is the most frequently used classifier (usage frequency ranked #8, lower number indicates higher usage frequency, Lexicon 2008) that goes with human related nouns and things. In informal speech it can be paired with even more nouns that are normally paired with other classifiers.

However, as discourse fillers, they assume the role of a place holder. As Hayashi (2003) suggests, the use of a distal demonstrative pronoun as a place-holder during word search may index a particular search domain. The following is an example that contains both fillers, which exemplifies the non-syntactic function of the two filler phrases: *jiu51shi* does not connect two NPs to function as a VP, and *nei51ge* does not precede an NP nor does it have any syntactic function in the utterance. The unit *nei51ge* 'that-classifier', plus the immediately following pause, appear to function as a place-holder while the speaker searched for proper formation of the question.

(8) 你们   学校   是   就是   那个 (0.45)
    Ni21m'   xue35x'iao51 shi51   jiu51shi41 **nei51ge** (0.45)
    2pl   school   be   exact-be   that-Cl
    就是   外面儿   包   包   那   食堂   吗?
    jiu51shi2 wai51miar **bao55** bao55   nei51 shi35tang35 ma?
    exact-be outside   contract contract   that   cafeteria   Q
    'Does your school (three filler phrases) contract out your cafeteria?'
    (Beijing Dec.04)

Example (8) came from a conversation between two girls from two different high schools. They had been best friends since elementary school and when they met they naturally shared their school life, including food. This utterance, a question, is at a turn-beginning phase with a new topic. There was no overlap during this utterance, but this topic switch did not seem to be smoothly uttered. The speaker first initiated a repair after expressing the verb *shi51* 'be', then recycled the verb with an added adverb for an emphatic phrase *jiu51shi51* 'exactly be', followed by the filler phrase *nei51ge* 'that-classifier' (see (7a, b)) plus a short pause. Then *jiu51shi* was recycled again before the rest of the utterance was produced. However, the filler phrases might not have offered enough time for the speaker to complete her word search. The main verb *bao55* 'contract out' became the site of another repair initiation.

The site of repair initiation may also fall on a two-syllable unit. Again, the unit may not be a dual-syllabic compound word or even a grammatical unit (Feng 2009), as exemplified below.

(9) 二姑　　　那个（0.1）　你那儿[14]（0.1）　你那儿
    Er51gu55　**nei51ge** (0.1)　**ni21nar51** (0.1)　ni21nar51
    2nd aunt　that-Cl　　　2sg there　　　　2sg there

    有　　　email　　　是　　吧？
    you35　e21mail31[15]　shi51　ba5?
    have　email　　　　be　　Q
    'Second Aunt, you have email at your place, right?'
    (Beijing_97 p. 27)

Example (9) illustrates a simple recycling repair on an NP. The utterance was made at a turn-beginning, with a question that was unrelated to the previous turn. The speaker first uttered a filler phrase *nei51ge* 'that-classifier' plus a short pause, signalling a trouble spot. Then he replaced the phrase with an NP *ni21nar51* 'your place[16]'. The filler phrase, if taken verbatum, would mean 'that-classifier', which is not part of the following NP.[17] Therefore this dual-syllable unit can only be taken as a filler that serves as a place holder (holding a discourse beat, Fox et al. 2009; Schegloff 2000b) to help the speaker formulate the question. The NP 'your place' started another repair sequence with a pause and a recycled NP.

In the next two exmaples the site of repair initiation also falls onto two-syllable units, and the two words do not necessarily form a grammatical unit either. This practice could be due to Mandarin Chinese speakers' preference of dual-syllablic prosodic units (Feng 2009).

(10) （说）　　　在我　　　在我　　　　眼里头　　　那就是
     (sh)'uo5　**zai51wo21** zai51wo21　yan35 li21tou5　na31jiu51r'1: (0.8)
     say　　　at　　　　1sg at　　　1sg eye　inside　that right be

     到时候　　　　一掰的事儿（.）　一拧　　　　的事儿。
     dao51r'35'ou5　yi51 bai55 de r'i31 (.)　yi51ning21　de sh'r51
     arrive time　　one-break DE matter　one-twist　DE matter

---

14 The last character represents a coda of the syllable as a retroflexed /r/ in Beijing Mandarin.
15 This is a common Mandarin Chinese term for the English word 'email', which added tones to the two syllables.
16 This is an idiomatic expression for locations (pronoun +locative 'here/there').
17 A classifier is needed when an NP begins with a numeral or a demonstrative. In (9) the NP starts with a possessive pronoun, which usually goes before the entire NP, including the numeral/demonstrative, not after them.

'To me (in my eyes) when the right time comes that's merely a matter of a simple bend, a simple twist'.
(Beijing04_July_end p.3)

Example (10) came from a discussion about a social issue of stealing bikes for profit (see (6b)). The specific utterance is a reiteration of a thief's arrogant boast of the ability to crack open any special locks. The site of repair in this example was initiated right after the two words *zai51wo21* (with no delay or any indication of a trouble source), whose interpretation is ambiguous at the site of initiation. The coverb *zai51* 'in/at', similar to a preposition, normally takes a locative nominal. But the first person pronoun *wo214* 'I', is not a location. So the two words only form a dual-syllabic prosodic unit for repair initiation, which does not fall under any syntactic construction. The pronoun may function in a variety of roles, one of which is a possessor when expressing inalienable possessions (from one's own body parts to intimate relationships such as family members, Fox 1981), part of an NP. The meaning was made clear right after the recycled repair when the rest of the coverb phrase was completed with the noun 'eye', plus the postposition *li21tou* 'inside' (Biq 2009). The coverb plus the postposition together form a completed circumposition phrase to express the meaning 'in my view' or 'as I see it'.

Example (11) below contains two instances of repair. The first was initiated at the end of a two-syllable unit containing a grammatical subject and a transitive verb.[18] The unit was recycled as the repair proper itself (line 1). The verb is transitive so it is the head of the VP; therefore the repaired dual-syllabic prosodic unit breaks down the verb phrase.

(11) → 1. 那叫: (0.8)   那叫: (0.73)   呃
Nei51j'iao41:: *(0.8)*   *nei51j'iao41:*   *(0.73)e*
That be-called   that be-called   eh

→ 2.   **b**-北烤   我们   这儿   算   南烤
     b- *Bei35kao21*[19]   *Wo21m'4*   *zher51 suan51*   *Nan35kao21.*
     north grill   1pl   here count-as   south grill

---

18 The verb *jiao51* 'call' can indicate the name of someone or something. The most closely matched meaning in English is 'be-called'. Syntactically the verb does not form a passive voice.
19 Both words *bei214kao214* have the 3rd tone. The two tones are realized in '35' and '21' by following tone sandhi rules as explained in (5).

1. 'That (restaurant) was (called) e::
2. Northern Grill. Ours (restaurant) here was the Southern Grill'.
(Beijing04_2 p.7)

The first recycling repair in (11) was initiated at the turn beginning. The repair initiation and the recycled repair units (line 1) both contained a clear vowel extension and a pause, which seem to reflect the speaker's effort to search for the next item due. The second repair initiation at line 2 started at the beginning of an NP, the object of the transitive verb *jiao51* 'be-called'.

The initiation of the second repair (line 2) presents a rare case in Mandarin Chinese where the site falls on the onset of a syllable, a bilabial stop /b/,[20] with only an articulatory gesture (lip closing) without releasing the explosive. After a slight delay, the /b/ was released to produce the word *bei35* 'north'. In this case the repair initiation is signaled by the bilabial speech gesture and delayed release of the stop, which naturally would not produce a recognizable word.

The two instances of repair in (11) are accompanied by additional bodily-visual practices, which is discussed in section 4.4. This section just discusses how Mandarin Chinese speakers utilize possible syntactic and phonological resources that are offered in Chinese grammar for the practice of repair. Generally speaking, at the lexical level speakers seem to prefer initiating repair on single syllables. On the syntactic level speakers seem to reflect a prosodic preference of dual-syllable units, be it a grammatical unit or not. The next section presents another grammatical feature that occurs on the site of repair initiation, Mandarin Chinese phonotactics.

4.3 Phonotactics of Mandarin Chinese

Mandarin Chinese phonotactics may be one of the major grammatical features responsible for the characteristics of the site of repair initiations in Mandarin Chinese, including the preferred dual-syllable structures and tone sandhi rules in the language. This section discusses the site of repair initiations specific to Mandarin Chinese, which is due to specific phonotactics of the language.

---

[20] Phonetically this should be an unaspirated /p/.

4.3.1 Mandarin Chinese syllables and site of repair initiation

Fox et al. (2009) find that repair initiations in Mandarin Chinese predominantly fall on or after the last element of a word, and this site of repair initiation results in a fully recognizable word being produced when a simple repair was initiated. Furthermore, they also find that the majority of simple repair is initiated on a monosyllabic word in Mandarin Chinese. While this preference is not shared by all languages, as found in that study, it makes perfect sense for Mandarin Chinese if we examine the phonological format of its syllable structure.

A syllable in Mandarin Chinese always ends in a vowel. The only two nasals /n, ŋ/ that may end a syllable are usually fused with their preceding vowels to form nasalized vowels.[21] This syllable structure gives rise to the following Mandarin Chinese phonotactic preferences: consonants, especially explosives and liquids, have to be produced with a vowel.[22] Therefore, a repair initiation on a monosyllabic word is almost always on or after the last sound/nucleus of the syllable (i.e. the vowel). Furthermore, with vowels come tones. Consequently, as soon as a consonant is produced, it brings out a vowel with at least a pitch register as the initial pitch of its designated tone (See (1)).

Initiating a repair on the first sound of a word entails a cut-off. English speakers often utilize this "device" to initiate repair (Fox et al 1996; Fox et al. 2009; Schegloff 1984). Yet due to the phonotactic constraints, Mandarin Chinese speakers do not seem to be used to cut-offs to initiate repair. When they do cut-offs, the consonant would often bring out its following vowel and at least a pitch register that can be extended to a tone. As a result, cut-off is rarely done on the first sound, the consonant of a monosyllabic word.

The data of this study offer supporting evidence to this proposal. Out of a sample of 260 instances of self-initiated repair by Beijing Mandarin Chinese speakers, there were 44 instances of cut-offs, of which 31 (about 70%) had repair initiations on the final vowel, with both the vowel and its designated tone cut short (i.e., only one beat rather than two beats of a full tone). There were 13 instances of cut-offs on the first sound, the consonant, without producing a vowel. It is interesting to note that of the 13 instances, two of them contained unreleased

---

[21] For instance, in informal speech, *Tiananmen* is always pronounced /tiã55 ã55 mẽ35/, and Chang'an (street) is produced as /chã^{n}35 ã55/, where the velar and alveolar nasals are completely fused with their preceding vowels. But this is not true of all Mandarin dialects.

[22] The phonotactic constraints are strictly followed. For instance, The English-based loan words in Mandarin Chinese would undergo syllable adjustments by either dropping the last consonant (coda), or adding a vowel to the last consonant. Compare: Denmark: *Dan55 Mai51*; Brook: *Bu51 Lu214 **Ke51*** (Lin 2011: 432).

stops /t, b/. The other 11 consonants that were released without bringing out a vowel (thus making the word unrecognizable) were all affricates and voiceless fricatives (e.g., z, sh::: ; s:::, etc. See Appendix).

The following are some examples of repair initiations that illustrate this practice, including initiation on the first sound (12), on the vowel (13a-c), and after the last sound/vowel (14). Full explanation of the examples is provided later on in Section 4.4.

Example (12), a repetition of (11), contains a rare case of repair initiation on the onset consonant bilabial stop /b/. The speaker made a clear bilabial gesture with a slight delay (0.01). Then he released the /b/ to produce the whole word *bei35*: north. The repair initiation was not a recognizable word (See (11) for the full utterance).

(12) **b-**北烤
 b- *Bei35kao21*
 north grill: 'Northern Grill' (name of a restaurant)
 (Beijing04_2 p.7)

Examples (13a-c) present repair initiations that also involve cut-offs. In all three cases the vowels were clearly shortened, and each carried a pitch register at a different height, clearly indicating an intended tone of the syllable. The word at the repair initiation could not be guessed because in (13a-b), part of the syllables were cut off (i.e. *ji3-jiao21* and *ji3-jin55* respectively). In (13c) the vowel was cut short as the first syllable of a three-syllable compound word, also making it impossible to guess the word at the repair initiation site.

(13) a. ...**ji** (0.325)   铰弯了
    ji'3[23] *(0.325)*   *jiao21* *wan55 le:*
    twi- twist   bend   Asp:
    '... bend it by twisting'
    (Beijing04_July_end p. 1-2)

  b. ... **ji** 今天   晚上   看
    ji5-jin55tian5 *wan21r'ang5* *kan51.*
    to- today   evening   look at:
    '(I'll) look at it tonight'.
    (Beijing_Kids_Dec.04)

---

[23] Some phoneticians (e.g., Lin 2011) consider the /i/ following the alveolo-palatal as part of the palatal consonant, instead of a semi-vowel. But in this study /i/ is still considered part of the diphthong /iao/ since it carries a pitch as the initial part of a tone.

c. ... 那个   **li-**   离合器   挂着锁,
   nei51ge3 **li2-**   li35h'e5q'i51   gua51r'2 suo21
   that Cl   clu-   clutch   hang-Dur lock
   '... that clu-clutch had locks hanging on it'.
   (Beijing_04_end p.3)

The cut-offs as illustrated in these examples may illustrate the influence of Mandarin Chinese phonotactic constraints. For instance, in (13b) the site of repair initiation was the first syllable of a two syllable word *jin55tian55* 'today'. The initial consonant /j/ (an alveolo-palatal affricate /dʒ/) was produced with its following vowel /i/ and a high pitch register that can be extended to the high-level first tone. But the syllable coda, the nasal /n/, was not audible. Due to the CV syllabic preference in Chinese phonotactics, cut-offs are typically made on or after the vowel. The same could be true of (13a, c).

Example (1), reproduced as (14) below presents an instance of recycling plus addition, in which the repair initiation occurred after the syllable was produced. However, the tone remained high, which means it was not produced in preparation for the low pitch of the following syllable. The short pause signals a repair initiation. In this case, the word 'gold' is clearly recognizable. Please see (1) for more detailed explanations.

(14)   ... 获过   金- (.)   全国   金奖
       Huo51 guo **jin55**- (.) *quan35guo35* *jin55jiang214*
       obtain-Asp   gold-   whole-nation   gold medal
       '(She) once won a gold- national gold medal'.
       (Bejing_04 Dec. Kids)

The final example of this section, (15), presents an instance of cut-off that was clearly motivated by the speaker's realization of a speech error. The utterance was at the turn-beginning and the speaker initiated a question about the whereabouts of one of their old neighbors, a lawyer with the last name *Ni35*. From the very beginning the speaker used a phrase *nei51shei35* 'that-who', a commonly used filler phrase in Beijing Mandarin to refer to someone's name that the speaker cannot readily think of.

(15)   1. 那   谁   呢?   那个   倪   呢?
           Nei51 *shei35* *ne?* *nei5'e* *Ni35* *ne?*
           That   who   Q   that-Cl   NI   Q

  →   2. 那个   姓   律师   那个   **li-** (0.4)   ^倪! (0.3)
           Nei51'ə xing51   *lü51shi* *nei51ge* **li-** (0.4)   ^*NI35* (0.3)
           that-Cl surname   lawyer   that-Cl   li-   NI

→ 3. 姓　　倪　　的　　那个　　律师　　呢?
   <u>Xing51 Ni35　de　nei51ge　lü51shi</u> ne?
   Surname Ni　DE　that-Cl　lawyer　Q

   1. 'What about what's his name, what about that Ni?
   2. That surnamed Lawyer that li-, NI35!
   3. That lawyer with the surname Ni?'
   (Beijing_97 p.1)

The speaker in this example made a speech error possibly because of the simultaneous mental activation of two NPs, *Ni35*, a surname, and *lü51shi* 'lawyer', which were uttered out of sequence.[24] While anticipating the next item due for the utterance '*surname NI the lawyer*', the utterance came out as '*surname lawyer*'. In Mandarin Chinese word order, the full NP 'the lawyer with the family name Ni' should be: *xing51 Ni35 de* lü51shi. Instead the speaker uttered: *xing51* lü51shi 'urname lawyer.'[25] By producing the onset of the last syllable /l/ after '*nei51ge* 'that-Classifier' the speaker must have realized the error, so a cut-off was made. By the general practice of Mandarin Chinese phonotactics, the liquid /l/ was produced with a vowel, though barely audible. This vowel had a reduced feature: instead of the high-front rounded /ü/, a high-front /i/ was produced with a very low pitch register. After a very brief pause, the repair attempt was made with a single syllable and a clearly pronounced full tone *NI35*, followed by a slight pause. It could be that by repeating only the surname the speaker reinforced her activation of the correct surname *NI35*. This syllable was produced with a higher pitch and volume than the other part of the utterance, and the duration was a bit longer than the same syllable in the properly repaired utterance. The higher pitch and volume was maintained in the following utterance, which was a fully repaired utterance, a practice that may have strengthened the activation of the right NP. Throughtout this struggle it seems that the speaker used prosody to help aid a 'mental fight' between the two NPs.[26]

Cut-offs, as with repair initiations in general, seem less preferred by Mandarin Chinese speakers, most likely due to the syllabic preference as summarized

---

24 This practice can be best explained in the cascade model of language production (Menn 2017; Morsella and Miozzo 2002), which indicates that lexical activation is not in line with the syntactic pattern, and activated words may be produced out of sequence.
25 The * indicates an ungrammatical or nonsense expression.
26 This type of speech error is well defined in the spreading-activation model of sentence production (Menn 2017).

in the Chinese phonotacitc constraints. The majority of repair cases have repair initiated after the full syllable was produced with tones.

4.3.2 Tone-related repairs

Mandarin Chinese has a set of tone sandhi rules that speakers follow closely (see (5) for some of the rules). When a tone violates a sandhi rule, speakers tend to recycle the syllable to get the right sandhi tone (Tao et al. 1999). The site of repair initiations in this case are always after the full syllable and its tone are clearly produced, and the word is recognizable. The practice often involves simple recycling of the syllable.

(16) a. =两　　两　　　两　　秒钟
Liang21 liang21　liang35 miao21zh'ong55
Two　　two　　two　　second o'clock
'two　　two　　Two seconds'
(Beijing04_1 p. 1)

b. 也:　也　　不是　　　特别地　　　说得来
ye35: ye21　bu35shi51　te51bie35de　shuo55de lai35
still　still　Neg-be　especially-Adv compatible
'(They) don't get along that well either'.
(Beijing13 p. 4)

c. 哎　踩碎　　　是把　　那个　　鬼祟
Ei55 cai21sui51　shi5 bai21 nei51'ə ^gui21sui51
Eh step-smash　be BA　that-Cl devil-ghost
给踩　　给踩啦[27]
gei35 cai35-　gei35 cai21 la55.
to-its-loss step to step – Asp.
'Eh crashing by stepping means to get the demons crashed'.
(Beijing97 p. 23)

---

[27] Example (16c) reports an old Beijing tradition during Chinese new-year's celebration: to cover the yard with dried sesame stalks for people to crash by stepping on them. The word 碎 sui51 'broken, smash', rhymes exactly with 祟 sui51 'demon'. The practice of 踩碎 cai21sui51 'crash by stepping', rhymes with 'crashing demons'. The phrase also rhymes with a good wish 彩岁 cai21sui51 'colorful year'.

All three instances of repair in (16) appear to be caused by tone sandhi violations at repair initiation, as explained in (5). The initiations reflect three different approaches: without delay (16a), a slight vowel extension (16b) and a slight cut-off (shortened vowel, 16c). In (16a), the first third tone, *liang214* 'two', should have changed to a rising tone *35* when preceding another third tone *miao214* 'second', but it was produced with a low tone *21*. The word was recycled twice before the tone was correctly hit. Notice that *miao214* 'second' takes a low tone *21* because it is followed by a high-level first tone *55* (sandhi rule (5a)). In (16b), *ye214* 'still' (emphatic), should take the low tone (sandhi rule (5a)) before a rising tone *35*, but it was produced with a rising tone. The speaker may have realized the wrong tone so she made a vowel extension to initiate the repair. In (16c), the speaker produced a rising tone on *cai214* 'step on', or 'crash by stepping', in anticipation for another dipping tone (sandhi rule (5b)). But the next syllable had a high level tone *55*, so the sandhi rule was wrongly applied. The speaker may have noticed this on the spot so he shortened the vowel and its tone to initiate the repair. Notice that in (16c), a two syllable unit, part of a verb phrase, was recycled, a malefactive particle plus a single-syllable verb. The perfective verb-final particle *la55* (a phonologically fused word that combines the perfective *le* and the interjection *a*, Chao 1968) was left out. This practice illustrates the dual-syllable preference in spoken Chinese (Feng 2001, 2009).

All instances of tone related repair seem to follow a general pattern: The site of repair initiations is always at the place after the syllable and its tone are produced. Repair is always initiated by the speaker right at the trouble source, as in same-turn self-repair, and the mechanics of repair always involve recycling.

This section introduces two types of phonotactics that Mandarin Chinese speakers utilize to conduct repair. Due to the CV syllable structure of the language, speakers rarely initiate a repair on the onset consonant of a syllable, and the predominant practice is to initiate a repair on or, more frequently, after the last segment of the syllable is produced. Furthermore, speakers initiate and recycle a single syllable or a dual-syllable phonological unit to adjust its tone to adhere to the tone sandhi rules, which is also a phonotactic practice of the language.

The next section discusses some embodied practices associated with repair.

4.4 Embodiment of repair in interaction

There are certain interactional needs that may trigger repair cross-linguistically (Ford and Fox 1996; Fox et al. 1996). Same-turn self-repair reflects a speaker's effort to deal with some ostensible problems (Schegloff 1979) that may break the progressivity of the utterances. For instance, the speaker may realize another description would deem more proper for the hearer to follow (e.g. Example (1), repeated in (14)), or they may be searching for proper expressions at different stages of a turn (e.g. Example (11) where repair initiations were at the beginning and middle of the turn). Repair often occurs when there is a change of discussion topic (e.g., Examples (8), (9) and (15)). Recycling repair often happens at the transitional period when the next speaker's turn-beginning overlaps with the end of the current speaker's turn (Schegloff 1987).

Accompanying utterances in conversations also include multimodal activities, which Ford et al. (2012) propose to be bodily-visual practices, including, for instance, head turning/tilting, gaze shifts, nodding, and gestures (Cienki and Müller 2008; Ford et al. 2012; Fox 2002; Kendon 2004; Schegloff 1984; Seyfeddinipur 2006; Stivers and Sidnell 2005). Vocal hesitations (such as cut-offs, pauses, etc.) are also frequently accompanied by body-movements (Ragsdale and Sylvia 1982). Ford et al. (2012: 197) propose that "talk and other modalities can mutually elaborate and contextualize one another." Bodily-visual practice during conversations may be highly correlated with repair, and may even be utilized as a means for communication, with as important of a role as linguistic means, because the coordination of the two aspects offer projectability in conversation (Ford, Fox, and Thompson 1996; Hayashi 2003; Sacks et al. 1974). Projectability allows speakers the prospective orientation of future course of actions in conversation (Ford et al. 1996; Ford and Thompson 1996; Hayashi 2003; Sacks et al. 1974).

The correlation of verbal (i.e., linguistic) and non-verbal (i.e., bodily-visual and other non-linguistic behaviors) practices can be found deeply rooted in human brains (Menn, Online summary). Contemporary researches have offered scientific support to this belief. For instance, Gibbs (2006: 158–207) proposes the embodiment of language that combines body movements and speech to emphasize meaning. Goldin-Meadow and Wagner (2013: 275) suggest that hand gestures are part of human beings; they provide building blocks "that can be used to construct a language." They also enhance language learning, and assist comprehension during conversations. Hayashi (2003: 112) demonstrated that a simultaneous gesture and the distal demonstrative pronoun as a place-holder enhance "the projectablity and specificity of the searched-for item." Hauk, Johnsrude, and Pulvermüller (2004) and Just et al. (2010), based on findings from event-related fMRI, suggest an overlapping activation of neurons that process action words (from the language sensitive areas, Menn 2017) and the neurons that process actions (at the motor and premotor cortex), in a somatotopic manner. They suggest that the connection must be due to frequent correlation of language usage and physical actions, (See also Chui 2013; He 2011; and Li 2013). These findings certainly support what Ford et al. (2012) propose that bodily-visual practice is not secondary or supplemental to verbal turns in conversation, but is rather in coordination with verbal expressions.

Three types of gestures are observed during repair in the data of the present study: emblems, iconic, and beat gestures. Emblems carry meanings of their own without the help of linguistic expressions. They reflect conventionalized gestures within a particular culture (Kendon 1995). For instance, moving sideways of either the hand or the head indicates disapproval or negation in many cultures. An iconic gesture is "in form and manner of execution" that exhibits a meaning relevant to the linguistic meaning expressed simultaneously (Beattie and Coughlan 1999: 36). An iconic gesture correlates with speech to express the speaker's intent (Chui 2013). The beat gesture describes a rhythmic movement of a finger, hand or arm, which may consist of a single strike or a series of beats. Experimental studies find that the speed of word retrieval may be significantly enhanced by simple beat gestures (simple, repetitive hand movements, Beattie and Coughlan 1999; Lucero, Zaharchuk, and Casasanto 2014; Ravizza 2003).[28] Lucero et al. (2014) suggest that beat gestures are motor actions, and repetitive motor actions produce cognitive consequences because they enhance neural activations in the whole brain.

Studies on non-visual eye movements (Ehrlichman and Micic 2012) propose that certain eye movements could reflect specific sensory components in thought (Dilts, Online Summary; Ehrlichman and Micic 2012; Ehrlichman et al. 2007; Buckner et al. 1987). Shifting gaze from the hearer could imply the speaker's mental efforts in information searching (See, Ehrlichman and Micic (2012) for a summary). During conversations, speakers may encounter uncertainty in the midst of descriptions, so word search and repair are often unavoidable. In this situation speakers "routinely withdraw their gaze" from the hearer while engaging in word search, and they resume the gaze to their recipients at the end of the search (Ford and Fox 1996: 155).

Included in this section are instances of repair that are associated with head turns, gaze shifts from the recipients, and hand gestures. Presented here are four cases, which share some or all of the above three bodily-visual practices. The instances are not exhaustive and future studies may reveal more multimodality or embodied cognition in interactive communication, especially concerning others-initiated self-repair. The four cases are listed below. The first three involve only the speaker who carried out the repair. They illustrate how the speaker coordinated verbal and bodily-visual practices to try to involve the

---

28 Those studies often involve examination of the tip-of-the-tongue state (TOT). Lucero et al (2014) found that beat gestures, but not iconic gestures, helped participants to find and activate words faster.

recipient for mutual stance building. The last example displays an instance of interactional exchange that involves both speakers while trying to reach intersubjectivity. The multimodal examples below include the following:
a. Gaze shifting and repair (Section 4.4.1);
b. Beat gesture and gaze during repair (Section 4.4.2);
c. Posture shifts and repair (Section 4.4.3); and
d. Interplay of gaze shifting, iconic gesture, and repair (Section 4.4.4)

4.4.1 Gaze shift and repair

Eye movement may coordinate with repair (Ford et al. 2012), which offers an extra signal at repair initiation when a trouble spot was detected. In (17), speaker A, sitting on the left, was telling B about the inconvenience of construction going on in her neighborhood. Line 1 appears to be the end of the turn. At line 2 speaker B oriented to A's turn as possible completion at the end of line 1, and immediately initiated her turn in a question. The question, however, overlapped A's turn by two syllables at line 3, which seemed to be the continuation of line 1. During the overlap, an error was produced by A on the second syllable of line 3. The word *bei214* 'north' was uttered as *bai21*. Speaker A made a cut-off at the error, the first syllable of the two syllable name *bei214guan55* 'northern gate'. Concurrent with the cut-off, speaker A displayed a "thinking face" – a gaze to an empty space away from the recipient while conducting word search (Goodwin and Goodwin 1986: 57; Ehrlichman and Micic 2012). Concurrent with the repair initiation at line 3, speaker A shifted her gaze away from the recipient, speaker B, and gazed up into an empty space above (Figure 1a, where A is on the left and B on the right). The gaze was shifted back toward B (Figure 1b) as soon as the repair started. Notice that although the trouble spot is the start of an NP (*Bei21guan55* 'Northern Gate'), the recycle started on the preceding verb, indicating how a unit is defined in the speaker's mind.

(17) 1. A: 得   挖   那个   二十米   深
             Dei21 wa55 nei51ge   er51shi mi21 shen55
             Need dig   that-Cl   twenty meter deep
             的一个 地下   通道。
             de yi35ge di41xia51 tong55dao51.
             DE one-Cl underground tunnel

→   2. B: [干   嘛   呀]?
             Gan51 ma35   ya
             Do   what   Q

Self-repair in Mandarin Chinese: The multimodality of conversation —— 281

→ 3. A: [叫: bai1-]
         Jiao51 bai1-
         Be-called bai

Figure 1a: *jiao51 **bai1-***. The boldface indicates the syllable produced at the moment as shown in the figure.

4.   叫   北关   环隧。
         jiao51   Bei21guan55   Huan35sui35
         be-called Northern Gate   circle-Underground.

Figure 1b: *Bei21guan55 huan35 **sui35***.

5. B: 北关?
        Bei21guan55
        Northern gate

1) A: '(They) had to dig an underground tunnel that's twenty-meters deep'.
2) B: '[Why did they do that]?'
3) A: '[(It's) called **bai21-**]
4)   called Northern Gate Underground-Roundabout'.
5) B: Northern-gate?
      (Beijing_14)

Example (17) presents an instance of interactional work during repair, which was done in coordination with non-verbal practices. The gaze shift at line 3 (Figure 1a) displays a thinking-face, possibly signaling a name search (Goodwin 1986; Goodwin and Goodwin 1986; Ford et al. 2012; Hayashi 2003). During the process of repair by speaker A, speaker B (on the right) kept her gaze toward A, showing attentiveness. As the repair was completed at line 4, A resumed her gaze to B, resulting in mutual eye contact, demonstrating the achievement of mutual stance. This behavior has been well-documented: during word searches, where recipients "characteristically" gaze to the speaker, presumably showing their attentiveness while allowing the speaker to finish the search (Goodwin and Goodwin 1986).

4.4.2 Beat gesture, gaze and repair

In the next example, ((18) reproduction of (6b)), a repair occurred concurrently with a beat gesture. The repair involved a cut-off and recycling of a single-syllable word, possibly caused by utterance overlapping. The entire repair process was concurrent with the speaker's constant gaze toward the recipient, an iconic gesture (i.e., holding a note to read), plus a striking motion superimposed to the iconic gesture. Repair initiation was done by coordination of verbal behavior and the beat gesture.

Example (18) is part of a discussion about the social issue of bike theft reported on TV. An expensive mountain bike was parked on a sidewalk with six different types of locks on it. A thief left a note on the bike, claiming that if they wanted to, the thief could have broken the six locks within a minute. Speaker A was retelling the story. At line 1 speaker B cut into A's turn with a question, which overlapped with speaker A at line 2. At the onset of line 2, *shuo55* 'say' speaker A stretched out his left arm towards B, with the palm tilting up towards himself in an iconic "reading" gesture (Figure2a).

Speaker A moved his left arm up and down as 'beats' throughout his turn at Lines 2 and 3. At line 2, A made three hand beats, each coordinated with two to three syllables that were marked by prosodic contours (Chafe 1994). These units were meaningful segments: a verb ('say', two syllables), a noun phrase ('a minute' three syllables) and a commonly used phrase ('within' two syllables). The beats certainly added emphasis to the effect of the reiteration. Specific to repair is the beat at the beginning of line 3. Speaker A's left arm raised up first (Figure 2a), and stroked down emphatically at repair initiation (Figure 2b), a cut-off of the numeral *liu51* 'six'. This beat differed from the previous ones because it did not coordinate with any meaningful segment of the utterance. Instead it correlated with the prosodic signal of the cut-off. The next beat resumed its concurrence with a full NP, *liu51ba35suo21* 'six locks', which is the repair proper. The last beat occurred with the final segment of line 3, 'all pry-open'. Observe:

(18) Speaker A just mentioned what the note said, and repeated it at line 2.

    1. B: 拿　　[什么　　　撬啊?]
            Na35 [shen35me　qiao51 a?]
            Take　what　　　pry-open Q

    2. A: [说(是²⁹)　一分钟]　　　之内
            [Shuo5'r　yi51 fen55'ong5]　zh'r55nei51
            Say be　　one-minute　　　within

→ 3.　　　把(你)　六　　六把锁　　　全　　撬开。
            ba35 n'1　**liu53**-　<u>liu51ba35 suo21</u>　quan35 qiao51 kai55.
            BA 2sg　six　　six Cl　lock　　all　　pry-open

a. Left arm up at the onset of **ba35**.　　**b.** Strike completed at end of **liu53**-.

Figure 2a–b: Beat gesture and repair.

    4. B: 他　　没有　　　偷走　　啊?
            Ta55 mei35you5　tou55 zou21　Ah
            3sg. Neg-Perfective　steal – go　Q

    1. B:　'Used　[what to pry-open (the locks)]?'
    2. A:　'(He)　[said that within one minute]'
    3.　　　'(I can) get all six locks of yours broken-open'.
    4. B:　Didn't he steal it?
            (Beijing04_July_end, p. 2).

Notice that at line 2, the beats were concurrent with intonation units, units that were marked by a prosodic contour with slight pauses in between (Chafe 1994). But at repair initiation (line 3), the strike was done at the cut-off, *liu53* 'six', a

---

29 The verb 是 *shi51* 'be' is reduced to a barely audible syllabic /r/, typical of Beijing Mandarin (Chao 1968).

numeral that does not form either an intonation unit or a semantic unit. Its tone was shortened so the falling tone did not reach its low pitch point, and there was no delay or pause between the repair-initiation and the repair proper, which was done by recycling the numeral and additional words to form an NP *liu51ba35 suo21* 'six locks'. This strike, therefore, coordinated with the verbal part of the repair-initiation, which may very well have added emphasis to the repair (Gibbs 2006). Additionally, the entire utterance in lines 2–3 and the beats were concurrent with eye contact – Speaker A maintained his gaze to B, possibly holding solidarity with B. The hand gesture, in coordination with speaker A's utterance in (18), exemplifies how a speaker made full use of different modalities to try to reach mutual stance with speaker B. Speaker B at line 4 uttered a question concerning information from A, which illustrates alliance and total involvement in this short narrative.

4.4.3 Posture shifts and repair

The next example ((19), repeated from (11)) also involves both gaze shifts and the beat gesture, except that the two bodily-visual practices were not completely in alignment with word search, which is different from findings of previous studies (Fox and Heinemann 2015). When a speaker shifts the gaze to an empty space away from the recipient during word search, the gaze usually is resumed to the recipient at the end of a search (Ford and Fox 1996; Goodwin and Goodwin 1986). The beat gestures are often thought to concur with or to assist word search (Lucero et al. 2014; Ravizza 2003). In example (19), the speaker's gaze was resumed to the recipient before his search was completed; yet the gesture came after the sequence of the repair was completed.

Prior to the first repair initiation, speaker A was facing speaker C, the recipient (where the camera was), with both hands resting on a table in front of him. The utterance was part of a short narrative about A's career working as a chef in a restaurant. At line 1 the speaker was trying to recall the nick name of the restaurant he had worked for, but the name did not seem to come to his mind at the moment. As a result, after the verb *jiao51* 'to be-called', speaker A made a sound extension and a pause to initiate a repair. Concurrent with the repair initiation, at the onset of the two-syllable subject-verb unit (*nei51jiao51* 'that was called'), speaker A shifted his gaze (line 1, Figure 3a; compare also, Figure 1a) to an empty space away from the recipient, demonstrating a "thinking face" (Goodwin and Goodwin 1986: 57). This "thinking face" coincided with repair initiation, clearly showing the speaker was conducting a name search.

The recycled unit *nei51jiao51* 'that be-called' (end of line 1) might not have been a completed repair because it ended with an extra sound *e*, which aided the sound extension and extended the utterance. While uttering *e*, speaker A resumed his gaze to speaker C (line 2). Usually gaze to an empty space is brought back to the recipient at the close of a name search (Ford and Fox 1996; Goodwin and Goodwin 1986). However, at line 2 the gaze was resumed to the recipient but the name did not come out right away. Speaker A turned to the recipient, facing the camera, with a clearly unreleased bilabial /b-/ and a slight pause, the initiation of a second repair (Figure 3b). In this case, A's gaze was resumed to the recipient prior to the completion of the name search: the onset of the syllable was activated (i.e., /b-/), but the whole name had not been; therefore, the release was delayed (Figure 3b). Right after releasing the name *bei35kao21* 'Northern Grill' to complete the second repair (line 2), at the onset of the pronoun *wo21men* 'we/our' (line 3), A's left hand made a quick strike (Figure 3c). Immediately after A's turn ended at line 3, Speaker C (line 4) uttered two syllables, acknowledging acceptance of A's stance.

(19) → 1. A: 那叫: (0.8)   那叫: (0.73) 呃
            Nei51j'iao41:: *(0.8)*   nei51j'iao41: *(0.73)*e
            That be-called   that be-called e

Figure 3a: "thinking face" ***Nei21***.

→ 2.   b-北烤
       b- *Bei35kao21*[30]
       north grill

---

30 Both syllables 北烤 *bei214kao214* 'northern grill' have the 3rd tone. The two tones are realized in '35' and '21' by following tone sandhi rules as explained in (5).

Figure 3b: Un-released *b-*.

→ 3.　我们　　　这儿　　算　　　南烤 =
　　　Wo21m'4　zher51　suan51　Nan35kao21=
　　　1pl　　　here　　count-as south grill

Figure 3c: Hand strike at *wo21men*.

4. C:　=嗯　　嗯
　　　　=En4　en41

1.　A: 'That (restaurant) was called – that was called -
2.　b-Northern Grill.
3.　Ours (restaurant) here was the Southern Grill'.
4. C: 'uhn uhn'
　　(Beijing04_2 p.7).

This example shows that speaker A spent quite a lot of effort to produce the information. It illustrates how different modalities collaborated during the process of repair while the speaker tried to engage the recipient in the conversation. The linguistic means of repair initiations include sound stretch and pauses (line 1), and a delayed sound-release as a cut-off (line 2). The two instances of repair in this example, and especially the second one (Figure 3b), showed typical behavior during the tip-of-the-tongue (TOT) state (Kohn et al 1987; Menn 2017).

Other bodily-visual behaviors are also observed, including gaze shifts (Figures 3a and 3b) and a hand strike (Figure 3c). Reiterated here are further explanations of the multimodal practices in this example. When speaker A shifted his eye contact from the recipient to gaze at an empty space (line 1, Figure 3a), a typical "thinking face" is displayed (Fox et al. 1996; Goodwin and Goodwin 1986). This practice could help the speaker to hold his turn during name search. When the gaze is brought back to the recipient, previous studies find that it signals the end of the name search (Fox et al. 1996; Goodwin and Goodwin 1986). Nevertheless, in example (19) the search was not completed at the moment. The *early* return of the gaze to the recipient might have occurred due to the speaker's attempt to engage the recipient, even though the name had not been fully activated. Speaker A therefore made a speech gesture of an unreleased bilabial stop /b-/ (Figure 3b). This cut-off, a very clear unreleased bilabial stop, initiated the second repair. After the repair proper 'Northern Grill' was produced, speaker A raised and stroke down his left hand once as one beat at line 3. Strikes as beat gestures are usually concurrent to word search, which could enhance word activation (Lucero et al. 2014). The hand strike at line 3 does not appear to add emphasis to the utterance, so this beat could constitute a *post-repair hand-strike*, a delayed motor response to the searching process. The dis-synchronized repair and bodily-visual practices have not been reported before so further research is needed to confirm this speculation.

In examples (17) – (19), speakers engage the recipients by either fixating their gaze toward the recipients (18), or resuming their gaze to the recipients after their gaze shifted away for word search (17, 19). In the meantime, the recipients kept their gaze to the speakers, showing their attentiveness and involvement (17).[31] The "thinking face" does not just indicate the speaker's internal processes in name searching. The behavior also displays forgetfulness and uncertainty, which "not only enable[s] a speaker to display to others some of the information processing, or other 'back-stage' work involved in producing an utterance, but also provide[s] participants with resources for shaping their emerging interaction" (Goodwin 1987: 115–116; also cited in Ford and Fox 1996: 155). In all three examples, the actions of the recipients were displayed in their proper responses, showing their understanding of the stance and their engagement in the conversation.

The concurrence of bodily-visual practice and repair suggests that different modalities "work together to elaborate the semantic content of the talk and

---

[31] Due to technical issues the recipients in examples (18) and (19) were not recorded in the picture of the video. But these recipients properly responded immediately at the end of the speakers' turns, presumably having maintained their attentiveness to the speakers.

constitute a coherent course in the conversation" (Stivers and Sidnell 2005: 1). However, just as ostensible problems may occur during speech production that may require repair (Sacks et al. 1974), as illustrated in (19), different modalities, linguistic and bodily-visual practices, might not always be organized in synchrony during interactional communication.

4.4.4 Interplay of gaze shift, iconic gesture, and repair

In the next example (20), different modalities mutually elaborate and contextualize one another in the practice of repair (Ford et al. 2012). It exemplifies how intersubectivity (Du Bois 2007) is collaboratively and contingently achieved through participants' verbal and bodily-visual practices in their effort to achieve epistemic stance in the conversation.

Three types of gestures are involved here: emblems, iconic, and beat plus gaze shifting in concurrence with repair. In this simple exchange, the non-verbal behaviors occurred prior to, during, and post repair initiations, further reflecting the fact that verbal and non-verbal behaviors might not always be in synchrony, but they collaborate as an integral part of the interactional conversation. In this example, the two speakers are siblings. A is the woman, and B is the man. This part of the conversation is reminiscent of their childhood events. The tiger-bone-pill in the conversation is a type of Chinese traditional children's medicine formed in tiny balls.

The first repair process by speaker A is reported here before the example is shown. Speaker B's response is discussed after the example. At the start of this exchange, speaker A was sitting on a couch facing speaker B to her right side. Speaker B was sitting in a chair facing A (Figure 4a). The video camera was set up on the left side of A, so B was facing the camera as well. Speaker A had her right hand resting on her knee. B had both his hands on his knees. Both speakers had eye contact before line 1, which was at a turn beginning with a new discussion topic.

There were two instances of repair in (19). The first one is done by the woman, which is discussed here before showing the example. The second repair is discussed after the example.

The first repair initiation started at line 2, which was done on the phrase *nei51ge* 'that-Cl'. This "demonstrative + classifier" unit may serve as a placeholder to hold the turn, and to offer some extra "discourse beats" (Fox et al. 2009) to help speaker A in her name search. This unit may have been turned into a place holder because of its highly frequent usage with an indexical nature for the domain of the concept being searched for (Fox 2007; Hayashi 2003).

The bodily-visual practice started at the same time – the speaker withdrew her gaze from the recipient, tilted her head slightly down, and shifted her gaze to an iconic gesture of her right hand, which formed a small circle with the thumb and index finger (Figure 4a). Shifting gaze to her own iconic gesture may display that speaker A oriented to the gesture as relevant to the conversation (Streeck 1994). Furthermore, the filler phrase and the gaze on the iconic gesture indicate that the image of the object *hu35gu21dan55* 'Tiger-bone Pill', had been activated before the word came to mind.

At the end of the first pause in line 2, speaker A lowered her right hand to rest it on her knee, and the gaze was further lowered to the ground (Figure 4b), showing a 'thinking face' (Goodwin and Goodwin 1986). The downward gaze continued throughout the recycled filler phrase *nei51ge* 'that-Cl', with sound extension and a second pause. Here the linguistic and non-linguistic modalities coordinated to display to the recipient speaker A's forgetfulness and her mental search for the right word.

At the end of the name search, A raised her head and brought her gaze back to B (Figure 4c) while she uttered the word 'Tiger-bone Pill'. The concurrence of the gaze shift (back to the recipient) and the repaired utterance offer an indication of a successful word search.

During the first repair (Lines 1–2), while A withdrew her gaze away from the recipient, speaker B, B kept his gaze toward A (Figures 4a–c, where speaker A, the woman, is sitting on the right, and B, the man, is on the left), a usual behavior showing total engagement in the conversation (Goodwin and Goodwin 1986). Here is the example.

(20) 1. A: 那时候　　　我们　　家里　　　　还　　施舍
        Nei51 shi55'ou　*wo21m'n*　*jia55 li21*　*hai35*　*shi55she21*
        That time　　　1pl　　　home-inside　still　give-as-charity

→ 2. 那个　　　(0.8)　那个　　呃　(0.7)　虎骨丹。
     nei51ge3　(0.8)　*nei51'e1::　e21*　(0.7)　*Hu35gu21dan55.*
     that-Cl　　　　　that-Cl　e　　　　　Tiger-bone pill

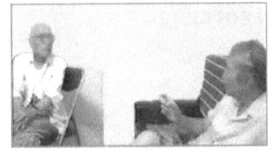

a. A: *Nei51ge* (first repair).　**b.** A: *Nei51ge e21* (second).　**c.** A: *Hu35gu21dan55.*

Figure 4a–c: Name-search and Repair by Speaker A (the woman on the right?).

3. B: 那个   虎骨丹   我   到   现在
      Nei51'e33 Hu35'u3dan55 wo21 dao51 xian51z'ai
      That-Cl   H   1sg   arrive now

d. B: *xian51zai51* (Speaker B on the left).

Figure 4d: Gaze-shift and gesture, prior to repair, by speaker B.

→   4.   那个   (0.36) 那个 方子   我   也   不   知道   了。
          nei51'e (0.36) **nei51ə ^fang55zi** wo35 ye5 bu51 zh'i55dao51 le.
          that-Cl   That-Cl formula 1sg also Neg know   CRS

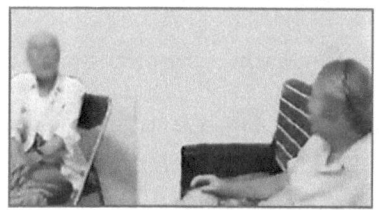 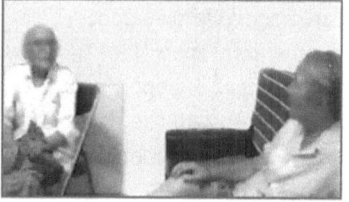

e. B: *nei51ge* (line 4).   f. B: (*bu51zhi55*) *dao51 le* (lines 5 and 6).

Figure 4e–f: Repair initiation (4e) and intersubjectivity nod (4f).

5. A: 奥 Ao51 [::
6. B: [呃 ə1

1. A: 'At that time our family also donated as charity
2.   that that eh Tiger-bone Pills'.
3. B: 'That Tiger-bone pill,
4.   I till now, that that formula I don't know (it) anymore'.
5. A: 'Ou:::'
6. B: 'E'.
(Beijing_97 p. 26)

Line 3 starts B's turn responding to A's recollection. Similar to A, when B tried to formulate his utterance he withdrew his gaze from A while uttering the NP *nei51ge hu35gu21dan55* 'that Tiger-bone Pill'. Speaker A, on the other hand, maintained her gaze toward B throughout Lines 3–4. Speaker B shifted his gaze toward an empty space away from speaker A, possibly indicating he was contemplating on formulating his utterance. Furthermore his utterances were fragmented, showing that the utterance formulation was done through talking and hand gestures. For instance, the name 'Tiger-bone Pill' at line 3 appeared to be a stand-alone NP because it was unrelated to the second part of the utterance in line 3. The second part of line 3 was an incomplete utterance formed with a subject and a predicate: *wo21 dao51 xian51zai51* 'I till now'. At the onset of *wo21* in line 3, B raised his left hand and pointed his index figure to a space away from him, and made a beat that ended at *xian51zai* 'now'. This indexical display of pointing plus the beat gesture could signal the effort B was making to formulate the utterance (Figure 4d). Right after the strike the utterance was abandoned.

Speaker B kept his gaze away from A at line 4 while he started a new NP. But the utterance did not come out smoothly either; so a repair was initiated at *nei51ge* 'that-Cl' plus a pause (Figure 4e). The unit *that-Cl* was recycled, then the rest of the NP was produced to complete the repair at line 4. Syntactically, the repaired NP (*nei51ge fang55zi* 'that formula') served as a fronted object to the utterance immediately following: 'I don't know any more', in the order of OSV.

At the onset of the negative predicate *bu51zhi55dao51 le* 'don't know anymore' (line 4), B shook his head in an emblem gesture that corresponded with his negation and, at the onset of the second syllable of *zhi55dao* 'know', B brought his gaze back toward speaker A. So B shook his head while resuming his gaze to A (Figure 4f). During B's utterances, including the gaze shifts and repair processes (Lines 3–4), A kept her gaze toward B, also showing total engagement (Goodwin and Goodwin 1986). The resumed gaze from B to A probably offered a resource for A to shape her emerging interaction – the resumed eye contact plus B's utterance (line 4) both displayed a possible end of the TCU. So, speaker A made a verbal acknowledgement plus nodding at line 5, which B also responded to with a verbal response and head nodding (line 6), signaling the two speakers reached intersubjectivity on the topic.

This example illustrates a collaborated effort both at repair initiations and name searching (Lines 2 and 4), and at the successfully performed repairs (end of Lines 2 and 4). The short exchange also reflected the interactive participation of the two speakers in both information exchanging and self-mental processes during speech production. The gaze shifts by both speakers could "not only enable a speaker to display to others some of the information processing, or other 'back-stage' work involved in producing an utterance, but also provide participants with re-sources for shaping their emerging interaction" (Goodwin 1987: 115–6; also cited in Ford and Fox 1996: 155). The syllable *ou* at line 5 functions as a "change-of-state" receipt token, registering the prior informing as delivering something that speaker A didn't know (Heritage 1984). The mutual gaze and speaker A's verbal acknowledgement and head-nodding (line 5) probably prompted B to reciprocate the interaction (line 6), offering receipt of A's acknowledgement, a typical sequence-closing third receipt (Schegloff 2007).

4.4.5 Interim summary

The interplay of repair and bodily-visual practices examined in this section offer a glimpse into how multimodality is closely intertwined in the interactive communication. The examples in this section have displayed how different modalities are coordinated during the process of repair. The use of gaze at or away from recipients may indicate realization of a trouble spot, thus prompting a repair (17). It may signal solidarity during repair (18), and the practice may also signal repair initiation, the effort of word search, and the end of the search (19–20). Gestures also coordinate with repair to assist recycling repair (18), to signal repair initiation and word search (20), and post-repair emphasis (19–20). Some of the multimodal coordination are synchronized (17, 20), but some are not (18, 19). The data reflect the possibility that bodily-visual practices and speech production could be explained by the cascade model (Dell 2013; Levelt 1989; Levelt et al. 1999; Menn 2017) that explains the processes of language production: word activation is not linear by following syntactic constructions. Sometimes words are produced out of sequence. This phenomenon is often demonstrated in speech errors (Menn, 2017). Similarly, the bodily-visual practice sometimes may be activated before the intended utterance is made, so the pace of activation may not be completely aligned.

5 Summary

This report presents a preliminary exploration on same-turn self-repair by Beijing Mandarin speakers during face-to-face conversations. The study has examined mechanisms in repair initiations and the recycling and replacement practice of the repair, including both language specific characteristics as revealed in the types of repair initiations, and general human interactional behaviors that involve a variety of non-linguistic means, which reflect the embodiment of language.

Unique to Mandarin repair, likely due to the resources of the grammar of the language, include the preference of repair initiation on single-syllables (Sections 4.1), and also on two-syllable prosodic units that may or may not form syntactic constructions (Section 4.2). Also specific to Mandarin repair are repair initiations that could be the outcome of resources from phonotactics and tone sandhi rules, which native Mandarin Chinese speakers follow (Section 4.3). Furthermore, repair practices in the data may reflect some general human behavior in the social organization of conversations, which include, for instance, two possible types of recycling practice: recycling the trouble source, and recycling plus adding additional information after repair initiations (Section 4.1–4.3), as well as different modalities collaborating in the process of repair (Section 4.4).

The multimodal nature of repair as illustrated in this study may offer further support to previous findings that utterances and gestures are possibly interconnected somatotopically. Simple hand beat gestures are often associated with recycling repair that display a speaker's mental processes when searching for the proper utterance (Section 4.4). It is highly probable that the somatotopy has been developed and strengthened over language use, and the usage in turn further strengthens the synaptic connections of neurons in the whole brain (Hauk et al. 2004), which may further enhance collateral activation of language and bodily-visual practices such as the multi-faceted practice of gaze and gestures. If this proposal is true, then language usage not only shapes grammar (Fox 2007; Tao 2006) but also offers the fundamental condition for the development of multimodality in human communication (Carnegie Mellon University).

The correlation of bodily-visual practice and repair can be observed more frequently during others-initiated self-repair (Schegloff 2000a), in which both speakers and recipients collaborate to reach mutual stance in communication. For instance, the display of uncertainty as repair initiation could signal the need of assistance from the recipients. There are many instances of such practice in the Mandarin Chinese data, which can offer other rich resources for the study of multimodality in communication.

In summary, the practice of repair in correlation to bodily-visual behaviors may be a universal phenomenon that can be observed in all conversations cross-linguistically. The practice may also reflect characteristics unique to speakers of individual languages. It is hoped that the findings from this study complement previous findings on the multimodal nature of repair in Mandarin Chinese, and on language and human cognition.

References

Beattie, Geoffrey and Coughlan, Jane. 1999. An experimental investigation of the role of iconic gestures in lexical access using the tip-of-the-tongue phenomenon. *British Journal of Psychology* 90(1). 35–56.

Biq, Yong-U. 2009. Locative particles in spoken Taiwan Mandarin. In Janet Xing (Ed.), *Studies of Chinese linguistics: Functional approaches*, 133–154. Hong Kong: University of Hong Kong Press.

Buckner, Michael, Meara, Naomi M., Reese, Edward J. and Reese, Maryann. 1987. Eye movement as an indicator of sensory components in thought. *Journal of Counseling Psychology* 34 (3). 283–287.

Bybee, Joan. 2006. From usage to grammar: The mind's response to repetition. *Language* 82(4). 711–733.

Carnegie Mellon University. (2010, January 13). Identifying thoughts through brain codes leads to deciphering the brain's dictionary. http://www.sciencedaily.com/releases/2010/01/100112201347.htm (accessed November 10, 2014).

Chafe, Wallace. 1994. *Discourse, consciousness, and time: The flow and displacement of conscious experience in speaking and writing*. Chicago: University of Chicago Press.

Chao, Yuen Ren. 1968. *A Grammar of Spoken Chinese*. Berkeley: University of California Press.

Chen, Helen Kai-yun. 2011. *Sound Patterns in Mandarin Recycling Repair*. Ph.D. dissertation. University of Colorado, Boulder.

Chui, Kawai. 1996. Organization of repair in Chinese conversation. *Text – Interdisciplinary Journal for the Study of Discourse* 16 (3). 343–372.

Chui, Kawai. 2013. Gesture and embodiment in Chinese discourse. *Journal of Chinese Linguistics* 41 (1). 52–64.

Cienki, Alan and Müller, Cornelia. (eds.). 2008. *Metaphor and gesture*. Amsterdam: John Benjamins.

Dell, Gary S. 2013. Cascading and feedback in interactive models of production: A reflection of forward modeling. *Behavior Brain Science* 36 (4), 351–352.

Dilts, Robert. Eye movement and NLP. http://www.nlpu.com/Articles/artic14.htm (accessed August, 2015).

Du Bois, John. 2007. The stance triangle. In Robert Englebretson (ed.), *Stance taking in discourse: Subjectivity, evaluation, interaction*, 139–182. Amsterdam: John Benjamins.

Ehrlichman Howard and Micic Dragana. 2012. Why do people move their eyes when they think? *Current Directions in Psychological Science* 21 (2). 96–100.

Ehrlichman Howard, Micic Dragana, Sousa, Amber and Zhu, John. 2007. Looking for answers: eye movements in non-visual cognitive tasks. *Brain Cognition* 64 (1). 7–20.

Feng, Shengli. 2009. Minimal word and its function in Mandarin Chinese. In Janet Xing (ed.), *Studies of Chinese Linguistics: Functional approaches*, 47–64. Hong Kong University Press.

Feng, Shengli. 2001. The Multidimentional Properties of "Words" in Chinese. 当代语言学 [Contemporary Linguistics] 3 (3). 161–174.

Ford, Cecilia E. and Fox, Barbara. 1996. Interactional motivations for reference formulation: He had. this guy had, a beautiful, thirty-two O:lds. In Barbara Fox (ed.), *Studies in Anaphora* 145–168. Amsterdam: John Benjamins.

Ford, Cecilia E., Fox, Barbara A. and Thompson, Sandra. A. 1996. Practices in the construction of turns: The "TCU" revisited. *Pragmatics* 6. 427–454.

Ford, Cecilia, and Thompson, Sandra A. 1996. Interactional units in conversation: Syntactic, intonational, and pragmatic resources for the projection of turn completion. In Elinor Ochs, Emanuel Schegloff and Sandra Thompson (eds.), *Grammar and interaction* 134–184. Cambridge: Cambridge University Press.

Ford, Cecilia E., Thompson, Sandra A. and Drake, Veronika. 2012. Bodily-Visual Practices and Turn Continuation. *Discourse Process* 49 (3–4). 192–212.

Fox, Barbara. 1981. Body part syntax: Towards a universal characterization. *Studies in Language* 5. 323–342.
Fox, Barbara A. 2002. The embodied nature of grammar: Embodied being-in-the-world. In Joan Bybee and Michael Noonan (eds.), *Complex Sentences in Grammar and Discourse: Essays in honor of Sandra A. Thompson*, 79–99. Amsterdam: John Benjamins.
Fox, Barbara A. 2007. Principles shaping grammatical practices: an exploration. *Discourse Studies* 9 (3). 299–318.
Fox, Barbara A., Hayashi, Makoto and Jasperson, Robert. 1996. Resources and repair: A cross-linguistic study of the syntactic organization of repair. In Elinor Ochs, Emanuel Schegloff and Sandra A. Thompson (eds.), *Interaction and Grammar*, 185–237. Cambridge, New York: Cambridge University Press.
Fox, Barbara A. and Heinemann, Trine. 2015. The alignment of manual and verbal displays in requests for the repair of an object. *Research on Language and Social Interaction* 48 (3). 342–362. DOI: 10.1080/08351813.2015.1058608
Fox, Barbara A., Wouk, Fay, Hayashi, Makoto, Fincke, Steven, Tao, Liang, Sorjonen, Marja-Leena, Laakso, Minna and Hernandez, Wilfrido Flores. 2009. A Cross-linguistic investigation of the site of initiation in same-turn self-repair. In: Jack Sidnell (ed.), *Conversation analysis: Comparative perspectives*, 60–103. Cambridge: Cambridge University Press.
Gibbs, Raymond W. Jr. 2006. *Embodiment and Cognitive Science*. New York: Cambridge University Press.
Goldin-Meadow, Susan and Wagner Martha A. 2013. Gesture's role in speaking, learning, and creating language. *Annual Review of Psychology* 64. 257–283.
Gomez de Garcia, Jule. 1994. *Communicative strategies in conversational Kickapoo*. PhD Dissertation. University of Colorado, Boulder.
Gomez de Garcia, Jule. 1995. Repair strategies in conversational Kickapoo. In William O. Bright (ed.), *Colorado Research in Linguistics*.
Goodwin, Charles. 1986. Gesture as a resource for the organization of mutual orientation. *Semiotica* 62(1–2). 29–49.
Goodwin, Charles. 1987. Forgetfulness as an interactive resource. *Social Psychology Quarterly* 50. 115–135.
Goodwin, Marjorie H. and Goodwin, Charles. 1986. Gesture and coparticipation in the activity of searching for a word. *Semiotica* 62 (1–2). 51–75.
Hauk, Olaf, Johnsrude, Ingrid and Pulvermüller, Friedemann. 2004. Somatotopic representation of action words in human motor and premotor cortex. *Neuron* 41 (2). 301–7.
Hayashi, Makoto. 2003. Language and the Body as Resources for Collaborative Action: A Study of Word Searches in Japanese Conversation. *Research on Language and Social Interaction* 36 (2). 109–141.
He, Agnes Weiyun. 2011. The role of repair in modulating modal stances in Chinese discourse. *Chinese Language & Discourse* 2(1). 1–22.
Jefferson, Gail. 2004. Glossary of transcript symbols with an introduction. In Gene H. Lerner (ed.), *Conversation analysis: Studies from the first generation*, 13–23. Amsterdam & Philadelphia: John Benjamins. http://www.liso.ucsb.edu/liso_archives/Jefferson/Transcript.pdf (accessed August 21, 2015).
Joue, Gina, Boven, Linda, Willmes, Klaus, Evolaa, Vito, Demenescub, Liliana R., Hassemera, Julius, Irene Mittelberga, Klaus Mathiakb, Schneiderb, Frank and Habel, Ute. 2018. Handling or being the concept: An fMRI study on metonymy representations in coverbal gestures. *Neuropsychologia* 109. 232–244.

Just, Marcel Adam, Cherkassky, Vladimir L., Aryal, Sandesh and Mitchell, Tom M. 2010. A neurosemantic theory of concrete noun representation based on the underlying brain codes. *PLoS ONE*, 2010; 5 (1): e8622 DOI:10.1371/journal.pone.0008622.

Kendon, Adam. 1995. Gestures as illocutionary and discourse structure markers in southern Italian conversation. *Journal of Pragmatics* 23. 247-279.

Kendon, Adam. 2004. *Gesture: Visible action as utterance.* Cambridge: University of Cambridge Press.

Kohn, Susan E., Wingfield, Arthur, Menn, Lise, Goodglass, Harold, Berko Gleason, Jean and Hyde, Mary. 1987. Lexical retrieval: The tip-of-the-tongue phenomenon. *Applied Psycholinguistics 8.* 245–266.

Kok, Kasper and Cienki, Alan. 2014. Taking simulation semantics out of the laboratory: towards an interactive and multimodal reappraisal of embodied language comprehension. *Language and Cognition.* 1–23.

Lee, Jee Won. 2010. Systematic repetition of the first person singular pronoun wo in Mandarin conversation: Negotiation of conflicting stance in interaction. *Chinese Language and Discourse* 1 (2). 183–219.

Levelt, Willem J. M. 1983. Monitoring and self-repair in speech. *Cognition 33*(1). 41–104.

Levelt, Willem J.M. 1989. *Speaking: From intention to articulation.* Cambridge, Massachusetts: MIT Press.

Levelt, Willem J.M. and Cutler, Ann. 1983. Prosodic marking in speech repair. *Journal of Semantics* 2 (2). 205–218.

Levelt, Willem J.M., Roelofs, Ardi and Meyer, Antje S. 1999. A theory of lexical access in speech production. *Behavioral and Brain Sciences.* 22. 1–75.

Li, Charles and Thompson, Sandra A. 1981. *Mandarin Chinese: A functional reference Grammar.* Berkeley: University of California Press.

Li, Xiaoting. 2013. Language and the body in the construction of units in Mandarin face-to-face interaction. In: Beatrice Szczepek Reed and Geoffrey Raymond (eds.), *Units of Talk – Units of Action*, 343–376. Amsterdam: John Benjamins.

Li, Xingshan, Gu, Junjuan, Liu, Pingping and Rayner, Keith. 2013. The advantage of word-based processing in Chinese reading: Evidence from eye movement. *Journal of Experimental Psychology: Learning, Memory, and Cognition* 39 (3). 879–889.

Li, Xingshan, Rayner, Keith and Cave, Kyle R. 2009. On the segmentation of Chinese words during reading. *Cognitive Psychology* 58. 525–552.

Lin, Yen-Hwei 2011. Loan word adaptation in standard Mandarin and phonological theory. In: Yun, Xiao, Liang, Tao and Hooi Ling Soh (eds.), *Current issues in Chinese Linguistics*, 426–451. Newcastle upon Tyne: Cambridge Scholars Publishing.

Luke, Kang-Kwong and Zhang, Wei. 2010. Insertion as a self-repair device and its interactional motivations in Chinese conversation. *Chinese Language and Discourse* 1 (2). 153–182.

Lucero, Ché, Zaharchuk, Holly and Casasanto, Daniel. 2014. Beat gestures facilitate speech production. In P. Bello, M. Guarini, M. McShane, B. Scasselati (eds.), *Proceedings of the 36th Annual Conference of the Cognitive Science Society.* Austin, TX: Cognitive Science Society. http://casasanto.com/chelucero/papers/LuceroZaharchuk&Casasanto_CogSci_2014.pdf (accessed October 2, 2014)

Menn. Lise. 2nd edn. 2017. *Psycholinguistics: Introduction and application.* San Diego: Plural Publishing.

Menn, Lise. *Neurolinguistics.* http://www.linguisticsociety.org/resource/neurolinguistics (accessed September 1, 2015)

Morsella, Ezequiel and Miozzo, Michele. 2002. Evidence for a Cascade Model of Lexical Access in Speech Production. *Journal of Experimental Psychology: Learning, Memory, and Cognition* 28 (3). 555–563.

Ravizza, Susan. 2003. Movement and lexical access: Do noniconic gestures aid in retrieval? *Psychonomic Bulletin and Review* 10 (3). 610–614.

Ragsdale, J. Donald and Silvia, Catherine Fry. 1982. Distribution of kinesic hesitation phenomena in spontaneous speech. *Language and Speech* 25. 185–190.

Research Team on the Lexicon of Common Words in Contemporary Chinese. 2008. 现代汉语 常用词表 [Xiàndài Hànyǔ Cháng Yòng Cí Biǎo: *Lexicon of Common Words in Contemporary Chinese*]. Beijing, China: 商务印书馆 Commercial Press.

Sacks, Harvey. 1992. *Lectures on Conversation*. Cambridge, MA: Blackwell.

Sacks, Harvey, Schegloff, Emanuel A and Jefferson Gail. 1974. A simplest systematics for the organization of turn-taking for conversation. *Language* 50. 696–735

Schegloff, Emanuel A. 1979. The Relevance of Repair to Syntax-for-Conversation. in Tom Givon (ed.), *Syntax and Semantics, Volume 12: Discourse and Syntax*, 261–286. New York: Academic Press.

Schegloff, Emanuel A. 1984. On some gestures' relation to talk. In J. Maxwell Atkinson and John Heritage (eds.) *Structures of social action: Studies in conversation analyses*, 266–296. Cambridge: Cambridge University Press.

Schegloff, Emanuel A. 1987. Recycled turn beginnings: A precise repair mechanism in conversation turn-taking organization. In Graham Button and John R. E. Lee (eds.), *Talk and Social Organization* 70–85. Clevedon, England: Multilingual Matters.

Schegloff, Emanuel. 2000a. When "others" initiate repair. *Applied Linguistics* 2 (1–2). 205–243.

Schegloff, Emanuel 2000b. Overlapping talk and the turn-taking organization for conversation. *Language in Society* 29. 1–63.

Schegloff, Emanuel. 2007. *Sequence organization in Interaction: A primer in conversation analysis* (Vol. 1). Cambridge, England: Cambridge University Press.

Schegloff, Emanuel A. 2013. Ten operations in self-initiated, same turn repair. In Makoto Hayashi, Geoffrey Raymond and Jack Sidnell (eds.), *Conversational Repair and Human Understanding*, 41–70. Cambridge, UK: Cambridge University Press.

Schegloff, Emanuel, Gail Jefferson and Harvey Sacks. 1977. The preference for self-correction in the organization of repair in conversation. *Language* 53. 361–382.

Sidnell, Jack. 2009. Comparative perspectives in conversation analyses. In Jack Sidnell (ed.), *Conversation analysis: Comparative perspectives*, 1–27. Cambridge: Cambridge University Press.

Seyfeddinipur, Mandana. 2006. *Disfluency: interrupting speech and gesture*. MPI Series in Psycholinguistics, n39. Nijmegen, NL: Radboud University of Nijmegen.

Stivers, Tanya and Sidnell, Jack. 2005. Introduction: Multimodal interaction. *Semiotica* 156 (1). 1–20.

Stivers, Tanya, Enfield, N.J., Brown, Penelope, Englert, Christina, Hayashi, Makoto, Heinemann, Trine, Hoymann, Gertie, Rossano, Federico, Peter de Ruiter, Jan, Yoon, Kyung-Eun and Levinson, Stephen C. 2009. Universals and cultural variation in turn-taking in conversation. *Proceedings of the National Academy of Sciences of the United States of America* (PNAS) 106 (26). 10587–10592.

Streeck, Jürgen. 1994. Gesture as communication II: The audience as co-author. *Research on Language and Social Interaction* 27 (3), (Special Issue: Is Gesture Communicative? Ed. by Adam Kendon), 239–267.

Tao, Liang. 1995. Repair in natural Běijīng Mandarin Chinese. In Branner, David P. (ed.), *Yuen Ren Treasury*, 55–77. Yuen Ren Society.

Tao, Liang. 1996. Topic discontinuity and zero anaphora in Chinese discourse: anaphora: Cognitive strategies in discourse processing. In Barbara Fox (ed.), *Studies in Anaphora*, 487-513. Amsterdam: John Benjamins.

Tao, Liang. 2001. Switch Reference and Zero Anaphora: Emergent Reference in Discourse Processing. In Alan Cienki, Barbara J. Luka and Michael B. Smith (eds.), *Conceptual and discourse factors in linguistic structure*, 253–269. Stanford, CA: CSLI Publications.

Tao, Liang. 2006. Classifier loss and frozen tone in spoken Beijing Mandarin: The *yige* phono-syntactic conspiracy. *Linguistics* 44 (1). 91–133.

Tao, Liang. 2010. Conversational Repair. In Hogan, Patrick C. (ed.), *The Cambridge encyclopedia of the language sciences* 225. Cambridge: Cambridge University Press.

Tao, Liang. 2011. Serial verb construction in Mandarin Chinese: The interface of syntax, semantics and language development. In Xiao, Yun, Tao, Liang and Soh, Hooi Ling, (eds.), *Current Issues in Chinese Linguistics*, 197–234. Newcastle upon Tyn, UK: Cambridge Scholarly Publications.

Tao, Liang, Fox, Barbara and Gomez de Garcia, Jule. 1999. Tone-choice repair in Conversational Mandarin Chinese. In Fox, Barbara, Jurafsky, Dan and Michaelis, Laura (eds.), *Cognition and function in language*, 268–281. Sanford: CSLI Publications.

Wolf, Dhana, Rekittke, Linn-Marlen, Mittelberg, Irene, Klasen, Martin and Mathiak, Kaus. 2017. Perceived Conventionality in Co-speech Gestures Involves the Fronto-Temporal Language Network. *Frontiers in Human Neuroscience*. doi: 10.3389/fnhum.2017.00573

Wouk, Fay. 2005. The syntax of repair in Indonesian. *Discourse Studies* 7(2). 237–258.

Wu, Ruey-Jiuan Regina. 2006. Initiating repair and beyond: The use of two repeat-formatted repair initiations in Mandarin conversation. *Discourse Processes: A multidisciplinary journal* 41 (1). 67–109.

Wu, Ruey-Jiuan Regina. 2009. Repetition in the initiation of repair. In Jack Sidnell (ed.) *Conversation analysis: Comparative perspectives*, 31–59. Cambridge: Cambridge University Press.

Zhang, Qing. 2005. A Chinese yuppie in Beijing: Phonological variation and the construction of a new professional identity. *Language in Society* 34 (3). 431–466.

Zhang, Wei. 1998. *Repair in Chinese Conversation*. Ph.D. dissertation. University of Hong Kong.

Appendix

List of transcription notations and glossary abbreviations used in this study (Following Jefferson 2004; Li and Thompson 1981)

()	Pause time in seconds
(.)	A very short pause, less than 1/10 of a second
^x	Sudden raise of pitch or stress on the lexical item
::	Sound stretch

'x	Missing or unclearly pronounced sound, often the onset of a syllable.
x'	The onset has turned into a voiced continuant /r/ or /I/ (Chao 1968: 37)
=	Immediately connected speech (e.g., between two utterances)
[	Start of overlapping between speakers
]	End of overlapped utterance
1st-sg	First person singular (including: 2nd-sg: second person singular, etc.)
Asp	Aspectual particle or oblique marker (no detailed semantic classification)
BA	The direct object marker in the pattern *ba-Object NP-Predicate*
Cl	Classifier
CRS	Currently Relevant Status, perfect aspect marker (Li & Thompson 1981)
DE	Noun modification marker (after the modifier before the noun)
Dur	Durative particle
Int	Interjection
Neg	Negative particle
Q	Question particle
x-	Sound cut-off
XX-One digit	Tone cut-off – the tone is not fully pronounced (e.g., *jin5-*)
Boldface	Trouble spot where a repair is initiated
<u>Underline</u>	Repair proper

I-Ni Tsai
A multimodal analysis of tag questions in Mandarin Chinese multi-party conversation

1 Introduction

Questioning is one of the most common and essential practices in daily talk-in-interaction. In everyday conversation, questions are prototypical first pair parts used to initiate action in an adjacency pair (Steensig and Drew 2008). Sacks (1992: 55) notes that "as long as one is doing the questions, then in part one has control of the conversation." Questions (and answers), observably ubiquitous, are also central resources through which many institutional interactions, such as interviews, medical encounters, and classroom discourse, are organized and constituted (Freed and Ehrlich 2010; Heritage and Roth 1995). Studies of questions and responses, therefore, can serve as a point of departure to understand the interactional mechanism in a language. They also offer a locus to look for intersubjectivity in turns at talk. The present study focuses on one particular type of question, the tag question, in talk-in-interaction in Mandarin Chinese.

In English, tag questions are a weak question format for eliciting information. The speaker seems to display his/her belief in the truthfulness of the declarative preceding the tag and to seek confirmation or affiliation from co-participants, depending on the participants' epistemic status (Heritage 2012b; Holmes 1982; Keisanen 2007; Quirk and Crystal 1985; Sadock and Zwicky 1985)[1]. Scholars in Chinese linguistics also suggest that tag questions are used for interpersonal purposes – mainly to seek confirmation and support (Li and Thompson 1981;

---

[1] Holmes (1982) distinguishes tag questions into two types: modal and affective questions. The former displays the speaker's uncertainty toward the information and seeks confirmation, while the latter serves to build interactional/social solidarity and seek alignment. Affective tag questions are particularly seen in a conversation with one of the speakers having epistemic authority (Cameron, McAlinden, and O'Leary 1988; Harres 1998). Under such a circumstance, the use of a tag question provides a negotiation space for less authoritative recipients to take part in the evaluation or corroboration of the information. Similarly, Heritage (2012b: 14) has proposed that tag questions are generally understood in the following two ways, depending on the epistemic status of the speaker. First, they can be understood as an information request, usually a confirmation request. Second, they can be used as a way to mobilize responses when speakers seek support for their point of view.

I-Ni Tsai, National Taiwan University

Liu, Pan, and Gu 1996; Shao 1996; Zhang 1997).² Although previous research in Chinese linguistics has pointed to the interactive nature of tag questions, to date, researchers have yet to explore how seeking confirmation or support is sequentially and locally accomplished as collaborative work in Mandarin talk-in-interaction.

In a more recent study, Gao and Zhang (2009) investigate Mandarin tag questions from an interactional point of view. They demonstrated that the action the tag question accomplishes is closely associated with the form the question tag takes and the ongoing interaction between participants. In talk-in-interaction, seemingly straightforward actions – such as seeking confirmation or seeking affiliation – can, in fact, involve complex moment-by-moment stance negotiation. Based on videotaped, naturally occurring everyday talk-in-interaction, this paper aims to investigate how Mandarin speakers and hearers in daily conversations orient to turns that tag questions are used and how the associated sequences are collaboratively achieved as the conversation unfolds. The primary focus of this paper is on how the general actions of tag questions – seeking confirmation and seeking affiliation – are locally interpreted. A secondary focus lies in understanding what other actions are sequentially accomplished through tag questions in multi-party conversations.

In Mandarin Chinese, the construction of a tag question commonly contains two parts: a statement and a question tag attached at the end. These attached question tags are minimal bundles built around verbal or modal elements (e.g., the copular verb *shi* 'to be') in either the final particle format (e.g., *shi-ma/shi-ba/shi-a*) or the V-not-V format (e.g., *shi bu shi*). Although question tags can be constituted in both forms, the V-not-V format has been shown to prevail overwhelmingly in Mandarin tag questions (Chu 1998; Li and Thompson 1981; Shao 1996); of these, V-not-V tags *shi bu shi* – built around the copular verb *shi* 'to be,' *hao bu hao* – built around the adjective *hao* 'good, okay,' and *dui bu dui* – built around the adjective *dui* 'right' – rank highest according to frequency analysis (Hu 2002; Tsai 2017). Similarly requesting confirmation, questions with the tags *shi bu shi* ('COP not COP') and *dui bu dui* ('right not right') provide a good point of departure to understand Mandarin tag questions in talk-in-interaction. To make a finely detailed analysis possible, the examples under examination in the present study are limited to examples with these two question tags in spoken Mandarin: *shi bu shi* ('COP not COP') and *dui bu dui* ('right not right').³

---

2 Question tags can also manifest as pragmatic markers to fulfill different communicative functions (Chen and He 2001; Hu 2002).
3 It is also important to note that a number of studies point out that some *shi bu shi* ('COP not COP') and *dui bu dui* ('right not right') tags manifest as grammaticalized stance markers, more

To analyze the turns at talk in detail, this paper adopts conversation analysis (CA) as an analytic framework that views talk as collaborative social interaction (Goodwin and Heritage 1990; Heritage 1984b; Lerner 2004; Pomerantz and Fehr 1997; Schegloff 1995, 2007). Individual utterances, therefore, are inextricably embedded in ongoing activities and accomplished through both speakers' and hearers' collaborative courses of actions (Goodwin 1981, 1986, 2000, 2007). As Goodwin and Heritage (1990: 283) described, the major concern of CA is to "seek to describe the underlying social organization – conceived as an institutionalized substratum of interactional rules, procedures, and conventions – through which orderly and intelligible social interaction is made possible." Methodologically, it is only through the detailed microanalysis of conversation and interlocutors' conduct in natural settings that the orderly social organization mentioned above can possibly be uncovered and described. Some CA concepts and analytic tools that are significant to the current analysis will be introduced below.

Using CA, the present paper considers question tags – particularly cases with *shi bu shi* ('COP not COP') and *dui bu dui* ('right not right') – as a feature of turn design, a linguistic resource in building and designing the turn. According to Drew (2013), the turn design refers to the way a speaker constructs a turn-at-talk to do and to be interpreted as doing the action it is designed to do. The study of turn design, as Drew (2013: 134) has suggested, should consider at least three interrelated principles that shape it: *recipient, sequence*, and *action*.

One principle that shapes turn design is to whom the turn is addressed, also known as recipient design (Goodwin 1979, 1986; Sacks, Schegloff, and Jefferson 1974). Speakers may design the turns-at-talk for their recipients by considering their personal relationships. Speakers may also consider what and to what extent their recipient(s) know(s), in terms of epistemic access and rights to the information. Further, they consider the epistemic status of the

---

to firmly indicate a stance than to mobilize response (Stivers and Rossano 2010). Participants orient to these usages as pragmatic or stance markers (Chen and He 2001; Fang 2005; Hu 2002; Shao and Zhu 2005) instead of as a question tag. For example, Chen and He (2001) examined the question tag *dui bu dui* in classroom interaction. They show that *dui bu dui* can be used as a stance marker to reinforce the illocutionary force of the sentence proposition. In addition, *dui bu dui*, as a pragmatic marker, can signal transitions of interactional sequences, which makes it easier for the speaker to maintain the addressee's attention in the talk. As the present study takes an interest in tag questions associated with question-answer sequences, cases of *shi bu shi* and *dui bu dui* as pragmatic or stance markers are excluded from the study since they are not used to mobilize response.

speakers and hearers relative to each other. Accordingly, speakers then claim their epistemic stance of information in the speech – being certain to uncertain – relative to the recipient(s) (Heritage 2012a, 2012b, 2014; Nir and Zima 2017; Raymond and Heritage 2006). Questions eliciting information normally represent speakers' less knowledgeable (K-) position relative to recipients' more knowledgeable (K+) position, indexing a relatively larger 'K- to K+' gap between speaker and recipient. Tag questions, displaying a speaker's belief in the proposition in the statement, on the other hand, indexes a relatively narrower 'K- to K+' gap. Relative epistemic status plays an important role in interpreting what a particular tag question is doing. A tag question posed by a relatively unknowing (K-) speaker is commonly interpreted as seeking confirmation; a tag question posed by a relatively knowing (K+) speaker is commonly interpreted as seeking affiliation. To understand the epistemic status of the tag questioner relative to the recipient, it is essential to determine to whom the tag question is addressed, particularly in multi-party conversations. In this respect, nonverbal resources such as the direction of eye gaze and body position (Frischen, Bayliss, and Tipper 2007; Goodwin 1979, 1986; Ho, Foulsham, and Kingstone 2015; Kok 2016; Rossano 2013) of the questioner are significant elements to make such determinations.

The second principle shaping turn design is the location of the turn in a sequence. Each turn of talk is produced in a sequential context and is designed to be responsive to and display its connection to the prior turn. The connection can be structurally displayed by an ellipsis, pro-forms, or repetition. Speakers also connect to the prior turn by designing the current turn to respond to the actions of the prior turn. Sequential context is then closely related to the final principle that shapes turn design: what is being accomplished in that turn. It is necessary to discover what particular grammatical forms – vocal-aural signs – are systematically selected in certain sequential environment to do certain actions (Ochs, Schegloff, and Thompson 1996). As face-to-face conversation is essentially multimodal interaction, the visuospatial modality often works together with vocal-aural modality to accomplish the intended actions (Kok, 2017; Langacker 2008; Mittelberg 2017; Stivers and Sidnell 2005).

In English assessment sequences, for example, the tag question can do quite opposite actions in different sequential positions (Heritage 2014; Raymond and Heritage 2006). The first assessment in the sequence (e.g., A in A: It's a beautiful day. B: It's gorgeous.) implies epistemic primacy. The use of the tag question in the first assessment (e.g., A: It's a beautiful day, isn't it? B: It's gorgeous.) marks epistemic downgrade, claiming both parties' equivalent rights to the situation. The second assessment is epistemically inferior in nature. The use of the tag question in the second assessment, however, marks an upgrade of the epistemic rights (e.g., A: It's a beautiful day. B: It's gorgeous, isn't it?). Hepburn and Potter (2010) have documented that child protection officers who take calls on child protection helpline commonly use tag questions. In an environment where callers are unresponsive because they are crying or in distress, tag questions are selected to articulate the potential problem for the callers and to solicit response. The turn is designed to display affiliation, ease the caller's distress, and encourage participation.

Using the analytic tools introduced above, this study analyzes in detail the examples of tag questions formulated by the two most frequent question tags in spoken Mandarin: *shi bu shi* ('cop not cop') and *dui bu dui* ('right not right'). It is found that in multi-party conversations, the tag questions were deployed in two common ways (1) to embody speaker's differential states of knowledge in relation to different co-participants, and (2) to seek affiliation in a disaffiliating move. These two practices will be respectively discussed in sections 3 and 4 below. Examples will be provided to describe how the tag questions are locally designed and interpreted in the dynamic process of interaction.

2 Data

The data for this study consist of nine videotaped, spontaneous, face-to-face conversations collected during the period of 2005–2009 in the United States and in Taiwan. All the participants – from teenagers to people in their thirties – are native speakers of Mandarin Chinese from Taiwan. Conversations – each lasting around an hour (thus, nine hours in total) – are multi-party interactions among three to four friends or acquaintances. These interactions took place in everyday hangout/chitchat scenarios if participants attended the same school or lived in the same neighborhood, or once-in-a-while gatherings if participants were old friends living at a distance from one another.

The data analyzed in this study are transcribed using the Mandarin pinyin system. In the transcripts, each line of original Mandarin utterance is aligned with two other lines: the second line provides a word-by-word gloss and the third line offers the English translation of the whole utterance. The data are primarily transcribed according to the conventions developed by Jefferson (2004). Also, remarks on bodily-visual aspects of the interaction, such as body movement, body position, eye gaze and so on, are provided after the English translation inside double round parentheses. In each extract, any identifiable proper names, such as names for persons, locations, schools, and stores, are changed to pseudonyms or abbreviations to protect the participants' privacy.

3 Tag question: Resource to embody differential states of knowledge in relation to multiple co-participants

This section will focus on interactions when a tag question is deployed as a resource to embody differential states of knowledge on a single matter or event in relation to different co-participants; that is, the tag question is commonly deployed when speakers have some knowledge on the matter being discussed relative to unknowing co-participant(s), but they have limited epistemic rights relative to the co-participant(s) that has epistemic authority. In a turn, within the format of a statement plus a question tag, speakers are able to make a statement, displaying their independent access to the matters at hand; they then use the question tag to indicate their epistemic inferiority, seeking confirmation from the one who is more knowledgeable. The format of the turn, capable of providing information and soliciting confirmation simultaneously, serves as a device for speakers to properly provide what they know to the ongoing talk and asserts their non-authoritative epistemic rights over information, leaving the final say to the authority.

This practice also serves as a way for speakers to enter an ongoing sequence in which they are the non-addressed recipients in the prior turns. Speakers, through tag questions, contribute what they know by supplementing additional information to the ongoing line of talk, while maintaining their non-focal participating role by conceding the ultimate rights to the authority.

Fragment (1), a case in point, is taken from a dinner table conversation at Jack and Brad's residence in Los Angeles, California, with Anne and Hana as their guests. Anne has just returned before dinner from her trip to visit a friend in another state. Jack first asks Anne about who showed her around on her visit (line 1). Anne mentions that her friend and her friend's boyfriend did. Jack then poses a follow-up question as to whether Anne's friend and boyfriend are students or working (lines 3 and 5). The target line is in line 7, when Hana poses a tag question.

(1) (001-00-003233, Boyfriend)

01 Jack: na   ta   nanpengyou fuze   kaiche lo.
          then   3s   boyfriend   in.charge   drive   FP
          'Then her boyfriend was the one who was driving (you) around?'

02 Anne: dui   a.   ta   nanpengyou shi   meiguoren ma.
          right   FP   3s   boyfriend   COP   American   FP
          'Yeah. Her boyfriend is a local American.'

03 Jack: *tamen shi   haizai nianshu haishi:*
           3s   COP   still   study   or
           'They are students or-'

04 Anne: *hum:[:*
           IP
           'Mm::' ((Eating))

05 Jack: [*gongzuo le.*
                [work   FP
                '(They are) working?'

06   (.)

07 Hana: → *ta   nanpengyou zai   gongzuo le, >shi m   shi<.*
            3S   boyfriend   ASP   work   FP   COP   NEG COP
            'Her boyfriend is working, *shi bu shi*?' ((Turning her head toward
            Anne))

08 Anne: *ta (.) nanpengyou zhiqian:, jiushi: (.) zai GC.*
           3s   boyfriend   before   DM   in   NAME
           'Her boyfriend um (.) used to work at GC earlier.'

09 Jack: °*mm.*
           mm
           'Mm.'

10 Anne: *keshi ta: (0.7) jin   nian di   jiu   (.) >cizhi le<.*
           but   3s   this year end just   quit   FP
           'But he quit his job at the end of this year.'

11 Jack: *ou, [la(h)o- lao   dao   yib(h)i.   huhuhuh.*
           IP   [fish.up fish.up reach an.amount huhuhuh
           '(He must have) earned a lot. huhuhuh.' ((Turning his head and
           talking to Brad))

12 Anne: [*ta zai nian Ph-*
                [3S ASP study
                'When he studied Ph-' ((Anne intends to say Ph.D.))

Hana's tag question – confirming whether the boyfriend is working – is addressed to Anne. Hana's tag question (line7) and Anne's answer (line8) constitute a question-answer pair. The people being discussed are Anne's friends and the friend's boyfriend, whom she just visited. It stands to reason that Anne has full access to the information and thus has epistemic authority among the participants. Hana and Anne are close to each other, and Hana may have heard before about Anne's friend and the boyfriend. Hana thus positions herself as a knowing party, contributing what she knows in the statement before the question tag. Compared to Anne, Hana has a lower epistemic status. Jack is the unknowing party. With both Anne and Jack present, Hana has differential states of knowledge in relation to different co-participants; she resorts to the tag question format and seeks confirmation from Anne. Facing such a confirmation request, Anne displays her authority over the matter by giving a transformative answer (Stivers and Hayashi 2010), resisting a simple confirming or disconfirming response. She responds with specific details: The boyfriend used to work, but just quit his job (lines 8 and 10). She then shares more details regarding the boyfriend's status even after this sequence (line 12).

Of note at this point is that this question-answer sequence is embedded within a larger ongoing activity of the inquiry-response sequence between Jack and Anne. As mentioned before, Anne has just returned, before dinner, from her trip to visit the friends. This sequence begins with Jack inquiring into who showed her around (line 1) and then asking whether Anne's friend and the boyfriend are students (line 3). Before Anne can actually respond (line 4), Jack adds the second part ('they are working') of his disjunctive question to complete his inquiry (line 5). As Anne does not immediately respond (line 6), Hana self-selects to talk at that moment (line 7). Hana expresses what she knows ('her boyfriend is working') and also displays her limited knowledge. Such display of stance is packaged in a tag question. In response to Hana's tag question, Anne elaborately describes the status of the boyfriend rather than offering a simple (dis)confirmation token[4]. This

---

[4] In typological studies, three systems for minimal answers to yes/no questions are proposed: the yes-no system, the agree-disagree system, and the echo system (Sadock and Zwicky 1985). The languages that belong to the yes-no system, like English, contain a single token, such as the particle "yes," for a positive answer and a corresponding token, such as the particle "no," for a negative answer. Unlike English, Mandarin has no such specific response particles. Instead, the two other answering systems work in parallel in Mandarin—the agree-disagree system and the echo system. For tag questions formulated by the question tags *shi bu shi* ('COP not COP') and *dui bu dui* ('right not right') that are seeking confirmation, the canonical affirmative response is the agreeing lexicon *dui* 'right' (Chui 2002; Wang, Tsai, Goodman, and Lin 2010) or the echo system, repeating the key lexicon in the question. The canonical negative responses are *bushi* (the negator *bu* 'no' and the copular *shi* 'to be') and *meiyou* (the negator *mei* 'none' and existential verb *you* 'have') (Wang 2008). However, a disconfirming response is also commonly displayed in a mitigated or non-straightforward way.

complicated nature of the boyfriend's status, along with Anne's being engaged in eating, may contribute to her failure to respond to Jack's inquiry (lines 6) in the first place.

In this exchange, Jack does not gaze at Anne (line 3) until he starts to utter the second part of his disjunctive question (line 5), connected by *haishi* 'or'. During this time, Hana gazes down eating and positions herself as a non-addressed recipient and a non-focal participant (Figures 1 and 2 below).

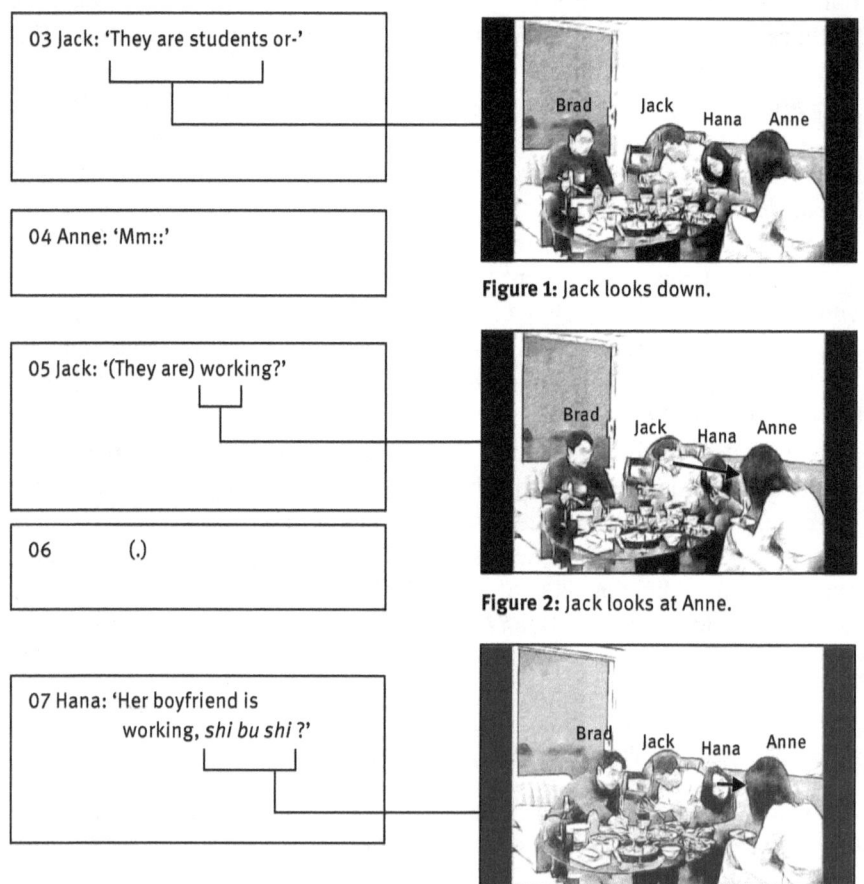

03 Jack: 'They are students or-'

04 Anne: 'Mm::'

Figure 1: Jack looks down.

05 Jack: '(They are) working?'

06   (.)

Figure 2: Jack looks at Anne.

07 Hana: 'Her boyfriend is working, *shi bu shi*?'

Figure 3: Hana looks at Anne.

When Anne delays replying to Jack's inquiry, Hana chooses to speak and thereby enters the conversation. At that point, she raises her head and gazes at Anne to pose the tag question (Figure 3). It seems that Hana provides what she knows and check with Anne when Anne fails to respond at the first possible opportunity. By designing her turn in a tag question format that seeks confirmation, Hana appears to find a way to display herself as a knowing party as well as acknowledge Anne as the one with epistemic authority and the legitimate right to respond to Jack's inquiry. By using a tag question format, Hana claims her complex epistemic stances concerning the information at hand – her lower epistemic right relative to Anne and her higher epistemic status relative to Jack. Hana's turn reflects how she manages this intricate interactional task.

In Extract (1), the speaker of the tag question self-selects to contribute to the talk with a tag question partly because the participant with authority fails to respond in the first possible position. In Extracts (2) and (3) below, the participant with authority does not fail to respond, but disaffiliation occurs between the authority and one of the co-participants. At this juncture, when speakers of the tag question confirm with the authority some relevant information, they contribute what they know, which seemingly helps to break the impasse and clear up the disaffiliation apparent in these two extracts.

Example (2) is taken from the same spate of conversation as Extract (1). Before the sequence, Jack and Brad, graduate students from the same department, have mentioned that Jack, in his third year, is scheduled to take the qualifying exam in the coming April. Anne finds that this piece of information conflicts with what Jack had told her earlier. Therefore, at the beginning of the sequence, Anne confronts Jack about having told her something different, namely, that the exam is taken in the second year (line 1), which leads to a tug-of-war between Anne and Jack regarding this matter.

(2) (001-00-003229, Qualifying exam)

```
01 Anne:      na    ni na   shihou zenme       jiang dier      nian=
              then  2s that time   how.come    say   second    year

02            =yiding yao    kao.
              must    need   test
              'Then how come you said that (you) had to take the exam in the
              second year?'

03            (1.5) ((Jack is drinking wine))

04 Jack:      dier   nian yiding yao    kao?
              second year must   need   test
              'Having to take the exam in the second year?'
```

05 Brad: *haoxiang ye   mei   you   zhege   guiding.*
              seem   also NEG   have this   rule
              'There seems to be no such rule.' ((Gazing at Jack))

06 Jack: *>meiyou, meiyou, meiyou. <wo you   jiang ma?*
              NEG   NEG   NEG   1S   have say   FP
              'No, no, no. Did I say (so)?' ((Gazing at Anne))

07   (1.1)

08 Anne: *meiyou ma?*
              NEG   FP
              'Didn't (you)?' ((Tilting her head))

09 Brad: °*aheh.* ((A light chuckle))

10 Jack: *yinggai shi   you   yixie   la.*
              should   COP   have   some   FP
              'Some (other departments) may have such a rule.'

11 Anne: *mm.*
              mm
              'Mm.'

12 Jack: *na   shi   [lingwai yi   ge   xi   de.*
              that COP   [other   one CL   department   NOM
              'It's another department.'

13 Hana: →   [*ou, na   ge   shi   nage (.) =*
                          [IP   that CL   COP   DM

14   →   =*ca:iliao,   shi   bu   shi.*
              material.science   COP   NEG   COP
              'Oh, it's the department of material science, *shi bu shi?*' ((Turning her head slightly towards Jack on her right))

15 Jack: *na   shi   [^Jerry.*
              that COP   NAME
              'It's Jerry.'

16 Hana: [Jerry   na   ge   x(h)i   de.
             NAME   that   CL   department   NOM
             'It's Jerry's department.'

17 Anne: sorry. wo   ba   ta   apply   dao   nimen   xishang   le.
          sorry   1S   BA   3S   apply   reach   2PL   department   FP
          'Sorry. I applied it to your department.'

Anne's questioning of the exam rules can be understood as a complaint against Jack. Both Jack and Brad, who are from the same department, respond and give disaffiliating responses in either explicit or implicit ways (Dersley and Wootton 2000; Dersley 1998). While Jack has recourse to question-intoned repeats (Wu 2006) to mark what Anne has claimed she heard from him as something out of the blue (line 4),[5] Brad directly states that there is no such rule (line 5). Jack then flatly rebuts in line 6, initially in a strong manner with three no's, but later he backs down by posing a final particle –ma question, opening up to the possibility of negotiation. As Anne insists on her claim and uses a repeat-formatted –ma question to maintain her belief about Jack having told her the second-year rule (line 8), Jack tries to ease the confrontation and gets around the discrepancies. He shifts the focus of the negotiation *away* from whether he said such a thing and *towards* whether such an exam rule exists. When he states that some other departments may have such a rule (lines 10 and 12), in a sense he makes efforts to affiliate with Anne's claim.

Overlapping with Jack's turn in line 12 ('it's another department'), Hana produces the target turn of a tag question in line 13. Note that Hana's turn is embedded within the aforementioned larger ongoing tug-of-war between Jack and Anne. As can be seen from the prior sequence, the stance negotiation concerns whether Jack has told Anne he has to take the exam in the second year. In this knowledge domain, Jack by nature has epistemic primacy. Hana displays her sudden recollection of a piece of relevant information, indicated by the turn-initial particle *ou*, similar to the English change of state token 'oh' (Heritage 1984a). She then brings the department of material science to the co-participants' attention. In a tag question format, Hana designs the turn to assert her relative

---

[5] Question-intoned repeats are proposed to "frequently serve to mark that which is being repeated as unexpected or having come out of the blue from the speaker's perspective" (Wu 2006: 104). Therefore, in this case, Jack uses question-intoned repeats to show that there is no way he would not know the exam system of his own department, and he has absolutely no idea why Anne would accuse him of saying something he himself has no thought of.

inferiority in epistemic rights to this knowledge as compared to Jack, but she also displays her access to the knowledge about the exam systems and the current confusion.

It is Hana's turn, with her tag question, that helps clear up the misunderstanding between Anne and Jack at the end of this segment. In the face of Hana's question, in the next turn Jack takes up what Hana says and asserts his authority by bringing up Jerry, who studies in material science (line 13). Hana's mention of the department of material science leads to Jerry, a mutual friend of theirs. The exam system that Anne accuses Jack of having previously mentioned is actually the system practiced in Jerry's department. Right before Hana's turn, Jack actively gets around the discrepancies by stating that some other departments may have the exam rule Anne purports he told her about. The statement in Hana's turn ('It's the department of material science') in line 14 fills in specific information for Jack's earlier turn ('some other departments') in line 10.

Using the tag question to confirm with an authority, Hana contributes – as an erstwhile non-addressed recipient – to an ongoing conversation, mainly between Jack, Anne, and Brad (lines 1–12). By selecting Jack as the next speaker and requesting confirmation, Hana gives back the speakership and leaves the right of the final say to him. In this case, Jack neither straightforwardly confirms nor disconfirms Hana's tag question; instead, he incorporates Hana's information and brings up Jerry, settling the ongoing dispute concerning Anne's accusation. Overlapping with Jack, Hana chimes in to state again that it is Jerry's department that has such an exam system. It seems to be the case that Jack and Hana collaborate to clear up the misunderstanding for Anne. In the end, to bring this extended dispute to a close Anne apologizes, with laughter, for her misunderstanding.

Fragment (3) is another case in point. The sequence is extracted from a casual get-together of three female friends on a Friday afternoon. Before this segment begins, participants talked about how to share the two cups of green tea from a teashop. In the end, they all agreed that they should split the tea into three portions and that they should do this over the sink in the kitchen. Although the conversation takes place at Faye's apartment, Kate volunteers to go get an empty glass in Faye's room and split the tea in the kitchen. When Kate brings back the divided drinks, in line 1, Faye expresses her gratitude to Kate for washing the cup. Later, Faye invites Kate to have some more tea, both verbally and by reaching out her cup to Kate (lines 3 and 5), which Kate declines (lines 4, 6, and, 8). This sequence demonstrates another instance of a tug-of-war – this time of invitation and decline. In Extract (2), a tug-of-war was also evident between Anne and Jack, through Anne's confrontation to Jack about having previously told her that he must take the exam in the second year.

(3) (002-00-002556, Friday afternoon)

01 Faye: xiexie ni   bang wo xi   beizi.
              thank you help   me   wash cup
              'Thank you for washing the cups for me.'

02 Kate: buhui, buhui.
              NEG   NEG
              'No problem, No problem.'

03 Faye: ni yao   bu   yao   he   (duo yidian).
              2s   want NEG want drink more a.little
              'Would you like some more?'((Picking up her cup))

04 Kate: [mei guanxi, mei   guanxi
              [NEG matter   NEG   matter
              'I am fine. I am fine.'

05 Faye: [wo qishi   bu   tai   neng he   z- lücha.
              [1s   actually NEG very able   drink   green.tea
              'I can't actually have too much green tea.' ((Reaching out to Kate))

06 Kate: mei guanxi, mei   guanxi
              NEG matter   NEG   matter
              'I am fine. I am fine.'

07   (0.5)

08 Kate: ni he   ba. (.)   qing   he.
              2s   drink FP   please drink
              'Go ahead and have it. Please have it.'

09 Beth: ehuhhuh. ((Bursting into a light chuckle))

10   (.)

11 Beth: na   ni [gei   wo   yidian   hao   le.
              then 2s [give 1s   a.little good FP
              'Why don't you give me some?' ((Reaching out to her cup))

12 Faye: [wo keneng zuihao buyao he   name duo.
             [1s probably best   NEG   drink so   much
             'It's better for me not to drink that much.'

13   (.) ((Faye is pouring tea into Beth's cup.))

14 Beth: →   ou, [dui hong. ni hui shui bu zhao], dui bu dui.=
             oh [rightFP   2s will sleep NEG asleep right NEG right
             'Oh, right. It keeps you awake, *dui bu dui*?' ((Faye is pouring tea into Beth's cup.))

15 Faye: [ni keyi zai   fen   yidiandian].
             [2s can again split a.little
             'You can have more.' ((Faye is pouring tea into Beth's cup.))

16 Faye: =*dui*.
             right
             'Right.'

17   (0.8)

18 Kate: he   lücha   jiu hui shui bu   zhao ou.
             drink green.tea just will sleep NEG asleep FP
             'Just drinking green tea keeps you awake?'

19 Faye: wo dui kafeiyin hen mingan.
             1s to caffeine very sensitive
             'I am sensitive to caffeine.'

20 Kate: zhende ou.
             really FP
             'Really?'

Initially, Faye invites Kate to have some more tea (line 3). When Kate declines (line 4), Faye gives an account for why she wants to give Kate more tea – she herself cannot drink too much green tea (line 5), which Kate declines again (line 6). Kate then persists in Faye having her own portion (line 8). This is the moment when Beth bursts into a light chuckle (line 9) and offers to break such an impasse (at line 11) by asking Faye to share the tea with her by reaching out with her cup. Overlapping with Beth, Faye again provides her account of giving out her portion of tea ('It's better for me not to drink that much.') (line 12). When Faye is pouring her portion of tea into Beth's cup, Beth produces the tag question in line 14.

Beth's line 14 is designed in the following way. Beth first displays her sudden recollection of a piece of relevant information about Faye, indicated by the turn-initial particle *ou* 'oh,' the change of state token, and an agreement token (*dui hong* 'right FP'). As what Beth confirms with Faye is something about Faye – green tea keeps Faye awake – and Faye by definition has the first-hand experience of this, participants are oriented to Faye as the authority. Beth's display of the recollection seems to indicate that she has heard this from Faye before. Beth designs her turn in a tag question format to display her different epistemic status relative to the different co-participants, with respect to the knowledge about the effect of green tea on Faye: she requests confirmation from Faye, the authority, indicating her relatively lower epistemic status, but she also expresses what she knows, displaying her higher epistemic status relative to the unknowing party, Kate.

In the earlier invitation-decline impasse between Faye and Kate, Beth plays a peripheral role as the non-addressed recipient. Beth first helps to break the impasse by asking Faye to share the tea with her. By confirming her information with Faye, Beth then contributes to give an ultimate account for why Faye gives out her portion of tea and not being able to drink much of green tea: Green tea may cause sleeping problems to Faye. By requesting confirmation, Beth gives back the speakership and leaves the right of the final say to Faye. In line 16, Faye gives a simple confirming response. Next to Faye's confirmation, Kate treats this piece of information as news receipt by the final particle *ou* (Wu 2004), which, in turn, serves as evidence for her role as an unknowing party.

In this section, the presented tag questions demonstrate a particular practice of Mandarin speakers and hearers in daily conversations to orient to turns with tag questions. Further, these conversation excerpts show how the associated sequences are collaboratively achieved. Apparently, that the tag question is deployed as a resource to embody a speaker' differential states of knowledge in relation to different co-participants, when a single matter is being discussed. The nature of a tag question is to contain a statement plus a question tag. Here the speakers are able to express what they know, indicating their independent access to the knowledge while using the question tag to seek confirmation from the one with authority, displaying their epistemic inferiority. The cases examined here show how seeking confirmation is sequentially and locally accomplished as a collaborative work in Mandarin conversation and how a speaker is oriented to such an intricate knowledge status in relation to the co-participants.

4 Tag question: Resource to make a disaffiliating move

The extracts above demonstrated that the tag question can serve as a resource for speakers to display their differential states of knowledge in relation to different co-participants. By requesting confirmation from the co-participant with epistemic authority, speakers who use tag questions can simultaneously contribute what they know to the talk, displaying knowledge when compared to the unknowing co-participant(s). In this section, examples are presented to demonstrate another practice associated with the tag question in multi-party conversations: the tag question serves as a resource to seek confirmation/ affiliation from the third party to make a disaffiliating move against particular co-participant(s).

The two-part format of the tag question is a turn design feature that allows speakers to simultaneously construct two different actions addressed at two different recipients in multi-party conversations. In such cases, the speaker uses the tag question to make a disaffiliating move – a complaint, a disagreement, or mockery – against a particular co-participant. However, the speaker completes such a move implicitly by addressing and requesting confirmation from the third party, thus seeming to seek support from and forge alliances with them. The turn manages interactional concerns of simultaneously seeking confirmation or support from the third party to make a disaffiliating move against a particular co-participant.

Extract (4) provides such an example. This sequence involves three teenage friends. The sequence starts with Jean's high praise of Sugar's dancing (lines 1–2), to which Dora strongly protests in lines 3 and 5, the target turns. Dora complains about Jean being too crazy about Sugar and talking about him too many times. Dora and Lisa have both heard Jean repeatedly mentioning Sugar since they went out for dinner earlier. Dora's target tag question is directed to Lisa for confirmation and support against Jean. Dora's turn consists of four major parts: (a) an exclamation expression (*hou* 'oh please'), (b) a statement (*women tingdao buzhi san ci le* 'we have heard that over three times'), (c) a question tag (*dui bu dui* 'right not right'), and (d) an address term ('Lisa').

(4) (010-01-002600, Three times)

```
01 Jean:     wo   shuo  Sugar  tiao   jiewu         hao=
             1s   say   NAME   dance  street.dance  very
```

02	=*ke'ai* [*ou.*
	cute [FP
	'I said Sugar is so cute when he does street dance moves.'((Saying with a big smile))

03 Dora: →	[*hou::,women tingdao buzhi=*
	[IP 1PL hear.reach not.only

04 Lisa:	[*huhuhhuh.*

05 Dora: →	= *san ci le. dui bu dui, Lisa.*
	three CL FP right NEG right NAME
	'Oh please, we have heard that over three times, *dui bu dui*, Lisa?' ((Facing Lisa and patting Lisa's arm when uttering dui bu dui))

06 Jean:	[*na you, cai dier-ci hao bu hao.*
	[where have only second- CL okay NEG ok
	'No such thing. Only the second time, okay?'

07 Lisa:	[*meiyou, cong- cong- cong cong ganggang qu chifan=*
	[NEG from from from from just.then go eat

08	=*kaishi.*
	start
	'Well, you started this when we went out for dinner.' ((Pointing forward))

09 Jean:	*wo meiyou jiang la.*
	1S NEG say FP
	'I didn't talk about this (back then).'

10 Lisa:	*ou, zhende ou.*
	IP really FP
	'Oh, really?'

Dora deploys multiple resources to select Lisa as the addressed recipient of her tag question. First, Dora specifically uses the address term "Lisa" at the end. Second, Dora directs her gaze to Lisa by turning her head and focusing her gaze on Lisa throughout her turn (Figures 6–7 below). Third, Dora pats Lisa's arm when she utters the tag *dui bu dui* (Figure 7). Fourth, Dora uses the first person plural form *women* 'we' at the very beginning to include Lisa. By the tag question, Dora seeks confirmation and support from Lisa to form an alliance against Jean. Dora seeks confirmation from Lisa about the number of times Jean has mentioned Sugar (*women tingdao buzhi san ci le, dui bu dui?* 'We have heard that over three times, *dui bu dui*?).

Note that produced right after Jean's praise of Sugar, Dora's turn constitutes a complaint about Jean's bombarding them with her fixation on Sugar. As mentioned before, the sequence starts with Jean's high praise of Sugar's dancing (line 1). Jean's gaze indicates that the turn is addressed to Dora (Figure 4). It appears that Jean has expressed such admiration before – presumably on many occasions – thereby leading to Dora's display of annoyance in response. Overlapping with Jean, Dora's display of annoyance starts with a lengthening turn-initial token *hou* 'oh please,' an interjection that indicates displeasure. This verbal display of annoyance also goes with her head movement and facial expression: Dora tilts her head with her eyes closed (Figure 5). Dora then seeks confirmation about whether it is the third time Jean has mentioned Sugar, to show how annoying Jean has been. By virtue of the tag question and the address term, Dora elicits Lisa's affiliation with her, forging an alliance with Lisa to complain about Jean.

Dora's turn simultaneously constructs two different actions (confirmation/support seeking and complaining) addressed at two different recipients (Lisa and Jean). On the one hand, Dora's tag question is directed at Lisa, seeking Lisa's confirmation and support; on the other hand, Dora's turn produced right after Jean's praise of Sugar can be considered as a protest or complaint against Jean. It is therefore appropriate for both Jean (line 6) and Lisa (line 7) to simultaneously respond in the very next position, and their responses overlap with each other. In response to the complaint, Jean undertakes to rebut Dora's gripe about her (line 6). Jean first utters a strong disagreement marker *na you* 'no such thing' as a protest. She then continues to defend herself, saying "it's only the second time," with the tag *hao bu hao* 'okay?,' indicating a refutation stance (Chen and Liu 2009). In the face of Dora's tag question, Lisa displays her orientation to Dora's utterance as a request for support. Instead of a simple agreement token, Lisa thus strongly backs up Dora's complaint. Specifically, she backs up Dora's claim by calling attention to the fact that Jean had been talking about Sugar since dinnertime (lines 7–8 and Figure 8). It is not clear though why Lisa initiates the turn with the negative marker *meiyou* 'no' (at line 7), considering she is affiliating with Dora at the moment. One possibility is that Lisa uses the marker to preface a 'correction/clarification' (Wang 2008).[6]

---

[6] The negative marker *meiyou* 'no' is a common response to a self-inquiry, a compliment, or

01/02 Jean: 'I said Sugar is so cute when he does street dance moves.'

Figure 4: Jean looks at Dora.

03/05 Dora: 'Oh please, we have heard that over three times, *dui bu dui*, Lisa?'

Figure 5: Dora tilts her head.　　Figure 6: Dora looks at Lisa.　　Figure 7: Dora pats Lisa on the hand.

06 Jean: ['No such thing. Only the second time, okay?'

07/8 Lisa: ['Well, you started this when we went out for dinner.'

Figure 8: Lisa points forward.

When Lisa provides her support, she does not neatly follow the way Dora formulates her complaints (this was the third time); instead, she describes Jean's behavior from a different angle (Jean had been talking about Sugar since dinnertime).

A similar pattern can be found in example (5), which involves the same three participants, whose conversation centers on a bag of french fries that Lisa brought for the gathering. In line 1, Dora responds to the sequence earlier, while Jean in line 2 turns to focus on the bag of french fries on the table and publicly launches a new spate of activity of fry tasting and assessing. Jean initiates the activity before

---

gratitude. It can also preface self-correction, correction/ clarification, and evasion.

line 2 by reaching out to the bag; it is when Jean takes a piece out of the bag that she utters line 2. Dora joins in this tasting activity in line 4. The target turn is in line 10.

(5) (010-01-000354, Salty)

01 Dora: [dui   a.
             [right FP
             'Yeah.'

02 Jean: [wo ye   yao   chi.=
             [1s also want eat
             'I would like to try, too.'

03 Lisa: =[wo you   cha[zi ou.
              [1s have fork   FP
             'I have forks.'

04 Dora: [> wo yao   [chi<.
             [1s want   [eat
             'I would like to try.'

05 Jean: [haochi   ma.
                          [delicious FP
                          'Is it good?'

06   (.)

07 Lisa: hai   bucuo.
             still not.bad
             'Not bad.' ((Jean takes a bite of the french fries.))

08   (.)

09 Jean: mmhuh. ((Bursting into a light chuckle))

10 Dora: →   hen   xian   hao bu   hao, dui   bu   dui.=
             very   salty ok   NEG ok   right NEG right
             'Very salty, okay, *dui bu dui*?' ((Facing Jean))

11	=wo keyi [chi ma.
	1s can [eat FP
	'Can I eat it?' ((Turning to Lisa))

12 Jean:	[hen xian ye.
	[very salty FP
	'Very salty.'

13 Lisa:	chi a.
	eat FP
	'Go ahead.'

14	(.)

Before Jean puts the french fries into her mouth, she poses a question to inquire about how the french fries taste (line 5), a question presumably directed toward Lisa, the one who brought the fries and had one earlier. After a short pause, Lisa responds in line 7 with the assessment *bu cuo* 'not bad.' It is to this assessment that Jean and Dora both give disaffiliative responses to. When Lisa makes the positive assessment in line 7, Jean concurrently has a bite of the fry she takes from the bag (Figure 9). Upon hearing Lisa's evaluation, Jean in line 9 bursts into a short and light chuckle and turns her head to look at Dora (Figure 10). The short chuckle ostensibly marks Lisa's turn as risible and, in turn, indicates a disaffiliating stance. Right after Jean's chuckle, Dora poses the target tag question in line 10.

In line 10, Dora first gives a negative assessment of the fries (*hen xian* 'very salty'). The first tag *hao bu hao* ('okay?'), serving as a stance marker, indicates displeasure or a refutation stance and heightens the sense of contradiction. The second tag here, *dui bu dui*, serving as a question tag, seeks support as well as confirmation. Dora's line 10 is specifically directed at Jean, as shown by eye gaze and body orientation (Figure 11). Selecting Jean as the recipient, Dora seems to seek confirmation and endorsement from Jean. Dora's negative assessment and her seeking support from Jean constitute a disaffiliating move against Lisa's positive assessment.

Lodged within a larger sequential organization, Dora's turn constructs two different actions addressed respectively to Jean and to Lisa. Jean responds with an affiliative assessment (*hen xian* ye 'very salty'). Lisa responds (*chi a* 'go ahead') only to Dora's request for permission to eat the fries in line 11. There is no uptake on the disaffiliating move.

07 Lisa: 'Not bad.' ((Jean takes a bite of the French fries))

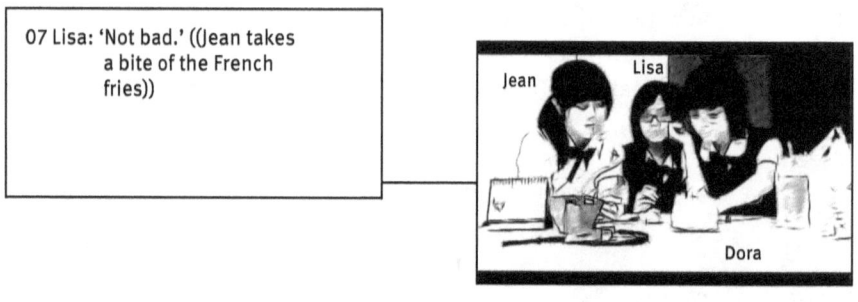

Figure 9: Lisa's not bad.

09 Jean: 'mmhuh.' ((Jean bursts into a light chuckle))

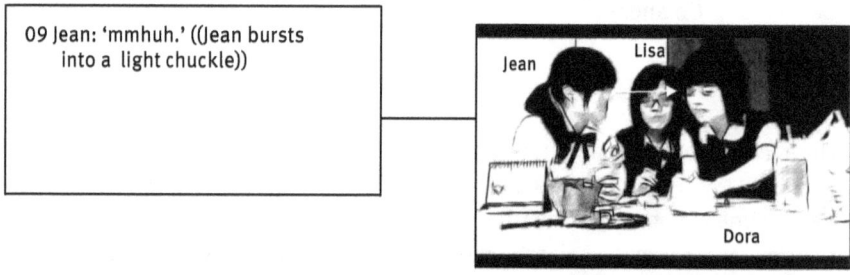

Figure 10: Jean looks at Dora.

10 Dora: 'Very salty, okay, *dui bu dui*?'

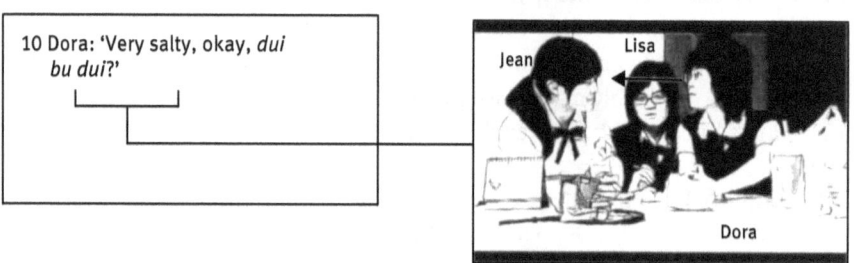

Figure 11: Dora looks at Jean.

Example (6) is taken from a casual after-school conversation among four teenagers from the same high school class. The whole sequence starts with Gary asking Cala whether an acquaintance of theirs, David, is handsome (line 1). Although Gary elicits the answer with a serious expression on his face and with persistence, the co-participants seem to treat the questions in a non-serious manner, with laughter throughout the sequence. Without getting a serious response from Cala, Gary later makes two more attempts ('how about compared with me' in line 9 and a clear comparative format 'of David and I, who is more handsome?' in line 15) to pursue the responses in the following lines. Gary never gets the serious answer he is looking for, even at the end.

(6) (009-01-002600, Handsome)

```
01 Gary:      ni    juede  David  shuai      ma.
              2s    think  NAME   handsome   FP
              'Do you think David is handsome?'

02 Abby:      bu    shuai.
              NEG   handsome
              'Not at all.'

03            (.)

04 Cala:      bu-yi-[wei-ran.=
              disapproving
              '(I) don't think so.'

05 Page:              [ta   shi    ke'ai ba.
                      [3s   COP    cute  FP
                      'He is just cute.'

06 Cala:      =bu(h)-yu-zhi(h)-[pi(h)ng. huhuhhhhuhuh.
              no.comment
              'No comment. huhuhhhhuhuh'

07 Page:                      [hhuhu[huhuhuh.

08 Abby:                      [huhuhu[huhuh.

09 Gary:                             [na-  na-  gen   wo   bi        lei.
                                     [then then with  1s   compare   FP
                                     'Then- how about compared with me?'

10            (.) ((Cala is looking at Gary, laughing))

11 Cala: →    [↑dangran   shu(h)ai    a,  [shu(h)ai   bao       le,  shi  bu   shi.
              [ of.course hadnsome    FP  [handsome   explode   FP   COP  NEG  COP
              '(David is), of course, handsome, totally handsome, shi bu shi?'

12 Page:      [ahauhuhuh              [huhuhuh=
```

13 Abby: [huhuh.

14 Page: =huhuhuhuh.

15 Gary: shi   David   bijiao   shuai   haishi wo   shuai.
            COP   NAME   compare   handsome   or   1S   handsome
            'Of David and I, who is more handsome?'

16   (.)

17 Cala: wo   bijiao   shuai.
            1S   compare   handsome
            'I am the handsome one.'

The first question, in line 1, receives responses from all three co-participants (lines 2, 4, 5, and 6); however, Gary's gaze and body orientation indicate that the question is specifically addressed to Cala (Figures 12 and 13). Although Cala responds in lines 4 and 6, she uses four-character idioms[7] to evade, refusing to comment. Therefore, Gary persists in pursuing Cala's assessment of David. It is Gary's second pursuit in line 9 that prompts Cala's turn in line 11 in the format of a tag question with the question tag *shi bu shi* at the end.

To understand Cala's turn in line 11 properly, it is helpful to first understand how Gary's turn in line 9 – his second attempt to pursue an answer from Cala – is interpreted. This second pursuit provides a new framework ('How about compared with me?') for Cala to make an assessment of David. This second attempt also transforms the type of question from a yes-no question (the first question 'Do you think David is handsome?' in line 1) to one in which Cala is asked to pick the most handsome one (an alternative question). After a short pause, Cala responds to Gary's pursuit in line 11. Cala's turn is designed in the following ways.

First, Cala gives positive assessments of David (*danran shuai a* 'of course he is handsome' and *shuai bao le* 'totally handsome'), which on the surface is a response to Gary's pursuits of her evaluation of David's looks. However, observably, Cala's turn is, in fact, mocking Gary in a non-serious interactional practice of

---

[7] In Mandarin Chinese, there are many idioms or idiomatic expressions that contain four characters, which form a special idiomatic group traditionally known as *chenyu*. In line 4, the four-character idiom *bu-yi-wei-ran*, which can be literally translated as 'not think it right' is roughly equivalent to '(I) don't think so.' In line 6, the four-character idiom *bu-yu-zhi-ping*, which can be literally translated as 'not give place comment' is an expression used to refuse to respond or to answer. It is equivalent to the English expression 'No comment.'

01 Gary: 'Do you think David is handsome?'

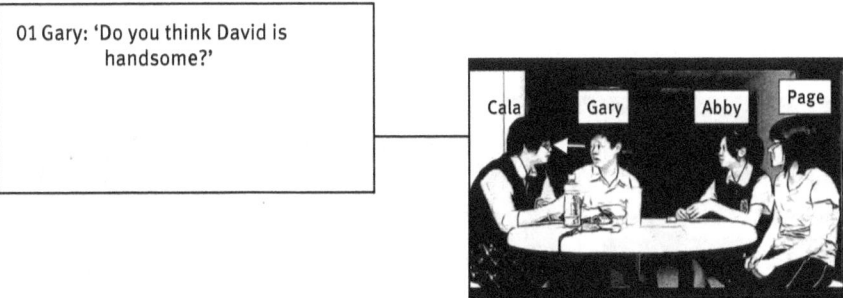

Figure 12: Gary asks question.

09 Gary: How about compared with me?

10   (.) (Cala is looking at Gary, laughing)

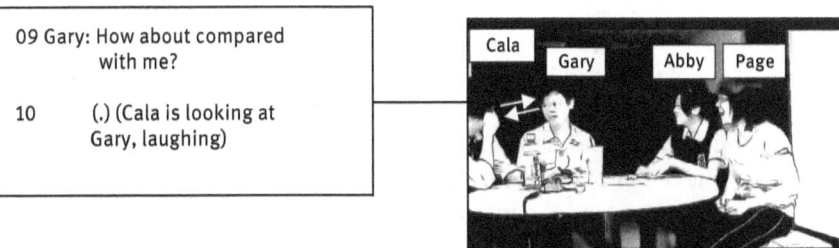

Figure 13: Cala fails to respond.

jocular mockery (Haugh and Bousfield 2012) for bringing himself into the comparison. Cala first initiates the turn with *dangran* 'of course' to challenge the "askability" of the question (Stivers 2011). Cala appears to indicate her stance that if Gary is the person with whom to be compared, David is then unquestionably more handsome, even though she may not evaluate David this way. Several practices show that Cala's turn is non-serious: her use of colloquial intensifying terms, such as *bao* 'explode,' the high pitch of her speech, and the smile and laughter accompanying her speech.

Second, Cala's turn is addressed to Abby and Page, as can be shown by Cala's eye gaze and body orientation. When Gary poses his question in line 9, Cala faces Gary and makes direct eye contact with him (Figures 13). However, when Cala starts her turn in line 11, she moves her gaze to Abby and Page (Figures 14 and 16). In terms of eye gaze and body orientation, Cala's turn is observably directed toward Abby and Page, who sit across the table from her. She shifts her gaze to look down in the middle (Figure 15) but gazes back toward Abby and Page right after she completes the turn (Figure 16).

Cala's turn similarly embodies two distinguishable participation frameworks and constructs two different actions. First, Cala's turn seeks support from Abby and Page, forming an alliance with them. It is reasonable to interpret here that

> 11 Cala: (David is), of course, handsome, totally handsome, *shi bu shi*?

Figure 14: Cala looks forward.   **Figure 15:** Cala looks down.   **Figure 16:** Cala looks forward.

Cala is seeking support rather than confirmation, for the following reasons. When Gary poses the question regarding the evaluation of David, his eye gaze is directed at Cala (Figures 12 and 13), showing that Cala is the addressed recipient entitled to make an assessment of David. In addition, Cala's turn, albeit in a tag question format, does not genuinely solicit verification; Cala's turn is what she uses to make fun of Gary. Cala thus is more likely to seek affiliation. Abby and Page also understand the turn this way; they affiliate with the non-serious stance by laughing along with Cala. Second, Cala's turn, produced in response to Gary's question, simultaneously makes disaffiliating moves to accomplish jocular mockery.

This section has shown examples in which the tag question serves as a resource in multi-party conversation to involve recipients in a disaffiliating move. In this environment, the speaker, employing the tag question, addresses to and solicits support from the third party against one particular co-participant. These tag questions thus simultaneously accomplish disaffiliating actions – a complaint, a contradiction, or mockery – in response to prior utterance(s).

5 Conclusion

Prior studies have shown that tag questions display certainty about the proposition rather than functioning to elicit information, and are mainly used to seek confirmation and support. Eliciting confirmation or support involves stance negotiation. However, little research in Chinese linguistics has examined how such stance negotiation is sequentially and collaboratively accomplished, and what other actions tag questions are sequentially doing.

Using the analytic tools from Conversation Analysis, this study analyzed in detail the turns of tag questions formulated by the two most frequent question tags in spoken Mandarin: *shi bu shi* ('cop not cop') and *dui bu dui* ('right not

right'). Examples were presented to show that in multi-party conversations the tag questions are associated with two common practices:
1. In the first practice, the tag question is mobilized to embody differential states in relation to different co-participants. The format of the tag question – a combination of a statement plus a question tag in a turn – makes it possible for speakers to make a statement that displays their independent access to the information while simultaneously seeking confirmation from the one that has epistemic primacy, thereby also displaying their epistemic inferiority. Through the tag question, speakers can provide what they know to the ongoing talk but leaves the final say to the participant that has epistemic authority.
2. In the second practice, speakers seek confirmation or support and forge an alliance, to accomplish an action of disaffiliation against particular co-participant(s) in interaction. They do this by addressing a tag question to participants who are not the co-participant(s) they aim to disaffiliate from. The format of the tag question makes it possible to constitute two simultaneous distinguishable actions and enables speakers engaged in this practice to manage intricate interactional concerns at the moment.

Based on videotaped naturally occurring everyday talk-in-interaction, this paper investigated how the general actions of the tag questions – seeking confirmation and seeking affiliation – are locally interpreted. Further, this analysis shows what other actions are understood to be sequentially doing in multi-party interaction. While tag questions may at first appear to be accomplishing a simple goal, such as pursuing confirmation of information or supporting an opinion, they are, in fact, doing much more: they become a way for speakers to manage complex moment-to-moment interactional concerns of knowledge status, affiliation, and disaffiliation.

Examples presented are reminder that conversation is a collaborative work accomplished by speakers and hearers. Participants in interaction concurrently make use of an array of multimodal resources, which mutually elaborate each other and contribute to the ongoing process of organizing and constituting in-situ social interaction (Goodwin 1981, 2000; Goodwin and Goodwin 2004; Stivers and Sidnell 2005). With a focus on Mandarin tag questions in talk-in-interaction, this paper demonstrates how interlocutors in conversation are finely attuned to different meaningful resources, moment-by-moment. These allow them to design and interpret turns at talk and the paper shows how the associated sequences are systematically and collaboratively achieved. It is only through a systematic, multimodal analysis of the situated context in talk-in-interaction that is possible to understand the inherent nature of tag questions as interactional and interpersonal.

References

Cameron, Deborah, Fiona McAlinden & Kathy O'Leary. 1988. Lakoff in context: the social and linguistic functions of tag questions. In Jennifer Coates & Deborah Cameron (eds.), *Women in their speech communities: New perspectives on language and sex*, 74–93. Sydney: Australian Professional Publications.

Chen, Jyun-gwang & Hsin-Yi Liu. 2009. A multi-level analysis of "hao" in Chinese with pedagogical applications. *Journal of Chinese Language Teaching (JCLT)* 6(2). 45–98.

Chen, Yiya & Agnes Weiyun He. 2001. Dui bu dui as a pragmatic marker: Evidence from chinese classroom discourse. *Journal of Pragmatics* 33(9). 1441–1465.

Chu, Chauncey C. 1998. *A discourse grammar of Mandarin Chinese*. New York: Peter Lang.

Chui, Kawai. 2002. Ritualization in evolving pragmatic functions: A case study of DUI. *Language and Linguistics* 3(4). 645–663.

Dersley, Ian & Anthony Wootton. 2000. Complaint sequences within antagonistic argument. *Research on Language and Social Interaction* 33(4). 375–406.

Dersley, Ian. 1998. *Complaining and arguing in everyday conversation*. York: University of York dissertation.

Drew, Paul. 2013. Turn design. In Jack Sidnell & Tanya Stivers (eds.), *The handbook of conversation analysis*, 131–149. Malden, MA: Wiley-Blackwell.

Fang, Mei. 2005. *Yiwen biaoji "shi bu shi" de xuhua–cong yiwen biaoji dao huayu-yuyong biao ji* [Grammaticalization of the question marker "shi bu shi": From a question marker to a discourse-pragmatic marker]. In Jiaxuan Shen, Fuxiang Wu, & Beijia Ma (eds.), *Yufahua yu yufa yanjiu II* [Grammaticalization and grammar studies II], 18–35. Beijing: The commercial press.

Freed, Alice F. & Susan Ehrlich (eds.). 2010. *"Why do you ask?": The functions of questions in institutional discourse*. Oxford: Oxford University Press.

Frischen, Alexandra, Andrew P. Bayliss & Steven P. Tipper. 2007. Gaze cueing of attention: Visual attention, social cognition, and individual differences. *Psychological Bulletin* 133(4). 694–724.

Gao, Hua & Wei Zhang. 2009. *Hanyu fujia wenju de hudong gongneng yanjiu* [The functions of tag questions in Chinese: An interactional analysis]. *Yuyan jiaoxue yu yanjiu* [Language Teaching and Research] 2009 (5). 45–52.

Goodwin, Charles. 1979. The interactive construction of a sentence in natural conversation. In George Psathas (ed.), *Everyday language: Studies in ethnomethodology*, 97–121. New York: Irvington.

Goodwin, Charles. 1981. *Conversational organization: interaction between speakers and hearers*. New York: Academic Press.

Goodwin, Charles. 1986. Audience diversity, participation and interpretation. *Text* 6(3). 283–316.

Goodwin, Charles. 2000. Action and embodiment within situated human interaction. *Journal of Pragmatics* 32(10). 1489–1522.

Goodwin, Charles. 2007. Participation, stance and affect in the organization of activities. *Discourse and Society* 18(1). 53–73.

Goodwin, Charles & Marjorie H. Goodwin. 2004. Participation. In Alessandro Duranti (ed.), *A companion to linguistic anthropology*, 222–244. Malden, MA: Blackwell.

Goodwin, Charles & John Heritage. 1990. Conversation Analysis. *Annual Review of Anthropology* 19. 283–307.

Harres, Annette. 1998. "But basically you're feeling well, are you? ": Tag questions in medical consultations. *Health Communication* 10(2). 111–123.

Haugh, Michael & Derek Bousfield. 2012. Mock impoliteness, jocular mockery and jocular abuse in Australian and British English. *Journal of Pragmatics* 44. 1099–1114.
Hepburn, Alexa & Jonathan Potter. 2010. Interrogating tears: Some uses of "tag questions" in a child-protection helpline. In Alice F. Freed & Susan Ehrlich (eds.), *"Why do you ask?": The functions of questions in institutional discourse*, 69–84. Oxford: Oxford University Press.
Heritage, John. 1984a. A change-of-state token and aspects of its sequential placement. In John Heritage & J. Maxwell Atkinson (eds.), *Structures of social action: Studies in conversation analysis*, 299–345. Cambridge: Cambridge University Press.
Heritage, John. 1984b. Conversation analysis. *Garfinkel and ethnomethodology*, 233–292. Cambridge: Polity Press.
Heritage, John. 2012a. The epistemic engine: Sequence organization and territories of knowledge. *Research on Language and Social Interaction* 45(1). 30–52.
Heritage, John. 2012b. Epistemics in action: Action formation and territories of knowledge. *Research on Language and Social Interaction* 45(1). 1–29.
Heritage, John. 2014. Epistemics in conversation. In Jack Sidnell & Tanya Stivers (eds.), *The handbook of Conversation Analysis*, 370–394. Chichester, UK: Wiley-Blackwell.
Heritage, John C. & Andrew L. Roth. 1995. Grammar and institution: Questions and questioning in the broadcast news interview. *Research on Language and Social Interaction* 28(1). 1–60.
Heritage, John & Geoffrey Raymond. 2012. Navigating epistemic landscapes: Acquiescene, agency, and resistance in responses to polar questions. In J. P. de Ruiter (ed.), *Questions: Formal, functional, and interactional perspectives*, 179–192. Cambridge: Cambridge University Press.
Ho, Simon, Tom Foulsham & Alan Kingstone. 2015. Speaking and Listening with the Eyes: Gaze Signaling during Dyadic Interactions. *PLoS ONE* 10(8). e0136905.
Holmes, Janet. 1982. The functions of tag questions. *English Language Research Journal* 3. 40–65.
Hu, Ching-chi. 2002. *Question tags in Taiwan Mandarin*. Taipei: National Taiwan Normal University MA thesis.
Jefferson, Gail. 2004. Glossary of transcript symbols with an introduction. In Gene Lerner (ed.), *Conversation analysis: Studies from the first generation*, 13–30. Amsterdam & Philadelphia: John Benjamins.
Keisanen, Tiina. 2007. Stancetaking as an interactional activity: Challenging the prior speaker. In Robert Englebretson (ed.), *Stancetaking in discourse: Subjectivity, evaluation, interaction*, 253–281. Amsterdam: John Benjamins.
Kok, Kasper. 2016. The grammatical potential of co-speech gesture: A functional discourse grammar perspective. *Functions of Language* 23(2). 149–178.
Kok, Kasper. 2017. Functional and temporal relations between spoken and gestured components of language: A corpus-based inquiry. *International Journal of Corpus Linguistics* 22(1). 1–26.
Langacker, Ronald W. 2008. Metaphoric gesture and cognitive linguistics. In Alan Cienki & Cornelia Müller (ed.), *Metaphor and gesture*, 249–251. Amsterdam: John Benjamins.
Lerner, Gene H. 2004. *Conversation analysis: studies from the first generation*. Amsterdam & Philadelphia: John Benjamins.
Li, Charles N. & Sandra A. Thompson. 1981. *Mandarin Chinese: A functional reference grammar*. Berkeley: University of California Press.

Liu, Yuehua, Wenyu Pan & Wei Gu. 1996. *Shiyong xiandai hanyu yufa [Modern Chinese grammar]*. Taipei: National Taiwan Normal University.

Mittelberg, Irene. 2017. Multimodal existential constructions in German: Manual actions of giving as experiential substrate for grammatical and gestural patterns. *Linguistics Vanguard* 3(s1). 20160047.

Nir, Bracha & Elisabeth Zima. 2017. The power of engagement: Stance taking, dialogic resonance and the construction of intersubjectivity. *Functions of Language* 24(1). 3–15.

Ochs, Elinor, Emanuel A. Schegloff, & Sandra A. Thompson. (1996). *Interaction and grammar*. Cambridge: Cambridge University Press.

Pomerantz, Anita & Barbara J. Fehr. 1997. Conversation analysis: An approach to the study of social action as sense making practices. In Teun A. van Dijk (ed.), *Discourse as social interaction*, 64–91. London: Sage.

Quirk, Randolph & David Crystal. 1985. *A comprehensive grammar of the English language*. London: Longman.

Raymond, Geoffrey & John Heritage. 2006. The epistemics of social relations: Owning grandchildren. *Language in Society* 35(5). 677–705.

Rossano, Federico. 2013. Gaze in conversation. In Jack Sidnell & Tanya Stivers (eds.), *The handbook of conversation analysis*, 308–329. Malden, MA: Wiley-Blackwell.

Sacks, Harvey. 1992. *Lectures on conversation* (Vol. I). Oxford, England: Blackwell.

Sacks, Harvey, Emanuel A Schegloff & Gail Jefferson. 1974. A simplest systematics for the organization of turn-taking for conversation. *Language* 50(4). 696–735.

Sadock, Jerrold M. & Arnold M. Zwicky. 1985. Speech act distinctions in syntax. In Timothy Shopen (ed.), *Language typology and syntactic description.*, Vol. 1. Cambridge: Cambridge University Press.

Schegloff, Emanuel A. 1995. Discourse as an interactional achievement III: The omnirelevance of action. *Research on Language and Social Interaction* 28(3). 185–211.

Schegloff, Emanuel A. 2007. *Sequence organization in interaction: A primer in conversation analysis*. Cambridge: Cambridge University Press.

Shao, Jingmin. 1996. *Xiandai hanyu yiwenju yanjiu* [A study on questions in modern Chinese]. Shanghai: East China Normal University Press.

Shao, Jingmin & Yan Zhu. 2005. Shi bu shi VP de dendingxing qinxiang jiqi leixingxue yiyi [The affirmative inclination of the shi-bu-shi + VP question and its typological significance]. *Shijie Hanyu Jiaoxue* [Chinese Teaching in the World] 2. 23–36.

Steensig, Jacob & Paul Drew. 2008. Introduction: Questioning and affiliation/disaffiliation in interaction. *Discourse Studies* 10(1). 5–15.

Stivers, Tanya. 2011. Morality and question design: "Of course" as contesting a presuppostion of askability. In Tanya Stivers, Lorenza Mondada, & Jacob Steensig (eds.), *The morality of knowledge in conversation*, 82–106. Cambridge: Cambridge University Press.

Stivers, Tanya & Makoto Hayashi. 2010. Transformative answers: One way to resist a question's constraints. *Language in Society* 39(1). 1–25.

Stivers, Tanya & Federico Rossano. 2010. Mobilizing response. *Research on Language and Social Interaction* 43(1). 3–31.

Stivers, Tanya & Jack Sidnell. 2005. Introduction: Multimodal interaction. *Semiotica* 2005(156). 1–20.

Tsai, I-Ni. 2017. Wenda zhijian: Shi-bu-shi wenda ju zai huihua zhong de zhishiqingtai lichang yu xieshang [Between question and answer: *Shi-bu-shi* initiated questions, epistemics,

and stance negotiation]. *Taida Dongya Wenhua Yanjiu* [The NTU Journal of East Asian Culture] 4. 69–100.
Wang, Yu-Fang. 2008. Beyond negation: The roles of meiyou and bushi in Mandarin conversation. *Language Sciences* 30(6). 679–713.
Wang, Yu-Fang, Pi-Hua Tsai, David Goodman & Meng-Ying Lin. 2010. Agreement, acknowledgement, and alignment: The discourse-pragmatic functions of hao and dui in Taiwan Mandarin conversation. *Discourse Studies* 12(2). 241–267.
Wu, Regina Ruey-Jiuan. 2004. *Stance in talk: A conversation analysis of Mandarin final particles*. Amsterdam: John Benjamins.
Wu, Ruey-Jiuan. 2006. Initiating repair and beyond: The use of two repeat-formatted repair initiations in Mandarin conversation. *Discourse Processes* 41(1). 67–109.
Zhang, Bojiang. 1997. Yiwen ju gongneng suoyi [On functions of questions]. *Zhongguo Yuwen* [Chinese Languages] 2. 104–110.

Appendix

Transcription conventions (Jefferson 2004)

[	the point of overlap onset
=	no break or gap
-	a cutoff or self interruption, often with a glottal stop
::	prolongation of the immediately prior sound
^	stress or emphasis
°	talk following it was markedly quiet or soft
<	left push, indicating a hurried start
><	the talk between them is rushed or compressed
↑↓	shifts into especially high or low pitch
.hh	an inbreath
.	falling intonation
?	rising intonation
(h)	plosiveness associated with laughter, crying, or breathlessness
(0.0)	elapsed time by tenths of seconds
(.)	a brief interval; a beat
( )	the transcriber's inability to hear what was said
(( ))	Author's descriptions rather than transcriptions
(word)	possible hearings
↓	head nods

Abbreviations of interlinear gloss

1S/2S/3S	first/ second/ third person singular pronoun
1PL/2PL/3PL	first/ second/ third person plural pronoun

ASP	aspect marker
BA	*ba* construction
CL	classifier
COM	complementizer *(de)*
COP	copular verb *(shi)*
DM	discourse marker
FP	final particle
IP	initial particle
NAME	proper name
NEG	negation words
NOM	nominolizer *(de)*

Index

Action 2, 5, 6, 7, 14, 17, 24, 26, 28–31, 33, 35–37, 39, 43, 46, 50–52, 56, 68, 70, 89, 103, 108, 110, 111, 114, 123, 126, 136, 158, 170, 181, 183–186, 192, 194, 197, 207, 213, 214, 216, 217, 238, 242, 278, 300, 301, 302, 327
Affiliation/ Affiliative 6, 7, 66, 106, 150, 151, 152, 156, 157, 161, 165, 167, 168, 173, 192, 193, 195, 199, 300, 301, 303, 304, 309, 316, 318, 321, 326, 327
Arm tap 6, 108, 111, 112, 113, 115, 116

Bidding (for speakership) 101–111, 116
Bodily visual behavior 5, 6, 13, 18, 32, 43, 50, 99, 100, 101, 183, 185, 186, 187, 201, 206, 207, 214, 245, 247, 265, 287, 293
Bodily-visual practice 5, 7, 28, 29, 30, 245, 255, 256, 278, 279, 284, 287, 288, 289, 292, 293

Cantonese 6, 17, 41, 99–117
Chinese linguistics 16, 24, 300, 301, 326
Coda 67, 269, 272, 274
Cognitive process 255, 257, 258
Common ground 120, 124, 125, 126, 132, 136, 141, 142
Composite gestures 5, 70, 73, 74, 79–82
Confirmation 110, 204, 249, 267, 300, 301, 303, 305, 307, 309, 312, 315, 316, 318, 321, 326, 327
Conversation analysis 2, 4, 5, 13–15, 24, 25, 28, 35, 45, 101, 150, 156, 185, 302, 326
Coverb (preposition/postposition) 257, 259, 264, 265, 267, 270
Coverbal gesture 257
Creaky voice 33, 53, 184, 195, 201, 206, 208, 225
Cross-linguistic perspective 1, 2, 4, 33
Current speaker 6, 99, 100, 101, 105, 108, 112–116, 151, 152, 167, 181, 215, 225, 278

Declination unit 224
Demonstrating 29, 46, 66, 68, 74, 95, 99, 130, 282, 284

Disaffiliating move 7, 304, 316, 321, 326
Disaffiliation 156, 157, 167, 199, 309, 327
Discourse-functional linguistics 7, 16
Discursive psychology 66
Divergence 2, 181, 205

Embodied completion 185, 186–197
Emergent speakership 99–117
Emergent structure 14
Epistemic access 302
Epistemic right 305, 309, 312
Epistemic stance marker 149, 153, 156, 159, 161, 165, 168, 173
Epistemic status 300, 302, 303, 307, 309, 315
Epistemics 5, 46, 104, 149–153, 155, 156, 159, 161, 165, 168, 171, 173, 174, 288, 300, 302, 303, 305, 307, 309, 311, 312, 315, 316, 327

Final particles 16, 17, 148, 157, 164, 174, 229, 277, 301, 311, 315
Framing 66, 74, 95
Functional linguistics 5, 7, 13–15, 16, 25

Gaze 1, 5, 7, 15, 24, 25, 28–31, 33, 36, 39, 43, 47–51, 54, 78, 99, 102–106, 109, 110, 114, 115, 120, 141, 143, 148–175, 184, 185, 206, 208, 213, 245, 246, 256, 265, 278, 279, 280–285, 287, 288–293, 303, 304, 308, 317, 318, 321, 324, 325, 326
Gestural repetition 6, 119–144
Gesture (emblem, iconic, beat) 279, 288
Gesture units 2, 43, 54, 71, 72, 78, 206
Grammar 1–5, 13–17, 25, 26–27, 32, 150, 156, 185, 214, 221, 232, 247, 255, 261, 262–264, 265, 271, 292, 293
Grammar-in-interaction 5, 13–15
Grounding 6, 119–144
Grounding sequence 6, 120–123, 125, 126, 130, 132, 142

Head shake 6, 128, 143, 194, 195, 197, 208
High-level discourse units 95

Holistic and atomistic perspectives 33
Home position 54, 100, 105, 108, 192, 204, 206

Incipient speaker 99, 101, 116
Increment 215, 216, 217, 257
Interactional linguistics 2, 7, 13, 16, 24, 28, 29, 35, 36, 45, 46, 149, 156, 185
Intersubjectivity 52, 213, 280, 290, 291, 300
Intonation units 65, 67, 84, 98, 262, 283, 284

Language production 257, 275, 292
Latching 53, 98, 174, 205, 207, 225, 228, 231
List 5, 65–96, 108, 117, 195, 218
List gestures 65–96

Mandarin grammar 181–209
Meta-interaction 5, 89–93, 94
Mimicked gestures 121, 123, 125, 126, 133, 136, 141, 142, 143
Modal 142, 143, 300, 301
Modalities 15, 24, 28, 35, 36, 46, 69, 93, 95, 142, 174, 206, 213–250, 278, 284, 286–289, 292, 293
Multimodal 1–7, 24–53, 65–96, 150, 181–209, 213, 214, 255, 258, 278, 280, 287, 292, 293, 300–327
Multimodal grammar 26–27
Multimodal interaction 1, 5, 7, 24, 26, 27–31, 32, 33, 35–51, 52, 65–96, 214, 303
Multimodality 1, 2, 5, 7, 13–18, 24–54, 95, 100, 185, 214, 247, 248, 255–293
Multiple-party 68

Next speaker 6, 101, 103, 107, 108, 111, 116, 151, 152, 164, 167, 168, 170–173, 214, 215, 216, 225, 278, 312
Non-current speaker 6, 99, 100, 101, 105, 112, 115, 116

Onset 7, 35, 67, 222, 224, 225, 263, 271, 273, 275, 277, 282, 284, 285, 291, 299
O-space 78, 107, 108
Overlapping talk 50, 100, 101

Palm up open hand (PUOH) 27, 201, 202, 206
Parallel structure 88

Participants' orientation 29, 32, 45, 46, 47, 151
Participation 6, 33, 47, 51, 101, 104, 111, 112–116, 149, 151, 152, 156, 161, 164, 165, 167, 168, 173, 174, 183–186, 195, 213, 291, 304, 325
Participation framework 47, 51, 101, 104, 111, 112–116, 164, 186, 325
Phonological unit 7
Phonotactics 255, 262, 264, 265, 271–277, 293
Place-holder 267, 268, 278
Possible turn completion 3, 4, 47, 50, 52, 181, 183–187, 192, 195, 195, 199, 201, 202, 204–207, 222, 224, 245
Private action 108
P-space 108
Public action 108
Punch line 114, 116

Question 7, 15, 30, 34, 41, 45, 46, 47, 50, 72, 74, 93, 94, 101, 106, 107, 110, 112, 113, 114, 115, 116, 133, 134, 156, 164, 170–173, 238, 242, 246, 247, 248, 264, 268, 269, 274, 280, 282, 284, 300–327

Raised hand/finger 6, 116
Recycling 50, 158, 161, 255, 257, 258, 259, 260, 261, 262, 264, 266, 267, 269, 271, 274, 276, 277, 278, 282, 284, 292, 293
Referential 74, 82–84, 120, 121, 136, 186, 190
Reiterative gesture 5, 70, 71, 73, 74, 82–93
Relevance of bodily-visual conduct 32
Repair 6, 7, 17, 34, 103, 110, 195, 255–293
Repeat 45, 66, 78, 88, 94, 121, 128, 134, 139, 142, 157, 201, 204, 205, 207, 238, 257, 259, 263, 275, 278, 283, 284, 307, 311, 316
Rhetorical effects 5, 74, 79, 82
Right-headed syntax 231, 232, 233, 242, 247
Rush-through 6, 201, 205, 215, 228

Semiotic resources 25, 26, 30, 33, 46, 213, 214, 216, 231, 247, 248
Semiotic structure 213
Sequence 5, 6, 7, 15, 26, 28, 29, 36, 44, 47, 50, 68, 70, 74–94, 101, 113, 114, 115,

120–126, 130, 132, 133, 136, 139, 142, 151, 173, 190, 192, 204, 225, 232, 240, 244, 257, 269, 275, 279, 284, 292, 301, 302, 303, 305, 307, 309, 311, 312, 315, 316, 318, 319, 322, 327
Serial verb construction 6, 233, 234, 235, 246
Social semiotics 2, 25, 26, 28
Somatotopy 293
Speaker change 94, 288, 291
Stance 5, 6, 17, 148–175, 190, 192, 194, 195, 197, 199, 201, 216, 245, 246, 280, 282, 284, 285, 287, 288, 293, 301, 302, 303, 307, 311, 318, 321, 325, 326
States of knowledge 7, 304, 305–315, 316
Story recipient 114–116
Storytelling/ storyteller 107, 114–116
Syntactically incomplete turns 6, 181–209

Tag question 7, 172, 300–327
Thinking face 280, 281, 284, 287, 289
Third party 111, 316, 326
Three-partedness 67, 94
Through-produced 50, 225, 228, 229
Tone 2, 4, 7, 41, 42, 52, 78, 237, 256–261, 263, 264, 270, 271–277, 284, 285, 293
Tone (tone sandhi) 7, 263, 264, 270, 271, 276, 277, 285, 293

Topic-comment 2, 3, 6, 34, 195, 235–238, 246
Tracking 5, 74, 84–88
Transcription of visual behavior 43
Transcription systems 32, 35–38, 42, 43, 45, 156, 208, 219
Turn competition 99–117
Turn-continuation 6, 213–250
Turn-taking 44, 68, 99, 100, 101, 107, 116, 152, 183, 184, 215, 256
Turn transition 30, 51, 100, 181, 184, 201, 205, 228, 232

Unexpressed nominal argument structure 238–242

Verb-resultative complement construction 242–247
V-not-V 301

Word 7, 14–16, 28, 34, 41, 42, 67, 71, 104, 120, 121, 124, 128, 132, 133, 141, 148, 151, 158, 204, 220, 222, 228, 231, 232, 235, 246, 248, 256, 257–262, 264, 265, 267–280, 282, 284, 287, 289, 292, 304
Workplace studies 28, 30, 31

www.ingramcontent.com/pod-product-compliance
Lightning Source LLC
Chambersburg PA
CBHW032055230426
43662CB00035B/416